Ancient Maya Cities of the Eastern Lowlands

Ancient Cities of the New World

UNIVERSITY PRESS OF FLORIDA

Florida A&M University, Tallahassee
Florida Atlantic University, Boca Raton
Florida Gulf Coast University, Ft. Myers
Florida International University, Miami
Florida State University, Tallahassee
New College of Florida, Sarasota
University of Central Florida, Orlando
University of Florida, Gainesville
University of North Florida, Jacksonville
University of South Florida, Tampa
University of West Florida, Pensacola

Ancient Maya Cities of the Eastern Lowlands

Brett A. Houk

Foreword by
Marilyn A. Masson,
Michael E. Smith,
and John W. Janusek

University Press of Florida
Gainesville / Tallahassee / Tampa / Boca Raton
Pensacola / Orlando / Miami / Jacksonville / Ft. Myers / Sarasota

Copyright 2015 by Brett A. Houk
All rights reserved

Printed in the United States of America on acid-free paper

This book may be available in an electronic edition.

21 20 19 18 17 16   6 5 4 3 2 1

First cloth printing, 2015
First paperback printing, 2016

Library of Congress Cataloging-in-Publication Data
Houk, Brett A. (Brett Alan), 1967– author.
Ancient Maya cities of the Eastern Lowlands / Brett A. Houk ; foreword by Marilyn A. Masson, Michael E. Smith, and John W. Janusek.
pages cm — (Ancient cities of the new world)
Includes bibliographical references and index.
ISBN 978-0-8130-6063-7 (cloth)
ISBN 978-0-8130-5415-5 (pbk.)
1. City planning—Belize—History. 2. Mayas—Belize—Antiquities. 3. Mayas—Belize—History. 4. Excavations (Archaeology)—Belize. 5. Indians of Central America—Belize—Antiquities. 6. Indians of Central America—Belize—History. I. Masson, Marilyn A., author of introduction, etc. II. Smith, Michael Ernest, 1953– author of introduction, etc. III. Janusek, John Wayne, 1963– author of introduction, etc. IV. Title. V. Series: Ancient cities of the New World.
F1445.H675 2015
972.82'01—dc23
2014040226

University Press of Florida
15 Northwest 15th Street
Gainesville, FL 32611-2079
http://www.upf.com

For my parents

Contents

List of Illustrations   ix
List of Tables   xii
Foreword   xiii
Preface   xv

1. Ancient Maya Urbanism in the Eastern Lowlands   1
2. Studying Maya Cities   13
3. The Setting in Space and Time   46
4. Preclassic Foundations   69
5. Southern Belize   84
6. Vaca Plateau and Maya Mountains   119
7. Belize Valley   147
8. Northwestern Belize   168
9. Northern Belize   201
10. Comparisons and Urban Planning   232
11. Deciphering Meaning in Maya Cities   265

References Cited   285
Index   327

Illustrations

1.1. Map of the Maya area   xviii
1.2. Map of the eastern lowlands   4
2.1. Structure B-3 at Cahal Pech with plaster restored over facing masonry   29
2.2. Idealized cross section of a vaulted masonry building   30
2.3. Structure A-32 on the north face of the Castillo at Xunantunich   31
2.4. Restored Structure E-1 at Cahal Pech   32
2.5. Photograph of a partially collapsed building in Courtyard 100B at La Milpa   41
2.6. Shaded relief map of Chan Chich Structure A-5 with 0.25-m contours overlaid   43
2.7. Contour map of La Milpa Courtyard 100 with rectified map of structures and architectural plan of eastern courtyard wall overlaid   44
4.1. Map of Cahal Pech   72
4.2. Simplified plan map of superimposed Late Preclassic Structures 14 and 15 buried in the plaza at the Tolok Group, Cahal Pech   73
4.3. Eastern profile Structure B1 at Blackman Eddy   74
4.4. Map of Cerros with inset of Central Precinct   81
5.1. Map of southern and central Belize   85
5.2. Map of Pusilhá   88
5.3. Map of Moho Plaza at Pusilhá   91
5.4. Map of Uxbenka   96
5.5. Map of Uxbenka's Stela Plaza   97
5.6. Map of Uxbenka Groups B–F   99
5.7. Map of Lubaantun   105
5.8. Photograph of Structure 12 at Lubaantun   106
5.9. Photograph of Plaza V at Lubaantun   107

5.10. Photograph of the stepped-perpendicular style of construction at Lubaantun 108
5.11. Map of Nim Li Punit 113
6.1. Map of Minanha 122
6.2. Map of Caracol's epicenter 130
6.3. Map of B Group at Caracol 131
6.4. Photograph of Caana at Caracol 132
6.5. Photograph of Structures B4–B6 at Caracol 133
6.6. Map of A and D Groups at Caracol 135
6.7. Photograph of the eastern structures in Caracol's E-Group 136
6.8. Map of the Caracol *sacbeob* network 137
7.1. Map of Xunantunich 150
7.2. Photograph of the Castillo from Structure A-1 151
7.3. Photograph of the replica of the eastern frieze on Structure A-6 152
7.4. Photograph of Structure A-11 153
7.5. Photograph of Structure A-1 155
7.6. Map of El Pilar 162
7.7 Map of the eastern groups at El Pilar 163
8.1. Map of northern Belize 169
8.2. Generalized northern cross section of the Three Rivers region 170
8.3. Map of La Milpa 173
8.4. Reconstruction drawing of the frieze on Structure 3 at La Milpa 174
8.5. Photograph of Structure 27 at La Milpa 175
8.6. Map of Dos Hombres 183
8.7. Illustrations of Yaloche Cream Polychrome lid with a macaw head from the Dos Hombres Structure B-16 tomb 186
8.8. Illustrations of Dos Arroyos Orange Polychrome vessel from the Dos Hombres Structure B-16 tomb 187
8.9. Map of Chan Chich 192
8.10. Reconstruction drawing of Structure A-5 at Chan Chich 193
8.11. Map of Kaxil Uinic 195
8.12. Tomb 2 at Chan Chich 197
8.13. Illustration of Terminal Classic anthropomorphic bowl from Burial 8, Structure C-6, Chan Chich 198
9.1. Map of Nohmul 204
9.2. Plan maps of Structures 9 and 20 206
9.3. Map of Lamanai 212
9.4. Photograph of fiberglass replica of Early Classic mask on Structure N9-56 at Lamanai 213

9.5. The High Temple at Lamanai as it appears today 214
9.6. Lamanai's Terminal Classic ball court 215
9.7. Map of Altun Ha 223
9.8. Map of Altun Ha Central Precinct 224
9.9. Perspective drawing of Structure A-6, B at Altun Ha 224
9.10. Perspective drawing of Group B at Altun Ha 225
9.11. Photograph of Structure B-4 at Altun Ha 226
10.1. Site core areas shown at common scale 237
10.2. Cities in this volume presented at a common scale 238
10.3. Simplified site maps used to calculate orientation 261

Tables

3.1. Maya chronology in the eastern lowlands   46
5.1. Political history of Pusilhá   93
6.1. Political history of Caracol   142
10.1. Site core area calculations   236
10.2. Comparisons of cities   240
10.3. Definitions of terms used to study coordination among buildings and spaces   251
10.4. Measures of coordination among buildings   253
10.5. Definitions of terms used to assess standardization among cities   255
10.6. Measures of standardization between cities   256
11.1. Comparison of cities to the Petén template   271

Foreword

During the Pre-Columbian era, the Eastern Maya Lowlands housed a populous network of Maya cities and towns, which are now mostly shrouded beneath the jungle canopy or farmlands of the modern Caribbean nation of Belize. In this book, author Brett Houk puts back together the pieces of the inner urban landscapes of the Maya archaeological sites of Belize. Some of these sites are well known, and others remain obscure today. His comparisons reveal principles of monumental works that were designed and built by Classic-era Maya lords, informed by an approach to these built environments that considers the dynamic and changing relationships of monuments and political power. The chapters of this book encapsulate and explain the variation among centers of different sizes, geographic locations, and time periods. The case studies show that no single model can explain the organization of Maya cities from southern Belize, the Vaca Plateau and Maya Mountains, the Belize Valley, northwestern Belize, and northern Belize. Each city's local setting provided the key political and economic resources that influenced its size, power, longevity, and opportunity.

An especially compelling aspect of this book is its use of scientific, archaeological data. This approach is necessary as the hieroglyphic records of this part of the Maya lowlands were fewer in number and were carved on less durable stone than the better-studied Petén (Guatemala) "core" area of the southern Classic Maya realm. While many archaeologists have ignored these eastern cities due to a general paucity of preserved hieroglyphic inscriptions, Brett Houk turns this circumstance into an opportunity to focus primarily on the architecture of downtown precincts of Maya centers. These data allow him to place these cities on interesting comparative ground with scientific analyses of the political monuments of ancient states in other parts of the world. However, where the eastern lowlands sites do have dynastic records, he folds this information into his broader reconstructions of monumental landscape histories.

The study of urban planning has garnered much recent attention in the archaeology of complex societies. Older work tended to classify New World cities as either "planned" or "unplanned," depending on whether or not they met western expectations of an orthogonal layout. Newer research assesses planning as a matter of degree. Cities were constructed through both top-down (elite) and bottom-up (commoner) processes, and regional factors affected their growth and position in broader geographic hierarchical networks. The surface features of monumental centers represent an amalgamation of cumulative human engineering through time, and in the case of some Maya centers, construction occurred over the course of a millennium or more. Monumental epicenters tend to exhibit more evidence of planning than their associated residential zones for many Mesoamerican cities.

Brett Houk evaluates evidence for the coordination and standardization of buildings, as well as their practical and symbolic functions in the built environment. The author also considers historical factors that contributed to variations in the monumental centers of Maya city states. Monumental features that are analyzed include plazas and courtyards, *sacbeob* (raised roads), temples, ballcourts, palaces and other noble residences, stelae, altars, and reservoirs from the Formative through the Late/Terminal Classic Periods. Planning and organization differed at centers of various sizes according to the goals of specific political regimes. Some smaller central precincts were geared toward performance and gatherings, while others exhibit more expansive and functionally diverse infrastructure as might be expected for political capitals of significance.

The eastern Maya lowlands region has been branded in a number of ways in prior research. Most commonly, sites of this area have been assessed with respect to their hinterland relationship to Petén region core sites. This book evaluates this model anew, and complexity arises in the details of varied regional relationships that are reflected in the diverse organization of individual sites. The sites of Belize are not easily lumped under one interpretive rubric, and their changing political and economic ties to the north, south, and west attest to a pluralistic and dynamic process of societal adaptation and transformation.

Archaeological tourism has become a thriving industry for the nation of Belize, and this work fills an important niche in the literature. This book offers a sustained intellectual consideration of Maya urbanism and also serves as a handbook for fourteen important political centers, many of which are visited by tourists today.

Marilyn A. Masson, Michael E. Smith, John W. Janusek
Series editors

Preface

Like many archaeological endeavors, the idea for this book involved beer. While we sat in the hotel bar at end of a long day of papers at the annual meeting of the Society for American Archaeology in Sacramento, California, Marilyn Masson asked if I would be interested in writing a book about Maya cities in Belize for a series she coedited with Michael Smith and John Janusek. I was at a point in my career where such a project made sense. However, until that conversation, I had not considered this particular topic, and, before agreeing to take this on, I had to contemplate the obvious question of "why a book about Maya cities in Belize?" The answer to that question, which is explored in more detail in the first chapter, is ultimately what compelled me to embrace this project. Basically, many of the Maya cities in the eastern lowlands are not well known outside of the tight-knit circle of archaeologists working in Belize. Much of the information on these cities is scattered in obscure technical reports, theses, and dissertations and simply out of the easy reach of the nonspecialist. These cities have much to contribute to our understanding of Maya urbanism and culture history, yet they remain largely unknown.

A different archaeologist would have probably written a very different book about the same broad topic. My book is heavily site-centric, focusing on the monumental epicenters of 14 Classic-period Maya sites in Belize. This is a very elite-focused approach, and many other archaeologists would have proceeded differently, preferring to stress economics, agricultural systems, the rolls of the non-elite in Maya society, and so on.

As I began thinking about the structure of the manuscript, I realized that compiling the data on a representative sample of cities from across the country of Belize and presenting it in a standardized format would be important because it had never been done before, and doing so would facilitate comparisons. Specifically, I wanted to pull out what was known about each city's urban plan, chronology, and political history, and summarize it for the reader.

The book, however, needed to do more than simply present data. Toward that end, the concluding chapters take the data and analyze them in terms of urban planning and meaning. The approach I follow to address these two themes derives from my personal research interests. For years I have been fascinated by site planning, basically the study of the meaning behind the urban plan of ancient cities, popularized in the Maya area by Wendy Ashmore (1991). I construe "meaning" broadly to encompass all the things that contribute to the final design of a place including mundane things like where water drains to esoteric things like worldview and cosmology. As for the theme of urban planning, it was my colleague Greg Zaro who suggested applying an approach put forth by Michael Smith (2007), which is discussed in Chapters 2 and 10, to frame the analysis and comparisons, and ultimately that is the route the study took.

Data in this book mostly derive from the efforts of other scholars and their published accounts of their work. In three cases—Dos Hombres, La Milpa, and Chan Chich—I was involved in some aspect of the research and had a hand in deciding what questions to ask, what structures to excavate, and where to place units. Only in the case of Chan Chich, however, have I been involved in all phases of excavations. In all other instances, I am presenting data collected wholly or in part by others. The goal is not to step on toes but to take what has been presented in various forms, repackage it, and present it in a new and consistent format. Part of that data presentation involves the maps of sites. To ensure consistency between maps and to highlight features mentioned in the text, all of the maps of cities in this book, with the exception of the map of Caracol's epicenter, have been redrawn following a common set of cartographic styles based on original published maps.

No one book on any topic can be all things to all readers, but hopefully a wide variety of readers will find at least some of this book useful. Students of ancient urban studies may find the comparisons of cities to be applicable to other parts of the ancient world, and Mayanists working outside of Belize should find the descriptions of individual cities useful. The nonspecialist reader may appreciate the background information and comparisons the most, and may find that skimming the site descriptions is adequate. The intrepid tourist, hell bent on seeing Maya ruins, however, may find those descriptions to be the most valuable part of the study. Hopefully, though, everyone who reads this will be as amazed as I am by the inherent flexibility in Maya city planning, which is a core trait of Maya urbanism.

There are many people to thank for helping directly or indirectly with this book. First, I would like to thank my parents and brothers for all their encouragement along the way. My dad deserves special thanks for reading drafts of the chapters and flagging things that might be confusing to a non-Mayanist. I owe a great deal to my first three mentors who shaped my early thinking about Maya cities. Fred Valdez first pointed me in the direction of Wendy Ashmore's site-planning work, which became the basis for my initial research. Vern Scarborough, through his water management research, showed me that Maya cities are heavily engineered artificial landscapes. Nicholas Dunning's regional approach to Maya settlement taught me the importance of looking around the place you are working, instead of just looking at it.

Discussions with other colleagues have continued to inform my understanding of and approach to ancient urbanism including Richard E. W. Adams, Wendy Ashmore, Jaime Awe, Geoffrey Braswell, Arlen Chase, Diane Chase, Norman Hammond, Jon Lohse, John Morris, Terry Powis, Carolyn Tate, Chris Witmore, and Greg Zaro. A paper entitled "The Cities on the Edge of History" that Greg Zaro and I presented at a Society for American Archaeology conference was the first step toward writing this book and helped frame the research orientation. The process of actually writing a book benefited from insight and advice from friends who have done this before, including Lisa Lucero, Jennifer Mathews, Carolyn Tate, and Chris Witmore. Lisa Lucero reviewed the first draft of this book and the second draft of Chapter 1. She made substantial comments that helped shape the final product. In addition to Lisa, I would like to thank Geoffrey Braswell, Marilyn Masson, Carolyn Tate, and an anonymous reviewer for reading and commenting on early drafts of one or more chapters.

Six graduate students in my seminar on Maya archaeology helped with background research before I started writing the book. I would like to thank them all: Sarah Boudreaux, Matt Harris, Krystle Kelley, Rose Leach, Vince Sisneros, and Brenda Snowden. Vince Sisneros also contributed a photograph to this book.

I would also like to thank the Office of the Provost at Texas Tech University for a faculty development leave to work on this project. The majority of the writing was accomplished during that semester, and without the time away from teaching, I never would have finished the first draft of the manuscript on schedule.

I would like to thank the series editors—Michael Smith, Marilyn Masson, and John Janusek—and the staff at University Press of Florida, especially the director, Meredith Morris-Babb, for all their help along the way. I would also like to acknowledge the fine copyediting done by Patricia Bower of Diligent Editorial and Book Production Service for the University Press of Florida. Finally, the hard work of my colleagues and their students, the support of the staff at the Institute of Archaeology in Belize, and the hospitality of the Belizean people made the research summarized in this book possible.

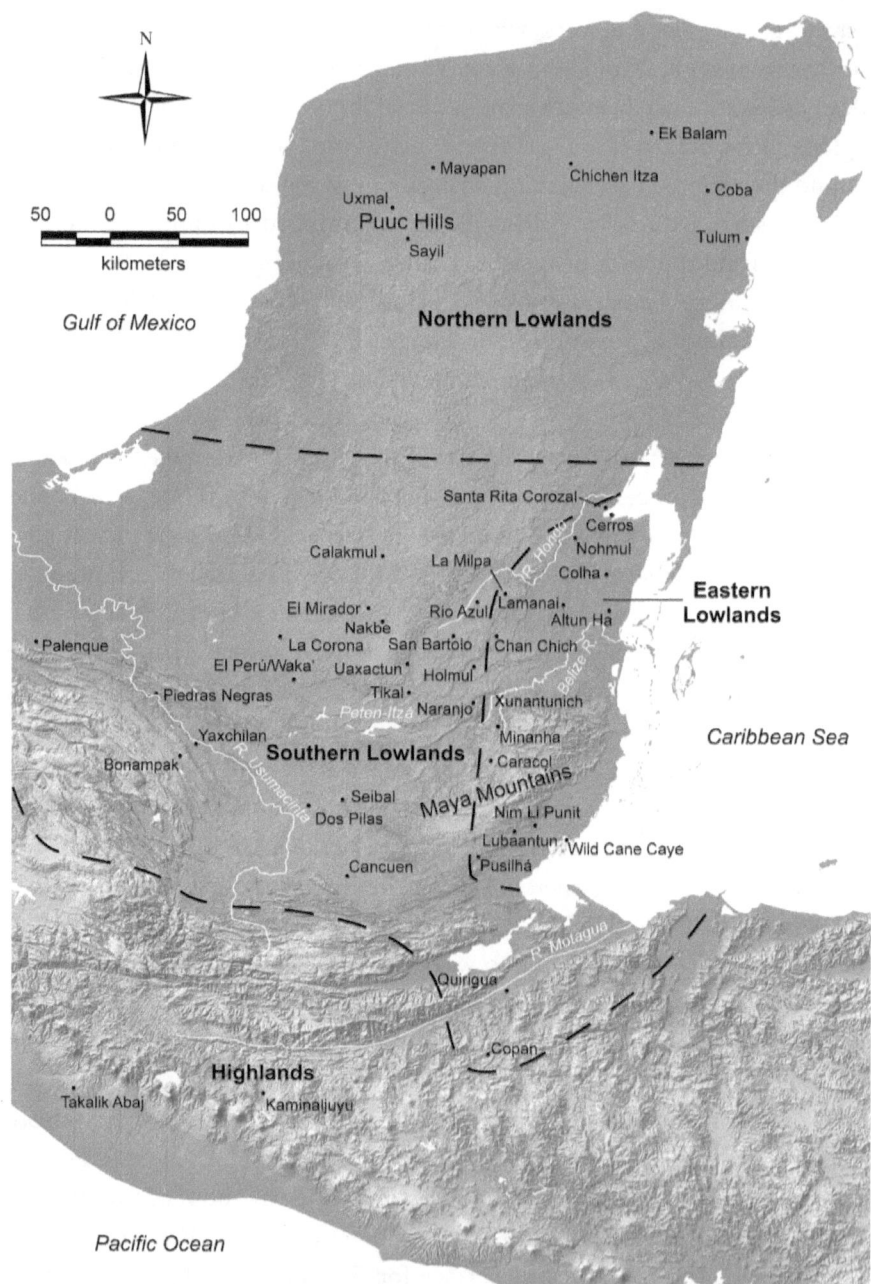

Figure 1.1. Map of the Maya area showing geographic areas, modern political boundaries, and selected sites. Base map courtesy NASA/JPL-Caltech, SRTM mission.

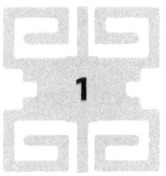

1

Ancient Maya Urbanism in the Eastern Lowlands

This book is about the ancient cities of the eastern Maya lowlands—roughly corresponding to the modern nation of Belize—the area between the Caribbean Sea and the Petén region of Guatemala (Figure 1.1). It is not only about how old the cities are and what they looked like; it is also about how the Maya planned the cities and the significance behind that planning.

The eastern lowlands are but a small part of the homeland of the Maya, which extends from western Honduras and El Salvador to eastern Mexico, encompassing all of Guatemala and Belize. This part of the world demonstrates incredible natural diversity, from volcanic highlands in southern Guatemala to karstic lowlands of the Yucatán Peninsula. With a generally hot and humid climate and dense forests, the Maya lowlands are seemingly inhospitable. Yet, in this setting, the ancient Maya developed a rich and unique urban tradition that persisted and evolved for almost 2,000 years. Over a century of archaeological research in the Maya area has identified a complicated array of villages, towns, and cities—complete with causeways, reservoirs, ball courts, pyramids, plazas, and palaces—that are part of this urban tradition.

Although we often talk about the ancient Maya as if their culture was monolithic and homogenous, they had a rich and diverse culture, and Maya cities are each unique. Maya cities share common elements, to be sure, but each is a variation on the theme, shaped by location, available resources, the natural environment, and the thousands of individual decisions made by kings, architects, and builders.

Some of the largest Maya cities are the best known; it was these that drew the early and lingering attention of archaeologists. Scholars have studied places like Tikal, Palenque, Copán, Calakmul, and Chichén Itzá for decades, and the discoveries at those cities have largely shaped our perception of Maya urbanism and culture. However, there are literally thousands of smaller places that have been mapped and studied, and they have much to contribute to our understanding of the Maya.

There are many possible ways to approach the subject of ancient Maya urbanism, but this volume examines what we know about 14 Classic period (250 to 900 CE) Maya cities in Belize, teasing out from published technical reports, journal articles, theses, dissertations, and books information on the site plan, chronology, and political history for each city. The purpose of this study is not simply to present facts about these places; rather, the goal is to examine planning and meaning in eastern lowland urban traditions in the larger context of ancient urban studies. These 14 Maya sites run the gamut from well-known places featured in television shows and documentaries, like the massive city of Caracol, to locales that even few archaeologists have ever visited, like the hard-to-get-to center of Dos Hombres. What the data in this book show are remarkable and nuanced variations in architectural assemblages across space and time, varied levels of political control over suburban landscapes, shared planning concepts combined with wildly different ideas about how to build a Maya city, and intriguing hints at possible relationships between cities based on planning principles.

One thing that makes the study of ancient urbanism intriguing in any part of the world is the underlying fact always lurking in the back of the researcher's mind that, until the first city appeared in a particular part of the world, no one ever lived in a city before. It sounds like a silly statement, but a "city represents a new social order" (Smith 2010:1). Building and living in cities, now the norm, are relatively recent facets of daily life in the history of our species.

The development of cities is, therefore, a fascinating field of study. While not its primary focus, this book touches on that topic by peering into the Preclassic period (1000 BCE to 250 CE) to examine the foundations for Maya cities in Belize at a sample of key sites. These Preclassic places show evidence for important religious, economic, and social structures that made subsequent urban institutions possible. In the Belize Valley archaeologists have uncovered evidence for one of the oldest Maya villages anywhere in the lowlands at Cahal Pech and have documented the significance of the continuity of place and an important transition in ritual architecture at Blackman Eddy. In northern Belize, at Cuello, the mass sacrifice of over 30 people accompanied a similar transformation in community ceremonial architecture, suggesting that sacralized warfare played an important role in the development of social complexity. A few dozen kilometers from there, at Colha, immense deposits of debris from stone tool production provide evidence for craft specialization on an almost industrial scale during the Late and Terminal Preclassic periods (400 BCE to 250 CE). Finally, on the northern coast of Belize along the shore of Corozal Bay, the radical transformation of Cerros from bayside village to ritual center attests to a new type of political and social order at the end of the Preclassic period as the first divine kings arose in the lowlands.

Cities did not appear overnight in the Maya lowlands. Nor did divine kings, but, as we shall see, Maya cities arose in lockstep with this new form of political and social order. The way the Maya of the Classic period built their cities—the types of buildings they constructed and how they arranged structures and spaces—tells us a lot about the social and political functions of cities and the changing nature of Maya political organization as it grew from its Preclassic roots.

Kingdoms on the Edge of History

The obvious question of "why the eastern lowlands?" has a three-part, not-so-obvious answer. First, the incredible diversity of the eastern lowlands makes the region a fascinating laboratory in which to study urbanism (Figure 1.2). For example, if you were to pluck a city like Pusilhá from southern Belize and drop it next to La Milpa in northwestern Belize so that you could compare their plans and architecture side by side, you might conclude they were built by two different cultures or were separated in time by hundreds of years. Of course, neither assumption would be correct; they are both Maya cities dating to the same time period, and they are nothing alike.

Second, there are rich data on the cities of the eastern lowlands. As the latter half of this chapter reveals, archaeologists have been investigating Maya sites and landscapes in Belize for over 100 years, and the number of individual research projects has literally exploded since the 1980s. The amount of raw archaeological data that exists for sites in Belize is staggering, yet much of the data are scattered in technical reports, theses, and dissertations. When published in journal articles and book chapters, the data are often presented piecemeal in the service of some specific research question.

Finally, the eastern lowlands represent a significant gap in the more mainstream archaeological literature on Maya cities and culture. In almost every major textbook about the ancient Maya, the eastern lowlands are treated as peripheral to the major cultural developments of the Classic period, despite the wealth of available data. Two things account for this: the cities in the area are generally smaller than their counterparts in the adjacent Petén region, and most lack carved stone monuments with legible texts, although there are important exceptions to this statement.

Although there are some impressive Maya buildings at sites in Belize, and Caracol is one of the largest Maya cities in the lowlands, when archaeolo-

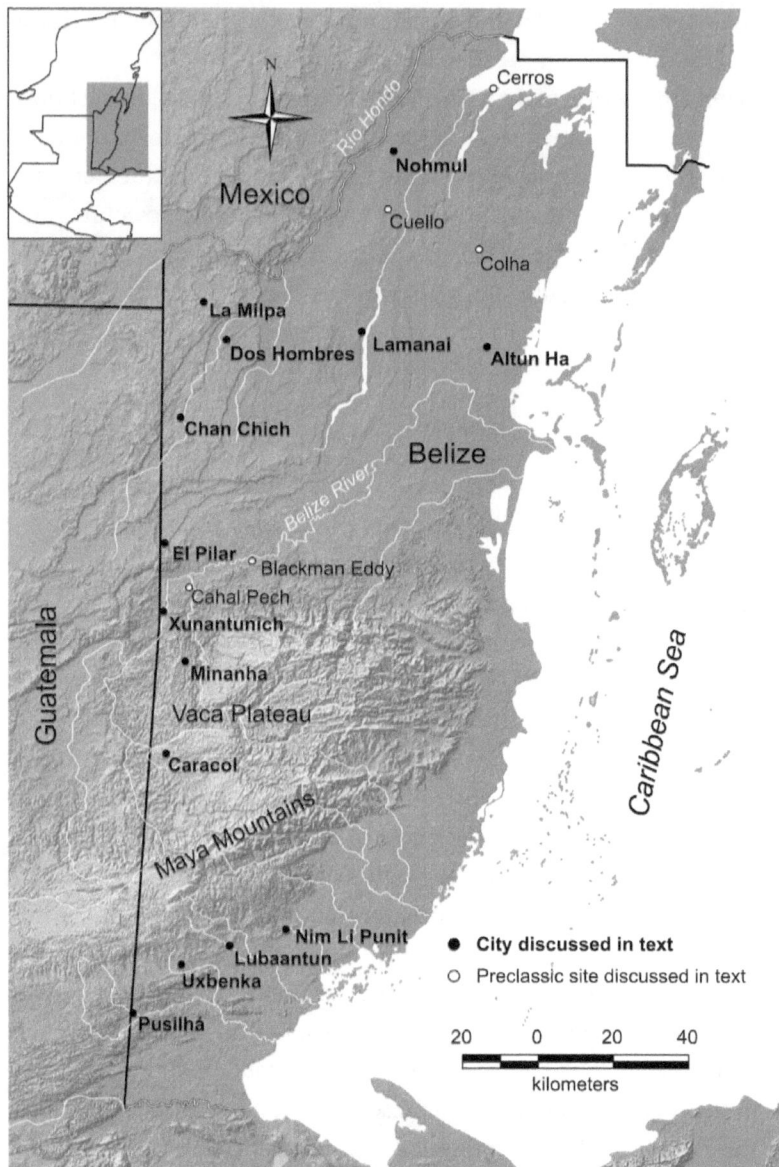

Figure 1.2. Map of the eastern lowlands area showing modern political boundaries and sites discussed in this book. Base map courtesy NASA/JPL-Caltech, SRTM mission.

gists were just beginning to explore the Maya world, it was the large ruins in Guatemala and Mexico that drew the most attention. What archaeologists learned through their excavations at Tikal, in particular, shaped, and continues to influence, our view of many aspects of Maya culture.

Around the time that large-scale projects like the one at Tikal were under way, epigraphers began to decipher Maya hieroglyphs, and sites with well-preserved stone monuments became even more important in the minds of many researchers. Breakthroughs in decipherment have allowed archaeologists and epigraphers to reconstruct the political history of the Classic period Maya in great detail, not only providing detailed stories of rulers at individual cities but also offering unparalleled information about the relationships between cities. Without a written account, for example, would we ever suspect that the powerful dynasty at Calakmul waged war against Palenque, a city some 245 km away as the quetzal flies (Martin and Grube 2008:159–60)? Maya political history, however, is largely confined temporally to the Classic period and geographically to the southern lowlands, and the narration in most Maya archaeology textbooks is heavily biased in favor of the cities with significant hieroglyphic texts.

Because most Maya cities in the eastern lowlands do not have many monuments with surviving texts, they have been ignored in the discussion of Classic period political history, in which the specific deeds of individual rulers are placed in time and space. Thus, the majority of Maya sites in the eastern lowlands, large and small, exist on the edge of history, full of important data but left out of the intellectual conversation about the historical flow of events. However, the cities of the eastern lowlands participated in the larger cultural developments of the Maya area and have much to offer to our understanding of Maya urbanism; with the proper datasets, it is possible to integrate text-free cities into the discussion of Maya political history.

History of Maya Archaeology in Belize

Books such as this one build on the work of countless other archaeologists who sweated in the trenches, sorted thousands of pottery sherds in mosquito-netted labs, and painstakingly reconstructed the chronologies and histories of the sites where they worked. Because this book is concerned with the cities of the eastern lowlands, I limit the review of the history of Maya archaeology largely to work conducted in Belize (known as British Honduras until 1973 but referred to throughout this volume as Belize), and I have had to be selective in the projects covered because there is enough material on the history of Belizean archaeology for its own book. Even though the ancient Maya had no concern with the political borders that the nations of Central America would impose on their homeland, those borders have done much to structure the nature of archaeological research since the mid-twentieth century. Different countries have different excavation, conservation, and exportation policies, which combine to shape the nature of archaeological research.

The transformation of Belizean archaeology from its beginnings as the colonial playground of Thomas Gann to one of the most important training grounds for the next generation of Mayanists is a remarkable story in its own right. Other sources treat the subject in more detail, including Norman Hammond's (1983a) account of the development of Belizean archaeology and David Pendergast's (1993) review of archaeological research in Belize from 1809–1992. Heather McKillop (2004) provides an excellent summary of the history of research in the Maya area, with a strong focus on work in Belize, and Stephen Black's (1990) PhD thesis, using a decidedly cultural-historical approach, divides the history of research in the lowlands into six developmental phases from the first explorations in 1517 up to the study's completion in 1990. Black's (1990) study actually builds on an earlier essay written by Norman Hammond (1983b) and uses some of the same phase names. Most recently Jaime Awe (2012) presents an insider's view—from the perspective of a native Belizean and a government archaeologist—of the current state of archaeology in Belize.

The earliest explorations of Maya ruins were unsystematic in nature and predated the establishment of archaeology as a science. Spanish travelers reported ruins as early as 1517, and official expeditions to visit sites in the late 1700s culminated with Captain Antonio del Rio's drawings and excavations at Palenque in 1787 (Hammond 1983b:8–9). Systematic exploration did not begin, however, until John Lloyd Stephens (1841, 1843) and Frederick Catherwood made their now famous trips to Mexico and Central America in 1839–1842, exposing the cities of the Maya to the western world in dramatic fashion (Black 1990:46).

A number of explorers, adventurers, and early archaeologists followed in their footsteps. In Belize, one of the first was Dr. Thomas E. F. Gann, a medical officer who explored and excavated Maya ruins as a hobby (McKillop 2004:41). Gann (1925, 1926, 1927) published accounts of some of his exploits, writing in the style of the travelogues that were so popular at the time. He is rather infamous for excavating—reputedly using dynamite on occasion—and not backfilling at numerous sites across the country. As Pendergast (1993:4) observes, Gann's methods "remained more destructive than protective of evidence from beginning to end." Gann's most notable expeditions were to Lubaantun in southern Belize (McKillop 2004:45).

Gann's exploits took place near the end of the era of early explorers, and in the 1920s public institutions began to dominate archaeology in the Maya area. First among these was the Carnegie Institution of Washington, which conducted long-term excavation projects at Uaxactun, Chichén Itzá, Kaminaljuyu, and Mayapan between 1924 and 1958 (Black 1990:75). Although Uaxactun is in Guatemala, the Carnegie Institution expeditions to the site began in Belize, where they purchased supplies and equipment (Shook 1998).

The Carnegie Institution sponsored Oliver Ricketson's (1924) excavations at Baking Pot in Belize in 1924, and the British Museum sponsored excavations at two sites in southern Belize around this time: Lubaantun in 1926–1927 and Pusilhá in 1928–1930 (Black 1990:101). J. Eric S. Thompson, a member of the 1927 British Museum expedition to Lubaantun, discovered carved stelae at Pusilhá, prompting the British Museum's move to that site the following year (Black 1990:101–102).

Thompson left the Carnegie to become an assistant curator at the Field Museum in Chicago and led several expeditions to Belize sponsored by Marshall Field. In 1928 and 1929, he worked at Mountain Cow, Hatzcap Keel, and Tzimin Kax in the Maya Mountains (see Black 1990:106; Hammond 1983b:23), and Thompson (1963:160) admits in his autobiography that a primary goal of that work was "to obtain exhibitable material for Field Museum."

In 1931 Thompson arrived in Belize on the Third Marshall Field Expedition with the intention of excavating at Kaxil Uinic, a small ruin near a modern Maya village of the same name, but was forced to change plans because the Belize Estate and Produce Company had closed the village and moved its inhabitants (Houk 2012a:34–35; Thompson 1963:6, 228). He worked instead at San José that season and returned in 1934 (under a joint Field Museum and Carnegie Institution project) and in 1936 (sponsored solely by the Carnegie Institution) for two additional seasons. The Carnegie Institution published the resulting report (Thompson 1939). Black (1990) notes the San José excavations were much more professional than Thompson's work at Mountain Cow, due presumably to A. V. Kidder's influence as Thompson's new boss at the Carnegie Institution. Thompson (1938) excavated at Xunantunich, which was then called Benque Viejo, and first recorded the site of La Milpa in 1938 as part of his last Carnegie Institution project in Belize.

After World War II, the pace of research in the Maya area accelerated. In general, the period was dominated by the University Museum of the University of Pennsylvania's Tikal Project, which began in 1956 and continued until 1969. In the span of 14 years, the interdisciplinary research project transformed the remote, jungle-covered ruins into what would become a UN World Heritage Site. The project's two most-enduring legacies are its combined reconstruction of the architectural and political history of the city through archaeological and epigraphic research and the training of dozens of graduate students who later went on to be professors, ultimately training their own graduate students. In this manner many of the field methods used at Tikal have been passed down from one generation of archaeologists to the next (Black 1990:151–153).

Although the Tikal Project dominated Maya archaeology in the 1950s, other researchers undertook important work elsewhere. In Belize, Linton Satterthwaite launched a small project at Caracol in 1950 aimed at preliminary mapping and recording as well as moving some of the site's monuments (Pendergast 1993:7). More significantly, Gordon Willey conducted the first settlement pattern study in the Maya area at Barton Ramie in the Belize Valley over the course of three field seasons between 1954 and 1956 (Willey at al. 1965). The work was important not only for its pioneering field methods but also because it was the first Maya research project funded by the U.S. government, through the National Science Foundation (NSF), an agency that has been an important partner ever since (Black 1990:144).

The Royal Ontario Museum (ROM) became a significant institution in Belizean archaeology in the 1960s. William Bullard (1965; Bullard and Bullard 1965) excavated at Baking Pot and San Estevan in the early 1960s, and David Pendergast conducted significant excavations at Altun Ha between 1964 and 1970 (Black 1990:169–173; Pendergast 1979, 1982, 1990a). Pendergast (1981) ran another long-term ROM project at Lamanai from 1974 to 1980.

The end of the twentieth century witnessed a fundamental change in the nature of archaeology in the Maya area, which was part of a larger paradigm shift in the discipline in the United States. A number of influential archaeologists argued that understanding cultural process should be the primary aim of archaeological inquiry, and processual archaeology, also known as the New Archaeology, swept the halls of academia (see Trigger 1989). Intellectually, Maya archaeology post-1970 became problem oriented, a direct result of the rising popularity of the New Archaeology and its concerns with cultural process (Black 1990:182; Hammond 1983b:28). This shift was due in part to the importance of funding from the NSF, which favors problem-oriented proposals (Hammond 1983b:28). Questions about the origins of Maya "civilization," the Classic Maya collapse, ecological adaptations, and economic systems were in vogue at the time (Black 1990:182).

On top of these intellectual changes in Maya archaeology, there were practical ones as well that helped fuel the growth of archaeology in Belize after 1971 (Pendergast 1993:9). McKillop (2004:51) observes that political unrest in Guatemala and a 15 percent surcharge on projects in Mexico led many Maya archaeologists to begin fieldwork in Belize. Long-term field projects became less common around this time, and smaller thematic projects became popular. Concurrently, the individual members of the massive Tikal Project's professional staff were training more graduate students than ever before, and Belize became a popular spot for dissertation research (McKillop 2004:51).

One such graduate student was Norman Hammond (1975), who carried out his dissertation research at Lubaantun in 1970. Hammond went on to become a significant figure in Maya archaeology in Belize for the next three decades. Following his dissertation work, Hammond shifted his interests to northern Belize, conducting the Corozal Project, a regional survey (Black 1990:196) that led to the discoveries of two of the important Preclassic sites mentioned above and discussed in chapter 4: Cuello and Colha. The Corozal Project led to excavations at Nohmul (Hammond [editor] 1985) and Cuello (Hammond, ed. 1991) in the 1970s and 1980s. The work at Cuello was particularly important because of its focus on Preclassic deposits using large horizontal exposures (Black 1990:199). The project also exemplified the beginnings of what is now an established practice: the publication of results in "interim reports" and the presentation of findings at professional conferences (Black 1990:201). Prior to the 1970s, institutions published their research in well-produced monographs that took years or even decades to complete. Interim reports allow data and preliminary interpretations to be disseminated quickly.

Following its discovery, David Freidel (1986a), then at Southern Methodist University, directed a survey and excavation project at Cerros over the course of seven seasons between 1974 and 1981. The work there is best known for uncovering elaborate stucco masks on Structure 5C-2nd, but also contributed important information on Late Preclassic urban planning.

Colha drew interest from Thomas Hester and Harry Shafer because of its dense deposits of lithic debitage associated with over 100 stone tool workshops. The University of Texas at San Antonio and associated institutions conducted research at Colha over the course of eight seasons from 1979 to 1989 (Black 1990:205). The work there, particularly during the first few seasons, focused heavily on studying the "procurement-processing-distribution sequence" of stone tools at the site (Hammond 1983b:30). The discovery of Middle and Late Preclassic settlement and lithic workshops prompted Cuello-like excavations of the earliest Maya deposits at the site (Anthony and Black 1994:40; Sullivan 1991).

Other problem-oriented studies focused on Maya agriculture at Pulltrouser Swamp (Harrison and Turner 1978) and Albion Island (Pohl 1990), Archaic settlement patterns in coastal Belize (MacNeish et al. 1980), and preceramic occupation at Colha (Lohse 1993; Wood 1990). The pre-Maya occupation of Belize continues to be an important research topic as new evidence is discovered, often through chance finds of Archaic points on the surface (Lohse 2010; Lohse et al. 2006; Rosenswig 2004).

Both the Cerros and Colha projects were part of a growing trend to involve undergraduate students and paying volunteers in archaeology. Since the 1980s the number of research projects run as archaeological field schools has exploded, particularly in the Belize Valley and northern Belize. In part, this has to do with the increasingly competitive nature of external grants, but the willingness of the Belizean government to allow field schools is equally responsible.

Today field schools are the norm in Belize, and pure research projects are increasingly rare. Field schools tend to be short duration seasons (usually one month long), and field school students do not excavate as much dirt as skilled workers do. As a result, projects tend to focus their efforts on one or two excavation areas, meaning that each season of work adds only incremental clarity to the questions at hand.

Archaeological projects launched after 1980 investigated many of the cities discussed in the subsequent chapters of this book. Some of the longest-running research projects ever to be conducted in the Maya area fall into this group, most notably the Caracol Archaeological Project under the direction of Arlen Chase and Diane Chase, which has operated since 1985 (UCF Anthropology 2013), the Programme for Belize Archaeological Project (PfBAP) under the direction of Fred Valdez Jr. (2012), which has investigated a number of sites and research issues on the vast holdings of the Programme for Belize (PFB) in the northwestern corner of the country since 1992, and the Maya Research Program (2011), which has studied the area around Blue Creek north of PFB since 1992.

Organization of the Book

Chapter 2 presents the approaches this book uses to investigate Maya cities: the built environment and site planning (or an analysis of ancient urban planning). These are the analytical screens through which the data are sifted, and they affect the discussion profoundly. For example, my approach to Maya cities places particular emphasis on their relationship to elite culture and political organization. Screening the data through the filters of the built environment and site planning highlights the monumental core of a particular city at the expense of the hinterland settlement, which, many colleagues would argue, made the city possible in the first place. Chapter 2 introduces Michael Smith's (2007) framework for examining planning in ancient cities, which is applied to the cities of the eastern lowlands in chapter 10. Beyond describing the book's analytical approach, the chapter looks at the component architecture of cities and how the Maya engineered and modified the world around them. The chapter discusses not only how archaeologists collect mapping data but also how they portray that data.

It is difficult to discuss the Maya cities of the eastern lowlands without first putting them in a geographic and temporal context. Toward that end, chapter 3 provides important background information on the physical setting of the Maya world as well as the chronology and political history of the Maya. The intent of the chapter is not to provide an exhaustive review of any of the topics but to give the non-Mayanist reader enough information to make the subsequent discussions of individual sites meaningful.

Developments in the Preclassic period set the stage for the Classic period cities that are the focus of this book. Of all the areas of the Maya world, the eastern lowlands have produced some of the best data on the first Maya and their predecessors, and chapter 4 targets five Preclassic sites to highlight different aspects of Maya culture during the transition from village life to urbanism.

Chapters 5 through 9 discuss five different geographical areas of Belize from south to north. While chapter 3 provides a general overview of the physical setting of the Maya area, the introductions to these five chapters highlight the incredible diversity that characterizes the natural setting of the eastern lowlands. This diversity had important consequences for the Maya as it meant that resources—raw materials for building cities, soils for growing crops, fresh water, lithic materials for making tools, and so on—were differentially distributed across the landscape. Many of the nuanced differences in the style of architecture and the layout of cities in the eastern lowlands stem from this physiographic and ecological diversity.

Chapters 5 through 9 present data from two or more cities in a consistent format to facilitate comparison. These chapters serve two main purposes. First, they pull together concise discussions for each city regarding setting, history of investigations, site plan and urban features, chronology, and political history. For most of these cities, this is the first time all of this information has been presented together. Second, these chapters provide the data that are used in chapters 10 and 11 to examine planning and meaning in eastern lowland centers.

The five geographical areas are southern Belize, the Vaca Plateau and Maya Mountains, the Belize Valley, northwestern Belize, and northern Belize. The cities described include Pusilhá, Uxbenka, Lubaantun, and Nim Li Punit in southern Belize; Caracol and Minanha in the Vaca Plateau; Xunantunich and El Pilar in the Belize Valley; Chan Chich, Dos Hombres, and La Milpa in northwestern Belize; and Altun Ha, Lamanai, and Nohmul in northern Belize.

Chapters 10 and 11 tackle the topics of planning and meaning in the Maya cities of Belize. It is in the final two chapters that the data on the individual cities are considered together, manipulated, spun around, and reconfigured in a search for understanding. It is also here that the wildly varied approaches to city building become most clear. Although they highlight the differences between cities, the final two chapters stress their similarities while searching for evidence of planning and meaning.

Studying Maya Cities

There are many possible ways to tackle the topic of Maya cities. This book takes a decidedly site-centric approach by focusing on the monumental precincts of the eastern lowland cities at the expense of their hinterland settlement areas. This chapter begins by describing the analytical approach applied to the cities in our sample and then considers what Maya cities are in the grand scheme of urban studies. This chapter also looks at multiple aspects of Maya cities to make the regional summaries more understandable to the non-Mayanist in the crowd. Because studying a Classic period Maya city requires deciphering the ruins of a place that the forces of nature have been patiently gnawing at for over 1,200 years, it is useful to understand not only how the Maya built their cities but also how those cities fell apart. Related to those topics, this chapter describes the architectural inventories common to Maya sites and considers the engineering concerns Maya architects and builders had to overcome. All of these things—what a Maya city is, how it was built, how it decays—are important considerations relevant to the two primary types of data, excavation and mapping, used in this study. The former heavily influences reconstructions of chronology and political history while the latter impacts discussions of planning and interpretations of meaning in site plans. To facilitate an understanding of how we read Maya maps, this chapter concludes with a discussion about how archaeologists collect and portray mapping data.

The Built Environment and Site Planning: Approaches to Studying Maya Cities

As mentioned in Chapter 1, this book views the cities of the eastern lowlands through two analytical filters: the built environment, which is perhaps best suited to studying the development of an individual city, and ancient urban planning analysis, which can be used to examine the relationship between cities (Houk and Zaro 2012a). The two approaches are described below.

Studying the Built Environment

While the built environment encompasses many elements across the landscape, this study is particularly concerned with monumental architecture, including formal plazas, palaces, causeways, reservoirs, ball courts, temples, and tombs. These types of constructions require not only significant planning and engineering but also the appropriation and supervision of both skilled and unskilled labor to complete them. Trigger (1990:126) argues that monumental architecture among early civilizations was "the most public material embodiment of the power of the upper classes." Furthermore, monumental architecture in early complex societies reinforced and served as highly visible reminder of that political power to all levels of society (Trigger 1990).

Archaeologists studying the Maya often link the first appearance of monumental architecture with the rise of social complexity. As is discussed in Chapter 3, in the Middle and Late Preclassic periods, the precocious use of monumental structures, cut stone masonry, and expensive (in terms of labor and resources) and extensive causeways at the sites of Nakbe and El Mirador are evidence for early powerful rulers (Hansen 1998, 2001; Sharer and Traxler 2006).

The scale and elaboration of individual structures make statements about the power of their creators. Particularly with funerary temples, but also with palaces and other buildings, individual structures were often associated with a particular ruler, and archaeologists have come to realize just "how much the personification of monumental components of the Classic Maya built environment embody assertions of power" (Webster 1998:36).

My colleague Gregory Zaro and I have argued elsewhere that abandoned or unfinished construction projects form a particularly important subcategory of the built environment (Houk and Zaro 2012a). Whereas a massive royal acropolis conveys a message of power to all who see it, buildings left unfinished make statements about the loss of power and control just as effectively. They speak to the disintegration of political influence and may be related to the abandonment of a particular site or region. In some cases it is possible to associate architecture and artifact deposits related to the collapse of a particular city to examine how fast and how uniformly the city was abandoned (Houk and Zaro 2012a). While it might be possible to link a particular building into the recorded flow of Maya history—the dedication of buildings was something the Maya wrote about on their carved monuments—and to a known historical figure, the abandonment of Maya cities is always an event outside the limits of recorded political history. For that and other reasons, a built-environment approach is just as useful at a site like Tikal, for which we have a detailed political history, as it is at La Milpa, a site for which we know the name of only one ruler (e.g., Zaro and Houk 2012).

Ancient Urban Planning Analysis

An analysis of the built environment is helpful for reconstructing the story of an individual site, but it is not useful on its own for trying to tease out the relationships between sites. The second approach of this study, ancient urban planning or site-planning analysis, is more helpful with that. There are really two prongs to this analytical skewer: one pokes at "planning" and the other takes a stab at "meaning."

Michael Smith (2007:7) published a compelling article outlining a new method to studying planning in ancient cities that argued in favor of examining multiple variables to assess cities on a "series of ordinal scales." The approach looks at coordination among buildings and spaces, which can be done for one particular city, and at standardization among cities, which involves comparing multiple cities to one another. Applying it allows a researcher to classify a city as "more planned" or "less planned," for example, and seeks to avoid the old dichotomy of "planned" versus "unplanned" that is common in the literature on early cities. The approach, however, is not necessarily easy to operationalize, and Smith (2007:7) observed that "the scale of planning is complex and multifaceted." In Chapter 10, Smith's (2007) method is applied to the cities presented in this book. That chapter also includes more detail on the subcategories within coordination and standardization.

The second prong of the urban planning approach "is to elucidate the meanings and social contexts of ancient buildings and urban settlements" (Smith 2007:7). Meaning is much harder to identify than is evidence for planning. However, for decades the two have been intertwined in archaeological studies of ancient urbanism. Wendy Ashmore (1989, 1991) began talking about what she called Maya site planning in the late 1980s and early 1990s, referring to the deliberate aspects of the arrangement of caches, structures, sites, and landscapes. A subset of that could be called "royal precinct planning," or site planning at the city scale (Ashmore and Sabloff 2003:232). While the recently popularized term "ancient urban planning analysis" may have wider appeal than the term "site planning," the older phrase is firmly embedded in not only the title of my dissertation but a wider body of literature on Maya cities.

Ashmore (1989, 1991, 1992) championed site-planning analysis in a series of publications, in which she linked a set of planning principles to a concern on the part of the builders for cardinal directions and Mesoamerican cosmological beliefs. In her 1991 article, Ashmore (1991) suggested that many Maya cities in the central lowlands followed a particular site-planning template based on cosmological principles. The template Ashmore (1991:200) recognized was one that stressed the north-south axis of Maya cities. Often with a ball court serving as an architectural transition between the two groups of architecture, the north and south ends of a site in this template were formally and functionally complementary. The relationship between the north and south in her model is one of opposition in which the southern end is dominated by elite palaces and enclosed private spaces while the northern end is home to the open plazas, where public rituals and community activities took place (Houk 1996:74; see also Ashmore 1989; Coggins 1967). Both Coggins (1967) and Ashmore (1989) recognized that this north-south focused template was most common in the northeastern Petén area, and I therefore refer to it as the "Petén template."

Ashmore (1991:200) observed this was but one of several templates recognized at Maya sites, a point that was later lost in subsequent critiques and applications. In fact, Hammond (1981:165) previously observed a pattern for sites in northern Belize in which the architecture was split into two groups, separated from one other by open ground or connected by a *sacbe*. My own analysis of Hammond's pattern concluded that these northern Belize sites had their public plazas in the south and their elite residential palaces in the north, the opposite of the spatial arrangement of the Petén template (Houk 1996).

Ashmore (1989, 1991, 1992) linked the Petén template to pan-Mesoamerican cosmological concepts, associating the north with up and the heavens and the south with down and the underworld. In Maya myth, confrontation between the Hero Twins and the Lords of the Underworld played out on the ball court, and Ashmore (1989:279) proposed that in Maya site plans the ball court often served as the metaphorical transition between the two cosmological realms. Thus, an important but ultimately controversial conclusion in her site-planning study was that the Maya created "microcosms, arranging architecture so as to symbolically equate the architectural center of civic power with the center of the universe" (Ashmore 1991:201). My own dissertation research applied her model to sites in northwestern Belize and concluded that a variation of her template was evident at several large sites in the region (Houk 1996, 2003).

Ashmore and Jeremy Sabloff (2002:201) more recently observed "it is increasingly clear that maps of [Maya] civic centers evince considerable planning and meaningful arrangement in the placement of buildings, monuments, and open spaces." They proposed "the spatial expressions of Maya cosmology and of Maya politics constituted the most prominent ideational foundations for planning" (Ashmore and Sabloff 2002:202). They used four sites in their study, including Xunantunich, and concluded that the individual site layouts were the product of multiple influences but that cosmological directionality and political emulation were two prominent factors.

Somewhere along the way an overriding and narrow focus on what Ashmore (1991:199) called worldview maps or microcosms hijacked many site-planning studies. In recent literature the term "Mesoamerican cosmogram," a concept first mentioned in studies dating back to the late 1980s (e.g., Freidel and Schele 1988a) and ultimately defined by Julia Hendon and Rosemary Joyce (2004:326) as "a representation of the entire universe through symbolic shorthand or artistic metaphor," commonly replaces the term "microcosm" (see Smith 2005). The idea that the Maya created representations of the universe in caches, sites, and even landscapes became commonplace in the 1990s, and many researchers used the Mesoamerican cosmogram as an interpretive tool without considering the implications. Smith (2005:220) was justifiably critical of many of these studies for "presenting highly speculative interpretations as if they were reasoned and unproblematic conclusions based on empirical evidence."

My own theoretical approach to urban planning bypasses the cosmogram detour many studies took and proceeds from Ashmore's (1991) original intent and Smith's (2007) more recent critique: to search for meaning in the layout and design of Maya cities. As Chapter 11 demonstrates, meaning can be construed in a number of ways, and on one level this book applies a rather broad definition to address the question "why does a Maya city look the way it looks?" In other words, what factors—symbolic, historical, functional, and so on—contributed to the final plan of the city?

On another level this book considers meaning as described by Amos Rapoport (1988). Rapoport, a professor of architecture and founder of the field of environment-behavior studies, wrote extensively about the study of meaning in the built environment and turned to archaeological research to give his work greater time depth. Rapoport (1988:325) argued that the built environment communicates meaning on three levels, which he called high-level, middle-level, and lower-level meanings. Ashmore's (1991:199) proposed microcosms or worldview maps, which convey information about worldviews and cosmologies, are examples of high-level meaning, the most difficult level to study in the archaeological record.

The other two levels of meaning are easier to examine through archaeology. Middle-level meanings communicate information about status, wealth, identity, and power (Rapoport 1988:325). The use of monumental architecture at Maya sites is an example of how cultures express middle-level meaning. Huge temples, plazas, and palaces express information about political and religious ideology and about the wealth and power of the rulers who commissioned their construction (Smith 2007). High-level meaning is usually culturally specific and may, in fact, be understood only by a small group of people in a society; for example, among the Maya, it is likely that only the elite understood any cosmological significance in their city plan. However, middle-level meaning is not as culturally specific; even modern-day visitors to Tikal immediately admire the grand scale of the site's epicenter.

Lower-level meaning is what Rapoport (1988:325) called everyday and instrumental. It includes architectural cues about how to behave, where to walk, the function of a structure, or the private nature of a room. Rapoport (1988:326) observes that lower-level meanings "enable people to judge the situation, to act appropriately . . . to know *who does what, where, when, including/excluding whom*" (emphasis in original). Thus, without a complete understanding of social roles and expectations, archaeologists may not be able to recover all lower-level meaning. A particular setting could provide different social cues to different members of society. Still, architectural features such as steep steps, causeways, entrances to buildings, and so on can inform us about political control, class structure, social inequality, and ritual (e.g., Smith 2007:36–37).

Although as archaeologists we may not be able to recover all the meaning from the built environment, it is still important to be able to recognize when symbolic communication has occurred, even if we cannot fully understand it (e.g., Ashmore and Sabloff 2003; Houk and Zaro 2011). As is discussed in more detail in Chapter 8, my project at La Milpa employed an urban planning approach to investigate part of the site's ceremonial epicenter, finding evidence for symbolic communication, planning, and what we called "ritual engineering" in the construction of Plaza B (Houk and Zaro 2011). Along with civil engineering concerns, which reflect low-level meaning and include practical considerations like where to direct rainfall runoff, the architects of the Late Classic expansion of Plaza B also took into account the location and placement of ritual deposits, which integrated the physical space of the plaza on a symbolic level (high-level meaning). Furthermore, the mat design—a motif associated with rulership—found on three ceramic lids from two plaza caches reflects middle-level meaning and suggests royal sponsorship of the plaza plan, or at least royal participation in the rituals surrounding the creation of the caches. As Smith (2007) has noted, the drivers behind city planning in the ancient world were often kings and other members of a restricted urban elite class. Other elements of meaning in the ritual deposits at La Milpa, however, are unclear to us, but we are able to recognize that symbolic communication took place via the diverse contents of the two plaza caches (Houk and Zaro 2011).

What Is a Maya City?

Just as Maya settlement systems changed through time, so too has our understanding of them. This is a common trait in science; old ideas are constantly reevaluated in the face of new data, and often what we thought was true turns out to be false. How archaeologists have conceived of Maya urbanism has changed over the past century as more and more data became available, but the question George Andrews (1975:14) asked decades ago—"are the complexes of structures and open spaces . . . really cities?"—still lingers. Large Maya settlements do not look like cities to us because they lack nice, neat grids to organize streets and architecture. In fact, they lack "streets" for the most part. And, the density of settlement at even the largest Maya centers seems low when compared to modern towns and cities and even the cities of other preindustrial cultures.

Early on, one of the most prominent Maya archaeologists of the twentieth century, J. Eric Thompson (1954), characterized Maya cities as "vacant ceremonial centers" inhabited by priests and visited only periodically by the simple farmers from the countryside. Today the downtown core of Maya cities is still commonly referred to as the "ceremonial center" or the "epicenter," but the notion of the center being vacant has long since been discarded (e.g., Smith 2011). Similarly, the dispersed nature of the settlement surrounding the epicenter is now regarded as an adaptation to the tropical environment (Sharer and Traxler 2006:71; Smith 2011:66). When you consider the architectural openness of the ceremonial core of Maya cities alongside their dispersed settlement, it is no wonder that Maya cities are considered "among the most open structures in Mesoamerica" (Hansen 2008:75).

Michael Smith (2008:4) and Bruce Trigger (2003:12), among others, espouse a functional definition of the city. Cities perform specialized economic, administrative, political, and religious functions that affect their hinterlands. Towns, too, are urban centers, but they are smaller than cities and perform fewer urban functions (Smith 2007:5). Applying this functional definition of urbanism to Maya centers removes most of the confusion caused by their unique urban tradition.

Another crucial feature of ancient urban centers is that they were the places that the elite lived (Trigger 2003:121). They were also home to other non-food producing members of society: merchants, priests, scribes, sculptors, retainers, and members of the ruling family. The city, therefore, depended on the countryside for basic subsistence in exchange for performing the functions mentioned above (Trigger 2003).

Ancient cities were also part of elite culture. Many of the artistic and cultural "elements that so impress us were created by or for elite people who most benefited from a strongly hierarchical political and economic status quo" (Webster 2002:70). Like the Long Count calendar and hieroglyphic writing, Maya cities were inextricably linked to the elite class. While commoners undoubtedly came to the city for various reasons—to visit the markets, to adjudicate a complaint, to work, or to witness a ritual or spectacle—the monumentality of the buildings, the beauty of the temples' facades, and the elaborate attire of the city's inhabitants would reinforce the distinction between elite and commoner (for both parties).

Beyond that, David Webster (2002:154, 157) argues that Maya cities, or what William Sanders and Webster call regal-ritual centers (Sanders and Webster 1988; see also Fox 1977), were essential trappings of rulership and primarily "huge royal households." A city housed not only the living members of the royal family but their ancestors as well. With stelae, temples, and royal palaces serving as constant reminders of not only a king's earthly power but also his divine ancestry, Maya rulers were strongly tied to their cities (Webster 2002:154). This is a very important observation for the purposes of this book, which in part seeks to bring the kingdoms on the edge of history back into the larger discussion of the political history of the Classic period. Because Maya rulers were so intimately tied to their cities, the developmental history of a Maya city is a proxy for the political and economic success of its ruler. Archaeologists are often criticized for spending too much time talking about artifacts and sites while losing track of the people. In the case of Maya cities, however, the history of the site is a surrogate for the history of its ruling family.

The Classic period Maya sites discussed in this book were all regal-ritual centers that affected their hinterlands and were arguably homes to royal courts; therefore, the term "city" is appropriate following the functional definition outlined earlier. Undoubtedly, some researchers will consider more than one of the sites discussed in this book to fall below some minimum threshold for a city in terms of size or settlement density, but all of the sites, save for one, covered in the regional chapters have what might be considered the architectural inventory (plazas, a ball court, temple-pyramids, monumental buildings—all terms described in the following chapter) required to provide a wide range of urban functions to the surrounding hinterland. The exception is Altun Ha, which does not have a ball court; the site is an oddity for a number of reasons. However, Altun Ha undoubtedly affected its hinterland to a greater degree than any site near it and was arguably home to a surprisingly wealthy royal court.

Royal Courts

What then constituted royal courts among the ancient Maya, and what were their functions? David Webster (2002:157) suggests they were similar to royal courts in other preindustrial societies, composed of not only the royal family but also "lesser nobles and their families, advisors and officials, guards and military personnel, visiting dignitaries and ambassadors, political prisoners and hostages, priests, scribes, scholars, physicians, entertainers, artists and artisans, and sundry other retainers, servants, dependents, guests, and general hangers-on." Although the list of potential members of a Maya royal court is long (see also Jackson 2013:15), the most important feature of a royal court is that it is organized around the king (Inomata and Houston 2001:6). The centrality of the *k'uhul ajaw*, the divine king, is reflected in Maya art; on Late Classic polychrome ceramic vessels, the king is not only the most frequently portrayed member of a court but his image often takes up the most space in and is usually at the top of the composition (Reents-Budet 2001:213). Additionally, the *k'uhul ajaw* is often shown in the most elaborate clothing, seated, with the other people in the scene shown facing and gesturing toward him (Reents-Budet 2001:213).

Another important title that shows up in texts, especially in the western lowlands, is *sajal*. The title refers to an important subordinate to a *k'uhul ajaw*, but whether the title is military or bureaucratic is not entirely clear. Sarah Jackson (2013:66) suggests that some *sajalob* may have been subordinate leaders within a royal court and some may have held a degree of independence, in charge of secondary centers but loyal to the king of the polity capital.

It is likely that many of the things we associate with Classic Maya society (writing, the calendar, advanced mathematics) were restricted to the nobility found at the royal courts (Webster 2002:158). Stephen Houston and colleagues (2000) proposed that the language of the Classic period hieroglyphic texts was an ancestral form of the modern Mayan language of Ch'orti' and not Yukatek or Ch'olan, as widely believed by other researchers. Relevant to the discussion of royal courts, Houston et al. (2000) speculate that Classic Ch'olti'an, as they call it, was a prestige language shared by the Maya elites of the Classic period. This prestige language—think of it as a "high" language—was a marker of social distinction that created lateral solidarity among the elite across the borders of kingdoms and at the same time separated the elite vertically within their kingdoms from the majority of the populace who spoke a "low" language (Houston et al. 2000:335–336).

Maya royal courts were probably the central administrative body for their polities, but the members of the court likely carried out other specialized tasks like scribal work or judicial responsibilities (Inomata 2001:49). The degree to which the royal court directed the affairs of the non-elite in their kingdom is a matter of debate, and David Webster (2002:163) proposes that Maya polities were not tightly centralized bureaucracies in most respects. The average non-elite probably went about his or her daily routine with no interference from the royal court most of the time.

One area in which the royal court must have been particularly active, however, was the arena of planning, scheduling, and engineering the construction and maintenance of monumental structures, water management features, and the symbolic or ritual elements of the built environment. We have little understanding of the processes involved in scheduling construction activities, but each stage of a project was probably a balancing act: labor had to be divided among multiple ongoing construction projects along with routine maintenance work and scheduled against the seasonal demands of an agricultural society (Zaro and Houk 2012).

A particularly important facet within this area of royal court concern was water. Rainfall is seasonal in the Maya area and is therefore a precious commodity during the dry months of the year. Vernon Scarborough (1998) has argued that the elite were the architects and managers of elaborate hilltop water catchment and management systems at several Maya cities, including Tikal, Calakmul, and La Milpa. A significant concern for the managers of these hydrologic systems was maintaining water purity during the dry season as the standing water in reservoirs faced the risk of stagnation (Lucero 2002:815). In fact, Lisa Lucero (2002:815) suggests that Classic period Maya royalty adopted the water lily symbol because of the important relationship between royal power and maintaining potable water; the water lily only grows in clean water and is thus a good indicator of water quality.

Scarborough's (1998) research and work done by Lucero (2002, 2006) bring in the importance of royal/elite ritual activity associated with water. The rulers of places like Tikal, with its archetypical water management system, acquired power by appropriating mundane water management activities through various water rituals (Lucero 2002:816; Scarborough 1998:148). Water, however, was only one aspect of ritual activity at the great Maya centers. Takeshi Inomata (2006) argues that Maya kings were the central actor in elaborate public spectacles, which involved large audiences of commoners. In fact, the need for public spaces large enough to host all the people living in a kingdom may have been a "primary concern in the design of Maya cities" (Inomata 2006:818).

The Role of the Non-Elites

Although the focus of this book is the epicenters of Maya cities where the largest architecture is found and the ruling families lived, the vast majority of the population of a Maya city comprised non-elites living in the surrounding hinterland (Lohse and Valdez 2004). For the most part, these were farmers who had little or no kinship ties to the elite living in the nearby epicenter. Undoubtedly, though, these farmers, through their labor, built the monumental structures where the elite lived and ruled.

One of the most interesting questions related to the rise and maintenance of social inequality is one asked this way by Lisa Lucero (2006:5) in her book, *Water and Ritual: The Rise and Fall of Classic Maya Rulers*: "how do a few people get others to contribute their labor, goods, and services without compensating them equally?" While this is obviously a complicated issue, a partial answer to this question appears to be that the elite sponsored public ritual events to reinforce their own connections to the supernatural forces that affected the affairs of humans and to integrate their otherwise dispersed communities (Inomata 2006:818; Lucero 2006:156). As noted earlier, in some kingdoms with large populations and little surface water, a significant source of royal power was apparently the control of elaborate water management systems; in the dry season, rulers would have been in positions of power to extract surplus food and labor from non-elites in exchange for keeping the water flowing to fields, farms, and families (see Lucero 2006:178). Surplus food production was necessary to feed the non–food producing citizens of the city—royals, elites, full-time crafts persons, and so on—and corvée labor likely accounted for the construction of large-scale projects like water management features, intensive agriculture fields, and monumental architecture. One thing is certain: the elite certainly did not build the cities in which they lived.

Emblem Glyphs and Geopolitics

In the 1950s Heinrich Berlin (1958) made the important discovery of a class of compound glyphs called emblem glyphs, which he thought referred to the names of cities or perhaps the ruling dynasty of each city. We now know that emblem glyphs include a main sign that is linked to a particular city and affixes that translate as "holy or divine lord." Taken together, an emblem glyph can be read as "holy lord of somewhere" and are titles apparently reserved for the ruler of that place (Stuart and Houston 1994:7).

While specific emblem glyphs occur at particular cities, Marcus (1973:913) suggests they actually refer to the entire territory controlled by each city. If that assessment is accurate, then it might be more accurate to think of emblem glyphs as referencing not just a particular city—like Tikal, for example, with its main sign of "Mutul"—but an entire polity or kingdom. The difference is subtle but important. Whereas a city represents a single site on the landscape, a polity or kingdom represents a capital city, its surrounding secondary centers and countryside, and its ruling family.

In addition to emblem glyphs, Stuart and Houston (1994) have identified place names in Maya texts. An emblem glyph refers to a large political unit, but a place name refers to a specific feature on the landscape such as a hill, a particular Maya site, or even a specific building at a site (Stuart and Houston 1994:2). However, to stress the role of Maya cities as essential accessories of rulership, it is worth noting that the place name for the capital of a polity served as the main sign in its emblem glyph in most cases. As Grube (2000:553) notes, "the capital was the state; it was the seat and origin of divinely legitimized power and therefore provided the name for the entire unit." In other words, the city, as home to the royal court, was equated with the polity itself (Grube 2000:553).

Since Berlin's initial breakthrough, the number of known emblem glyphs has expanded to approximately 50 (Webster 2002:163). Peter Mathews (1991:29) has proposed that each emblem glyph represents a different independent polity and its dynasty, meaning that there were at least as many kingdoms as there were emblem glyphs during the Classic period.

If Mathews' (1991) hypothesis is correct and there were up to 50 or more dynasties of divine kings in the lowlands, it raises the issue of Maya Classic period geopolitical organization. Besides arguing about whether or not the Maya had "true" cities, archaeologists also love to debate how the many kingdoms of the Classic period were organized politically. If each city was home to a royal court, then by the end of the Late Classic there were literally hundreds of kingdoms scattered across the lowlands. How were they organized, if at all? Were they all equal in power and authority?

The two most prominent and enduring models are the regional-state model and the city-state model (Grube 2000:547; A. Smith 2003:119), with variations of each cropping up from time to time. The one thing all models agree on is that the Maya area was never under the control of one city, no matter how powerful.

Under the regional-state model, researchers like Richard E. W. Adams (1991) proposed that the Late Classic lowlands were divided into a handful of regional states, each with a major city serving as its capital. Adams' (1991) particular spin on the model was based in part on the work he and colleagues had done previously on rank-ordering Maya cities based on site size—derived from volumetric assessments and by counting courtyards at each center using published site maps, as discussed in Chapter 10 (Adams and Jones 1981; Turner et al. 1981).

Mathews' (1991:29) hypothesis that emblem glyphs represented individual dynasties carried with it the idea that, because they were part of the titles of Maya lords, all dynasties were equal, thus refuting the regional-state model. This line of reasoning was one used to support the city-state model, which envisioned small polities each with a royal center that was home to a ruling dynasty. If all kings and, by extension, all polity capitals were equal, why were some cities clearly larger than others? In fact, it was the clear difference in size, evident in the rank ordering of Maya sites, that had led supporters of the regional-state model to propose that a small number of cities controlled large territories and numerous smaller cities and towns.

More recent decipherment has identified glyphs that clearly indicate some kings were subordinate to others (Grube 2000:550). While each kingdom may have been under the control of a dynasty of divine kings, not all divine kings were created equal, it would seem. As Nikolai Grube (2000:550) observes, "some kingdoms are consistently more dominant than others and seem to be manipulating the affairs of weaker ones." Thus, the emerging view is a complicated geopolitical landscape during the Classic period, with some kingdoms, particularly Tikal and Calakmul, holding "lesser ones in their sway" (Grube 2000:550). The kings of these Classic period city-states, we now know from deciphered hieroglyphic texts, practiced a wide range of activities to establish, maintain, and manipulate political relationships. Gift giving, royal visits, marriage, and shared ritual activities maintained alliances, while warfare reflected the ongoing competition between the groups of city-states (Grube 2000:550).

Despite these complicated arrangements and alliances, Maya city-states apparently remained largely autonomous. Even after being defeated in battle, kings—or in some cases the next in line for the throne—were allowed to remain on the throne and rule their polity without interference (Grube 2000:550). In a rather stunning discovery, archaeologists working at La Corona in Guatemala found an indication that Yuknoom Yich'aak K'ahk' of Calakmul visited La Corona in 696 CE (Bueche 2012). For decades archaeologists had assumed he had been killed or captured several months earlier following a defeat by Calukmul's great rival, Tikal.

The model of the Classic period Maya that I have outlined here fits what Hansen (2000:16–17) has called a city-state culture. The region that is today marked by the archaeological remains of the ancient Maya was occupied by people who shared a common culture and spoke related languages but were divided politically into a large number of polities spread across the lowlands. The polities, or kingdoms, varied considerably in size, but no one kingdom was ever powerful enough to control the entire region. Antonia Foias (2013:230) concludes that not all Maya states employed the exact same political structure, yet different kinds of states and different sized kingdoms coexisted during the Classic period. Political power in these kingdoms, however, was "precarious and fragile," and that fragility shaped the dynamic nature of Maya geopolitics (Foias 2013:230). As with other city-state cultures around the world, war was endemic between these Maya kingdoms, but at the same time there was considerable interaction between kingdoms economically and culturally, even across borders between states.

The occasional but always temporary and fluid domination of other city-states by the two great powers of Tikal and Calakmul is also a characteristic of city-state cultures. As Hansen (2000:17) observes, "the city-states of a city-state culture are not necessarily 'peer polities,' but can be hierarchically organised systems of polities, of which some are hegemonic, some independent, and some dependencies." Thus, the model this book favors for the geopolitical landscape of the Classic period is one of numerous kingdoms, each ruled by its own dynasty of divine kings, and each operating fairly autonomously, at least in terms of the management of their own internal affairs. Each kingdom had a capital city, which was the home of the royal court and the symbol of authority for the entire polity. In many ways, the capital city was a regal-ritual center (e.g., Webster 2002:151), home to the elite and high culture.

Another way to think of these kingdoms is as territories. Thomas Garrison (2007) used this model in his dissertation, which examined the geopolitical organization of northwestern Belize and northeastern Guatemala. A territory includes the "area of land and population under the control of a particular capital" (Garrison and Dunning 2009:526). In this model, territories include not only a capital but also minor centers and rural household groups, and they operate as independent, social, and economic units (Garrison and Dunning 2009:527).

Clearly, not all Maya cities and dynasties were equal in power; the affairs of many kingdoms were affected either directly or indirectly by the political maneuverings of Tikal and Calakmul for centuries during the Classic period. Through what Simon Martin and Nikolai Grube (2008:185) call "overkingship," the most powerful polities directed the affairs of lesser kingdoms. This system of political patronage in effect reduced the smaller kingdoms to client states of the more powerful dynasties and accounts for the fact that seemingly autonomous kingdoms ruled by divine kings could differ so greatly in scale (Martin 2001:185).

In many cases, the royal families of smaller kingdoms participated in this seemingly eternal competition by being allies with or vassals to the king of one of the two powers. Royal visits, marriages, rituals, and joint military action created and maintained ties between the kingdoms of the lowlands (A. Smith 2003). To complicate this picture, the geopolitical landscape was a dynamic and complex network of relationships; some kingdoms switched sides, some broke away from their overlords, and others fought another member of the same alliance.

Making a Maya City

The Maya cities of the eastern lowlands all comprise the same basic architectural building blocks, which are configured in unique ways at each city. Maya architects had plentiful limestone in most areas of the lowlands with which to work and employed other lithic materials, such as sandstone in southern Belize, where limestone was not available. As a rule, however, limestone served as the primary facing material and was used to make not only cut stone blocks but also mortar and plaster. The Maya also had a variety of perishable materials at their disposal, including palm leaves and vines for thatching, and several species of hardwood trees for making lintels and perishable superstructures. Maya architects used these materials to design and build a wide variety of buildings and structures including temple pyramids, ball courts, multiroomed buildings commonly called palaces, plazas, causeways (*sacbeob*), shrines, city walls, and reservoirs. All around the ceremonial centers were smaller structures grouped around courtyards and surrounded by domestic features such as kitchen gardens, *chultuns*, and middens.

Except for the humblest of Maya structures, Maya buildings big and small shared a common architectural foundation: the platform. During the Preclassic, the earliest documented Maya domestic structures consisted of perishable buildings built on low platforms made of earth and stone that were faced by shaped or cut stones. The perishable buildings were likely constructed in the same manner as modern Maya houses with a wooden framework made of poles that supported a thatched roof and walls made of wattle and daub or simply smaller poles. As Robert Sharer (1994:631) observes, these early domestic structures became the prototype for the more elaborate monumental constructions of stone and plaster.

The Maya constructed platforms to create level surfaces to support other buildings and to serve as activity areas, such as plazas and courtyards. In the monumental architecture of the Classic period, platforms consisted of a core of rubble (cobbles, boulders, soil, and even midden material) usually encased in a core face composed of carefully laid but not necessarily shaped stones. Cut stones then formed the face of the platform; a lime plaster covered the cut stone face to give the platform a smooth surface, which could be painted or decorated (see Loten and Pendergast 1984). Today, at restored Maya ruins, the outer coating of plaster is usually absent, and visitors are left with the mistaken impression that the cut facing stones were visible when the city was occupied (Figure 2.1). The nature of the material used as the core, or the fill, in a platform was highly variable and changed through time. For example, in northwestern Belize my own excavations have encountered a wide range of fill types, from a mixture of earth and small cobbles in Late Preclassic structures, to small cobbles encased in mortar (what is called wet-laid fill) in Late Preclassic and Early Classic platforms, to cobbles and boulders with no mortar (what is called dry-laid fill) in Late Classic constructions. Typically, when building large platforms such as those used to create a plaza or a courtyard, the Late Classic architects would place unshaped boulders as the base. They would gradually transition to cobbles as the platform reached its desired height. Smaller cobbles and pebbles capped the cobbles and served as ballast for the plaster floor, which topped the platform. This method required very little consideration for which rock was placed where in the core; the irregularly shaped boulders create a strong physical bond and, just as importantly, leave large voids between them. This means that a percentage of the structural mass is actually air, allowing the construction of larger platforms with less material.

Most Maya platforms had slightly sloping (what is called "batter") faces instead of vertical ones, and tall platforms were often constructed of two or more terraces; both methods improved the stability of the platform. Another

Figure 2.1. Battered (sloping) platform face of Structure B-3 at Cahal Pech with plaster restored over facing masonry (photograph by the author).

feature seen in larger platforms is construction pens. These pens are essentially crudely built "cells" of unshaped boulders or large cobbles that contain discrete pockets of fill. In addition to adding stability, they may have been used to divide workers into groups with assigned tasks during the construction of the platform. In some cases, sequential construction projects would link two or more platforms into a single, larger platform (Sharer 1994:634). Stairs usually provided access to the summits of platforms, and stair placement, while variable, generally favored the centerline of the platform.

As noted earlier, platforms were constructed to create level surfaces to support buildings or to serve as activity areas themselves. Large platforms were used to level hilltops and create plazas, which in turn supported other smaller platforms and buildings.

In a typical Maya city, many of the buildings in the epicenter of the site were masonry or at least part-masonry structures (Figure 2.2). The walls of these structures—and internal features like benches—followed the same basic construction technique as the platform but used generally smaller stones: unshaped cobbles, usually with some kind of mortar or aggregate, formed the core

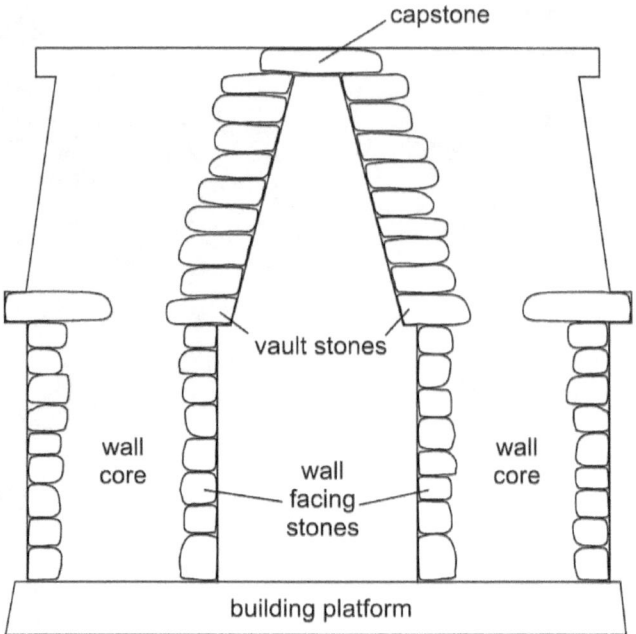

Figure 2.2. Idealized cross section of a vaulted masonry building.

of walls, and cut and shaped stones formed the face of the wall. Just as was the case with the platforms, the faces of the walls, on both the inside and outside of a building, were coated in plaster to give them a smooth surface.

The height of walls varied on Maya buildings; some structures had only low-height walls that supported perishable upper walls and roofs, while others had full-height walls topped by a perishable frame and roof. The most impressive buildings, however, were those with masonry ceilings. The Maya never developed the true arch; instead they relied on a corbeled vault, or false arch, that resembled an inverted "V" in cross-section (Sharer 1994:634). Maya builders placed a series of overlapping and projecting blocks to span the distance between two walls and create the ceilings of their masonry buildings, relying on the mass of the mortared core of the ceiling to support the weight of the projecting blocks. As David Pendergast (1990b:68) notes this method of vault construction was a major weakness in Maya architecture. Nevertheless, the Maya used this method to construct not only temples but also elite residences, particularly in the monumental precincts of cities.

Given the limitations of the corbeled vault, most Maya masonry buildings have thick walls and narrow rooms, usually not more than 2 m wide (Pendergast 1990b:68). In buildings with parallel rows of rooms, the center wall, or spinewall, had to be even thicker than the outer walls because it had to support the mass of two vaults (Figure 2.3). This necessity resulted in a significant percentage of the floor plan of a Maya building consisting of wall mass rather than useable space. Because the doorways to buildings and between rooms had to be spanned by stone or wooden lintels, they were usually not much wider than their walls were thick. The result was small, dark, private rooms. Often one or more low masonry benches occupied much of the floor space in a room. This construction technique also meant that most Maya buildings were only one story (Figure 2.4), although a few multistory buildings have been documented (Sharer 1994:637).

One result of the use of the corbeled vault was that it created large roof masses above rooms, the faces of which were often decorated with sculptural elements (Pendergast 1990b:69). In the case of temples, the height of the roof was occasionally increased by the addition of a roof comb, which served as an additional surface for artistic decoration (Sharer 1994:637).

The corbeled vault, already a poor architectural solution to creating interior spaces, faced other structural problems including highly variable—and generally decreasing through time—quality of raw material used to construct buildings and the deleterious effects of heavy rainfall on plaster exteriors, which

Figure 2.3. Structure A-32 on the north face of the Castillo at Xunantunich, facing west. Note the thickness of the spinewall in comparison to the two outer walls on this once vaulted building (photograph by the author).

Studying Maya Cities   31

Figure 2.4. Restored Structure E-1 at Cahal Pech. Although this appears to be a two-story building, the upper room is built behind the lower room, not on top of it (photograph by the author).

served as a protective barrier for the bulk of the architecture. The stone raw material available to the Maya varied from area to area, and, although limestone was the most common, other rock was used in constructions where it was available. The quality of stone, however, was not uniform across the Maya world, and architects without access to fine-grained or less-fractured raw material faced great challenges. Additionally, in areas with limited amounts of suitable construction material, each successive generation of builders found their supply of raw material more and more depleted and the quality of raw material to be lower (Pendergast 1990b:70).

The Maya living in the southern half of the lowlands, from eastern Chiapas, across the Petén and Belize, and into western Honduras, had to contend with seasonally high rainfall, which sometimes fell in hours- to days-long deluges (in 2008, I personally experienced 96 straight hours of rainfall during a tropical storm in Belize). Rainwater washing off buildings created drip lines that eroded plaster surfaces, massive runoff events flooded plazas and courtyards, and even short-term submersion under water weakened exposed plaster surfaces. Furthermore, high humidity and hot weather caused exposed plaster and limestone to discolor within only a few years.

As a result, Maya cities required nearly constant maintenance, and archaeologists commonly find evidence of floors having been resurfaced and walls having been repaired or modified. Another extremely important characteristic of Maya architecture, however, was the fact the Maya apparently did not intend for buildings to be in use forever. As David Pendergast (1990b:69) observes, the Maya were saved from the potentially dangerous effects of their flawed engineering—picture a corbeled vault collapsing on a royal family somewhere—"by their zeal in covering old buildings with new ones." Therefore, just as a coat of plaster could disguise defects in the masonry of a platform face, a new and larger building could eradicate structural problems with its predecessor. When constructing a new building over an old one, at times the Maya infilled vaulted rooms to serve as the core of an enlarged platform, and at other times they demolished the old superstructure entirely, using the debris for construction fill for the new building and presumably salvaging useful material in the process.

This brings up an important observation David Webster (2002:155) made about Maya cities that tends to be overlooked. When presented with detailed reconstruction drawings of Maya cities on the pages of *National Geographic* magazine, it is easy to forget that, like cities everywhere, Maya cities "were in a continual state of decay and renewal" (Webster 2002:155). Maintenance was an ongoing activity that probably stopped only when it rained so hard it could not be done (Pendergast 1990b:68). While some buildings were in use, others were likely abandoned, awaiting repair, and still others were under construction (Webster 2002:155). When scheduling construction activities, Maya city planners had to take all of these factors into consideration, along with the availability of labor and the need for other projects in the kingdom, and it is likely that major construction or renovation projects proceeded in stages (e.g., Zaro and Houk 2012).

Common Architectural Components of Maya Cities

Although each Maya city was unique, they all comprised a number of common building types as well as other urban features. Some of these features are found in other Mesoamerican cultures; some are uniquely Maya. The following section describes a wide range of common architectural features found at Maya sites to provide background for the descriptions of sites in the subsequent chapters and the comparison and analysis of site plans in the final two chapters. Not all of the features described in the following come back into play in the final analysis, but many do.

Plazas and Courtyards

The buildings in the epicenters of Maya cities are almost always grouped around plazas and courtyards. The former are large, open platforms that have been artificially leveled (Andrews 1975:37). The edges of a plaza are marked either by the faces of its platform or by buildings or walls. In most cases, plazas are rectilinear in shape and oriented within 15 degrees or so of a cardinal direction. We suspect that most Maya plazas were originally covered in a plaster surface, but it is rare to find the actual floor surface preserved today, except beneath stone monuments or at the base of buildings where it was protected from the elements by collapse debris. Plazas are considered to be public places and were likely the focus of community life, including elaborate spectacles put on by the king for the entire community (Inomata 2006:810). Plazas also tend to be the settings for carved stone monuments (discussed below), and Inomata (2006:811) suggests many stelae depict public performances put on by kings in their plazas in front of large audiences. In essence, the monuments serve as a reminder of the spectacle or ritual long after it took place.

As will become evident in the following chapters, the sizes of plazas varied dramatically from site to site, but plazas are the central organizing feature of Maya cities. It is also likely that they served multiple functions including artificial water catchments (Scarborough and Gallopin 1991), locations for community-wide gatherings (Inomata 2006), and marketplaces (Dahlin et al. 2007). New circumstantial evidence of Maya markets comes from the remarkable murals showing apparent merchants and consumers on Structure 1 in the Chiik Nahb complex at the massive Maya city of Calakmul in Mexico (Carrasco Vargas et al. 2009), and new archaeological evidence comes from promising geochemical prospection to look for residues of metals and minerals in plazas (Bair and Terry 2012; Dahlin et al. 2007; Rothenberg 2014). Hosting a market would have been another elite or royal strategy to promote community integration and to acquire tribute.

Courtyards are smaller open spaces, generally considered to be residential in function, although they may include private shrines. Like plazas, courtyards are artificially leveled surfaces, and buildings mark their margins. Unlike a plaza, a courtyard is defined by the buildings that surround it and cannot be thought of as separate from them (Andrews 1975:38). Courtyards may occur as isolated groups separated by some distance from other buildings, or they may occur within a contiguous group of architecture such as a palace or acropolis.

Causeways (*Sacbeob*)

Unique to Maya cities, *sacbeob* (the plural of *sacbe*) were important architectural features that likely served a wide variety of functions ranging from transportation, polity integration, water management, and ritual (Shaw 2001). Most Maya causeways are raised platforms constructed in the same basic manner as structural platforms, with stone-lined edges and a *sascab*-paved surface (Shaw 2001:261). In rare cases, such as at Chan Chich, causeways were not raised features but were essentially ground-level corridors defined by low walls or parapets along their margins (Houk 2003:60), and Andrews (1975:38) observes that some elevated causeways have low parapet walls along their margins, such as the Mendez Causeway at Tikal.

Most causeways connect plazas within the same site or link two cities together. *Sacbeob* vary widely in length, width, and height across the Maya area, but Shaw (2001:262) has proposed three basic types based on length and what they connect: local intrasite, core-outlier intrasite, and intersite. Those of the first type connect architectural groups within the site core and are comparatively short. The second type links the core to outlying groups and can be as long as 5 km, while the intersite *sacbeob* connect two different cities together and are longer than 5 km (Shaw 2001:262). All three types have been documented in the eastern lowlands, but intersite *sacbeob* only occur at Caracol (Shaw 2001:262).

Not all Maya cities had *sacbeob*; few have more than one in the eastern lowlands, while Caracol has many. Clearly, not every Maya city needed a *sacbe* to function, which raises the question of just what the functions of *sacbeob* were beyond transportation corridors. In some cases, they served as integrating features, such as at Caracol, binding an extensive settlement into one political and administrative entity (see A. Chase and D. Chase 1996). In other (or all) cases, they may have also had important religious and political roles as processional ways (Andrews 1975:38; Inomata 2006:817).

Whatever their function(s), causeways represented a significant construction expense. Despite their unimposing nature, they are often much wider than necessary if they were strictly transportation routes, and elevating them required large amounts of construction fill and masonry. Consider that a 20-m wide *sacbe* that is 1 m high requires 200 m^3 of fill for every 10 m of length. At 100 m long, our hypothetical causeway would require 2,000 m^3 of fill, enough to build a 20 by 20 m platform to a height of 5 m. At Caracol, stepping from the hypothetical to the real world, there are over 70 km of causeways between 3 and 12 m wide (A. Chase and D. Chase 1996:806).

Temple Pyramids

The most recognizable of Maya building types is the temple pyramid, most often simply called a temple. The pyramid portion of the assemblage is the substructure, usually square in plan and composed of multiple terraces that become progressively smaller with each level, and the temple is the building on top (Andrews 1975:39). The first lowland Maya pyramids were built during the Middle and Late Preclassic periods. These early pyramids often had elaborate stucco masks flanking their central stairway and flat summits to support perishable buildings (Lucero 2007:412). By the Classic period, masonry temples replaced the perishable structures.

Although temples already towered over the other buildings at a Maya city, by the Late Classic Maya architects often exaggerated the height of a temple by adding an elaborate roof comb on top of the structure (Andrews 1975:42; Sharer 1994:637). The temples themselves consisted of one or two small rooms with one central doorway. These small interior spaces and the generally steep stairway from plaza to temple indicate temples were not public structures (Andrews 1975:42) despite the fact they are most commonly found in public plazas. While rituals conducted at the top of the steps could be seen by people in the plaza below, any rites conducted inside the temple would have been private (Lucero 2007:412).

Some temples were clearly designed and built as funerary monuments for specific rulers; in some cases, rulers appear to have added a tomb chamber into an existing substructure. However, not all temple pyramids have tombs, nor are all tombs in temple pyramids.

Range Buildings, Palaces, and Acropoli

Much more common than temples at Maya cities are low platforms topped by multiple rooms. Range buildings, which tend to be longer than they are wide in plan, have two or more rooms placed side by side. Usually each room has its own entrance. Tandem range buildings have two rows of rooms, one behind the other. Building off these basic models is a wide range of possibilities involving additional rooms oriented perpendicular to the others (termed transverse). At larger sites, range buildings can be quite massive and support numerous rooms.

While range building is a rather inglorious label for some of the more impressive examples of the form, it is a label unburdened by implications of function. Early on, Spanish explorers referred to these buildings as *palacios*, and the term palace became rather uncritically applied by subsequent archaeologists to many buildings at Maya centers (Christie 2003:2). Borrowed from European concepts of architecture and government, the palace label assumes that the buildings in question functioned as residences (Harrison 2003:100). However, research at Tikal has shown that the term is misleading, as the numerous buildings sharing the palace label "do not serve the same—and often not even similar—functions" (Harrison 2003:100). The label tends to be applied to larger range buildings or a complex of range buildings arranged around one or more interior courtyards, sometimes called a palace group (see Andrews 1975:59). At Tikal, Harrison (2003:110) proposed the palaces there had features consistent with judicial, diplomatic, educational, and residential functions.

To complicate the classification of Maya architecture even further, Maya archaeologists borrowed the term "acropolis" from Classical European architecture and applied it freely to a wide range of building aggregates (Andrews 1975:67). To bring some order to the chaos, Andrews (1975:67) defined a Maya acropolis group as a combination of palaces or temples built on various levels of a large platform or series of platforms. Acropoli are elevated groups of architecture comprising a series of courtyards with limited and controlled access so that "movement from one space to another can only be accomplished along a predetermined path culminating at the most important building in the group, usually a temple" (Andrews 1975:67).

Ball Courts

One of the most recognizable architectural features at a Maya city is the ball court (or ballcourt, as some scholars prefer). The ball game was played across Mesoamerica, up into the American Southwest, into northern Central America, and even on several Caribbean islands. In the Maya area, ball courts consist of two parallel structures facing each other across a playing alley, or alleyway. The courts in the central and eastern lowlands are most often opened ended, as opposed to "I" shaped courts with well-defined end zones (Scarborough 1991a:134). The two structures generally have low benches and/or sloping faces that front the playing alley; in some cases the sloping faces were replaced by deep steps to give the structures a tiered form, as at Chan Chich. The summits of the structures sometimes supported masonry buildings but in many cases were only flat surfaces without a superstructure. Some, but not all, ball courts had one or more circular ball court markers placed in the alleyway.

Ball courts are almost always built in an open area not connected to other buildings, but there are exceptions. At a handful of centers in the eastern lowlands, one structure of the ball court is physically attached to a much larger building, while the other structure is freestanding. There is tremendous variation in length and width of the playing alley and in the size and height of the flanking structure, but Vernon Scarborough (1991a:137, Figure 7.3) suggests that the large number of courts with alleyways clustering between 2–6 m wide and 14–22 m long indicates that the game was standardized to a large degree.

Ball courts are found at most larger sites, but not all, and are not found at most smaller sites. They are almost always found in association with the monumental architecture of site cores, and most are oriented generally north–south (Scarborough 1991a:138–40). It is worth remembering that ball courts are often placed as architectural transitions between the northern and southern parts of sites fitting into Ashmore's (1991) Petén site-planning template, discussed below.

Stone Monuments

Another important feature of Maya cities are their stone monuments. In addition to ball court markers, which were sometimes carved, the Maya commonly placed stelae and altars in the plazas of sites. In most of the eastern lowlands, limestone was used to make stelae and altars, but in southern Belize sculptors used the available sandstone for their monuments (Sharer 1994:641). Stelae are stone pillars erected upright and often, but not always, carved. Those that show no evidence of having been carved may once have been covered in stucco and painted. The size of stelae varies widely across the Maya area, and even varies within the same site, but most stelae are at least 1.5 m tall.

Carved stelae often depict kings, and those stelae with hieroglyphic texts usually describe important historical events, often with accompanying Long Count dates. Sadly, over a millennia of rainfall has damaged many stelae, and looters have removed an unknown number from their original locations.

Not all Maya sites have stelae, and it is unclear what the presence of stelae indicates. For example, the lack of stelae erected by rulers at the great Maya city of Tikal after the defeat of that city by its enemies at the end of the Early Classic period is a common argument for Tikal's being a vassal of its conqueror, Calakmul (e.g., Sharer and Traxler 2006:377). If true, does the presence of a stela at a site indicate political independence? Does the absence of stelae indicate a subordinate role (and to what degree does looting of carved stelae bias such a conclusion)?

Altars are less common than stelae but are nonetheless found at many Maya sites. Altars are generally circular in plan and about 50 to 70 cm high, and some are carved. Some altars apparently sat on stone pedestals, and there is a possibility that altars served as thrones for Maya kings (e.g., Sharer 1994:641). Altars may occur alone or paired with a stela, in which case they are almost always placed in front the stela.

Quarries, Reservoirs, and Water Management Features

All the elements of Maya cities discussed so far are above-ground features that add material to the built environment, but some features subtract material from the landscape. Obviously, the construction material used to build masonry structures at Maya cities had to come from somewhere. It was quarried from pits and rock faces, often from sources close to the city since the resulting stones had to be carried by hand to their destination since the Maya did not have domesticated pack animals. Quarries created depressions on the landscape that could be modified fairly easily into reservoirs. In fact, Vernon Scarborough (1998:139) suggests that the quarry location was possibly as important a component of the built environment as the monumental structures the quarry supplied.

In some cases, best documented at Tikal, Maya cities included large-scale water management systems that included reservoirs, diversion weirs, and clay-lined channels to move water downhill to feed smaller reservoirs and agricultural fields (Scarborough and Gallopin 1991). Causeways, as noted earlier, were sometimes integrated into the water management system of a city, serving as catchment basins and/or dams (see Shaw 2001). At Tikal, Scarborough's teams have documented an amazingly complex and integrated system composed of rather simple technologies and engineered facets of the landscape that satisfied the city's water needs for centuries (Scarborough et al. 2012). Simpler versions of this system have been documented at smaller cities like La Milpa (Scarborough et al. 1995). Such systems undoubtedly required constant maintenance, and controlling them and their precious resource may have been an important source of political power for Maya rulers (Lucero 2002, 2006; Scarborough 1998).

Engineering Concerns of a Maya City

Reservoirs lead our discussion of Maya cities to engineering concerns faced by Maya architects and builders. A Maya city is nothing if not a heavily engineered built environment, and one of the greatest engineering concerns was water in all its forms: rainfall, runoff, and an important seasonally available resource to be managed. The epicenters of Maya cities comprised great expanses of impervious ground with their plaster-covered buildings and plazas. Maya engineers turned a potential problem—vast amounts of runoff during heavy rains—into an opportunity to engineer the built environment in such a way as to capture that runoff. Therefore, the plazas and other plaster surfaces, which acted as artificial catchment basins, formed another important element of the water management system described earlier. By engineering the slope of not only terraces on structures but the surfaces of plazas and courtyards, the Maya could direct runoff into reservoirs or channels (Pendergast 1990b; Scarborough 1998). Doing so required careful planning prior to any major construction event because every modification to the built environment could affect the water management system. In fact, the *sacbeob* at Tikal, for example, served multiple purposes: in addition to linking and integrating the city and serving as routes for ritual processionals, they also were functional components of the water management system, acting as catchment areas and doubling as dams (Shaw 2001:266–67).

How Maya Buildings Fall Apart

Maya architecture is almost never found intact. Time, rainfall, gravity, and a relentless succession of vegetation have been slowly but surely breaking down the Classic period cities since their caretakers abandoned them over 1,000 years ago. To understand how the mounds we see today once looked, it is useful to have an understanding of how Maya buildings fall apart.

When they were in use, Maya structures were a combination of perishable items like wood and thatch combined with masonry and plaster elements. Perishable materials could be used to make walls, roofs, lintels, partitions, supports, and a wide variety of other architectural elements. Masonry was used to construct platforms, floors, walls, benches, and, on the most elaborate structures, stone roofs. The stone elements were covered in a protective layer of plaster that required constant maintenance. Once that upkeep ended, the forces of nature began to impact the buildings unchecked.

Cracks in the plaster coating of exterior walls allow water to penetrate, and the plaster begins to peel away from the structure. The vaulted ceilings, which were structurally deficient even when new, weaken, particularly as their perishable components like lintels and cross beams rot away. Birds drop seeds on the roofs of buildings, and eventually plants begin to find purchase for their roots as cracks become more common. Tree roots burrow through structural cracks, forcing apart walls and breaking through floors. Chemically the matrix formed by the collapse of a Maya building is very similar to the soils that form as limestone weathers, and structurally a partially collapsed building provides a better hold for a tree's roots than the natural terrain across much of the lowlands. It is, therefore, not uncommon to find some of the largest and oldest trees in the modern forest growing on ruins rather than natural ground.

The result is that, slowly but surely, the buildings begin to fall apart, and as they do so the tops of buildings collapse and the outer walls of rooms fall outward, down the sides of the platform, creating the mounds we see today. On large structures, the thicker, load-bearing walls preserve better than the thinner outer walls. The spots where perpendicular walls meet are often where preservation is best. However, these spots are also where you are most likely to find large trees growing on the ruins. The back walls of buildings, which tend to be built above the steepest platform faces, are usually the worst-preserved walls, and it is not uncommon for the entire back wall of a building to fall away if the face of the platform gives way below it.

The process of deterioration is generally slow, but certain events can cause severe damage to Maya buildings very quickly. Generally, when a tree growing on a mound dies, it decays over the period of many years, but powerful hurricanes periodically sweep across the Maya lowlands knocking over living and dead trees alike. When this happens, the root system of the tree is often torn from the ground, and, if that tree happens to be growing on a Maya building, what was intact architecture is ripped apart as the roots are pulled from the ground.

A side effect of this process of collapse is that archaeologists must remove large amounts of debris before any intact architecture is encountered. When reading archaeological reports, you will see various terms such as "tumble" and "collapse debris" to describe the rubble created as a stone building breaks apart. Often excavations provide a snapshot of the process as tumbled stones are uncovered, literally frozen in the act of collapsing (Figure 2.5).

Figure 2.5. Photograph of a partially collapsed building in Courtyard 100B at La Milpa. Captured in the act of collapsing, the eastern wall of the building is falling outward, pulling away from the bench in the room, and the southern face of the doorway jamb has fallen to the east, down the face of the structure, and is actually inverted. Note the tree root growing through a ceramic cord holder in the wall and other collapsed wall stones visible in the north wall of the excavation unit (photograph by the author).

Generally speaking, the architecture covered by this collapse debris is protected from exposure to the elements. Because of that, plaza floors and plastered steps are often found intact at the base of buildings, but tops of buildings are usually poorly preserved. Within rooms, floors and the bottom of walls are better preserved than the tops of walls.

How Archaeologists Map Maya Sites

Maps of Maya sites may be confusing to those not familiar with Maya ruins or the conventions archaeologists use to map them. Most Maya maps are depicted in a rather unusual method—unless you happen to a Mesoamerican archaeologist, in which case it is not unusual at all—but there are many ways that archaeologists collect their mapping data. Most Maya sites are mapped using a variety of methods ranging from something as expedient as using a compass and a measured step (pace and compass) or a compass and a long tape measure (tape and compass) to as slow as using a surveying instrument like a total data station or even a global positioning system. The first two methods can collect simple two-dimensional data suitable to depict the arrangement of buildings and spaces while the latter can collect three-dimensional data that can show vertical relationships. Three-dimensional data can be used to produce topographic maps that record the shape of the built environment based on differences in elevation, expressed as contour lines.

Recently, archaeologists working in the eastern lowlands have turned to light detection and ranging (LiDAR) technology to collect mapping data for large areas of dense forest (Chase et al. 2012). Traditional mapping methods require teams of surveyors to hack their way through the forest to create lines of sight, but airborne LiDAR literally sees through the canopy and collects three-dimensional measurements of the ground surface; this allows archaeologists to generate detailed topographic maps of huge areas (Chase et al. 2012). Pioneered in the Maya area at Caracol where the Caracol Archaeological Project mapped over 200 km^2 of hilly, forested terrain in 2009 (Chase et al. 2011), LiDAR has since been used in southern Belize at Uxbenka (Thompson et al. 2013) and in the Belize Valley (Ford and Bihr 2013).

Archaeologists have also used related approaches on the ground to collect detailed mapping data of smaller areas. At Pacbitun, Terry Powis' team has been experimenting with a laser scanner—basically ground-based LiDAR—to map the monumental architecture at the site (Lund and Weber 2013). At Chan Chich, Chet Walker and Mark Willis successfully used Structure from Motion

(SfM) technology to produce a high-resolution digital elevation model (DEM) of a large building in the Main Plaza (Houk, Walker et al. 2013). SfM is an intriguing option because it is much cheaper than LiDAR or laser scanning; it uses off-the-shelf digital cameras to collect the mapping data. Specialized software takes the photographs and stitches them together into a photogrammetric block to produce a DEM, from which topographic maps, shaded relief maps, and so on can be derived (Figure 2.6). The technology is not able to penetrate vegetation like LiDAR can, but it is a powerful tool in many situations. For example, in January 2014 Eleanor Harrison-Buck's Belize River East Archaeology project relied on the technical expertise of the same SfM experts to map approximately 11 km^2 of cleared fields around the minor center of Saturday Creek (Harrison-Buck et al. 2014). Walker and Willis used a pair of small drones, less controversially known as unmanned aerial vehicles, to collect the data in one day of field time.

Although the methods mentioned here are capable of producing high-resolution topographic maps, they are not necessarily better at picking up features important to an archaeologist (e.g., Hutson 2012:288). As a result, even when archaeologists have topographic data, they still often draw maps of Maya sites following an old convention usually called "Malerization" (Figure 2.7).

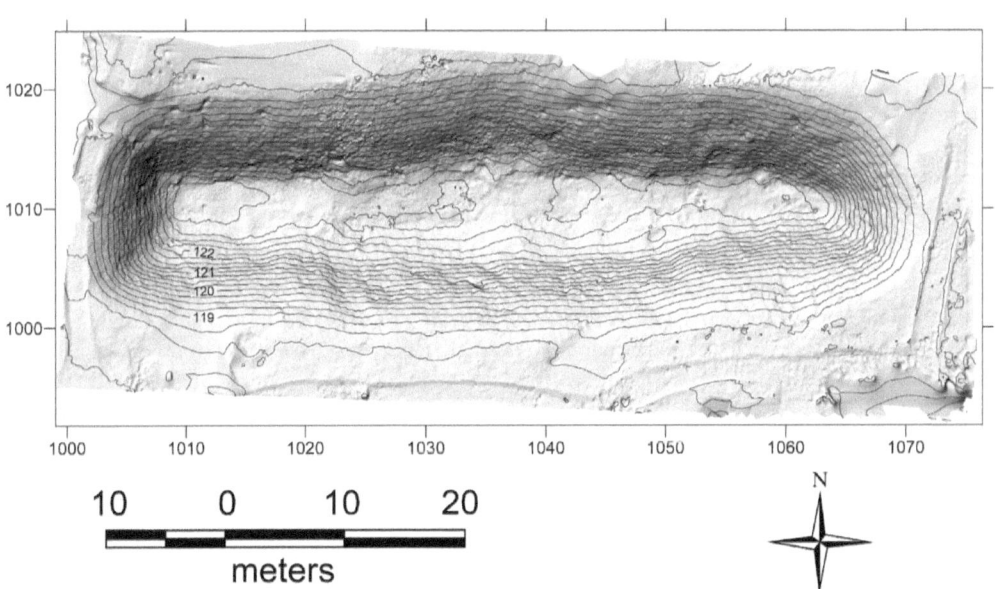

Figure 2.6. Shaded relief map of Chan Chich Structure A-5 with 0.25-m contours overlaid. This map was produced by Chet Walker and Mark Willis using SfM mapping, supported by funding from the National Geographic Society/Waitt Grants program. Map courtesy of the Chan Chich Archaeological Project.

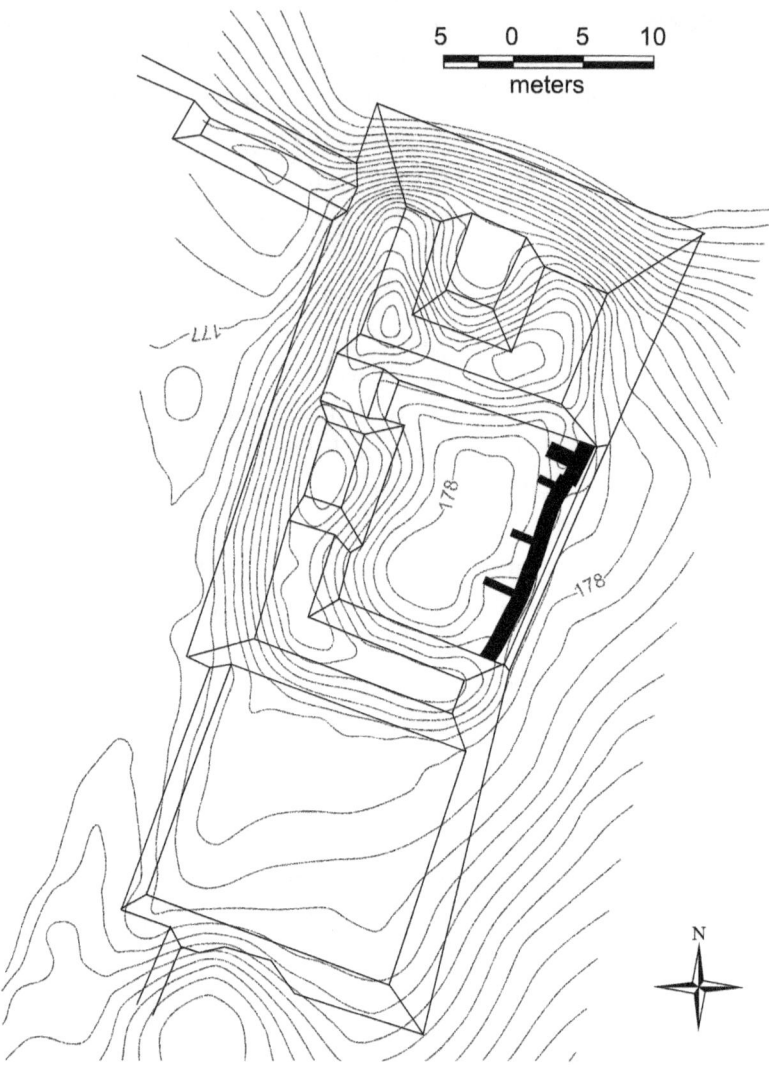

Figure 2.7. Contour map of La Milpa Courtyard 100 with rectified map of structures and architectural plan of eastern courtyard wall overlaid. Contour interval is 0.25 m. Map courtesy of the La Milpa Core Project.

Named after Teobert Maler, an early Maya explorer, who is incorrectly credited with inventing the convention, Malerization is a technique for depicting the mounds of earth and stone that make up a Maya site as rectified shapes (Hutson 2012:284–85). As Gair Tourtellot (1988:16) describes it, the convention uses geometrical prismatic forms to depict the ruins. When excavation data are available to provide more information on buildings, maps sometimes depict a mixture of prismatic shapes and more detailed architectural plans.

The system is meant to be able to convey not only the size of a mound but its height as well. Unfortunately, the convention for indicating height assumes that all mounds slope at the same angle, which they do not. Furthermore, archaeologists use "an unruly family" of techniques to create prismatic representations of mounds, and there is no standardized method for the convention (Hutson 2012:286).

Most archaeologists learn how to draw a prismatic or rectified map through field instruction. In other words, someone shows them how they would draw a particular structure while the two of them actually climb all over the mound, taking measurements and identifying architectural features. As it turns out, some people are better than others at interpreting what they see and depicting it as a prismatic shape. Most archaeologists can draw a prismatic version of an isolated mound, but not as many are good at conveying the complex arrangement of terraces, platforms, structures, and stairs that make up a massive acropolis, for example. Those who are not so good at it tend to create impossible prismatic shapes that look like something you might find in M. C. Escher's trashcan.

No two archaeologists would produce identical prismatic maps of the same Maya site, and you will no doubt notice differences in the way buildings are depicted on the various maps in this book. Almost all of the maps of cities in this book have been redrawn, but, unless noted, the shapes of structures have not been reinterpreted.

Summary

This chapter has covered a lot of ground from a conceptual framework for studying their cities to mundane facts about how the Maya piled rubble fill in their plazas. The concepts and definitions presented here, however, come into play repeatedly in the succeeding chapters as the case studies unfold. The final two chapters of the book filter those case studies through Smith's (2007) proposed approach to studying planning in ancient societies to look for patterns and meaning.

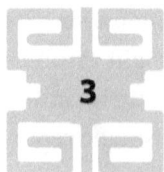

3

The Setting in Space and Time

This chapter is directed primarily at the non–Maya scholar reading this book; it provides a crash course on the geography of the Maya area, Maya cultural history (Table 3.1), and Classic period Maya political history. In many textbooks, the latter two topics are blended together, but they are separated here to mirror the structure of the case studies that follow. The agriculturally minded scholar may bemoan the surficial treatment given to soils in the

Table 3.1. Maya chronology in the eastern lowlands

Period	Dates	Cultural Developments	Important Eastern Lowland Sites
Early Preclassic	1100–1000 BCE	Earliest agricultural villages in the Maya lowlands	Cahal Pech, Blackman Eddy, Cuello
Middle Preclassic	1000–400 BCE	Spread of Maya farmers into interior; first monumental architecture	Cuello, Colha, Cahal Pech, Blackman Eddy
Late Preclassic	400 BCE–100 CE	Rise in social complexity; evidence for craft specialization; first cities, states, and divine kings	Colha, Cerros, Caracol, Nohmul
Terminal Preclassic	100–250 CE	Earliest divine kings in eastern lowlands; decline of earliest states	Chan Chich, Nohmul
Early Classic	250–600 CE	Spread of Maya kingdoms, Long Count, and writing	Caracol, Altun Ha, Lamanai
Late Classic	600–810 CE	Apogee of Maya kingdoms and peak rural populations	Caracol, La Milpa, Lamanai, Xunantunich, southern Belize cities
Terminal Classic	810–900 CE	Failure of divine kingship; Classic Maya collapse and widespread abandonment of southern lowlands	Caracol, Lamanai, Nohmul
Postclassic	900–1500 CE	Transformation of Maya civilization in northern lowlands	Lamanai

geographic section, but since the focus of this book is how the Maya built their cities, more text is devoted to talking about rocks than about dirt.

The Geographic Setting

This section summarizes the geographic setting of the Maya area; more detailed descriptions of the geography of the eastern lowlands are included in the subsequent regional chapters. One of the best ways to gain an appreciation for the accomplishments of the Maya is to excavate, even for a day, a Maya ruin. By deconstructing something others constructed by hand over a thousand years ago, the excavator gains an appreciation for the Maya that no textbook can convey. Removing bucket load after bucket load of rubble from a plaza test pit not only gives you an immediate understanding of the sheer amount of physical labor that went into creating the thousands and thousands of ancient buildings that dot the modern landscape, but it also conveys just how exhausting and difficult working in the heat and humidity of the lowlands really is. Yet the Maya persevered and even thrived under these difficult conditions for over 2,000 years and developed a remarkable culture and urban tradition tailored to the tropical setting.

The Maya occupied all of the modern nations of Belize and Guatemala, parts of western Honduras and El Salvador, and parts of eastern Mexico, including all of the Yucatán Peninsula (see Figure 1.1). Physiographically, the area is highly diverse and includes a narrow band of coastal plains along the Pacific Ocean, rugged volcanic and metamorphic mountains in the south, and predominantly karstic lowlands extending from the foothills of the mountains to the Caribbean Sea and Gulf of Mexico.

The mountainous area is known as the Maya highlands, and the Maya people who lived there followed a slightly different cultural trajectory than their neighbors in the lowlands. The highlands include a band of active and extinct volcanoes stretching from Chiapas, Mexico, into Central America; the tallest of these is nearly 4,220 m (15,000 ft) high (Sharer and Traxler 2006:35). The mountains formed during Tertiary and Pleistocene eruptions that covered the area in thick deposits of pumice and ash (Coe 2011:14). Between the young, active volcanic range on the south and the older range on the north is a tectonic depression through which the Motagua River flows. The highlands provided a number of mineral resources that were exploited and traded by the Maya including jade, granite, serpentine, and obsidian (West 1964).

The numerous valleys and basins in the highlands are characterized by fertile volcanic soils and have supported dense populations since Preclassic times

(Sharer and Traxler 2006:35–36). The largest is the Valley of Guatemala, home to Guatemala City today and the ruins of Kaminaljuyu, an important Late Preclassic–Early Classic period highland site.

The transition from the highlands to the lowlands takes place in the Alta Verapaz region of Guatemala where the northern slope of the highlands gives way to a large number of folded and faulted limestone ranges that have produced a series of depressions and ridges paralleling the mountains to the south. In general, elevation trends lower from south to north.

Researchers usually subdivide the lowlands into two or more broad subsections, with further subdivisions as warranted. Most schemes include the southern lowlands, from the highlands north to approximately Laguna Bacalar in Mexico, and the northern lowlands, which encompass the rest of the Yucatán Peninsula. This book follows that approach but includes the eastern lowlands as a subdivision of the southern lowlands.

While the southern and northern lowlands both occupy the same limestone platform, there are important differences in the physiography of the two regions. The southern part of the platform is slightly higher in elevation and has gently rolling to hilly topography north of the central Petén lakes. The terrain has isolated conical hills with *aguadas* and *bajos* occupying the intervening depressions (West 1964:72–73). *Bajos* are large karst depressions that cover between 40 and 60 percent of the southern lowlands (Dunning et al. 2002:268–269). Although now only seasonally inundated swamps, *bajos* may have once been shallow lakes that were ideal areas for wetland agriculture (Dunning et al. 2002). *Aguadas* are small ponds that typically hold water year round.

The Maya Mountains in Belize jut up quite spectacularly to elevations above 1,000 m (3,300 ft) and are a notable deviation from the broken karst topography that characterizes most of the southern lowlands. They are part of a larger mountain-building belt known as the Antillean orogenic belt. A horst of uplifted igneous and metamorphic rocks, the Maya Mountains are geologically unlike most of Belize (Rice 1993:15). From this region the Maya obtained granite, basalt, slate, and other minerals (Graham 1994; Sharer and Traxler 2006:46). The mountains extend eastward toward the Caribbean and are responsible for the significant differences in topography and vegetation between southern and northern Belize.

In the northeastern part of Guatemala and northwestern Belize, a series of southwest-to-northeast trending faults have created broad upland depressions through which a number of rivers flow, draining the eastern part of the Petén into the Caribbean Sea. These faults have created a stepped topography that dramatically transitions from the interior, at 120–300 m in elevation, to the coastal plain of Belize, at about 1–20 m in elevation (Dunning et al. 2002:269).

Other rivers originating in the highlands pass through the southern and western parts of the southern lowlands, discharging their flows in the Caribbean Sea and the Gulf of Mexico. These rivers were important sources of water but also provided natural transportation corridors that facilitated contact and trade across the Maya area.

The interior of the southern lowlands, however, is a series of internal drainage basins. In the center of the Petén is a large basin covering some 3,000 km^2 and highlighted by a chain of over a dozen small lakes, the largest of which is Lake Petén Itzá. The Mirador Basin, home to the earliest city in the lowlands, is a large internal drainage basin in northern Petén.

Low-lying topography, coastal marshes, and small inland lagoons characterize the eastern coast of the Yucatán Peninsula in Belize and southern Mexico. The largest of these lagoons is Laguna Bacalar in southern Quintana Roo. Off the coast lies the longest coral reef in the northern hemisphere, extending for 650 km. The reef, which is between 40 and 65 km from the mainland, has formed a protected area that is home to hundreds of small sand islands (cays, or cayes as they are called in Belize), shallow lagoons, and mangrove islands (West 1964:73).

The rivers, *bajos*, and small lakes of the southern lowlands highlight the significant hydrological differences with the northern area. In the northern lowlands, there are no surface streams. The flat limestone platform is dotted with hundreds of features known as cenotes, natural sinkholes resulting from caving of surface rock into underground stream channels (West 1964:72). Cenotes were important sources of water for the Maya in the northern lowlands (Sharer and Traxler 2006:53).

The only major topographic relief in the northern lowlands comes in the form of the Puuc Hills, also known as the Sierrita de Ticul, a curved ridge rising up to 50 m above the surrounding landscape (West 1964:70). During the tenth and eleventh centuries CE this area was home to a series of Maya cities expressing a regional style of architecture known as Puuc (Sharer and Traxler 2006:533).

Another difference between the southern and northern lowlands is soil thickness. Dunning et al. (1998:91) characterize nearly all of the soils of the lowlands as thin, calcareous clays. In the southern lowlands, soils can be up to 1 m thick, but in the northern lowlands most soils are only a few centimeters thick, and bedrock outcrops are visible on the surface in many areas (Dunning et al. 1998:91). The soils in the vicinity of the Puuc Hills are the exception to this pattern; these agriculturally productive soils are up to 1 m thick (Sharer and Traxler 2006:50, 533; Stevens 1964:303).

A number of scholars have researched the complicated relationship between soils, rainfall, natural vegetation patterns, and agricultural potential and systems in the Maya area. Scott Fedick (1996) and Nicholas Dunning and colleagues (1998), for example, have proposed that the mosaic of different soils and environments in the lowlands required regional agricultural adaptations. In other words, old approaches that stressed a one-size-fits-all approach to Maya agriculture are not useful. Dunning's more recent work has examined how Maya agriculture and declining forest cover "produced many interrelated, and often negative, effects on the regional environment" and differentially affected population collapse and recovery in the Terminal Classic of the ninth and tenth centuries CE (Dunning et al. 2012).

Two important stone resources that the Maya exploited across much of the Yucatán Peninsula were limestone and chert (Rice 1993:16). The former, which makes up the bedrock over most of the lowlands, is actually soft and easily quarried; the limestone hardens when exposed to air. Therefore, once the upper exposed surface had been removed, the underlying material could easily be shaped into blocks of various sizes. Limestone could also be burned to make lime and mixed with *sascab*—degraded limetone— and water to produce mortar. Chert in the form of nodules or seams in the bedrock provided raw materials to make stone tools (West 1964:73). As discussed in Chapter 4, the small site of Colha in northern Belize was strategically situated in a zone of particularly high-quality chert, which the Maya exploited extensively to make stone tools (Shafer and Hester 1983:519).

Although the climate of the lowlands is tropical, water was an important resource that had to be managed by the Maya because rainfall in the region is seasonal. Over 80 percent of the annual rainfall comes between May and October. The driest month of the year is March, and September is the rainiest (Vivó Escoto 1964:201). For the Maya, water was scarce for four months out of the year.

Rainfall is not uniform across the lowlands; amounts generally decrease from southeast to northwest (Rice 1993). The jungles of southern Belize can receive over 4,000 mm of rain in a year, while less than 1,000 mm falls in the extreme northwestern corner of the peninsula. On average, most of the southern lowlands get between 2,000 and 4,000 mm per year (Vivó Escoto 1964:Figure 11).

The vegetation of the lowlands is primarily tropical rainforest, but the height of the canopy decreases from south to north, mirroring rainfall and soil thickness. From south to north, the vegetation changes from mostly tropical forest, to subtropical forest, to dry tropical forest, to very dry tropical forest (Rice 1993:23). Within any zone the vegetation can be highly variable depending on the topography and soil conditions.

In Belize the vegetation diversity is greater than almost any other area of Central America (Lundell 1945). In his mid-twentieth century study of the vegetation of Belize, Cyrus Lundell (1945) described four main vegetation belts that occur in the country: mangrove swamps along the coast; pinelands and barrens, found primarily inland from the mangrove swamps in northern and central Belize and in the Mountain Pine Ridge of the Maya Mountains; inland swamps and marshes along rivers and in northern Belize; and quasi-rainforest and rainforest over much of the country.

Overview of Maya Cultural History

Although an exhaustive review of Maya cultural history is beyond the scope of this book, a short summary of the major cultural developments of ancient Maya civilization is necessary to place the cities of the eastern lowlands in a temporal and geographic context. This section begins with a general summary of the major chronological periods of Maya civilization, focusing primarily on the southern lowlands. As mentioned earlier, thanks to our ever-improving ability to read Maya hieroglyphs, we can now overlay a more detailed political history onto the general chronological framework. Readers interested in more comprehensive coverage of Maya culture history should consult any number of excellent textbooks, including Robert Sharer's and Loa Traxler's (2006) edition of *The Ancient Maya*, Michael Coe's (2011) frequently updated *The Maya*, or Heather McKillop's (2004) *The Ancient Maya: New Perspectives*, which includes more data from archaeological work in Belize than any other textbook. For political history, Sharer and Traxler (2006) is an excellent source, but *Chronicle of Maya Kings and Queens* by Simon Martin and Nikolai Grube (2008) is unsurpassed in its level of detail. Keep in mind that all of these sources, like this book, have out-of-date information, because new discoveries are constantly altering our understanding of Maya cultural and political history.

Maya cultural history is divided into three major periods, each with its own finer subdivisions: the Preclassic (or Formative), the Classic, and the Postclassic periods (see Table 3.1). These divisions are arbitrary constructs imposed on the Maya by archaeologists, and their names reflect early biases about the evolution of Maya society. As inaccurate or inappropriate as they may be, the terms are embedded in the archaeological literature. Preceding these periods is the long-lived Archaic period, during which the nomadic hunter-gatherers of northern Central America made important advancements in technology, subsistence, and economics that made settled village life possible.

The Eastern Lowlands Archaic Period (8000 to 1100 BCE)

A fascinating and wide-open field of study is the Archaic period—and the even older Paleoindian period (8000 BCE and older)—in northern Central America. So little is known about the peoples who inhabited the region during this long period of time that any new Archaic period discovery is an important one. Jon Lohse and colleagues (2006) attribute the state of affairs to a lack of stratified archaeological sites from that time period and a general lack of directed research into the topic, although a number of scholars are attempting to address the second factor (Lohse 2010; Rosenswig 2004; Prufer and Thompson 2013).

Prior to about 1100–1000 BCE, it appears that the Yucatán Peninsula was lightly populated by small, nomadic groups of hunter-gatherers (Lohse et al. 2006). Near the end of the Archaic period, sometimes called the Late Preceramic period, people began to experiment with horticulture (Lohse et al. 2006). Pollen studies indicate the inhabitants began clearing the forest and growing maize about 2500–2400 BCE, about 1,500 years before the first villages (Lohse et al. 2006:Figure 8). For a number of compelling reasons, Lohse (2010) sees the origins of the first Maya in the eastern lowlands in the economy, technology, and subsistence of their late Archaic predecessors.

The Preclassic Period (1100 BCE to 250 CE)

Although the earliest settled villages appeared in other areas of Mesoamerica at the beginning of the Early Preclassic period around 2000 BCE, the oldest indication for pottery-making people who lived in agricultural villages in the Maya area is from about 1100 BCE. The earliest evidence comes from the Belize Valley where excavations at a number of sites have recovered Cunil ceramics, dating to the Terminal Early Preclassic period (Garber and Awe 2009; Sullivan et al. 2009).

Throughout the Middle Preclassic, Maya farmers gradually spread across the lowlands, primarily by following rivers inland before colonizing the interior forests (Sharer and Traxler 2006:202). These earliest Maya lived in small, independent villages composed of pole-and-thatch houses and ancillary structures, usually built on low platforms. Shortly after the initial colonization of the lowlands by farmers, the first evidence for increasing social complexity appeared at several sites in the form of public buildings. Unlike constructing a house, which could be accomplished by a family, building public architecture required communal participation, signaling some form of authority to organize and direct the construction.

The site of Nakbe in Guatemala grew to be the largest of these Middle Preclassic villages with public architecture. The first monumental architecture at the site was built as early as 800 BCE, and by 450 BCE the town's architects and sculptors had created the first masonry buildings, built the first causeways and ball court, and erected the first carved stelae and altars in the Maya lowlands (Hansen 1991; Sharer and Traxler 2006:214).

The earliest public architectural assemblage in the lowlands, known as an E-Group, also appeared during the Middle Preclassic and originated at Nakbe or one of its neighbors in the southern lowlands (Hansen 1998:66). Named after the first one to be excavated at the site of Uaxactun, E-Groups consist of an elongated eastern structure—later versions have three distinct buildings sharing a common platform on the eastern side of the assemblage—facing a square-based pyramid on the western side. Originally interpreted to have astronomical significance as solstice or equinox observatories (Blom 1924; Ruppert 1940), subsequent researchers have found that not all E-Groups function in this manner and have suggested many are commemorative structures copying the form of the original but not its function (e.g., Laporte and Fialko 1990). Anthony Aveni and colleagues (2003:161–163), in a more recent study, concluded that the earliest E-Groups did indeed function as solstice observatories but that later versions operated as "orientation calendars" designed to mark 20-day intervals during the dry season as a means of scheduling crop planting. Regardless of their function, E-Groups are symbolically important. The first plazas and monumental architecture to appear in the Petén very often were associated with E-Groups (Doyle 2012:358). Arlen and Diane Chase (2007a:62–63) argue that the construction of an E-Group represents the "ideological founding" of a Maya center and established what would become the "downtown" of the city as it continued to grow. The E-Groups at Nakbe and a handful of other sites were precocious (Doyle 2012; Estrada-Belli 2011:69); most other examples were constructed during the Late Preclassic to Early Classic transition (Aveni et al. 2003:Table 1). Jaime Awe (2013) argues that many assemblages that have been called E-Groups, particularly in the Belize Valley, are actually three separate pyramid shrines placed in a line.

The process of colonization and expansion continued into the Late Preclassic period, and more, larger villages with public architecture indicate social complexity continued to rise as well. The Maya actually developed many of the traits commonly associated with the subsequent Classic period during the Late Preclassic period. El Mirador supplanted its neighbor Nakbe as the largest Maya settlement during this period. El Mirador was unlike any settlement before it; its site core contained two massive groups of monumental architecture, and its tallest building, the Danta pyramid, towered 70 m over the surrounding forests and fields. A series of causeways radiated out from the site core to connect it to other emerging towns, including Nakbe. Based on its impressive size, evidence for a larger population than any center before, and its central position in the network of causeways, Sharer and Traxler (2006:259, 262) conclude that El Mirador was the seat of power for the first archaic state in the Maya lowlands.

The Late Preclassic period witnessed a number of architectural innovations, many of them evident at El Mirador, including a new type of pyramid construction known as the triadic pyramid or temple. Triadic pyramids consisted of two smaller pyramids flanking a larger central pyramid, all built on a shared basal platform (Sharer and Traxler 2006:253). The arrangement created a small plaza-like area in front of the three temples. Examples include the Tigre and Danta complexes at El Mirador and the massive High Temple at Lamanai, Belize. The in-line triadic shrine assemblage, noted above, may be a variation on the original triadic pyramid design, rather than on an E-Group assemblage (Awe 2013).

At a number of sites, Maya architects and artists adorned the platform faces of temple-pyramids with elaborate stucco masks and friezes. Often interpreted as the portraits of Maya deities or creatures from Maya mythology, elaborate stucco masks flanking the central stairs of pyramids are now known from a large number of Maya sites including Nakbe, El Mirador, Cival, Uaxactun, Holmul, Blackman Eddy, and Cerros (Estrada-Belli 2011). Some of the first such masks to be excavated were discovered on the western radial pyramid of Uaxactun's E-Group, which dates to the end of the Late Preclassic (Ricketson and Ricketson 1937). The structures adorned with these masks also had large open spaces on their terraces and summits that rulers likely used for public rituals (Schele and Freidel 1990:105).

Along with the spread of Maya villages across the lowlands, the development of new architectural forms, and the rise of El Mirador as the first archaic state, the Maya made other significant advances during the Late Preclassic period that had previously been attributed to the Classic period. Perhaps most important among these were writing and the concept of divine kingship. Stela 2 from El Mirador has a vertical panel with small incised hieroglyphs (Hansen 2001), and several examples of perhaps even older writing have been found at the smaller Late Preclassic center of San Bartolo, Guatemala (Saturno et al. 2006).

The San Bartolo examples include a fragment of a painted wall, found in construction fill, with a column of 10 currently unreadable hieroglyphs that excavators estimate were painted between 300 and 200 BCE (Saturno et al. 2006:1281). A second, younger example is better preserved; it is part of an elaborate series of murals that cover the walls of a buried room in a building nicknamed Las Pinturas. Dated to approximately 100 BCE, the text includes one intelligible glyph, an early version of the sign for AJAW, meaning "lord, noble" or "ruler" (Saturno et al. 2006:1282). The column of eight glyphs appears near a scene showing a ruler seated on a scaffold, being handed an elaborate headdress by an attendant. The text is related to an apparent historical coronation of an early Maya king, although many other elements of the murals depict mythological scenes of the Maize God, an avian creature from Maya mythology known as the Principal Bird Deity, and other creatures (Saturno 2009).

Other evidence for early divine kings comes from a handful of Late Preclassic and Terminal Preclassic royal tombs. San Bartolo has a royal tomb dated to 150 BCE, about 50 years older than the murals in the Las Pinturas building (Saturno 2006:73). At Tikal, Burial 85, created around 100 CE, has been attributed to the founder of the royal dynasty there, a man named in later texts as Yax Ehb' Xook (Martin 2003:5; Sharer and Traxler 2006:310). Burial 85 employed a new architectural form in which the tomb chamber was cut into bedrock and capped by a low shrine in what would later become the North Acropolis at Tikal, and the tomb was richer than other burials from the same time frame (Loten 2003:238–239). At Chan Chich, a slightly later tomb dating to the Terminal Preclassic period or cusp of the Early Classic period followed the same architectural pattern and contained the remains of an early king, identified by a type of jade jewel worn by early rulers (Houk et al. 2010).

The Late Preclassic version of divine kingship differed rather dramatically from the Classic period manifestation of the concept. Kings tended to be portrayed in private settings, like the San Bartolo mural room, and the monumental temples of the Late Preclassic period emphasized cosmological forces (via their elaborate masks and friezes) rather than the deeds of individual rulers (Sharer and Traxler 2006:274). In fact, temples did not serve as funerary structures until the Classic period; the Late Preclassic kings were buried in plazas marked by small shrines (Houk et al. 2010:246). Kings, however, represented both religious and political power in Late Preclassic polities, as best evidenced by the use of sacred temples emblazoned with supernatural masks and imagery as the setting for royal ritual (Sharer and Traxler 2006:269).

The larger Preclassic cities, like Nakbe and El Mirador, demonstrate a strong east–west orientation of their monumental architecture. The civic/ceremonial core of El Mirador stretches 2 km along its east–west axis, anchored at either end by the triadic pyramids of El Tigre and Danta (Sharer and Traxler 2006:253). As is seen in many of the site plans of the cities discussed later in this book, the east–west axial arrangement of centers in the Late Preclassic gave way to a preference for north–south arrangements in the Classic period.

Another urban planning difference between the early centers and their successors was in their water management systems. Scarborough (1998:139) characterizes the Late Preclassic water management system as passive; centers were built near the bases of natural depressions to take advantage of runoff. This "concave microwatershed" system stands in direct contrast to the "convex microwatershed" system used at many Classic period cities (Scarborough 1998:139, Figure 2).

The Terminal Preclassic period witnessed not only the development and spread of the concept of divine kingship but also the collapse of several significant Maya centers, including the archaic state of the Mirador Basin and the sites of El Mirador and Nakbe (Estrada-Belli 2011:119; Webster 2002:189). Theories for the rapid and puzzling abandonment of the Mirador Basin include warfare and reduced agricultural productivity due to increased sedimentation, which choked once-productive *bajos* with clays (Estrada-Belli 2011:128; Sharer and Traxler 2006:295). Far from the Mirador Basin, near the Caribbean Sea, the thriving trade center of Cerros was also abandoned at the end of the Preclassic period (Freidel 1986a, 1986b). Still other centers, such as Tikal and Lamanai, weathered the turbulent end of the Preclassic period and found themselves in a position to grow and prosper in the third century CE.

The Classic Period (250 to 900 CE)

For several important reasons, we have more archaeological data from the Classic period than from the Late Preclassic or Postclassic. First, in the southern and eastern lowlands, Maya civilization reached its peak in terms of population size and number of settlements during the Classic period. Second, because the Maya tended to build over previous structures, archaeologist must excavate through a Classic period veneer of architecture and settlement to get to older structures and deposits. The Classic period buildings, therefore, get the most attention. Third, it was during the Classic period that the Maya recorded the achievements of their kings and queens in hieroglyphic texts and used the Long Count to fix those events in time. Therefore, in addition to having a large body of excavation data, we also have historical data for a growing number of important Maya centers. This makes it possible to discuss Classic period cultural history separate from political history. In this summary, the Classic period is divided into Early Classic (250 to 600 CE), Late Classic (600 to 810 CE), and Terminal Classic (810 to 900 CE) subperiods in the southern lowlands, roughly following Sharer and Traxler (2006:Table 2.2).

Classic Period Cultural History

The Early Classic period saw the emergence of Maya states across the southern lowlands, but the Mirador Basin remained largely abandoned. Although population estimates are always tricky, it appears that populations in most areas continued to grow during the Early Classic period with the expansion of existing settlements and the founding of new ones. Two of the largest cities during this period were Tikal, which had been settled during the Preclassic period, and the upstart kingdom of Calakmul, Mexico. The latter city was home to the Kan dynasty, which had perhaps originated at El Mirador in the Late Preclassic period (Sharer and Traxler 2006:357).

As the number of kingdoms expanded, the nature of kingship changed. Although large stucco masks adorned a number of Early Classic temples, these masks were depictions of kings, not deities (McKillop 2004:93). More common, however, were depictions of kings on stone stelae, frequently with Long Count dates and hieroglyphic texts. This new focus on the king as the symbol of dynastic power, rather than the deities of the Late Preclassic period, extended to architecture as well. The Early Classic period witnessed the development of palaces, which served as royal courts at cities with divine kings, and kings began to use temples as funerary monuments. The tombs of these Classic period kings were also larger and more richly furnished than those of their Late Preclassic ancestors. Kings became concerned with accumulating and displaying wealth and power and establishing their legitimate right to rule by reinforcing their dynastic lineage, best exemplified in the royal funerary cult.

While kingship was changing, so too was the structure of Maya society. During the Early Classic period, society became clearly stratified into two endogamous groups, the elite and the non-elite (Sharer and Traxler 2006:371). As is discussed in Chapter 2, the separation between these groups was reinforced and maintained through a number of mechanisms, including the use of a separate prestige language by the elite.

In general, our understanding of non-elite Maya society during the Classic period has improved tremendously since settlement surveys and household archaeology became more common toward the end of the twentieth century (see Lohse and Valdez 2004). Even as the elite directed the construction of monumental site centers, the non-elite may have been managing a decentralized agricultural system (Lohse 2004) and interacting with the elite in a variety of ways (Yaeger and Robin 2004). Importantly, the non-elite in Maya society may have enjoyed a much greater degree of residential mobility than their elite counterparts, a significant trait that placed additional burdens on the elite in terms of creating and maintaining a sense of community at their centers (Inomata 2004, 2006).

Tikal became the largest Early Classic kingdom under a series of divine kings. During the Early Classic period, the downtown heart of the city began to take shape around the Great Plaza, bounded by the North Acropolis—the Late Preclassic and Early Classic necropolis for the kings of Tikal—and the Central Acropolis, which was the seat of the royal court (Harrison 2001a:221). Both of those architectural groups had Late Preclassic antecedents, but the Early Classic construction substantially altered the core of the city.

A significant feature of the Early Classic period was increased interaction beginning in the fourth century CE between the Central Mexican city of Teotihuacan and the kingdoms of the lowlands. This interaction is indicated archaeologically at Tikal and other lowland cities by the introduction of new architectural styles, including talud-tablero platforms, and new artifact styles, including Central Mexican ceramics and green obsidian from the Pachuca source near Teotihuacan (Braswell 2003:3). The nature of this interaction is debated, but Teotihuacan appears to have directly influenced the political history of the southern lowlands during the Early Classic period, as discussed below.

Although the individual fortunes of Maya cities waxed and waned over the course of the Classic period as evidenced by construction sequences in their site cores, the overall pattern of growth continued in the Late Classic period. More and more Maya kingdoms emerged, and the population of the southern lowlands peaked around 800 CE. David Webster (2002:174) envisions a patchy distribution of population, even in the eighth century, with some areas very densely populated and others essentially uninhabited. Population estimates are notoriously difficult, but the core area of the lowlands, including Calakmul to the north, Belize on the east, Copán on the south, and Palenque to the west could have contained up to 4 to 5 million Maya during the eight century CE (see Webster 2002:174 for discussion of population estimates).

Archaeologically, the evidence for growth comes in the expansion of the built environment at many cities. At some cities, the Late Classic period witnessed the construction of entire sections of the ceremonial core without Preclassic or Early Classic antecedents, and many rural courtyard groups were first constructed in the Late Classic. Not surprisingly, this rapid growth led to competition and conflict. Although warfare had been a part of Maya society as early as the Late Preclassic—attested by the mass graves of warriors at the village of Cuello, Belize, circa 400 to 300 BCE (Robin and Hammond 1991)—it became endemic during the Late Classic period. The evidence includes hastily built walls and palisades, burned buildings, and even the capture and sacrifice of entire royal families (Demarest 2004a; Inomata 1997; O'Mansky and Dunning 2004; Sausnavar and Demarest 2011).

Despite increasing competition—or perhaps because of it—the Maya created some of their most fantastic art and architecture during the Late Classic period, including the beautiful murals from the site of Bonampak, Mexico. Those murals depict vivid scenes of courtly life at a small Maya kingdom and give us a rare glimpse into many aspects of elite life, ritual, and warfare (Miller 1999:171; Miller and Brittenham 2013). The murals, along with numerous codex-style polychrome vases from the Late Classic period, demonstrate that the Maya elite had an abiding interest in displaying personal wealth. As a result of an almost voracious appetite for prestige goods, the trade in elite or exotic artifacts continued unabated during the Late Classic, although the number of items from Central Mexico declined precipitously following the abandonment of Teotihuacan at the end of the Early Classic period.

The last century or so of the Classic period, known as the Terminal Classic, was characterized by the failure of the system of divine kingship, the abandonment of almost every major center, and near total depopulation of the countryside in the core area of the Maya lowlands in a series of events collectively known as the Maya collapse (Webster 2002). The collapse has long been a topic of intense interest, debate, and disagreement, and more than one excellent book has been written or compiled on the subject (e.g., Culbert 1973; Demarest et al., eds. 2004; Webster 2002). Decades of research on the topic has demonstrated that no one thing caused the Classic period kingdoms of the southern lowlands to collapse; nor did they all collapse at the same time. Lamanai, a major site in Belize, was never abandoned (Graham 2004), but is the exception that proves the rule. Problems with high populations and declining agricultural yields, intense competition and frequent warfare between kingdoms, and the rejection of the divine kings and the ideology that supported them all worked in concert to trigger the collapse (Webster 2002:327–328).

As higher resolution temporal and climatic data have become available, the role that droughts played in the downfall of the Classic period kingdoms has been intensely debated (Gill 2001; Iannone 2013; Lucero et al. 2011; Medina-

Elizalde et al. 2010). While Richardson Gill (2001) linked droughts in part to volcanic eruptions, scholars have more recently looked at global weather systems, such as El Niño, and highly refined climatic sequences from cave deposits to associate population expansion with times of plentiful rainfall and population decline with periods of drought (Kennett et al. 2012). In fact, Douglas Kennett and colleagues (2012) suggest that a drying trend from about 660 to 1000 CE triggered many of the stresses on Maya society during the Late Classic period and contributed to warfare, political fragmentation, and ultimately population collapse.

Although the individual circumstances were unique at each city, including the responses by the city's people to the events taking place around them, ultimately both the elite and non-elites at virtually every city in the southern lowlands died or left by the tenth century CE. Arthur Demarest (2004b:267) describes the processes and events of the Terminal Classic period in the eastern lowlands as more variable and a little later than those in the Petén, and Demarest et al. (2004:571) more prosaically describe them as a "crazy quilt of continuities and discontinuities—rapid collapses, gradual declines, smooth transitions, or striking transformations." While some cities were rapidly and completely abandoned, such as Xunantunich (Ashmore et al. 2004), Caracol persisted until 900 CE (A. Chase and D. Chase 2004a, 2007b), and Lamanai carried on uninterrupted (Demarest 2004b:267; Graham 2004). At a number of settlements in the eastern lowlands where there is evidence for Terminal Classic occupation, influences from the northern lowlands are evident in artifacts and particularly architecture, in the form of circular shrine structures (Harrison-Buck 2012:113; Harrison-Buck and McAnany 2006:287).

Classic Period Political History

During the Classic period, the Maya of the southern lowlands recorded many historical events in hieroglyphs, and they anchored these events in time with Long Count dates. The Maya hieroglyphic writing system is logosyllabic, meaning it uses logographs, or signs that stand for words, in combination with phonetic signs representing syllables or vowels (Coe and Van Stone 2005:18). Maya scribes could use this system to express any spoken thought, but they primarily restricted its use to historical information. They "wrote" this information by carving their hieroglyphs on stone stelae, panels, lintels, thrones, and altars, or by painting them on murals or walls. They also incised hieroglyphs on small objects of jade, bone, and wood, or painted them on ceramic vessels, although such texts were generally ownership statements (Martin and Grube 2008:12). They also recorded information in folding books called codices, none of which survive from the Classic period. The texts that have survived are almost entirely concerned with elite activities but are an invaluable source of information about individual Maya rulers, their kingdoms, and their deeds.

Of course, to record historical events, you must have a system of counting days and keeping track of time. Toward that end, the Maya developed an extremely sophisticated mathematical system, independently developing the concept of "zero." The Maya used a base-20 (vigesimal) system, which is different than our base-10 (decimal) system, and expressed numbers using bars and dots. A dot stands for "1," and a bar stands for "5." Numbers larger than 19 use a positional notation, similar to the way our base-10 system works in which each position to the left of the decimal point increases by a power of 10. In a base-20 system, however, each position increases by a power of 20: 1, 20, 400, 8,000, etc.

The Maya counted days in a number of calendars, all based on cycles of time, and had what Anthony Aveni (2009:67) calls a "preoccupation . . . with organizing time cycles . . . to fit together." The three most important calendar cycles were the Tzolk'in, a ritual calendar with a 260-day cycle composed of 20 named days paired with 13 numbers; the Haab, a 365-day solar calendar composed of 18 named months with 20 days each and a short 5-day period at the end; and the Calendar Round, a cycle combining the Tzolk'in and Haab together. In the Calendar Round, a combination of dates in the Tzolk'in and Haab repeats every 18,980 days (or once every 52 years).

Cycles of time such as these three calendars, while they have many uses, are not particularly good at keeping track of things that happened long ago. For example, referring to a past event using a Calendar Round date is kind of like saying something happened on January 15. Without a year specified, the event could have taken place on any January 15 in the past. Because the Maya, particularly the rulers, had an interest in recording events that took place hundreds or even thousands of years in the past, they developed another calendrical system called the Long Count. Often thought of as a count of days since a starting point in the past—akin to our count of days since January 1, 1 CE—the Long Count is really just another big cycle, itself composed of a succession of smaller cycles. Using a modification of the base-20 system, the Long Count is made up of cycles of *kins* (days), *uinals* (20 days), *tuns* (360 days, a deviation from the 400 days expected in a vigesimal system), *k'atuns* (7,200 days), and *bak'tuns* (144,000 days). Many Mayanists consider 13 *bak'tuns* to be one great cycle, equal to 5,125.37 solar years. Whether or not the Long Count reset itself at the end of 13 *bak'tuns* or continued counting forward to the end of 20 *bak'tuns*—as would seem logical in a base-20 system—on December 21, 2012, is a rather academic point because the Maya stopped using the Long Count before 1000 CE during the eleventh *bak'tun*. Archaeologists abbreviate Long Count dates as follows: 8.11.0.0.0 equals 8 *bak'tuns*, 11 *k'atuns*, zero *tuns*, zero *uinals*, and zero *kins*. How to correlate the Long Count system to our calendar has long been a question of Maya scholars, although most researchers accept the Goodman-Martinez-Thompson (GMT) correlation or GMT+2 correlation (Martin and Grube 2008:13).

The Long Count system allowed the Maya to look deep back in time, and it allows us to align their political history with our own calendar. The period of recorded history for the Maya extends from 292 CE, when the oldest known stela with a Long Count date was erected at Tikal, until 909 CE, when the last known stela with a Long Count date was placed at Tonina. As the number of kingdoms expanded in the Late Classic period, so too did the practice of erecting stelae; the peak of monument placement, and thus the period with the most historical texts, is between 731 and 790 CE (Webster 2002:209). Fortunately, the Maya also wrote about events in the past, so historical accounts extend back into the Late Preclassic.

Epigraphers have been reconstructing the political history of the Classic period since Tatiana Proskouriakoff (1960) recognized that the stelae at the site of Piedras Negras, Guatemala, depicted kings, not gods, and their texts recorded the births, accessions, and deaths of the rulers and their ancestors. The picture that has emerged is a more complex geopolitical history than early Mayanists could have ever imagined. The ruling dynasties of the two great Classic period cities of Tikal and Calakmul competed and fought against each other for centuries, and the ruling families of many other smaller cities found themselves embroiled in this conflict through a complex system of alliances that emerged across the lowlands.

Tikal's later kings credit Yax Ehb' Xook with founding the royal dynasty, probably around 100 CE (Martin and Grube 2008:26–27). The best documented of Tikal's early kings is Chak Tok Ich'aak I, who took the throne around 360 CE. He presided over the largest Maya kingdom in the lowlands at the time (Martin and Grube 2008:28), erected several Early Classic stelae, and used one of the buildings in Tikal's Central Acropolis as his royal palace (Harrison 2001b:87). At this time, Calakmul was an important center in its own right, but there is no written account of the ruling dynasty from this period.

An event known as the Entrada of 378 CE dramatically altered the fortunes of Tikal and the political landscape of the lowlands. A man named Sihyaj K'ahk,' or Fire Is Born, passed through the city of El Perú/Waka' in western

Petén and then arrived at Tikal on January 16, 378, the same day that the king of Tikal, Chak Tok Ich'aak I, died (Stuart 2000:479). The "arrival" verb used to describe this event connotes political takeover (Sharer and Traxler 2006:322). Shortly after arriving at Tikal, Sihyaj K'ahk' conquered the nearby city of Uaxactun and slaughtered its ruling family (Schele and Freidel 1990:146).

Sihyaj K'ahk' never took the throne of Tikal for himself; rather, he seems to have been a general acting on behalf of a man named Spearthrower Owl, the ruler of an unknown site, which some researchers suspect was Teotihuacan, the great Early Classic non-Maya city in Central Mexico (Stuart 2000:484). Within a year, Sihyaj K'ahk' installed a new king on the throne of Tikal named Yax Nuun Ahiin I, Spearthrower Owl's son. This new king is shown on Stela 4 dressed in Teotihuacan costume and not in the attire of a traditional Maya king (Stuart 2000:472). It is around this general time frame that Teotihuacan-style artifacts and architecture appeared at Tikal, although the Central Mexican architectural style known as talud-tablero was in use at Tikal as early as the end of the third century CE and continued to be used into the Late Classic at Tikal, long after Teotihuacan had declined (Laporte 2003:200, 203).

Although the exact nature of the Entrada, takeover or political contact, is a matter of debate and the subject of books in its own right (e.g., Braswell, ed. 2003), the changes that followed it were profound and undeniable. Yax Nuun Ahiin I, under the patronage of Sihyaj K'ahk,' launched a period of expansion at Tikal, subduing the Early Classic kingdom of Río Azul in northeastern Petén and consolidating his power at home through marriage to a woman from the former royal family (Sharer and Traxler 2006:324).

Yax Nuun Ahiin I was succeeded by his son, Sihyaj Chan K'awiil II, in 411 CE. Like his father, Sihyaj Chan K'awiil II followed an expansionist policy, apparently going so far as to send a trusted general to the distant city of Copán to found a new dynasty there in 426 CE (Sharer and Traxler 2006:333, 338). Unlike his father, Sihyaj Chan K'awiil II depicted himself in the traditional trappings of a Maya king, best exemplified by his portrait on Stela 31. That monument, which has the Early Classic dynastic history of Tikal recorded on its back, portrays Yax Nuun Ahiin I dressed as a Mexican warrior on its two sides, and Sihyaj Chan K'awiil II attired in decidedly Maya garb and headdress on the front (Martin and Grube 2008:34–35).

Tikal continued to be the most powerful kingdom in the lowlands through the remainder of the Early Classic period, although the rulers that followed Sihyaj Chan K'awiil II were not as powerful or successful. Toward the end of the Early Classic period, the Snake Kingdom of Calakmul began to grow in power and influence by assembling a far-reaching political network. The powerful king named Sky Witness brought the kingdom of Naranjo under his sway and managed to turn Tikal's ally, Caracol, the largest Maya city in the eastern lowlands, against it. In 562 CE, Calakmul defeated Tikal in battle, and Sky Witness may have overseen the sacrifice of Tikal's twenty-first king, Wak Chan K'awiil (Martin and Grube 2008:104).

At Tikal, what had been a period of political weakness became a full-blown political hiatus. The royal line was broken—the next king to take the thrown was not Wak Chan K'awiil's son—and a series of weak rulers governed the site until the late seventh century CE. Although limited construction took place in the core of the city, the rulers at Tikal did not erect any stelae for over a century; this is a testament to their reduced role on the political stage of the lowlands.

Calakmul flourished during this period and continued an aggressive stance, going so far as to attack Palenque, a western kingdom that had been an ally of Tikal (Sharer and Traxler 2006:381). The city reached its apogee at the beginning of the Late Classic period during the reign of Yuknoom the Great, who was responsible for the construction of much of the monumental architecture in the site's center and the placement of many of the city's stelae (Martin 2001:186). With Tikal weakened, Yuknoom the Great brought many smaller kingdoms under his control, practicing what Simon Martin and Nikolai Grube (2008:109) call "overkingship."

Calakmul's dominance ended during the reign of Yuknoom the Great's successor, a king named Yuknoom Yich'aak K'ahk,' who was defeated in battle by Tikal's king, Jasaw Chan K'awiil, in 695 CE (Sharer and Traxler 2006:393). That battle was only one of many that took place as part of the wider Tikal–Calakmul rivalry in the late seventh and early eighth centuries CE. Those wars, which involved the cities of Naranjo and Caracol as well and ultimately reduced Calakmul's power and broke most of their holds over client states, were precursors to the endemic warfare that followed in the late eighth and early ninth centuries.

As the cities of the lowlands began to succumb to the Maya collapse, the written record fell silent. The final monuments erected at the dying kingdoms of the lowlands provide no information about what was happening; that was not the nature of Maya written history. At Tikal, the 10.0.0.0.0 *bak'tun* event passed without comment, a sign of political weakness. Jasaw Chan K'awiil II, the last known king of Tikal, erected the final stelae at the city in 869 CE—importantly, that was the only stelae to be erected for three *k'atuns* (Martin and Grube 2008:52–53). The dynasty at Tikal's great rival, Calakmul, similarly appears weakened during this time period, also failing to commemorate the end of the tenth *bak'tun* in 830 CE. The last stela at that great city was probably erected in 909 CE, although Martin and Grube (2008:115) suggest a few crude stelae may have been set a little later.

Terminal Classic and Postclassic Cultural History

As the southern lowlands went into decline, the focus of Maya civilization transformed and recentered to the northern lowlands during the Terminal Classic period (Demarest 2004b; Sharer and Traxler 2006). This transformation involved three distinct regional developments in the northern Yucatán Peninsula centered on Cobá to the east, the Puuc area to the west, and Chichén Itzá in the center (Demarest 2004b:268).

Cobá's Terminal Classic florescence in many ways is more similar to the Late Classic kingdoms of the southern lowlands than it is to its Terminal Classic neighbors in the northern lowlands (Demarest 2004b:270–271). A dynasty of divine kings ruled its extensive polity from the Late Classic period into the Terminal Classic period, erecting 32 stelae, most of which are too eroded to read (Sharer and Traxler 2006:554). During the Late Classic, Cobá brought the distant city of Yaxuna in the center of the northern lowlands into its hegemony, linking the two cities by a 100-km-long *sacbe*, the longest in the Maya world (Suhler et al. 2004:483). The city's apogee was between 730 and 1000 CE; after a 200-year-long period of decline, Cobá was abandoned about 1200 CE (Sharer and Traxler 2006:554). The largest kingdom of the eastern third of the northern lowlands succumbed to the stress and conflict caused by competition with the other rising powers in the peninsula.

In the Puuc area a number of small kingdoms sharing a distinctive regional architectural style thrived between 770 and 950 CE (Carmean et al. 2004:424). The rulers of these cities blended the concept of divine kingship with a northern concept of shared rule while integrating Mexican traits into the architecture of their cities (Carmean et al. 2004:425).

The city of Uxmal developed into the largest of the Puuc polities. Although ruled by a line of divine kings who still erected stelae, certain visual elements on several monuments suggest that political power was shared. Some of Uxmal's most spectacular buildings, including the House of the Governor and the Nunnery Quadrangle, were built between 890 and 915 CE during the reign of Lord Chaak (Carmean et al. 2004:430–431). It appears that Lord Chaak managed to bring most of the western Puuc cities under his control through a combination of conquests and alliances (Demarest 2004b:269). Uxmal and its neighbors, including the important center of Sayil, declined in power and population shortly after their early-tenth-century peak, victims of Chichén

Itzá's aggression and increasing influence in the peninsula (Carmean et al. 2004:445).

The third of the Terminal Classic regional developments proved to be the most successful. Chichén Itzá's rise to power began in the Late Classic period and peaked around 1000–1100 CE, during which time it became a powerful regional state exerting control over most of the northern lowlands (Cobos 2004:537; Demarest 2004b:274; Sharer and Traxler 2006:559). The city features many iconic architectural and urban features including one of the largest ball courts in all of Mesoamerica; the round observatory building known as the Caracol; the four-sided temple pyramid and spring equinox observatory called the Castillo; the Temple of the Warriors and its colonnaded entrance with columns adorned with low relief sculptures of warriors; and the sacred *cenote*, connected to the site core by a large *sacbe*.

In many ways Maya society at Chichén Itzá at the end of the Terminal Classic period and beginning of the Early Postclassic period represented the culmination of a cultural transformation that began with the fall of the southern lowland kingdoms two centuries earlier. Even the average tourist who visits Tikal and Chichén Itzá is likely to be struck by just how dissimilar these two great Maya cities are. The imposing temples and massive palaces of Tikal stand in stark contrast to the open spaces and colonnaded buildings at Chichén Itzá. The architectural distinction reflects the differing political systems employed at the two cities as a system of shared rule, with which the Puuc cities experimented, was apparently firmly in place at Chichén Itzá (Sharer and Traxler 2006:580).

There is ample evidence at Chichén Itzá in architecture, artifacts, and sculpture of significant contact with groups to the west in Mexico, most strongly reflected in adoption of new religious icons associated with the Mexican god of Quetzalcoatl, known in Mayan as K'uk'ulkan (Sharer and Traxler 2006:582). There are differing interpretations on the nature of this interaction, with some scholars advocating for a Toltec intrusion into the Yucatán (e.g., Coe 2011) and others suggesting the Mexican elements were brought to the area by Chontal Maya from the Gulf Coast (Sharer and Traxler 2006:559). Chichén Itzá's period of dominance extended into the Early Postclassic period, but the city's grip on the peninsula was broken about 1100 CE, when the last great Maya city of Mayapan supplanted it (Sharer and Traxler 2006:592).

Mayapan is a unique expression of Maya urbanism (e.g., Smith 1962:171). The city's ceremonial precinct is much smaller than Chichén Itzá's, although it mimics it with its own version of the Castillo, a round structure, and colonnaded buildings (Masson et al. 2006:189–90). However, Mayapan's associated residential groups are tightly packed and enclosed by a wall that surrounds the city; as many as 4,000 buildings within the 4.2 km² inside the wall create the densest concentration of structures at any known city in the lowlands (Sharer and Traxler 2006:594; Smith 1962:171).

For approximately 260 years, Mayapan controlled much of the northern Yucatán Peninsula through a system of shared rule known as *mul tepal*, though it is likely that two families actually dominated the politics of the city and its state (Milbrath and Lope 2003:32; Sharer and Traxler 2006:595, 601). This style of government was radically different from the rule of divine kings in the Classic period, and it allowed Mayapan to exert control over a vast territory. Each province, however, maintained its own identity; once Mayapan collapsed, each became a separate territory (Milbrath and Lope 2003:31).

Mayapan's influence extended as far as the eastern lowlands of Belize, where population levels rebounded in the Late Postclassic period. Northern and coastal Belize were part of Mayapan's Chetumal province (Masson 2001:348). The Postclassic Maya of Belize favored "aquatic-oriented locations" for settlement, such as lagoons, swamps, rivers, and cayes (Masson 2000:15). These settlements participated in an extensive canoe-borne trading economy that was active along the eastern Yucatán Peninsula during the Late Postclassic period (Sharer and Traxler 2006:604). Although Lamanai (Graham 2004; Pendergast 1981) and Santa Rita Corozal (D. Chase and A. Chase 2004a) have long been known to have significant Postclassic construction and occupation, a number of recent projects have focused on smaller Postclassic settlements in Belize such as Laguna de On (Masson 2000), Progresso Lagoon (Oland and Masson 2005; Masson et al. 2004), Saktunja (Mock 2005), and Wild Cane Caye (McKillop 2005).

When the Spanish arrived in the Maya area in the sixteenth century, the peninsula was politically fragmented into at least 16 independent provinces (Marcus 1993:117). As described by Ralph Roys (1957), some provinces were administered from a head town and ruled by one individual, others were jointly ruled by local lords from the same lineage, and others were composed of loosely allied groups of towns. Joyce Marcus (1993) hypothesizes that this form of political organization represented a long-standing pattern in Maya political history extending back to the Classic period. At various times, one or more kingdoms would manage to form a regional state by integrating smaller kingdoms into their polity, but ultimately the larger states would breakdown into a series of smaller independent kingdoms (Marcus 1993:164).

Summary

Maya society arose, thrived, and transformed over the long span of nearly 2,500 years under the challenging conditions presented by the geography, climate, and vegetation of the lowlands. As noted at the beginning, the goal of this chapter is to provide larger geographical and temporal context for the subsequent discussions of the eastern lowlands. Although the summary of Maya cultural history included here spans the Archaic period through the Postclassic period, in the following chapters, with the exception of Chapter 4, the focus is squarely on the Classic period urban developments in the eastern lowlands. Chapter 4 provides important background on the Preclassic foundations for Classic period urbanism in the eastern lowlands.

4

Preclassic Foundations

Although the focus of this book is Classic period cities, the Preclassic developments in what is now Belize warrant discussion as they provided the basis for the architectural and planning innovations that followed (see Figure 1.2). Some of the best evidence for the origins of settled village life, a precursor to the rise of urbanism, and early monumental architecture comes from the eastern lowlands. This is not meant to diminish in any way the Preclassic period achievements that have been documented since the 1990s in the southern and northern lowlands (e.g., Estrada-Belli 2006; Estrada-Belli et al. 2003; Glover and Stanton 2010; Hansen 1990, 1991; Saturno 2006, 2009; Saturno et al. 2006). Stressing the eastern lowland data simply provides a foundation for the ensuing Classic period case studies.

Maya archaeologists are burdened by the connotations of cultural evolution that are inherent in labels like "Preclassic," "Classic," and "Postclassic." Although we now treat those periods as arbitrary time divisions, for decades they colored our understanding of the developmental trajectory of Maya civilization (Estrada-Belli 2011:1). The Uaxactun project's greatest discovery in the 1920s was arguably the Late Preclassic temple in Group E at the site, but scholarly interest soon gave way to an obsession with younger—Classic period—sites with carved monuments (Estrada-Belli 2011:28). As archaeology matured as a science, and Maya scholars fell under the spell of the New Archaeology in the 1960s and 1970s, interest in problem-oriented research took hold. The origins of complex society emerged as a hot topic in Mesoamerica, and a number of Maya archaeologists began to turn their focus away from Classic period ruins to seek out Preclassic sites.

In Belize, Norman Hammond's (1981, 1983b) Corozal Project documented several important Preclassic sites in northern Belize including Cerros, Nohmul, Cuello, and Colha, all of which have since been intensively studied. The work at those sites produced important new data about the origins of

Maya civilization and coincided with research by other scholars on Late Preclassic intensive agricultural systems in the same part of Belize (see Turner 1983; Turner and Harrison 1983).

The confirmation in the 1980s and 1990s that the massive northern Petén city of El Mirador was Late Preclassic in age and the subsequent realization that the nearby site of Nakbe was even older fundamentally altered our conceptions of the beginnings of Maya urbanism and social complexity and spurred a renewed interest in the topic (Hansen 2001). Based on recent work in eastern Guatemala at places like Cival, Holmul, and San Bartolo, we now know that large Late Preclassic centers are more common than the archaeologists at Uaxactun nearly 100 years before would have ever dreamed possible (Estrada-Belli 2011). The discovery of the painted murals at San Bartolo in 2001 shattered old notions about Preclassic art, the antiquity of Maya writing, and the origins of divine kingship in the lowlands (Saturno 2006, 2009; Saturno et al. 2006).

One of the challenges archaeologist face when studying the Preclassic period is that at most Maya sites Classic period architecture completely buries all evidence of earlier occupations. A number of my colleagues whose research focus is on the Preclassic period half-jokingly refer to the vast majority of Maya architecture as the "Classic period overburden." In rare cases, Preclassic cities were abandoned and never reoccupied, but in most cases deep excavations are required to reach the oldest occupations.

The following discussion highlights five Preclassic sites in the eastern lowlands: Cahal Pech, Blackman Eddy, Cuello, Colha, and Cerros. I have selected each to illustrate a different facet of Preclassic Maya culture as it relates to the foundations for settled village life and the development of urbanism. These are by no means the only Preclassic sites in the region—nor the only important ones—and, as is demonstrated in the following chapters, most of the large Classic period cities have their origins in the Middle or Late Preclassic period.

Belize Valley: The Earliest Maya in the Eastern Lowlands

Although the search for the earliest Maya is an ongoing topic and source of constant debate, the Belize Valley in western Belize has yielded some of the best data and oldest radiocarbon dates associated with ceramics and architecture. Jon Lohse (2010:343) recently reviewed the published radiocarbon results from sites in western Belize and northern Belize and concluded that the earliest deposits at Cahal Pech "could reasonably be between and 25 and 100 years older" than the earliest material from northern Belize.

The two sites with the best evidence for early settlement are Cahal Pech and

Blackman Eddy. The modern Belizean town of San Ignacio surrounds the hilltop center of Cahal Pech in western Belize. The site is in the upper Belize Valley about 2 km south of the confluence of the Mopan and Macal Rivers. Given that the site is easily accessible and has large structures, Cahal Pech has long been of interest to archaeologists, appearing on Thompson's (1939) list of sites in Belize as El Cayo, and has been studied almost continuously since the late 1980s (Aimers et al. 2000; Awe 1992; Garber and Awe 2008). Blackman Eddy is one of a string of sites occupying the hills and ridges above the Belize River terraces and floodplain. It is on the southern side of the river, approximately 15 km east-northeast of the confluence of the Mopan and Macal Rivers. The Belize Valley Archaeological Project (BVAP) directed by James Garber studied the site for over a decade beginning in 1990 (Garber et al. 2004).

Cahal Pech

The Classic period site core of Cahal Pech includes 34 structures, 6 plain stelae, and an uncarved altar grouped around 7 courtyards or plazas (Awe 1992:60). Plaza B occupies the center of the site and is dominated by Structures B-1, B-2, and B-3, three connected temple-pyramids on the eastern side of the plaza (Figure 4.1). The central pyramid is 12 m high (Awe 1992:98), and the combined group constitutes a possible E-Group, albeit one lacking a western structure (Aimers and Rice 2006:86), or possibly in-line triadic shrines (Awe 2013). The largest structure at the site is the 24-m tall Structure A-1, which towers over the small and tightly enclosed Plaza A (Awe 1992:71). Cahal Pech contains two Classic period ball courts (Awe 1992) and is linked by a *sacbe* to an outlining group to the south (Cheetham 2004; Healy, Cheetham, et al. 2004). Most of the structures in the site core are oriented approximately 16° west of north.

Although the Classic period remains at Cahal Pech represent an impressive development, they cover important Preclassic deposits, including some of the oldest evidence for Maya occupation found anywhere. Extensive excavations beneath and at the base of Structure B-4 discovered an impressive stratigraphic sequence beginning with Early Preclassic residential platforms associated with Cunil ceramics, the earliest documented pottery in the eastern lowlands (Powis and Cheetham 2007:180). Cunil pottery, with a Maya-twist on pan-Mesoamerican iconographic symbols (Garber and Awe 2009), has been dated to the end of the Early Preclassic period, within 100 years or so on either side of 1000 BCE (Awe 1992; Healy, Cheetham, et al. 2004:105; Sullivan and Awe 2012:108–10). These ceramics are associated with early residential structures built on 0.5-m high platforms with plaster floors and

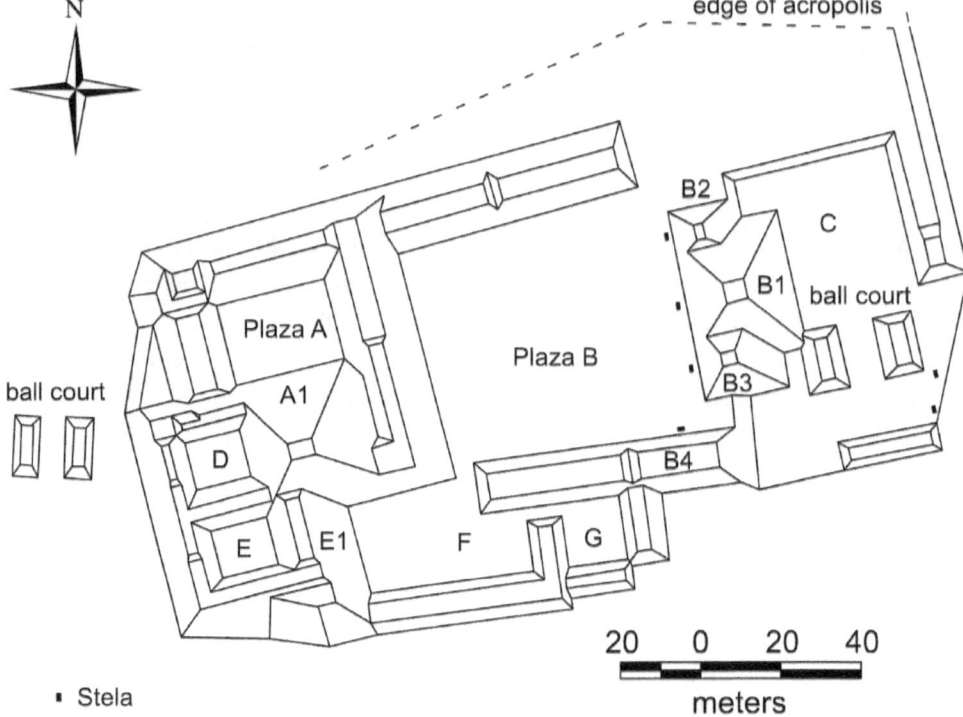

Figure 4.1. Map of Cahal Pech, after Awe and Healy (1994:Figure 3).

perishable superstructures. These buildings were wattle and daub structures with white plastered walls decorated in places with red vertical bands (Awe 1992:208). Based on posthole patterns and the shape of their platforms, these early houses were round or apsidal in plan (Healy, Cheetham, et al. 2004:107) and oriented slightly west of magnetic north (Powis and Cheetham 2007:180). Cahal Pech was likely a small village with perhaps eight residential structures during the Cunil phase (Healy, Cheetham, et al. 2004:108).

During the early Middle Preclassic period around 800 BCE, the Cahal Pech villagers transformed their settlement by leveling the southern and eastern sides of Plaza B to create a ceremonial plaza (Healy, Cheetham, et al. 2004:108). As part of this transformation, they constructed the first temple at the site, Structure B-4 9-Sub, atop the earlier Cunil residential platforms. Subsequent generations built a succession of temples in this location, culminating in the ninth and final version of Structure B-4 during the Late Classic period. As Powis and Cheetham (2007:180) note, this new civic/ceremonial structure maintained the west of north orientation that the initial buildings established in the Early Preclassic. During a late Middle Preclassic building episode, the villagers expanded Plaza B to its present horizontal extent and likely built the initial version of the plaza's eastern structures as a long rectangular platform beneath Structures B-1 to B-3 (Healy, Cheetham, et al. 2004:109–110).

While the Plaza B area was being converted from residential to public space, people began to construct residential groups in the periphery of the site. Consisting of clusters of mounds with both houses and likely ceremonial platforms, these Middle Preclassic settlements are often found buried in the plazas of Classic period ruins. Round platforms with cut-limestone-block platform faces and plaster floors that once supported perishable superstructures are common at Middle and Late Preclassic residential groups (Figure 4.2). The heights of these platforms varies from as low as 15 cm to as high as 3 m, and their diameters

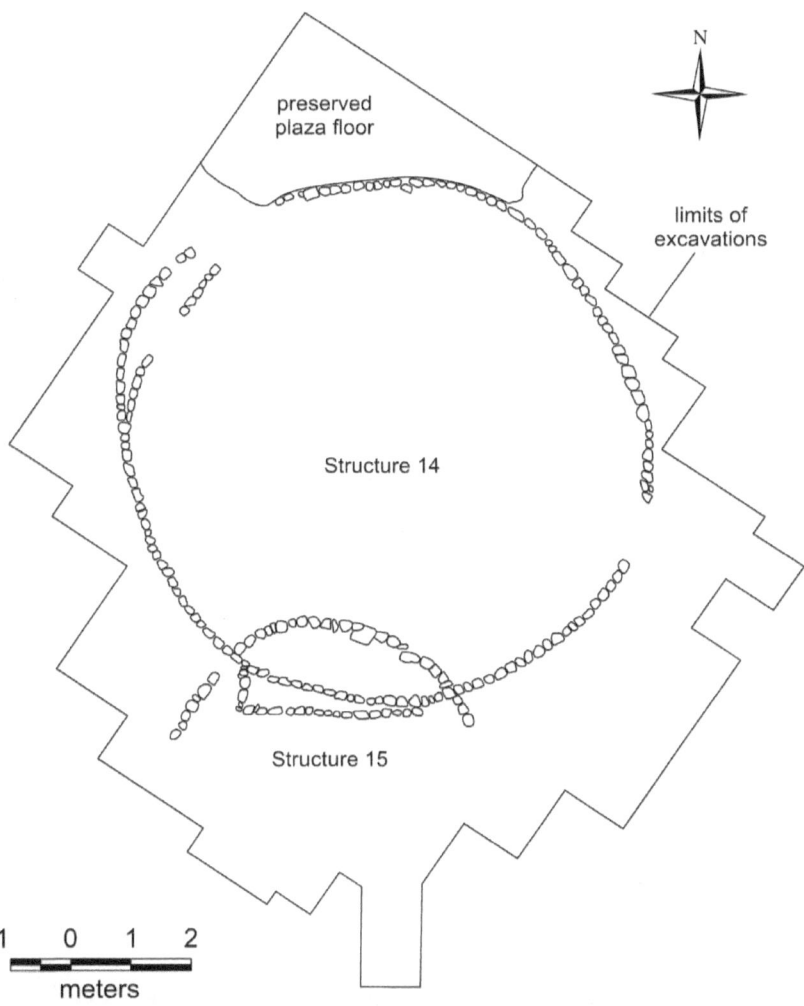

Figure 4.2. Simplified plan map of superimposed Late Preclassic Structures 14 and 15 buried in the plaza at the Tolok Group, Cahal Pech, modified from Aimers et al. (2000:Figure 7).

range from 3 m to 11 m (Aimers et al. 2000:Table 1). At Cahal Pech, the largest Preclassic round structure so far discovered is the third version of the Structure B-4 temple (7-Sub), which was 2–3 m tall and had a stairway on its northern side (Aimers et al. 2000:Table 1).

Blackman Eddy

Blackman Eddy's Classic period site core stretches across 200 m of a north–south oriented ridge and has a commanding view of the valley below. Twenty structures are grouped around two plazas. Plaza A, the largest plaza, contains a ball court, two 10-m-tall temple-pyramids, an altar, and three stelae (Garber et al. 2004:49, 59, 63). The two tallest mounds are part of an E-Group assemblage that is the focus of the Plaza A architecture (Aimers and Rice 2006:Table 1). Stela 1 is an Early Classic monument with a partially legible Long Count date that falls between 376 and 396 CE (Garber et al. 2004:63).

Of more interest to this discussion, however, is the northern group of architecture centered around Plaza B. In the mid-1980s unauthorized bulldozing activity destroyed the western half of Structure B1, the tallest mound at Plaza B (Figure 4.3). Upon inspection, the resulting profile revealed a 2,000-year construction sequence, and in 1994 the then Department of Archaeology asked BVAP to excavate the intact half of the mound to bedrock because the mound was too damaged to stabilize (Garber et al. 2004a:26). This rare opportunity allowed James Garber's team to study the architectural evolution of the structure phase by phase.

As was the case with Cahal Pech, the earliest settlement beneath Structure B1 dated to the Early Preclassic, ca. 1100 to 900 BCE, and consisted of low, ap-

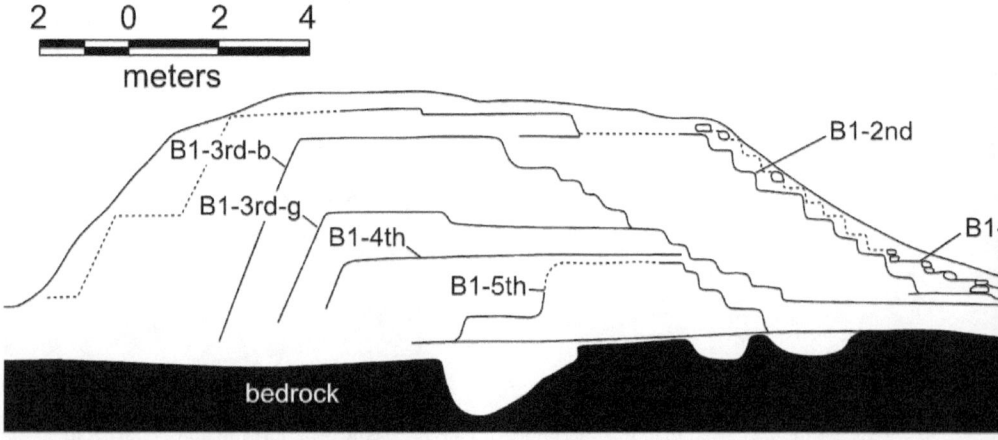

Figure 4.3. Eastern profile of Structure B1 at Blackman Eddy, after Garber et al. (2004a:Figure 3.1).

sidal platforms with tamped-earth floors (Garber et al. 2004b:15, 18). Postholes cut into the underlying bedrock demonstrate that the platforms supported perishable buildings, and a fragment of daub plaster with a red hematite stripe suggests the buildings were decorated like the contemporary structures at Cahal Pech (Garber et al. 2004b:18).

During the early Middle Preclassic period, low rectangular platforms, which Brown and Garber (2005:56) interpret as public buildings, covered the older apsidal buildings. From that point forward in time, the function of Structure B1 remained civic-ceremonial, and sequential construction phases gradually enlarged the building until the final temple-pyramid was completed in the Late Classic period (Brown and Garber 2005).

The emerging elite at the site may have used the earliest platforms to host communal feasts, as evidenced by debris associated with Structure B1-5th, the last early Middle Preclassic version of the structure (Brown and Garber 2005:59). Structure B1-4th, a Middle Preclassic platform, had masks flanking its inset stairs. This is the earliest known example of stucco masks in the Maya lowlands; unfortunately the structure and masks were burned and desecrated prior to the construction of Structure B1-3rd (Brown and Garber 2005:59).

Structure B1-3rd marked a change in the architectural form of the building from a low platform to an elevated pyramid, and a succession of renovations to this stage made the building increasingly taller (Brown and Garber 2008:162–163). The new style of building not only signals an increased investment in labor and material to renovate the temple, but it also marks a change in the nature of ritual as the large platform space was replaced by a pyramidal summit that was made increasingly higher and smaller with each of seven renovations to Structure B1-3rd (Brown and Garber 2008:160–162).

Two sets of masks flanked the outset stairs on the lower two terraces of Structure B1-2nd, the Late Preclassic–to–Early Classic version of the structure. Although badly damaged, enough detail remained on the masks for researchers to identify elements of creation mythology in the iconography (Garber et al. 2004:56–57).

Summary of Belize Valley Developments

The Preclassic architecture at both Blackman Eddy and Cahal Pech demonstrates the transformation from residential to ceremonial functions in the oldest settled areas at each site. Powis and Cheetham (2007:183–184) suggest that in these cases the Middle Preclassic temple-pyramid represents the metaphorical house of the founding lineage by occupying the same space on the landscape. We may be able to trace symbolic foundations for divine kingship in the ritual activities and iconographic programs associated with these first temples (Garber et al. 2007). Structure B1 at Blackman Eddy and Structure B-4 at Cahal Pech also demonstrate the importance the Maya placed on continuity of construction and use at sacred locations (see Brown and Garber 2008:168–169; Sharer and Traxler 2006:210).

Northern Belize

Swamps, lagoons, and slow-moving streams stretch across the gently rolling but low-lying terrain of northern Belize. In places, the low canopy of the forest is broken by stretches of pine forest that occupy bands of sandy soil. Today much of northern Belize is cropped in sugar cane. Prehistorically, this region of Belize witnessed not only some of the earliest Maya villages but also some of the latest, in the form of a Postclassic aquatic adaption that developed around the small lagoons and waterways (e.g., Masson 2000).

The Corozal Project first recorded the sites of Cuello, Colha, and Cerros, and identified different research issues at each. Cuello, which occupies the crest of a low ridge between the Rio Hondo and the New River, is just west of the modern town of Orange Walk. Following its initial discovery by the Corozal Project in 1973–1974, Norman Hammond (1991:8) and colleagues investigated the site between 1975 and 1987, specifically because of its potential to yield Preclassic remains, and produced an excellent monograph that distills six seasons of research into one volume. Hammond returned to Cuello for six additional seasons of research in 1990, 1992, 1993, 1997, 2000, and 2002 (Hammond 2005; Hammond et al. 1995). Colha is 27 km southeast of Cuello, adjacent to Cobweb Swamp, and was selected for study because of its high frequency of chert tools and lithic workshops (Shafer and Hester 1983:521). The Colha Project studied the site over the course of multiple but not always consecutive seasons beginning in 1979 and continuing until 1989. Other projects and researchers have returned to the site since the 1989 season to research specific topics, such as the Preceramic occupation of the area (Lohse 1993, 2010). Cerros, situated on a peninsula jutting into Corozal Bay, offered David Freidel (1986a:xix) the opportunity to study what appeared to be a Postclassic coastal trading site. Over the course of seven seasons between 1974 and 1981, Freidel's (1986a) teams mapped and excavated what turned out instead to be a major Late Preclassic center, with little Classic or Postclassic occupation. The Cerros Cooperative Archaeological Development Project subsequently returned for three seasons from 1992 to 1995 to focus on the Late Preclassic abandonment of the site (Walker 2005:6).

Cuello

Although Cuello has a moderately sized Classic period site core, the primary focus of investigations was always the Preclassic occupation at the site. During the first season of the Cuello Project, a test excavation through Platform 34 at the base of Structure 35, a small temple-pyramid south of the main architectural groups, produced a 3.4-m stratigraphic sequence of occupation punctuated by alternating layers of plaster floors and fill with some surprisingly early radiocarbon dates from the lowest levels (Hammond 1991:13). Based on what initially appeared to be Early Preclassic dates and ceramics beneath Platform 34, the Cuello Project excavated a 10-m wide, 30-m long block, known as the Main Trench, over the course of five seasons between 1976 and 1987 (Hammond 1991:14–16). Ultimately, the excavations documented a developmental sequence below Platform 34 beginning around 1000 BCE or slightly earlier and extending to the beginning of the Early Classic period, ca. 300 CE (Hammond et al. 1995; Hammond, Gerhardt, and Donaghey 1991).

The well-documented Middle Preclassic occupation at the site consisted of apsidal platforms that once supported timber-framed houses that had wattle and daub walls and thatched roofs. These platforms were tightly clustered around a small patio (Hammond and Gerhardt 1990). The occupants of the houses periodically stripped walls and floors before constructing new and larger platforms over the old ones. They buried their dead beneath their house floors, and graves of two children, each richly adorned with shell jewelry—one with a *Spondylus* shell pendant—indicate that Cuello's Middle Preclassic society was socially stratified to some degree (Hammond, Clarke, and Robin 1991:362). Refuse deposits associated with these houses indicate the villagers engaged in shell working and fishing, and they tapped into long-distance trade networks to acquire jade and obsidian from the Maya highlands far to the south (Hammond, Clarke, and Robin 1991:362). Toward the end of Middle Preclassic period, an important change occurred as people were buried for the first time in the patio between the houses, indicating new ritual practices and the importance of certain individuals to the entire social group, not just their immediate families (Hammond and Gerhardt 1990:469).

During the Late Preclassic period, the Middle Preclassic patio group was buried beneath the initial construction of Platform 34 (Hammond, Gerhardt, and Donaghey 1991:41). This radical renovation included the initial construction of a temple-pyramid on the western side of the newly created plaza. This was the first of three pyramids to be superimposed one on top of the other, culminating with the 9-m-high Structure 35 in the Early Classic period (Hammond and Gerhardt 1990:472–473).

The placement of a mass grave of at least 32 individuals in the platform fill signals that the construction event was more than a simple exercise in community revitalization. The burial population comprised 26 adult males, 1 adult (?) female, and 5 adults of unknown sex, most of whom had been butchered prior to burial (Hammond, Gerhardt, and Donaghey 1991:42). This remarkable deposit included two main individuals in the center of the group; "in their laps lay body bundles of nine severely mutilated" individuals, with the other bodies in the mass grave interred around the central group (Robin and Hammond 1991:211). This feature represents an apparent mass sacrifice of 32 people who may or may not have been members of the Cuello community that occurred in conjunction with the construction of Platform 34 (Robin and Hammond 1991:211).

Colha

Colha's Late Classic ceremonial center consists of approximately two dozen mounds, including a ball court, tightly grouped around a small main plaza and approximately six courtyards. Although the ball court was initially built in the Late Preclassic (Eaton and Kunstler 1980), the visible architecture in the epicenter of the site represents Late Classic and Terminal Classic construction (Anthony and Black 1994:39). Like its neighbor to the northwest, Colha's main plaza overlies buried Preclassic residential structures, and multiple seasons of excavations in the early 1980s documented a complex sequence of Middle Preclassic and Late Preclassic floors, burials, middens, and structures extending from near the surface of the plaza to 1.5 m deep (Anthony and Black 1994:39). In 1989 a month-long season of excavations exposed more Middle and Late Preclassic domestic round structures beneath the Main Plaza but did not find Early Preclassic deposits like those documented at Cuello (Sullivan 1991). The transformation from village to ceremonial precinct at Colha took place during the Late Preclassic period when the dimensions of the current Main Plaza were established (Anthony and Black 1994:39).

Colha is located in the heart of the Northern Belize Chert Bearing Zone, and lithic tool production constituted an important economic activity at the site during most periods of occupation. The Colha Project documented 89 chert debitage deposits or tool workshops across the site, 32 of which date to the Late Preclassic period (Shafer and Hester 1983:522, 524). Standardized tool production, however, took place as early as the Middle Preclassic, when Colha flint knappers produced T-shaped adzes in numbers that exceeded their own community's needs (Shafer and Hester 1991:82).

The Late Preclassic workshops comprise sheet deposits around *aguadas* or isolated mounds of debitage up to 1.75 m thick. Craft specialists took large flake blanks, which had been fashioned elsewhere, and reduced them at the workshops using hard hammer percussion to create four standardized tool forms: oval bifaces, tranchet bit tools, stemmed macroblade spear points, and large bifacial eccentrics (Shafer and Hester 1983:524, 1991:84–85).

Tranchet bit tools are unique to northern Belize. To produce one of these, a Colha flint knapper created a triangular biface and then removed a single, curved flake from the distal end—the tranchet flake—to create a sharp edge suitable for using as an axe or an adze (Shafer and Hester 1983:524, 1991). Because tranchet flakes are so distinctive and one primary flake was produced for each biface, researchers were able to count the flakes at a workshop to estimate the number of tranchet bit tools produced. The calculated number of tools produced is impressive: 75,562 tranchet bit tools at one workshop alone (Shafer and Hester 1991:87).

The flint knappers at Colha produced an estimated 4.5 million tranchet bit tools and oval bifaces during the Late Preclassic period, an average of 18,000 tools per year. In a village with only about 600 people during this time frame, the flint knappers fashioned many more bifaces than they needed for local consumption (Shafer and Hester 1991:87). Farmers in northern Belize and southern Quintana Roo served as the primary consumers for Colha-produced utilitarian tools. While oval bifaces and tranchet bit tools made their way to secondary peripheral consumers farther from Colha, stemmed macroblades and eccentrics are found in ritual deposits in northern Belize as well as distant sites like Tikal and El Mirador (Shafer and Hester 1991:90).

Cerros

As noted earlier, most Preclassic deposits are buried beneath the "Classic period overburden," a thick mantle of hundreds of years of stratigraphy and architecture that must be carefully excavated and documented before the Preclassic remains can be revealed. At Cerros, most of the visible mounds date to the Late Preclassic period, offering archaeologists a rare chance to study the settlement patterning and architecture across an entire site rather than through small excavation windows (Scarborough and Robertson 1986:156). Through survey and excavation, David Freidel's (1986a) crews documented not only the plan of a moderately sized Preclassic site but also its remarkable transformation from small seaside village to ceremonial center (Figure 4.4) in the span of only a couple hundred years.

Around 100 to 50 BCE, Cerros had 86 ground-level houses grouped around small patios or plazas on a spit of land projecting into the Corozal Bay portion of the larger Chetumal Bay. This small village was built right up to the edge of the bay and contained one small temple platform (Cliff 1986:55; Scarborough and Robertson 1986:159).

After 50 BCE, the community ritually terminated their small temple by smashing ceramic vessels and other artifacts on its surface and then buried their village under a thick layer of fill before constructing a new plaza and monumental temple-pyramids (Cliff 1986:53; Freidel 1986a:xviii). Once this remarkable construction project was finished, Cerros had been transformed into an impressive town with five large temple-pyramids, two ball courts, and expansive plaster-covered plazas and courtyards.

The Late Preclassic epicenter consists of a complex of monumental architecture at the northern edge of the site under which the older village is buried—known as the central precinct—and other courtyards, plazas, and structures encircling the north group to the southwest, south, and east in what is known as the core zone. A 1,200-m-long canal encircles the core zone and separates it from the peripheral zone of settlement (Scarborough and Robertson 1986:159–160).

Literally backed up to the edge of the bay, Structure 5C-2nd became the architectural gem of the remodeled Cerros. This southward facing temple-pyramid consists of a two-tiered platform with an outset central stairway and a masonry superstructure on its summit. This building, the only masonry superstructure at the site, had front and back rooms with walls painted pink and floors and basal moldings painted red. Flanking either side of the stairway on the faces of both platform tiers are elaborate stucco panels featuring large masks of deities presented in a "fully articulated symbol system" that appeared alongside the architectural remodeling of the site (Freidel 1986b:5–6). Linda Schele and David Freidel (1990:113–116) interpret the four masks to represent different aspects of the Jaguar Sun God in his daily journey through the heavens.

Constructed as it was over the span of a few decades, the Late Preclassic layout at Cerros probably represents a unified plan rather than an accretion of competing and conflicting design agendas. As is the case with the sites discussed earlier, the ceremonial precinct of Cerros was built over the initial settlement. Schele and Freidel (1990) link the sudden creation of the ceremo-

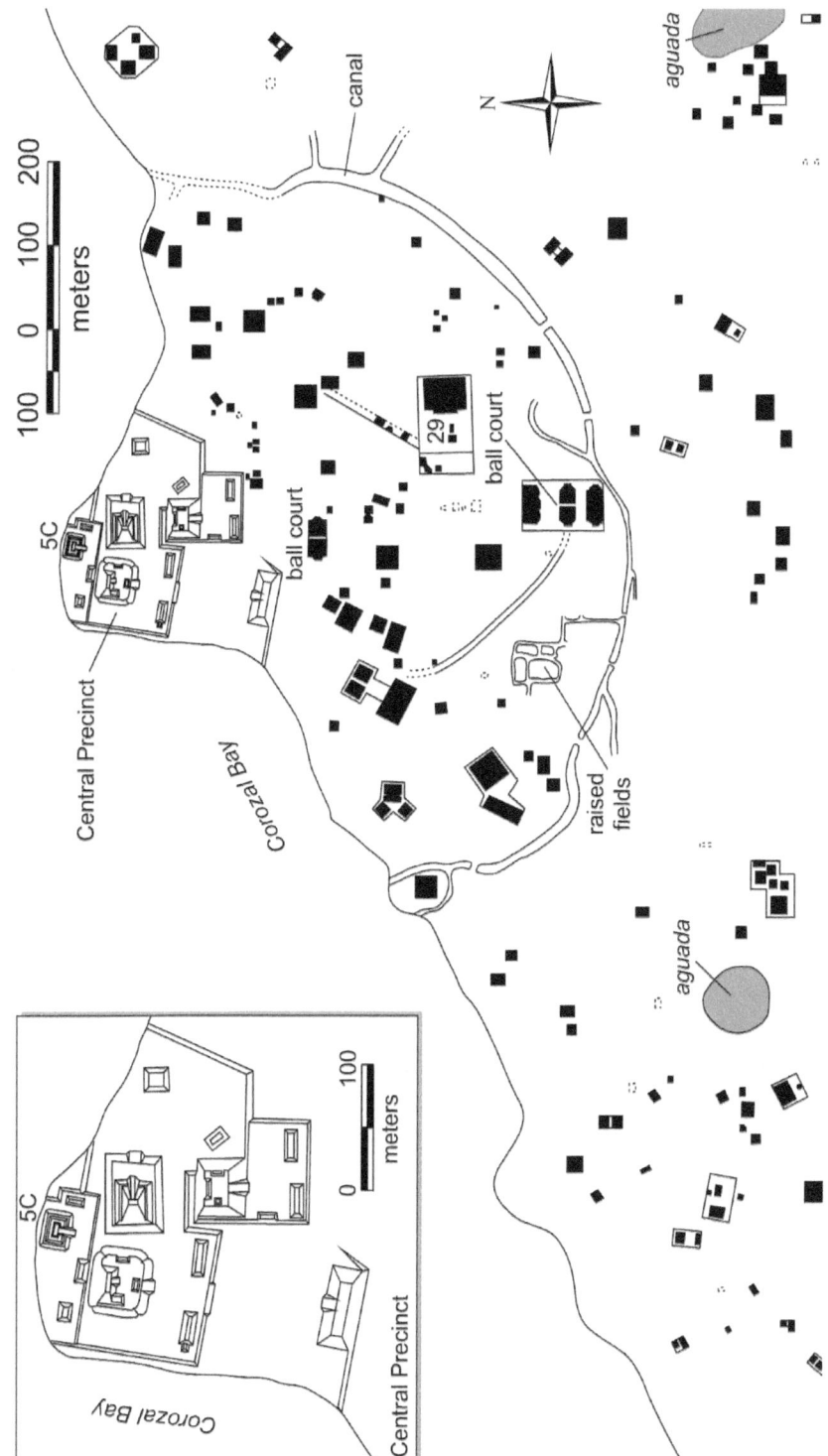

Figure 4.4. Map of Cerros with inset of Central Precinct, after Scarborough and Robertson (1986:Figure 3).

nial precinct with the advent of divine kingship at Cerros. The marshaling of labor and resources needed to transform a small fishing village into a sacred ceremonial center was certainly outside both the means and interests of someone other than an early king, who derived legitimacy from the accepted belief that he was divinely inspired and a conduit of supernatural power (Freidel and Schele 1988b:563).

The monumental structures at Cerros are oriented north–south or a few degrees east of north, and the largest temple-pyramids are all found in the central precinct with the exception of Structure 29, a 10-m-high pyramid with a triadic-temple arrangement on its summit (see Freidel 1986b:11). Structure 29 and the site's two ball courts are found within the core zone of the site but south of the ceremonial precinct; all three were constructed near the end of the Late Preclassic period, shortly before the site was abandoned (Freidel 1986b:Table 1.3).

Summary of Northern Belize Preclassic Developments

The Preclassic data from Cuello, Colha, and Cerros mirror the pattern seen at the two examples from the Belize Valley; the earliest domestic structures at each site were covered by Late Preclassic ceremonial centers. In the case of Cuello, a mass burial of over 30 sacrificial victims accompanied this transformation. At Cerros, the transition was rapid and extensive, and the builders of the remodeled town created impressive temple-pyramids adorned with complex imagery related to Maya cosmology and the emerging concept of divine kingship. Although the Preclassic monumental center that they created included urban features common at Classic period cities, the organization of the architecture expressed different concepts of city planning. Colha provides a unique example of the development of craft specialization during the Preclassic period. Although the temporal resolution of the workshops is not fine enough to correlate the development of Late Preclassic mass tool production to the Terminal Preclassic creation of a ceremonial precinct, it is nonetheless reasonable to see the control of lithic production and distribution as a source for early elite power at Colha.

The Stage Is Set

During the Preclassic period, Maya society in the eastern lowlands transformed from a scatter of small villages beginning around 1000 BCE to a densely settled region by the advent of the Early Classic period in 250 CE. Along the way, Maya society incorporated a number of crucial elements including craft specialization, intensive agricultural systems, warfare and sacrifice, and ancestor worship. Perhaps the most important development, from the viewpoint of power, social organization, and city building, was the advent of a new political system—directed by the first divine Maya kings—seen spectacularly at places like El Mirador in Guatemala but also manifest in the eastern lowlands at places like Cerros. The Classic period elite likely have the first kings of the Preclassic period to thank for institutionalizing this remarkable system whereby the many are convinced to contribute time and energy to building palaces and temples for the few.

Southern Belize

More so than any other area of the eastern lowlands, southern Belize developed a distinctive regional tradition. As Richard Leventhal (1990:138) observed, the region's geographical isolation contributed to greater "internal homogeneity and external heterogeneity" with respect to architecture and hieroglyphic traits. The similarities generally shared by the major sites in the region include a lack of vaulted buildings, tombs without vaults, the sequential reuse of tombs, rare masonry superstructure walls, the integration of major structures into the natural topography and modified hills with architectural facades, few freestanding pyramids, ball courts enclosed by walls, common hieroglyphic monuments, and inconsistent lunar series information on monuments (Braswell et al. 2011:115; Braswell and Prufer 2009:45).

The four largest and best-documented sites in the region are Pusilhá, Uxbenka, Lubaantun, and Nim Li Punit (Figure 5.1). Beyond these four, Phillip Wanyerka (2009:24) reports 32 major sites in the region, 10 of which contain readable hieroglyphic texts. As will become clear, the sites in southern Belize are the least urban of the eastern lowland kingdoms and represent a distinct style of settlement design, architecture, and political expression.

Setting

Southern Belize, due to its remoteness, is one of the most poorly understood regions of the Maya lowlands in general (see Prufer et al. 2011:202), despite having the greatest concentration of hieroglyphic texts in Belize (see Wanyerka 2009). The major sites in the region are found in the Toledo Foothills, part of a ring of eroded and dissected Cretaceous limestone that surrounds the uplifted and older volcanic and metamorphic horst of the Maya Mountains (King et al. 1992:37; Rice 1993:15). The Maya Mountains lie west and north of the foothills, and a narrow band of coastal plain extends from the base of the hills to

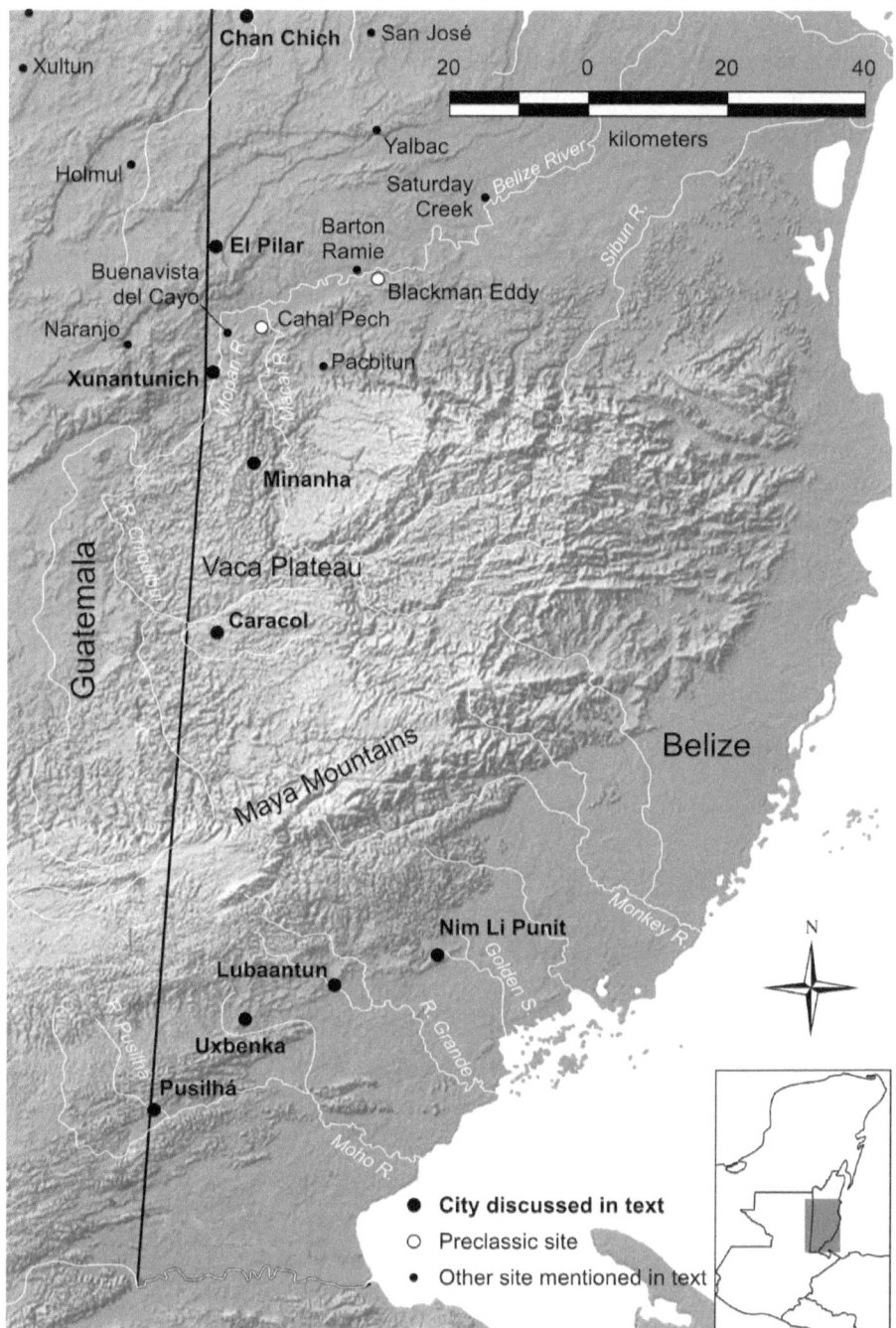

Figure 5.1. Map of southern and central Belize showing sites discussed in the text. Base map courtesy NASA/JPL-Caltech, SRTM mission.

the Caribbean Sea on the east. The swampy Sarstoon River basin to the south forms the modern border between Belize and Guatemala and was the final geographic boundary that made the area remote and isolated in ancient times, just as it does today (Prufer et al. 2011:202).

More rain falls in southern Belize than any other part of the country. This contributes to the region's lush tropical forests and feeds numerous short rivers and streams that drain the southern slopes of the Maya Mountains and the Toledo Foothills (Wright et al. 1959:27–28). These drainages include, from west to east, the Pusilhá River, which feeds the Moho River, the Río Grande, the Golden Stream, and the Monkey River.

The Maya of southern Belize had access to important volcanic rocks, including basalt and granite as well as slate and shale (Graham 1987:753–756). Beyond volcanic resources, the region also supplied limestone, mudstone, and sandstone, all of which make excellent construction materials and influenced the regional architectural style in southern Belize. The Maya found that cleaved pieces of sandstone and mudstone could be used to make massive stelae (Wanyerka 2009:155).

Pusilhá

Setting

Pusilhá is the westernmost and largest major center in southern Belize, situated less than 2 km east of the Guatemalan border and between 180 and 250 m above sea level (Hammond 1975:272). Uxbenka is approximately 19 km to the northeast. The ruins of Pusilhá occupy the hilly banks of the Pusilhá River, one of the small waterways draining the Maya Mountains in southern Belize. The Pusilhá River, also known as the Machaca River, joins the Poité River east of the site to form the Moho River, which flows into the Caribbean Sea some 40 km east-southeast of the ruins. Braswell (2002:2) reports the 6-km^2 settlement zone is sharply circumscribed by the Maya Mountains in all directions but the east, where the narrow Moho River valley passes through the hilly terrain. A northwest mountain pass provided access into the Maya Mountains.

Investigations

Acting on a report from the forestry department, members of the British Museum Expedition to British Honduras visited the ruins of Pusilhá in 1927, making note of an ancient Maya bridge spanning the Pusilhá River and substantial settlement in the vicinity (Joyce et al. 1927:315–316). The museum studied the ruins over the course of three subsequent field seasons, spurred by the discovery of numerous carved monuments with Long Count dates in a portion of the site known as the Stela Plaza. Ultimately, five of the best stelae from the site were cut up and transported to the British Museum where they remain (Braswell 2002:5; Braswell, Prager, and Bill 2005:65; Hammond 1975:273–274). The British Museum crews excavated structures in several groups at the site but were generally disappointed with the artifacts recovered, except from Pottery Cave, a nearby cavern that yielded many fine polychrome sherds (Braswell 2002:5). Sylvanus Morley (1938) subsequently visited the site and published an account of the inscriptions.

Despite the impressive collection of carved stelae, once Morley departed, Pusilhá largely languished in obscurity until Norman Hammond (1975:272–274) visited it as part of his project at Lubaantun. Hammond's (1975:274) work at the site was limited to clearing and photographing the bridge abutments and excavating a pottery dump in a cave near the site.

In 1979 and 1980, Richard Leventhal's (1990) Southern Belize Archaeological Project conducted mapping and excavation at Pusilhá, concluding the site had two distinct focal points: the Stela Plaza to the north and the Gateway Hill Acropolis to the south, characterized by contrasting architecture and urban features. Leventhal's teams conducted limited settlement survey and discovered two ball courts along with several previously unknown architectural groups.

Following a few minor studies of the monuments and ruins, which did not result in published reports, Geoffrey Braswell (2002) began the Pusilhá Archaeological Project in 2001. Braswell's teams spent eight seasons at the site, and the research resulted in numerous publications and five master's theses (Braswell et al. 2009:1). In 2008 Braswell's focus expanded to include much of the Toledo District, and the project was rebranded the Toledo Regional Interaction Project, or TRIP (Braswell et al. 2009:1).

Site Plan and Urban Features

Much of the monumental architecture at Pusilhá occupies a series of hills between the Poité River to the north and the Pusilhá River to the south, although the Gateway Hill group is south of the Pusilhá River (Figure 5.2). The surrounding countryside is dotted with smaller residential groups (Braswell, Prager, and Bill 2005; Volta 2007).

Braswell (2007:74) describes the Gateway Hill Acropolis as the most important architectural group at Pusilhá, noting that an ancient toponym for the site consists of a set of stairs and the glyph *witz*, meaning "mountain." Based

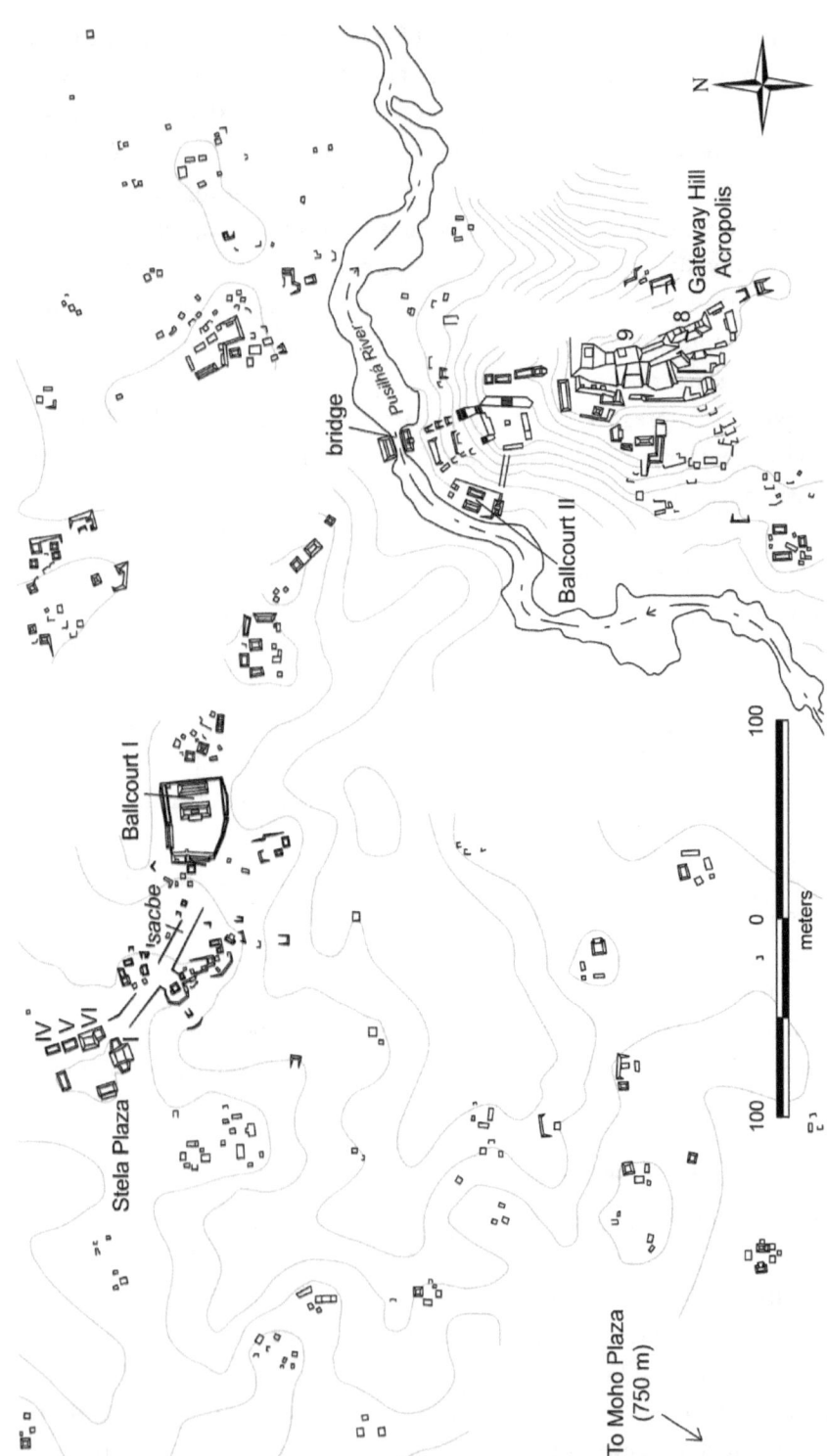

Figure 5.2. Map of Pusilhá, after Prager et al. (2014:Figure 10.3). Contour interval is 5 m, but contours are approximate and only intended to show general terrain features. Areas with no contour lines are unmapped.

on the physical appearance of the acropolis, it is likely that the toponym refers to this massive architectural group. The acropolis includes a series of platforms and structures that climbs a 79-m hill on the south side of the Pusilhá River. Following the natural north-northwest to south-southeast orientation of the hill, the group begins at the river where the British Museum expedition first documented bridge abutments (see Joyce et al. 1927:315–316) and extends south-southeast for over 500 m. The series of climbing platforms built into the hill face begins south of the bridge and leads to the first terrace of the acropolis. Two large boulders with low platforms below them are situated on the lower slope of the acropolis below the first terrace, flanked by two sets of stairs and terraced ramps (Braswell 2007:75). A 20-m-long ramp or *sacbe* leads down from the first terrace to the south end of Ballcourt II, which is bordered immediately to the west by the Pusilhá River.

A stair leads to the east from the first terrace up to the second terrace, a platform flanked by three structures on its eastern side. Atop this terrace near its southern end are two more large boulders that create the gateway after which the acropolis is named (Braswell 2007:75).

The mass of the acropolis lies to the south of the gateway boulders, covering the summit and western side of the hill with structures. The Operation 8 structure, the largest and tallest building, occupies the southern and highest level of the acropolis; it is a temple-pyramid with extensions to the north and south. This structure served as the royal funerary monument for a Late Classic ruler of the site, as discussed later (Pitcavage 2008:32–33). The Operation 9 structure, immediately to the north of the Operation 8 structure, is the second-largest pyramid at the site, but excavations showed it to be a stone facade covering a natural bedrock feature, in keeping with the southern Belize tendency to integrate the natural topography into the architecture (Braswell, Prager, and Bill 2005:79–80).

North of the river on a natural rise is the Stela Plaza, which was home to 22 carved stelae, 4 zoomorphic altars, and at least 4 round altars before the British Museum began working there (Braswell 2002:3). The plaza measures approximately 50 m north-northwest to south-southeast by about 40 m wide. Structure I, a temple-pyramid with extensions on either side, forms the southern boundary of the plaza, and a line of three structures (Structures IV, V, and VI) delineates the eastern edge. The northern and western edges are marked by single structures. The area to the north of Structure I was the setting for most of the carved monuments; a map from the 1928 British Museum expedition to the site shows 12 stelae in a row in front of the structure, with 3 others just north of the line and 2 more at the northwestern corner of Structure I

(Joyce et al. 1928:Figure 2). Braswell's (2002) initial cleaning of the plaza resulted in the discovery of 88 monument fragments primarily in the vicinity of this stela row, a previously unrecorded stela (the twenty-second), and a fourth zoomorphic altar, one more than reported by previous researchers.

Approximately 190 m to the east-southeast of the Stela Plaza on a bench of an adjacent hill is a walled platform that is home to Ballcourt I. A 15-m-wide *sacbe* connects the two groups, running across the undulating terrain for approximately 130 m—as mapped, the *sacbe* does not extend the full distance between the two groups. The midway point of the *sacbe* is flanked by groups of small structures on either side. Ballcourt I, like Ballcourt II across the river, is an example of the southern Belize style of walled ball courts noted by Leventhal (1990:138). The enclosures comprise freestanding walls with bases made of several courses of cut stones. The upper sections of the walls were presumably made of perishable materials (Leventhal 1990:138).

The Moho Plaza is on a low flat plain over 1.5 km southwest of the Stela Plaza and perhaps could be considered a secondary center within the Pusilhá suburban settlement (Figure 5.3). Despite being so far away from the rest of the monumental architecture, the Moho Plaza is the second-largest architectural group at the site, measuring approximately 105 m north-northwest to south-southeast and 75 m wide. The plaza is framed by three long platforms on its eastern side, a large range building (Structure VI) on its southern side, several smaller mounds on its western side, and a ball court on its northern side. This, the third ball court at Pusilhá, is the largest ball court in southern Belize (Braswell, Prager, Bill, et al. 2005:224). Two badly looted mounds in the southwestern corner of the plaza may be another small ball court (Braswell 2002:14). Structure VI on the southern side of the plaza has a hieroglyphic stair with a calendar round dedication date believed to fall in 798 CE (Braswell 2002:14).

Braswell (2007:72–73) observed a distinct architectural pattern at Pusilhá, which he termed "Special Function Group." Conforming to and perhaps establishing the idiosyncratic preference in Pusilhá architectural orientation, these Special Function Groups are defined by three structures on the eastern side of a plaza, accompanied by the two principal structures in the plaza occupying the northern and southern ends. These principal structures are often square in plan, rather than rectangular like the eastern buildings. Among the eastern buildings, the tallest is usually the southern structure, not the central one. Finally, the western side of the plaza is much more open and contains only one structure.

Braswell (2007:73) notes at least three Special Function Groups at Pusilhá,

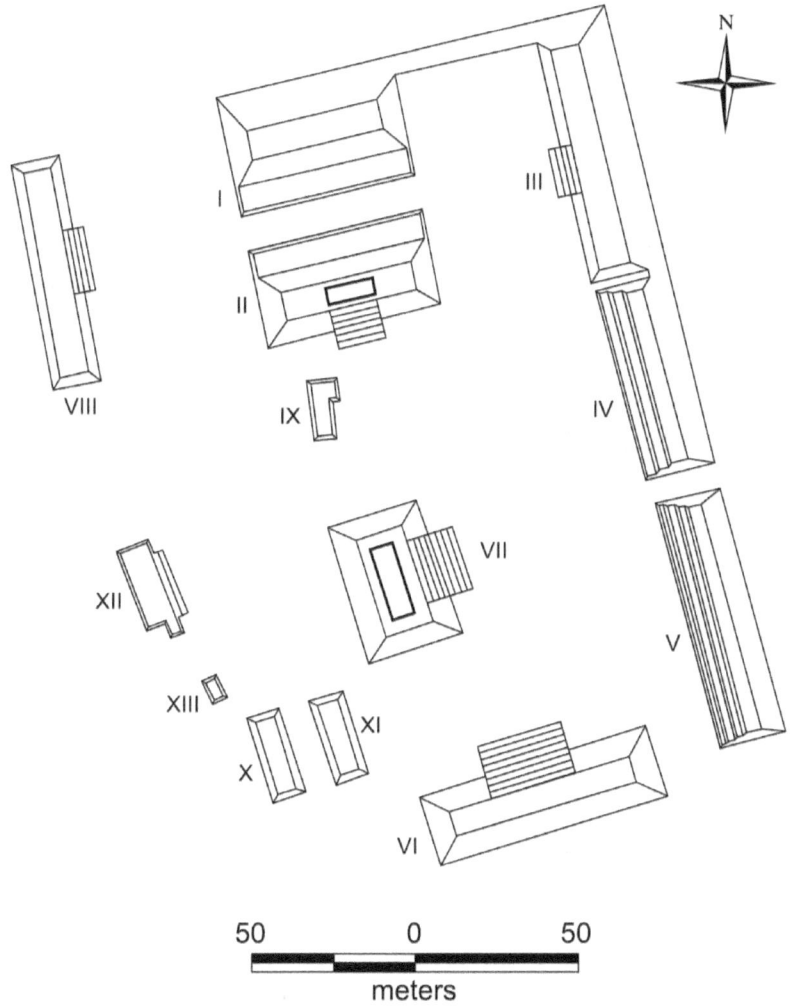

Figure 5.3. Map of Moho Plaza at Pusilhá, after Braswell (2002:Figure 4).

including the Stela Plaza and the Moho Plaza. The artifact assemblage from these groups contrasts with the typical pattern at Pusilhá. The ceramics commonly contain incense burner fragments, while utilitarian vessel forms are rare. Animal bones and river-snail shells are completely absent from these areas of the site but are common in residential contexts.

Chronology

Pusilhá was founded near the end of the Early Classic period, according to hieroglyphic texts at the site (Braswell and Prufer 2009:47). Ceramic material from this period, however, is only known from Pottery Cave, a group approximately 300 m north of the Gateway Hill Acropolis on the northern side of the Pusilhá River (Braswell et al. 2008:55). Based on ceramic data from the epicenter, Braswell, Prager, and Bill (2005:66) propose a four-phase sequence for the occupation at Pusilhá: early Late Classic (600–700 CE), late Late Classic (700–780 CE), Terminal Classic (780–850 CE), and Postclassic (950–1100 CE). The site's first inhabitants appear to have come from the southwestern Petén, based on ceramic data (Bill and Braswell 2005; Braswell 2007).

The Stela Plaza appears to be a largely Late Classic construction, based on the abundant Long Count dates from monuments there (see Braswell et al. 2004), and the Gateway Hill Acropolis has a strong Terminal Classic occupation, evidenced by numerous burials dating to that period (Pitcavage 2008; Pitcavage and Braswell 2010). Braswell, Prager, and Bill (2005:68) note finding large amounts of Terminal Classic ceramics from floor and surface contexts at the site. They also report that at least two people "were left dead on the surface of the plaza" in front of the Operation 8 structure at the end of the acropolis' occupation (Braswell, Prager, and Bill 2005:81).

Braswell, Prager, Bill, et al. (2005:224) speculate that the Moho Plaza dates to the Terminal Classic period as well, quite late in the occupation history of the site. The 798 CE date for the Structure VI hieroglyphic stair is the latest recorded date at the site, and there are architectural similarities to Lubaantun and Nim Li Punit, two sites that peaked after 800 CE. Additionally, Ballcourt III is oriented east–west, a typically late manner of building ball courts, and it is not walled like Ballcourts I and II. The group's setting, on a low-lying plain rather than hilltop, also differs from the older groups.

Evidence for a Postclassic occupation at the site was recovered at "the Bulldozed Mound" platform (Braswell 2007:70), a group about 600 m east of the Stela Plaza. In at least this area of the site, a small group of people using crude and nonstandardized ceramics eked out a living for several generations after the rest of the site had been abandoned.

Political History

With its numerous hieroglyphic texts, it is possible to reconstruct the political history of Pusilhá in more detail than nearly any other city in the eastern lowlands (Table 5.1). Within the texts are the names of 38 individuals. Eleven of them employ the title of divine ruler of the site, which was known in the Classic period as "Un," meaning "avocado" (Braswell, Prager, Bill, et al. 2005:228). Both Wanyerka (2009) and Prager (2002; and reported in Braswell et al. 2004; Braswell, Prager, Bill, et al. 2005; Prager et al. 2014) have completed epigraphic studies of the texts at Pusilhá and present slightly different

Table 5.1. Political history of Pusilhá

Ruler	Long Count	Gregorian Date	Events and Notes
K'awil Chan K'inich (Ruler A)	9.6.17.8.18?	June 17, 571	Accession
	9.7.0.0.0	December 5, 573	Celebrated period ending, Stelae O? and P
	9.8.0.0.0	August 22, 593	Celebrated period ending, Stela Q
	9.8.1.12.8	April 24, 595	War-related event, but it is unclear if Pusilhá suffered or won; antagonist may have been Altun Ha
K'ak' U Ti' Chan (Ruler B)	9.10.15.0.0	November 8, 647	Celebrated period ending to glorify deeds of father, Ruler A, Stelae D and P
Muyal Nah K'uhul [unreadable] K'ak'U Ruler C	9.11.0.0.0	October 12, 652	Accession at age of 66 years, celebrated period ending, and engaged in battle with another site and took a captive, Stela H
Ruler D	9.12.0.0.0	June 29, 672	Celebrated period ending, Stela K
Ruler E	9.14.0.0.0	December 3, 771	Celebrated period ending, Stela M
Ix Ich'ak ... K'inich (Ruler F)	9.14.0.0.1– 9.14.19.17.19	December 4, 771– August 19, 731	Maximum possible period of reign, only female named in dynastic texts
Ruler G	9.15.0.0.0	August 20, 731	Celebrated period ending with stone-binding ritual, son of Ruler F, Stela E
Ruler X5?	9.16.0.0.0	May 7, 751	Possible ruler, celebrated period ending and performed hand-scattering event, Stela F
Ruler X3?	9.18.7.10.3?	March 24, 798	Dedicated Hieroglyphic Stair 1

Source: After Prager et al. 2014.

interpretations of the political history of the site. The following summarizes the reconstruction put forth by the Pusilhá Archaeological Project (Braswell 2007; Braswell et al. 2004; Braswell, Prager, Bill, et al. 2005; Prager 2002; Prager et al. 2014). For a more detailed discussion, please refer to Prager (2002) and Prager et al. (2014).

Ruler A, K'awiil Chan K'inich, founded the Pusilhá dynasty in 571 CE. He used the title Ochk'in K'aloomte,' a rare title also used at Copán by the dynastic founder (Braswell 2007:68; Wanyerka 2009:379). During his reign, Ruler A may have had ties with Copán, and he named his son, Ruler B, after the eleventh ruler at Copán, K'ak' U Ti' Chan (Prager et al. 2014). Wanyerka (2009) indicates that a Pusilhá lord is shown on a bench witnessing the accession of Copán's sixteenth ruler in 763 CE, some 116 years later, which suggests that ties between the cities persisted deep into the Late Classic period.

Among the known rulers of Pusilhá, Prager identifies Ruler F as a queen who ruled sometime prior to 731 CE (Braswell, Prager, Bill, et al. 2005:229). Excavations at the Operation 8 structure in the Gateway Hill Acropolis possibly uncovered the tomb of her successor, Ruler G (Braswell, Prager, and Bill 2005:82; Prager et al. 2014).

Little is known of the final Terminal Classic rulers at the site. The final date at Pusilhá comes from the Moho Plaza's hieroglyphic stair in 798 CE (Prager et al. 2014), but occupation and presumably the royal dynasty continued past this date.

Braswell, Prager, Bill, et al. (2005:230) observe that the antagonistic nature of the political history of Pusilhá is notable, as at least eight conflicts are mentioned between 594 and 731 CE. However, where the enemy's name survives, it is invariably of some small polity whose location has not yet been identified, including a place called B'alam (Braswell, Prager, Bill, et al. 2005:230). Curiously, the larger centers of Classic Maya world (i.e., Copán, Quiriguá, Tikal, Caracol, and Calakmul) and the nearby southern Belize cities (i.e., Uxbenka, Lubaantun, and Nim Li Punit) are not named on the carved monuments at Pusilhá, although other hieroglyphic evidence suggests contacts with Caracol (Braswell, Prager, Bill, et al. 2005:231).

Discussion

Pusilhá has many standard urban features found at most of the cities in this book, including public plazas, private courtyards, a *sacbe*, carved stone monuments, an impressive number of ball courts, temple-pyramids, and an acropolis group. In its overall layout, the major architectural groups are more dispersed than is common at cities in other parts of the eastern lowlands but are similar to the pattern at Uxbenka. In large part, this is probably an engineering accommodation to the hilly terrain of southern Belize. The base of the Gateway Hill Acropolis is over 600 m away from the Stela Plaza, and the Moho Plaza is even farther away at 1.5 km.

In many ways Pusilhá fits the stereotype for a southern Belize city, demonstrating all of the traits mentioned in the beginning of this chapter that define the regional pattern. The temple-pyramids in its southern acropolis, particularly Structure 9, are examples of the illusion of monumentality created by blending natural topography with architectural facades, what Leventhal (1990:138) called the "Hollywood set" style of construction. Two of the city's three (possibly four) ball courts are surrounded by walled enclosures, and the large buildings lack masonry superstructures and vaulted rooms. The site's stela plaza also has counterparts at two of the other major southern Belize cities.

Pusilhá nonetheless has important idiosyncratic features that distinguish it from its neighbors. The persistent north-northwest to south-southeast alignment of structures and groups is uncommon at other sites, for example. The most obvious architectural feature of distinction is its bridge, an extremely rare type of construction among Maya cities. Less obvious is the Special Function Group. The pattern is reminiscent of the in-line triadic shrines noted by Awe (2013) in the Belize Valley.

The absence of textual references to the major sites of the southern lowlands seems to reflect the isolated nature of southern Belize during the Classic period. More difficult to explain, however, is the failure of Pusilhá's scribes to discuss the neighboring sites with emblem glyphs. If the isolation of the area contributed to the development of a regional style, why did it not also result in greater political interaction between the major centers of southern Belize?

Uxbenka

Setting

Uxbenka is approximately 19 km northeast of Pusilhá and 13 km west-southwest of Lubaantun in the rolling foothills of the Maya Mountains. The site is at the western end of an exposed formation known as the Toledo series, a sedimentary formation of primarily fine-grained siltstones and sandstones, which contrasts with the belt of limestone exposed in the foothills to the north. This formation is also home to Lubaantun and Nim Li Punit. Although Uxbenka is some 34 km inland, it had easy access to both coastal and inland trade routes (Braswell and Prufer 2009:46). The major architectural groups at the site occupy hilltops covered in broadleaf forest and dense patches of secondary growth.

Investigations

Leventhal's (1992:145) Southern Belize Archaeological Project first discovered Uxbenka in 1984, although Thompson (1939:280) may have visited an outlying group of the ruins previously (see also Hammond 1975:274). In 1989 and 1990, Leventhal's teams surveyed parts of the site and conducted limited testing excavations to collect chronological data (Prufer 2005:4). In 2005 Keith Prufer (2005) began the Uxbenka Archaeological Project, which completed its ninth season of research in 2013 (Prufer and Thompson 2013).

Site Plan and Urban Features

Uxbenka's monumental architecture, like that of neighboring Pusilhá, is dispersed over multiple ridges and hilltops (Figure 5.4). Prufer (2005:7–8) defines three clusters of architecture including Group A, a set of five plazas

(Groups B–F) arranged in a north–south line, and a hilltop acropolis (Group G). The most well-known architectural complex is Group A, which is home to 23 stela (see Braswell and Prufer 2009:46; Leventhal 1992:148). Located approximately 500 m southeast of Groups B and C, Uxbenka's stela plaza is at the eastern edge of the site's epicenter. The plaza itself is not large, measuring at its widest 55 m east–west by only 35 m north–south; its size was likely constrained by the size and shape of the hilltop upon which the plaza was built (Figure 5.5). Nevertheless, the final form of the plaza resulted in significant modifications to the hilltop, as over 3.5 m of fill was used along the southern and eastern edges of the plaza to expand and level the plaza floor (Prufer et al. 2011:208).

Six generally modest structures surround the plaza in a roughly circular arrangement. The tallest and most massive is Structure A-1, a 10-m-high temple-pyramid built on a much wider platform, which supports smaller flanking buildings. The majority of the plaza's stelae are found in an east–west line in front of Structure A-1. Leventhal's project excavated a collapsed but unlooted tomb in front of Structure A-4 in the plaza (Leventhal 1990:Figure 8.4; Prufer 2005:8).

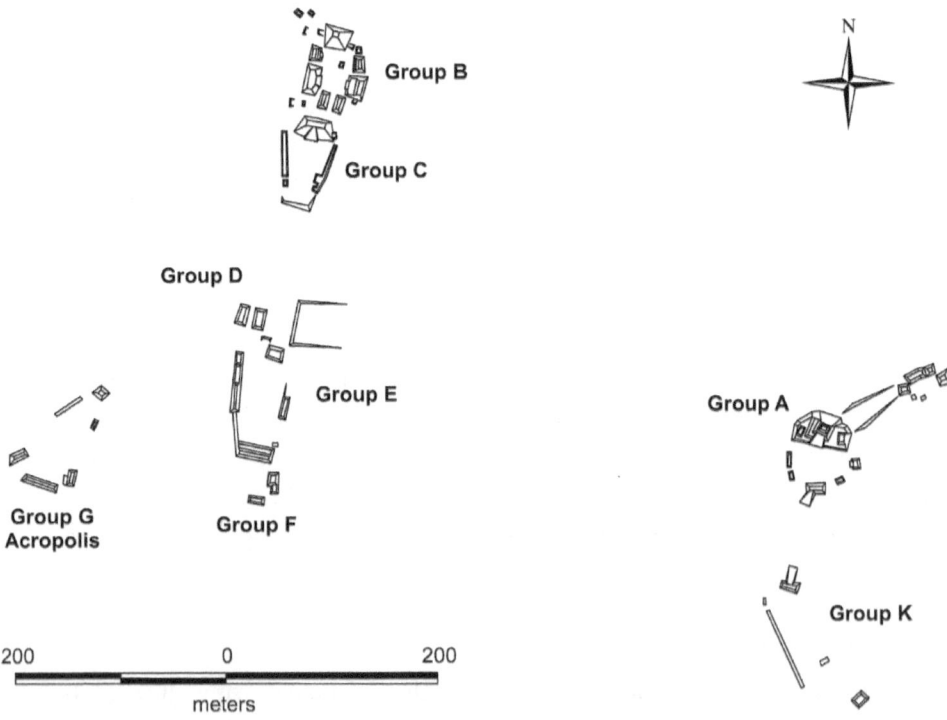

Figure 5.4. Map of Uxbenka, after Prufer et al. (2011:Figure 3).

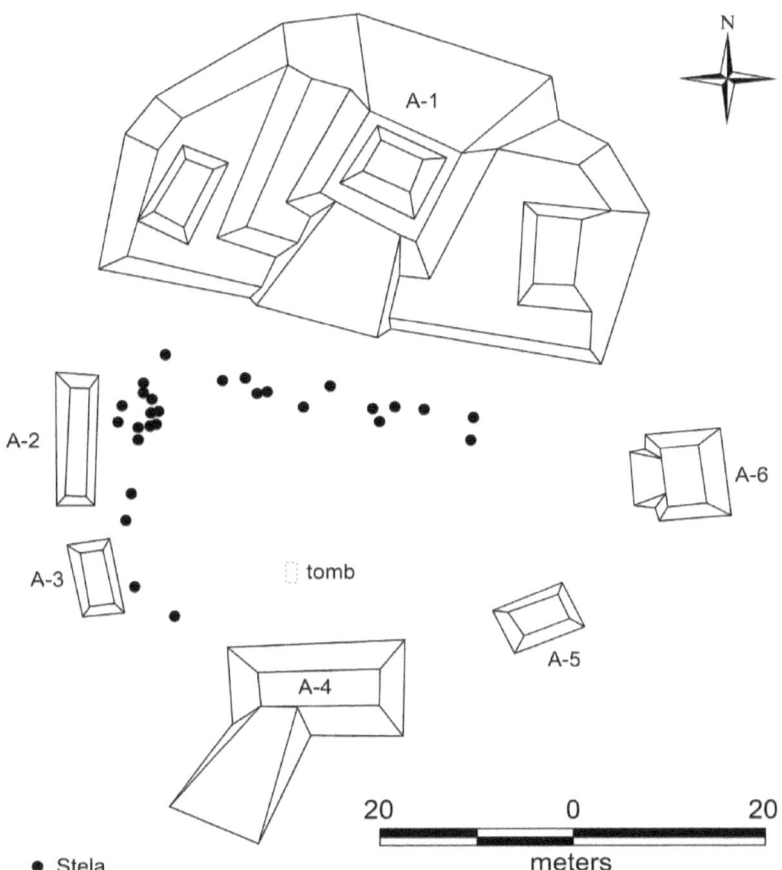

Figure 5.5. Map of Uxbenka's Stela Plaza, after (Prufer et al. 2011:Figure 4). Tomb location based on Leventhal (1990:Figure 8.4).

Approximately 75 m to the south of Group A on an adjacent hilltop is Group K. This large and open plaza has a long, low range building on its western edge and only four other structures. A stairway attached to the north side of the northern structure leads down from the plaza and faces its counterpart at the base of Group A (Prufer 2005:8).

The core of the city is arguably the 550-m stretch of modified ridge that is home to the plazas and buildings of Groups B through F (Figure 5.6). At the northern and highest end of this line of architecture is Group B, a narrow plaza measuring almost 70 m north–south by 30 m east–west. The steeply sloping hillsides at the plaza's margins are faced with cut stone terraces, visually exaggerating the monumentality of the group (Prufer 2005:13). The plaza and most of its structures are oriented approximately 15° east of north. At the northern end of the plaza is tallest structure in the group, Structure B-4, an

8-m-high temple-pyramid. The eastern and western margins are flanked by lower platforms. A badly looted ball court is located in the southern portion of the plaza, and Structure C-1 forms the southern edge of the plaza and the northern edge of Group C. Stairways on either side of Structure C-1 provided access between the two groups (Prufer 2005:12–13).

Group C's 60-m-long plaza is several meters lower in elevation than Group B and straddles the crest of the ridge, which narrows from north to south. Following the landform, Plaza C narrows from 45 m wide to 20 m wide. The eastern and western edges are defined by long, low mounds, and the southern end is a stone terrace that drops steeply. The only monumental building is Structure C-1 at the northern end (Prufer 2005:15).

Group D is located below and approximately 75 m south of Group C; here the ridge top widens and begins to rise as it turns to the east. Group D has a ball court along the western edge of the plaza and a large, low platform on its eastern side. Excavations in the ball court's alley recovered a massive central marker, which measured over 1.4 m in diameter. The upper face of the marker was decorated with a bas relief carving of a circle, raised about 5 cm above the surface of the stone. Prufer (2007:15) suggests only this smaller design was exposed on the surface when the ball court was in use. The eastern platform, which has no structures on its summit, is less than 2 m high but measures over 60 m on each side. Prufer (2005:15) reports that it "may have been partially or completely paved with large limestone slabs." A raised step and a low platform separate Groups D and E.

Group E occupies a finger of the ridge that juts southward. As is the case in Group C, the ridge's topography constrains the plaza in Group E. The 80-m-long plaza narrows from 40 m wide to 30 m from north to south. The architecture in the group consists of low range structures along the eastern, western, and southern edges of the plaza. The ridge and the line of architecture ends with Group F at its southern and lowest end. Group F's small courtyard is open on its western edge, allowing a view of the Group G Acropolis.

The acropolis at the site is separated from the other architecture by a saddle in the ridge and occupies two modified hilltops, which have been faced with cut stones to convey the appearance of a massive two-tiered platform. Despite the impression of monumentality created by modifications to the hilltops, the architecture in the acropolis consists of only six small structures, none taller than 3.5 m. Three buildings occupy the higher southern terrace, and three occupy the lower northern terrace; all six face inward onto their respective courtyards. Prufer (2005:16) reports three looted plaza tombs on the north face of the upper terrace.

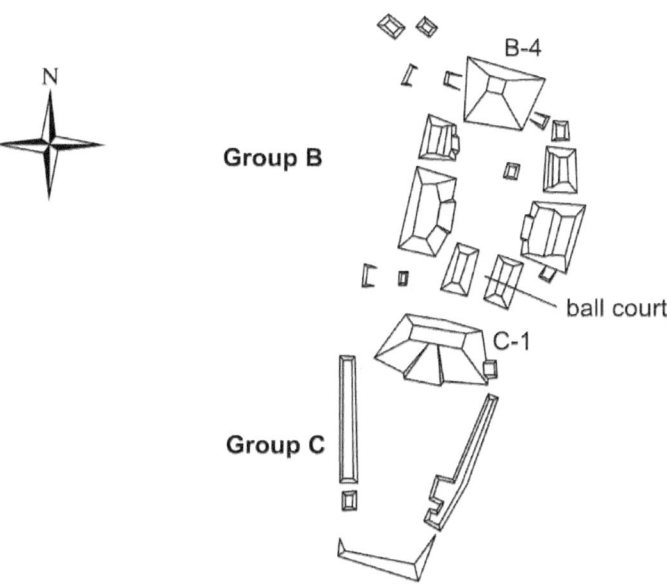
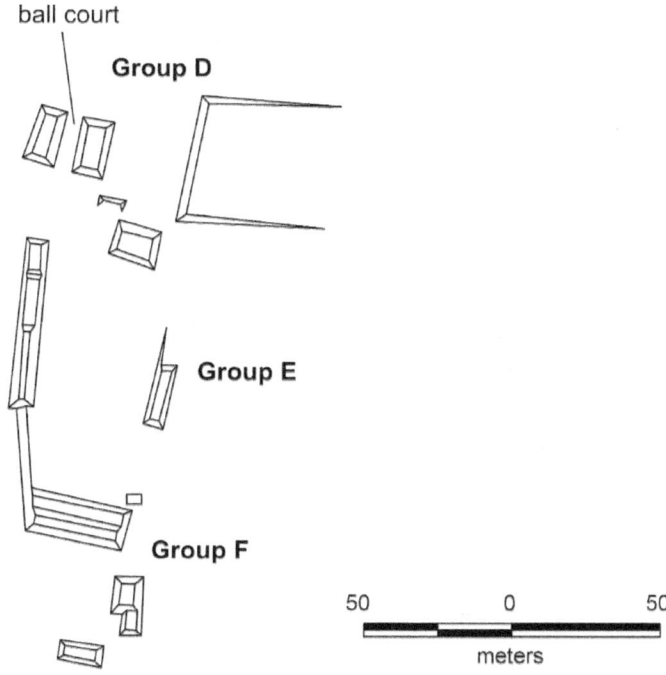

Figure 5.6. Map of Uxbenka Groups B–F, based on Prufer et al. (2011:Figure 4).

Chronology

The most remarkable thing about Uxbenka in a regional context is its antiquity. Radiocarbon dates from Group A indicate the first occupation of the site dates to the Late Preclassic period. The earliest structures on the hilltop were low, earthen mounds with plaster surfaces but no masonry construction (Prufer et al. 2011:208). Early Classic construction subsequently buried these mounds as the Stela Plaza began to take shape. Radiocarbon dating suggests the earliest stone buildings were constructed between 250 and 400 CE; most of the Early Classic structures show no evidence of subsequent remodeling other than frequently being replastered (Prufer et al. 2011:210, 212). Structure A-1, the largest building in the group, is the exception, showing an Early Classic remodeling of its western flank (Prufer et al. 2011:210). At least four of the stelae in the plaza date to this period (Wanyerka 2009:220), and the newly discovered Stela 23 has the earliest Long Count date (9.1.0.0.0, or 455 CE) in southern Belize (Braswell and Prufer 2009:47).

Initial construction also occurred at Group B during the Early Classic period, with construction episodes every 40 to 50 years. The visible structures in Group B, however, postdate 500 CE and demonstrate Late Classic use (Prufer et al. 2011:212).

The site grew to its maximum size and final configuration during the first part of the Late Classic period, but the Stela Plaza was not renovated after 500 CE. It functioned as a "monument garden dedicated to the founding ancestors," and the seat of political power at the site shifted to Plaza B (Prufer et al. 2011:219). The last dated monument in the Stela Plaza is Stela 15, which marks the 9.17.0.0.0 period ending in 780 CE (Wanyerka 2009:267). Braswell and Prufer (2009:47) report that the decline and abandonment of the site are not well understood but "likely coincided with the rapid abandonment of most political centers in the region" after 800 CE; however, detailed radiocarbon dating reported by Aquino et al. (2013:277) narrow the time frame for the site's abandonment to the beginning of the tenth century CE during the Terminal Classic period.

Political History

The hieroglyphic inscriptions at Uxbenka provide tantalizing data related to the early political history of the site. Although Stela 23 is the earliest dated monument, Stela 11 is even older. The monument was discovered in 1984, broken into three pieces. It depicts an Early Classic king holding a double-headed serpent bar. Stylistically, it resembles Early Classic monuments from the central Petén, and the iconographic motif of Tikal's king Chak Tok Ich'aak I (Jaguar Paw) is displayed on the loincloth of the ruler (Wanyerka 2009:220). The motif is not a retrospective mention of the ruler but rather appears to date to Chak Tok Ich'aak I's reign, which began in 360 CE and ended abruptly in 378 CE when Sihyaj K'ahk' (Fire Is Born) arrived at Tikal (Prufer et al. 2011:218; Wanyerka 2009:246).

Interpreting Stela 11 and what it signifies about the political relationship between Tikal and Uxbenka is challenging, but Wanyerka (2005:183) suggests that one of Tikal's kings (either Chak Tok Ich'aak I or his successor, Yax Nuun Ahiin I) could have founded Uxbenka as a vassal kingdom. Wanyerka (2005:184, 2009:245) also proposes that Stela 11 originally stood at Tikal and was "exiled" to Uxbenka following the Teotihuacan Entrada. Its placement at Uxbenka would have been part of the post-378 CE expansion of Tikal's hegemony across the southern lowlands. Even if that interpretation is not correct, the clear depiction of a Tikal king on a monument at Uxbenka indicates important ties between the two cities as early as the late fourth century CE (see Prufer et al. 2011:218).

The central Petén influence is seen in the other three Early Classic monuments at Uxbenka. Unfortunately, only Stelae 23, with its period ending date in 455 CE, can be dated on the basis of anything other than style. Aside from Stela 11, none of the Early Classic monuments contain preserved texts that illuminate the political history of the site.

The Late Classic corpus of monuments includes four stelae with legible dates. Stela 14 has a Long Count date between 9.12.0.0.0 and 9.13.0.0.0, or 672 to 692 CE. Stela 19 contains a tentative Long Count date of 9.12.11.13.11 (684 CE) among its 36 weathered glyph blocks, but no other information is legible. Stela 22 has a 751 CE period ending date and the outline of an emblem glyph. Though the main sign is not legible, the glyph demonstrates that Uxbenka was an independent kingdom at least during the Late Classic period (Wanyerka 2009:259–264). The rulers of Uxbenka claimed divine status by using the royal title of *k'uhul ajaw* on three of the Late Classic stelae (Wanyerka 2009:281). Stela 15 is the latest monument with a date and commemorates a fire-scattering ritual to celebrate the 9.17.10.0.0 period ending in 780 CE (Wanyerka 2009:267).

Unfortunately, despite its impressive number of stelae, Uxbenka's corpus of hieroglyphic texts is highly eroded and not terribly informative. Wanyerka (2009) suggests the early ties to the central Petén and Tikal waned at the end of the Early Classic as Tikal slipped into its hiatus. Uxbenka emerged from the Early Classic into a transformed southern Belize region marked by the rapid rise of three other emblem-glyph bearing kingdoms, and the southeastern part of the Maya world may have had greater influence in the region than did Tikal during the Early Classic (Wanyerka 2009). What is particularly curious, and frustrating for those of us trying to reconstruct the political landscape of southern Belize, is that none of the cities with stelae make mention of another kingdom in the region in their texts, as noted earlier (Braswell and Prufer 2009:51).

Discussion

Uxbenka currently holds the distinction of being the oldest site in southern Belize, although recent work at Nim Li Punit may be challenging that status (discussed in the following). The site provides the only evidence for Early Classic political contact in the possibly exiled Stela 11. Perhaps southern Belize was an area of interest for the Early Classic kings of Tikal, but any aspirations for long-term political ties were forgotten following the death of Chak Tok Ich'aak I.

Like Pusilhá, Uxbenka's monumental core is dispersed across a series of hills and ridges. Unlike Pusilhá, the architecture at Uxbenka generally follows a more standard orientation, approximately 13° east of north. The architects at Uxbenka, beginning in the Early Classic period, built their plazas on modified hilltops and enhanced the monumentality of their city by facing the slopes of those hilltops. In the case of the acropolis, such facing stones covered the top 18 m of the hillside (Prufer 2005:15). For the most part, the structures at Uxbenka are small, however. The tallest building is Structure A-1, but, at 10 m tall, it would only be a moderately tall building at most cities discussed in this book.

Among the architectural inventory are two ball courts, a *sacbe*, plazas, a stela plaza, temple pyramids, and an acropolis. As is the case with most other cities in the region, Uxbenka does not have a clearly defined palace group, and its buildings lack full-height masonry walls and vaulted ceilings. The city, given its antiquity, may have set the standard for urban architecture and influenced the designs of its later neighbors.

Lubaantun

Setting

Lubaantun is located in the lush broadleaf forest of the Maya Mountains' foothills, 15 km west-southwest of Nim Li Punit, 13 km east-northeast of Uxbenka, and 27 km northwest of the coast. The site's core is approximately 50 m above sea level (Hammond 1975:259) and occupies the strip of exposed rock known as the Toledo series, an interbedded sedimentary formation including fine-grained siltstone, sandstone, and limestone within 3 to 4 km of the site (Hammond 1975:15). This formation is well bedded and jointed, and the Maya found that the finer sandstone and limestone, in particular, made excellent and easily obtained facing stones for their monumental buildings (Hammond 1975:16).

The Cretaceous limestone hills north of the site have been severely eroded by the heavy rainfall of southern Belize, and the small streams and rivers draining them have steep-sided valleys and often disappear underground only to emerge again farther downstream (Hammond 1975:17). Lubaantun is 2 km east of the Río Columbia, one of the short rivers draining the Toledo Foothills. Feeding the river are creeks that run in deep gullies east and west of Lubaantun, forming natural borders for the site (Hammond 1975:17). Downstream of Lubaantun, the Río Columbia joins the Río Grande, which drains into the Caribbean Sea north of the modern town of Punta Gorda.

Investigations

Norman Hammond (1970; 1975:31–42) provides a detailed review of the early investigations at Lubaantun, the longest known and most frequently studied site in southern Belize. The ruins of Lubaantun, called Río Grande Ruins until 1924, have been known since at least the late 1800s, discovered shortly after the region was settled by Confederate expatriates following the American Civil War, and there is a possibility Spanish explorers visited the ruins prior to that (Hammond 1975:31).

Thomas Gann, acting on orders from the governor of the colony, visited the ruins in 1903, conducted limited excavations and mapping, and published various versions of his expedition in England over the next two years. Gann's accounts prompted R. E. Merwin to visit the ruins in 1915 as part of a Peabody Museum of Harvard expedition to eastern Yucatan. Merwin mapped the site, described its architecture, documented the site's ball court, and removed three carved ball court markers, which he shipped to the Peabody Museum. Merwin was the first researcher to point out the lack of masonry superstructures, a common trait in southern Belize (Hammond 1975:31–32).

The most infamous period of investigations at Lubaantun came in 1924–1925, when Thomas Gann returned, this time with F. A. Mitchell-Hedges and Lady Richmond-Brown. It was decades later that Mitchell-Hedges' adopted daughter, Anna, claimed to have discovered a crytal skull at the site in 1927 (Hammond 1978).

More scholarly research resulted from Gann's expeditions as T. A. Joyce at the British Museum became interested in the site. Joyce organized two seasons (1926 and 1927) at Lubaantun and an additional three at Pusilhá (1928–1930); although Gann was attached to these expeditions, so too was J. Eric Thompson (see Hammond 1975:39–41; Joyce et al. 1927).

In 1970 Norman Hammond (1975) conducted his dissertation research at Lubaantun and published a comprehensive monograph on the work entitled, *Lubaantun: A Classic Maya Realm*. Hammond (1975:2–4) selected the Toledo District to conduct his research in part because so little was known about its archaeology, but he was also interested in searching for Preclassic sites. He was drawn to Lubaantun because it "displayed a number of interesting and idiosyncratic features, including the absence of stelae and vaulted architecture, and the unusual 'stepped perpendicular' architecture of the main substructures." He returned in 1971 to conduct a survey of southern Belize, confirming the locations of 22 sites in the region (Leventhal 1990:131).

Peter Dunham (1990) conducted dissertation research at Xnaheb, a small Late Classic center situated midway between Lubaantun and Nim Li Punit. His work was an element of Leventhal's Southern Belize Archaeological Project and investigated the development of Xnaheb as a boundary center between the two larger centers (Dunham 1990).

In 1997 and 1998 the then Department of Archaeology conducted excavations, conservation, and restoration work at Lubaantun as part of the Maya Archaeological Sites Development Programme (MASDP), funded by the European Union (Awe 2012:75; Trein 2007:27). MASDP was the first project of its kind to be directed by Belizean archaeologists (Awe 2012:75). In 2009 Geoffrey Braswell and colleagues (2011) began a new study of Lubaantun as part of TRIP. The project focuses on the political and economic relationships between Lubaantun, Nim Li Punit, and Pusilhá (Braswell et al. 2011:116).

Site Plan and Urban Features

Lubaantun's epicenter covers a natural, north–south oriented ridge bordered by two creeks and their steep-sided gullies (Figure 5.7). The ridge, though undulating, generally rises in elevation from south to north. The monumental core of the site stretches 335 m south to north and is approximately 155 m wide at its widest point. Given the natural rise of the ridge top, the northern end of the site is 20 m higher than the southern end (Hammond 1975:66). As Hammond (1975:66–67) describes it, the core of the city comprises a number of "hill platforms" designed to flatten the slope of the ridge and provide level building surfaces; the first platforms occupied the spine of the ridge, and later

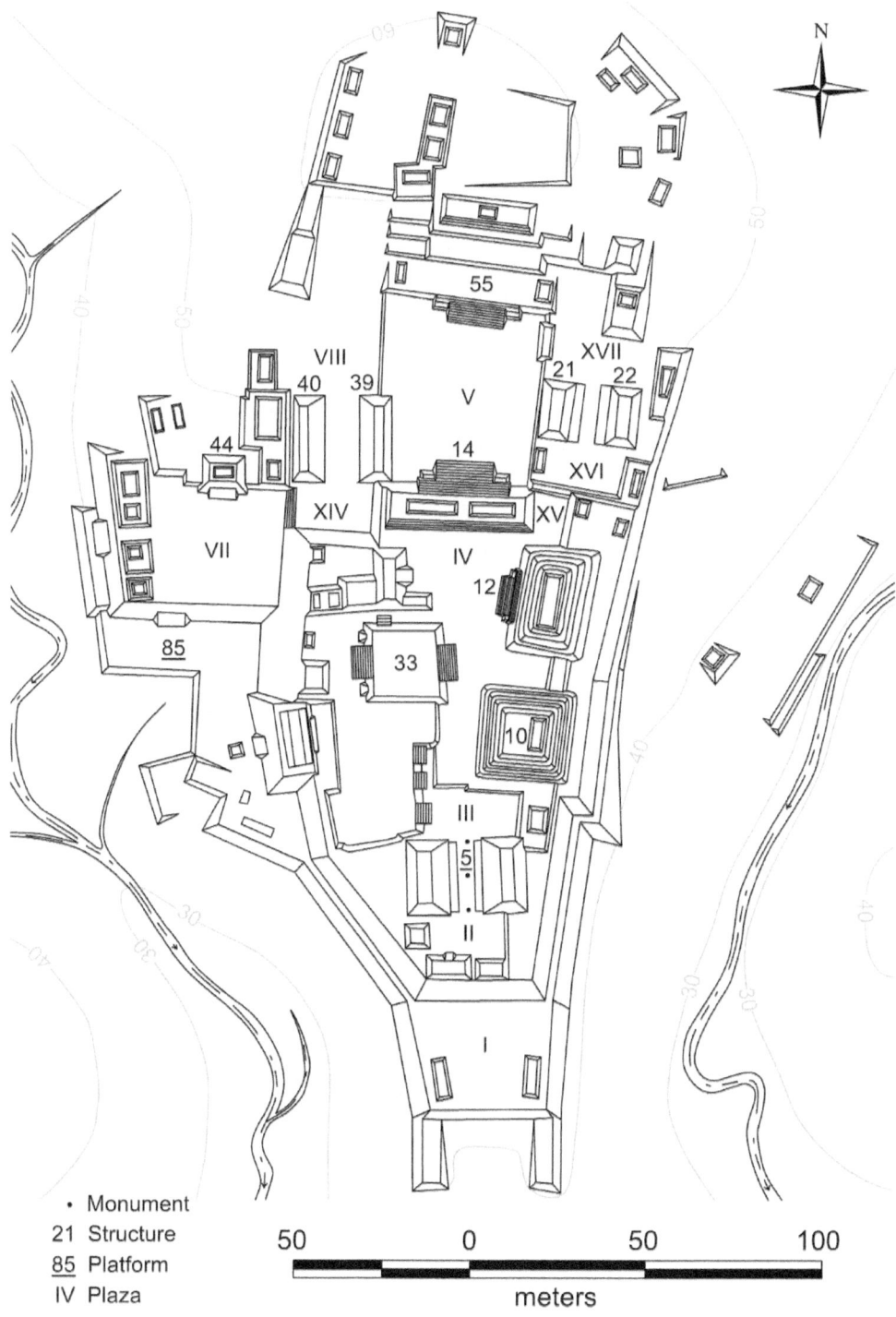

Figure 5.7. Map of Lubaantun, after Hammond (1975:Figure 21). Contour interval is 10 m.

ones developed along its sides. The plan of the site, therefore, "is the result of the way in which these platforms articulate and the extent to which they modify or are governed in form and location by the microtopography of the ridge" (Hammond 1975:66).

The city's layout demonstrates a pronounced north–south axis, mirroring the underlying ridge's orientation. As mapped by Hammond, the site core comprises over 100 structures, which are built around and/or on 20 courtyards/plazas and numerous platforms. The courtyards and plazas range in size from as small as 80 m^2 (Plaza XV) to as large as 2,250 m^2 (Plaza V).

Plaza IV occupies both the physical and symbolic center of the city. It is a 70-m-long plaza, bound on the north by Structure 14, a long, low building that provided access between Plazas IV and V via stairways on either side. Two large temple-pyramids, Structures 10 and 12, flank the eastern side of Plaza IV (Figure 5.8). On the western side are a series of low platform-like structures, including Structure 33, the third major temple-pyramid in the center of the city (Hammond 1975:72). The structure is a square platform measuring 22 m on a side with stairs on both its eastern and western faces.

Immediately south of Plaza IV are Plaza III and Plaza II, separated from

Figure 5.8. Photograph of Structure 12 at Lubaantun (photograph by the author).

one another by a ball court. It was from the alleyway of this court that Merwin removed the three carved ball court markers in 1915 (Hammond 1975:148). Two low structures form the southern edge of Plaza II, and behind them the retaining walls of Platform 5, which supports the ball court and Plazas II and III, drop steeply to Plaza I, an open space with only two low structures near either of its southern corners. This plaza and two structures that project off its platform to the south form the southern end of the site core.

The largest plaza at the site in terms of area, Plaza V, is north of Structure 14 and 3 m lower in elevation (Figure 5.9). Structure 55, a wide platform with a broad central stair and two smaller structures on either end, is across the open plaza from Structure 14. North of Structure 55 is a series of climbing platforms and buildings masking the southern face of a natural rise in the ridge. The extreme northern end of the site did not include any major structures and was at least partly residential (Hammond 1975:66).

On the eastern and western sides of Plaza V are elevated platforms supporting smaller plazas and primarily ceremonial structures. To the east are Plazas

Figure 5.9. Photograph of Plaza V at Lubaantun facing south from Structure 55. Structure 14 is in the center of the photograph, with Structure 12 visible behind it to the southeast (photograph by the author).

XVI and XVII, separated by a ball court (Structures 21 and 22). To the west are Plazas VIII and XIV, also separated by a ball court (Structures 39 and 40).

To the southwest of Plaza XIV and its ball court, the architecture steps down in elevation onto Plaza VII. Structure 44, a temple-pyramid fronting an elevated plaza behind it, marks the northern end of Plaza VII. Several low structures form the western edge, and the southern edge of the plaza is open, dropping steeply to Platform 85.

The architects at Lubaantun employed a stepped-perpendicular style of constructing terraces; every two or three vertical courses of stones on a platform face would be stepped back at least 10 cm, a technique that provided greater stability for high platform faces (Figure 5.10). A variation on this technique was employed to create stepped, rather than sloping, ball court aprons (Hammond 1975:147). The ball court markers found in the southern ball court, described below, all show the game being played in front of a stepped building. This style of ball court architecture is uncommon but is also found at Chan Chich in northwestern Belize.

Figure 5.10. Photograph of the stepped-perpendicular style of construction at Lubaantun (photograph by the author).

Geoffrey Braswell's team interprets the area south of, and possibly including Structure 33, to be "a small acropolis-style palace" (Fauvelle et al. 2013:243). Although this area, marked as Platforms 104 and 105 on Hammond's (1975) map, is depicted as a flat platform, Braswell's crew describes it as "a complex set of rooms and corridors" (Fauvelle et al. 2013:243).

Lubaantun does not have a *sacbe*, although *sacbeob* are present in the regional architectural inventory. Despite this omission, the site possesses other urban features expected of a city its size, including large plazas, temple-pyramids, and three ball courts, an impressive number.

Chronology

Lubaantun is an oddity in the sample of cities described in this book because it is an entirely Late Classic development. Hammond (1975) subdivided the construction sequence of the city into five phases, all of which took place between the early eighth century and the middle ninth century CE as defined by Tepeu 2 and Tepeu 3 ceramics (Hammond 1981:177). These phases, based on ceramics and construction sequences, are not further refined by calendar dates but represent a relative sequence of construction events spanning only 100 to 150 years.

What follows is a greatly condensed summary of the site's chronology based on Hammond's (1975:51–66) detailed account. The earliest occupation at the site was found beneath Plaza IV and comprised house platforms, middens, and several nondomestic structures built on the natural rise in the center of the site. The second phase involved a major expansion of the modified hilltop, extending the artificial platforms to the north and south. By the end of Phase 2, the ceremonial center "consisted of two broad platforms on different levels, linked by steps" and extending from Plaza II in the south to Plaza V in the north (Hammond 1975:53). The southern ball court at the site was constructed during this phase, as were three temple-pyramids: Structures 10, 12, and 33.

The next stage of construction saw the site core expand to the east and west. The eastward expansion accompanied renovations to Structures 10 and 12 and involved piling massive boulder fill along the eastern side of the hill, burying earlier retaining platforms and creating a wider and taller surface for the ceremonial structures. The westward expansion was due to the addition of new plazas and structures to the west of Structure 33, which was also enlarged in Phase 3 (Hammond 1975:55–56). North of Plaza V, new platforms and structures were added to the southern face of the natural hill at the northern end of the site as part of this phase (Hammond 1975:58).

Phase 4 growth was concentrated on the western side of the city as new platforms, plazas, and structures were built lower down the hillside and closer to the creek. This phase included a renovation to Structure 44 to convert it into the small temple-pyramid facing south into the newly created Plaza VII. The Structures 39 and 40 ball court also dates to Phase 4.

The site reached its greatest extent during Phase 5, which is dated to the Terminal Classic period based on associated Fine Orange ceramics (Hammond 1975:65–66). The Structure 21 and 22 ball court dates to this phase, as do the latest phase of Structure 55 and a series of climbing platforms leading up the hill slope north of Structure 55.

Hammond (1975:66) does not specifically address the abandonment of Lubaantun but notes that the entire length of occupation is estimated to be between 100 and 150 years, indicating an occupational period of ca. 700 to 850 CE. Braswell and Prufer (2009:50) suggest an 890 CE ending date for the occupation based on their reading of Hammond's work. The site was apparently not reoccupied, or even revisited, during the Postclassic period (Braswell et al. 2011:125).

Political History

Although southern Belize is known for its unusually high number of carved monuments relative to other parts of the eastern lowlands, Lubaantun has no stelae and only three carved ball court markers. Morley stylistically dated the three markers from the southern ball court to 780–790 CE, and that temporal frame remains an accepted estimate even today (see Wanyerka 2003:18). All three markers depict two players engaged in a ball game; they face each other with the ball between them and the stepped face of the ball court in the background. Although each marker contains between 6 and 13 glyph blocks, most of the text is too eroded to read. The damaged text on Ballcourt Marker 2 may reference either Quiriguá or Copán, two larger sites in Guatemala and Honduras, respectively. Ballcourt Marker 3 appears to have an emblem glyph for Lubaantun, and the same glyph appears on two broken ceramic figural plaques on display in the site's visitor center. The same glyph appears at Naj Tunich cave, 30 km west of Lubaantun (Wanyerka 2009:415).

This newly discovered emblem glyph has important implications for understanding Lubaantun's political role in southern Belize. Subsequent to his Lubaantun monograph, Hammond (1981:179) speculated that Lubaantun may have been the political and economic capital of a polity in which Nim Li Punit, discussed later, was the ritual center. Braswell and Prufer (2009:46) considered this unlikely given the distance between the two sites, and both sites' possessing emblem glyphs argues for their both being independent polities (Wanyerka 2009).

Discussion

Lubaantun's site core has a pronounced north–south axis and was constructed over the comparatively short span of 100 to 150 years but still demonstrates five major phases of expansion as documented by Norman Hammond's (1975) excavations. Lubaantun shares vernacular architectural traits with its southern Belize neighbors, including the technique of integrating structures and platforms into the natural topography, most obvious in the series of platforms and structures that climbs the face of the hill at the north end of the site core.

A striking trait of the southern cities, well displayed at Lubaantun, is size and quality of the stones used in the facings of walls and platforms. The builders employed both fine-grained limestone and Toledo sandstone to craft blocks up to 2 m long by 60 cm high (Hammond 1975:71). The result is a distinctly different feel to the architecture when compared to that of other areas of the eastern lowlands (see Figure 5.8).

In other respects, the city is very different from its neighbors. Its site plan is compact and stands in sharp contrast to the dispersed site cores of Pusilhá and Uxbenka to the southwest. Geoffrey Braswell (personal communication, 2013) compares the mapped portion of Lubaantun to the acropolis at Pusilhá, noting "what we call Lubaantun is just the acropolis of a larger center/community." The problem is that no one has mapped the wider settlement area beyond 600 m from the site core, leaving us with an incomplete understanding of the site.

Most striking, however, is that Lubaantun, despite its size and its apparent political independence, does not have any stelae. Perhaps its idiosyncratic elements can be explained by the city's late founding date. By the eighth century when Lubaantun was founded, stelae dedication was waning at the other cities in the region and the Stela Plaza at Uxbenka had already been relegated to a monument garden, rather than the architectural focus of dynastic power.

Nim Li Punit

Setting

Nim Li Punit is approximately 15 km east-northeast of Lubaantun. The two sites share similar settings as both are built in the band of Toledo series rocks in the foothills arcing around the base of the Maya Mountains. The site occupies a high ridge covered in broadleaf forest overlooking a tributary of Golden

Stream, one of the short waterways draining the foothills to the Caribbean Sea, approximately 13 km to the southeast.

Investigations

Less is known about Nim Li Punit than any other major site in southern Belize (Braswell and Prufer 2009:48), although that is changing. Despite its proximity to southern Belize's major road, Nim Li Punit escaped discovery until 1976, when an oil-exploration company bulldozed a stone substructure while running a seismic survey line. The archaeological commissioner, Joseph O. Palacio, visited the ruins and discovered the site's stela plaza. Inspired by the portrait of a king on Stela 14, Palacio named the site after the Kekchi Mayan term for large headdress. Palacio invited Norman Hammond to conduct a preliminary study of the ruins, and a small crew from the Corozal Project at Cuello (see Chapter 9) spent three days mapping, photographing, illustrating, and testing the ruins (Hammond et al. 1999:1–2).

Richard Leventhal's (1990) Southern Belize Archaeological Project began studying the ruins in 1983 and determined they are larger than Hammond et al. (1999) suspected. In addition to discovering two previously unmapped groups of buildings, Leventhal (1990) salvaged a royal tomb at the site. MASDP carried out limited excavations and more extensive conservation work at Nim Li Punit in the late 1990s (Awe 2012:75; Trein 2007:27), including salvage work on two additional royal tombs (Braswell and Prufer 2009:48).

In 2010 TRIP began a new study of Nim Li Punit as part of their regional investigations of southern Belize (Fauvelle et al. 2013). At Nim Li Punit, their focus has been on structures at the southern end of the site core, which they interpret to be a royal palace.

Site Plan and Urban Features

The epicenter of Nim Li Punit comprises three major groups of architecture (Figure 5.11). The South Group, home to the stela plaza, and the East Group are a connected line of architecture built along a north–south axis that extends for approximately 325 m. The West Group occupies a hilltop about 60 m from the other groups and separated by a narrow stream. The orientation of the architecture at the city is consistent internally but differs from the orientations seen at most other sites in Belize. Most of the structures in the South Group are 4–5° west of north; only Pusilhá has a similar west-of-north style of orientation.

The South Group anchors the southern end of the site core and includes about a dozen structures grouped around two platforms of different eleva-

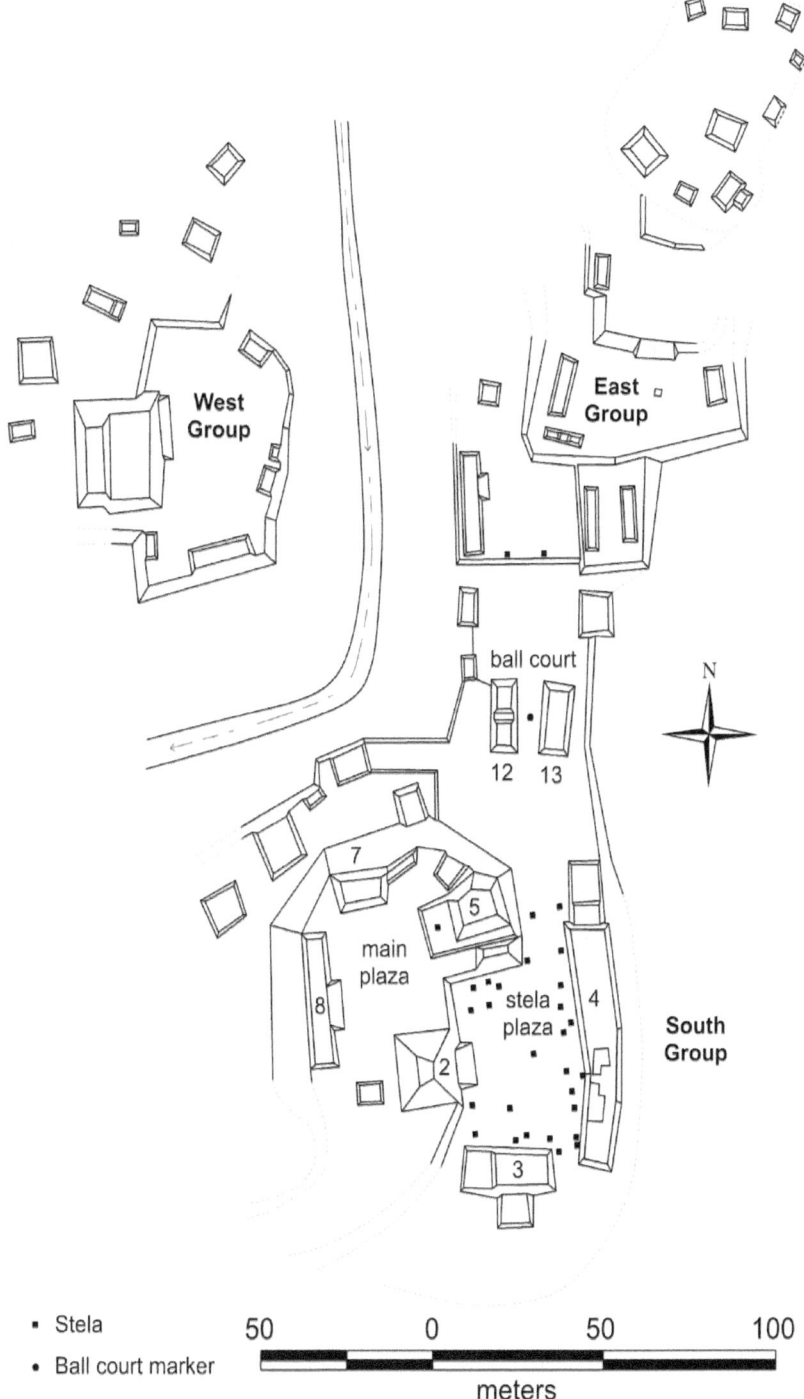

Figure 5.11. Map of Nim Li Punit, after Leventhal (1990:Figure 8.2).

tions. The main plaza, which occupies the lower of the two platforms, is elevated about 5 m above the natural terrain to the east and south and measures approximately 55 m north–south by 30 m east–west (Hammond et al. 1999:2). Access to the main plaza is from its northern end where a stairway leads down to another platform and the site's ball court. Hammond et al. (1999:Figure 2) mapped 23 stelae or stelae fragments in the main plaza, noting that several of the fragments probably could be refit. This appears to have been the case as Braswell and Prufer (2009:48) report 21 stelae at the site. Only Stelae 1 and 16 were standing when the site was first mapped (Hammond et al. 1999:4). At approximately 1,840 m^2, the main plaza at Nim Li Punit is the smallest of the three stela plazas found at the major sites in southern Belize. Uxbenka's Stela Plaza checks in at approximately 1,930 m^2, and Pusilhá's measures approximately 2,560 m^2.

Structure 2 is an 11-m-tall temple-pyramid with an outset stairway. It is the tallest structure at the site and dominates the western side of the main plaza. It faces Structure 4, a 63-m-long, 3-m-tall range building the marks the eastern edge of the main plaza. The lone structure on the southern edge of the plaza is Structure 3, a 24-m-long mound that is also 3 m tall.

Attached to the western side and northwestern corner of the main plaza is a higher platform that supports not only the bulk of Structure 2's pyramid-substructure but also six other buildings grouped around an irregularly shaped plaza. This is known as the Plaza of the Royal Tombs today; three collapsed tombs were excavated there in the 1980s and 1990s (Fauvelle et al. 2013:243). Leventhal's (1990:132) team excavated Tomb 1, a royal tomb with the remains of 5 people who were buried with 39 or 40 ceramic vessels and various other artifacts including jade diadems and stingray spines (see also Fauvelle et al. 2013:243), in front of Structure 5. The tomb fits the pattern of sequential tombs in the region as it held the remains of 5 individuals interred separately. MASDP excavated Tombs 2 and 3 in front of Structure 8, a 40-m-long and 2-m-tall mound that marks the western edge of the plaza (Fauvelle et al. 2013:243). The 3.5-m-tall Structure 7 marks the northern edge of the plaza.

Members of TRIP concluded the group of buildings and associated plaza constitute a "habitation group-style palace" (Fauvelle et al. 2013:243). They interpret Structure 8 to have possibly been a council house based on the lack of caches, burials, and middens (Fauvelle et al. 2013:247). Structure 7 and its two outbuildings they more confidently interpret to be the royal residence of the kings of Nim Li Punit (Fauvelle et al. 2013:248). The identification is based on the architectural form and elaboration as well as the content and number of caches found in the structure (Fauvelle et al. 2013:248).

The ball court at the site is located north of the main plaza and consists of Structures 12 and 13, two 20-m-long buildings separated by a 6-m-wide playing alley. Low benches at the base of each mound, however, restrict the alley's width to about 3.5 m. Excavations recovered a single plain limestone marker in the center of the alley (Hammond et al. 1999:4). Although not entirely evident from published maps, Leventhal (1990:138) describes the ball court as being walled.

The East Group is north of the ball court and consists of a complex series of platforms and four plazas that climb the gentle slope of the ridge as it rises to the north (Leventhal 1990:132). The highest platform in this series occupies the high point of the ridge and includes nine low structures rather haphazardly arranged around a common plaza.

Leventhal (1990:132) describes the West Group "as the smallest of the central architectural clusters, although still impressive in its scale." The group includes two terraces—an upper one and a lower one—and over a dozen structures. The largest structure occupies the western side of the lower terrace and is approximately 6 m tall.

Chronology

Until recently, little could be said about the chronology of Nim Li Punit outside of the 76-year period covered by its carved monuments. The limited excavations at the site prior to TRIP's work did not produce enough data to determine a construction sequence for the major groups, and the ceramics from the site had not been formally analyzed. Thankfully, the preliminary work accomplished since 2010 has sketched out a ceramic chronology for the site. The earliest ceramics thus far discovered come from fill and primary context in the southern part of the site and date to the Early Classic, ca. 400 CE. TRIP researchers attribute the bulk of the construction at the site including the West Group and the final phase of the South Group, however, to the Late Classic (600–830 CE) and early Terminal Classic (830–850/900 CE) periods (Fauvelle et al. 2013:246).

Political History

Stelae dedication at the site occurred in two bursts: the first (based on the latest historical dates on the monuments) between 734 and 741 CE in the Late Classic period and the second between 790 and 831 CE in the Terminal Classic period (Fauvelle et al. 2013:246). Recorded history at Nim Li Punit begins with Stela 15, which was erected in 734 CE. The stela depicts three individuals conducting a scattering ritual framed by upper and lower registers of hieroglyphs, which are supplemented by 19 secondary glyph blocks, including site's the emblem glyph, in the figural scene (Wanyerka 2003:74–75).

Stela 2 was apparently erected in 738 CE, although its text makes mention of a date in 726 CE and the 9.15.0.0.0 period ending in 731 CE. The monument depicts two standing individuals facing a third seated person. They are engaged in a scattering ritual atop an elaborate Witz' monster pedestal, which is accompanied by a water-lily jaguar and a snake. Wanyerka's (2003:46–49) reading of the text suggests it deals with the accession of a king of Nim Li Punit that was attended by a lord from the "Water-Scroll" site, which may be Altun Ha in northern Belize, and another lord from either Copán or Quiriguá—an interpretation that Braswell and Prufer (2009:49) do not favor.

Stela 1 also depicts a scattering ritual to commemorate the 9.15.0.0.0 period ending in 741 CE. Lajun Ka'an, a king of Nim Li Punit, faces a seated figure with a ceramic bowl on the floor between them. The figures are atop an unusual Witz' monster pedestal with a large mat design below it.

Braswell's TRIP team speculates that the 50-year hiatus in stelae dedication at the site after 741 CE could be related to an intriguing possibility. The royal dynasty may have pulled up its roots and relocated to the smaller site of Xnaheb, located approximately midway between Nim Li Punit and Lubaantun, where the only dated monument was dedicated in 780 CE (Fauvelle et al. 2013:246; Wanyerka 2003:88).

Monument placement began again with Stela 21 in 790 CE; this monument mentions a fire ritual and a scattering ritual associated with the 9.18.0.0.0 period ending. The king involved is a divine lord from Nim Li Punit, nicknamed "Macaw Jaguar God of the Underworld," who is shown alone, holding a K'awiil scepter. The main sign of the Nim Li Punit emblem glyph is spelled syllabically on this monument as Kawam, a word that may refer to a bird of prey (Wanyerka 2003:80–81).

Stela 14 is a remarkable monument because of its massive size. At 9.29-m tall, it is the second-tallest stela in the Maya world (Wanyerka 2003:68). The monument depicts a single person conducting a scattering ritual, probably to commemorate the 9.18.10.0.0 period ending in 800 CE. The stela names the same king seen on Stela 21, as well as his parents; his mother was a noblewoman from the as-yet-unidentified site of B'alam (Wanyerka 2003:68–69).

Stela 7 is a highly eroded monument that shows two standing figures atop a Witz' monster pedestal celebrating the 9.19.0.0.0 period ending in 810 CE. Unfortunately, its eroded text yields no additional information of note.

Stela 3 is an odd monument that includes a single 7 Ajaw glyph, curiously written backwards. This apparently represents a Short Count calendar date, a shorthand method of naming period endings based on their associated Tzolk'in date. In this case, the most likely Long Count date corresponding to 7 Ajaw is 10.0.0.0.0 in 830 CE (Wanyerka 2003:53). Braswell and Prufer (2009:49) suggest the stela is a post-abandonment monument.

Wanyerka (2003:74) believes the texts on Stelae 2, 15, and 21 provide political references to Copán and Quiriguá, two important centers in the southeastern lowlands of Honduras and Guatemala. Braswell and Prufer (2009:49) argue for a more cautious interpretation because the emblem glyphs for Copán and Quiriguá do not show up in any of the texts, nor do they name individuals known from those sites. Furthermore, none of the nearby emblem-glyph bearing kingdoms is mentioned in the texts.

Discussion

Using the methods to rank sites discussed in Chapter 10, Nim Li Punit is smaller than the other southern Belize Late Classic cities. Geoffrey Braswell (personal communication, 2013) points out that Nim Li Punit and Uxbenka have the least nucleation of large architecture. Despite its differences, Nim Li Punit shares much in common with them the other sites in the region, including the integration of the natural topography into the urban architecture and the lack of vaulted buildings. The ritual heart of the city was clearly the South Group with its almost two dozen stela, central temple-pyramid, elevated palace group, and royal tombs.

Our understanding of the city's age and role in the regional political arena is sure to change based on the recent and ongoing work by TRIP. Significantly, the discovery of Early Classic ceramics in primary contexts has the potential to challenge Uxebenka's status as the oldest city in the region.

Discussion and Concluding Remarks

Of all the regions discussed in this book, southern Belize is the most meaningful as a reflection of ancient Maya developments. In other words, not only is the region a useful geographic subdivision, but it also appears to be culturally significant. The centers of southern Belize developed and shared an architectural style that is distinct from the other areas of Belize. Were they really cities, however? Three of the four sites discussed here are clearly royal centers, and Lubaantun could easily be argued to be royal as well, assuming it had an emblem glyph. Geoffrey Braswell (personal communication, 2013) notes that there is little that is truly urban in the region, and he prefers to classify the sites as "royal manor houses embedded in a rural framework." For the purposes of this book, however, it is reasonable to view the major sites of southern Belize as functionally equivalent to the cities described in the following chapters. They are regal-ritual centers and the seats of independent royal courts. In terms of size, they certainly fall at the bottom of the rank ordering presented in Chapter 10, but they still served their rural hinterlands as the central administrative bodies for their polities.

The region is notable for its high frequency of carved monuments, its small stela plazas, and the curious lack of textual reference to neighboring cities. Furthermore, the complete lack of stelae at Lubaantun is puzzling given the site's size and the ubiquity of stelae at other sites in the region.

Another important characteristic of the region is that the major cities lacked Preclassic antecedent architecture, as the region apparently was not heavily settled until the Early Classic period. Most of the other major centers of the eastern lowlands are all built on the remains of Preclassic villages; those villages not only affected the location of urban developments but also influenced and constrained subsequent architectural growth to varying degrees.

Southern Belize, isolated and unique, is atypical when stacked alongside the rest of the eastern lowlands in terms of chronology, architecture, use of stone monuments, settlement patterning, and concepts of city building. In fact, no starker contrast exists than that between the southern kingdoms and the mighty site of Caracol on the other side of the Maya Mountains. Caracol represents a completely different kind of urban development and political force: it engulfed its neighbors, challenged the Early Classic power structure in the southern lowlands, and dominates Chapter 6 of this book.

6

Vaca Plateau and Maya Mountains

Separated from southern Belize by the rugged Maya Mountains lies the karstic landscape of the Vaca Plateau (see Figure 5.1). The southern part of the plateau served as the stage for the remarkable development of Caracol, easily the largest Maya settlement in the eastern lowlands. This chapter presents Caracol and, as something of a foil, Minanha, a much smaller center that thrived for a short period of time on the fringe of Caracol's realm. The two centers represent contrasting expressions of Maya urbanism but were likely linked politically by proximity.

Setting

The Maya Mountains in the south-central part of Belize are an uplifted block of quartz-rich and granitic rock with peaks over 1,000 m (3,300 ft) in elevation (Wright et al. 1959:23). Younger Cretaceous age limestone deposited around the uplifted volcanic and metamorphic mountains has subsequently eroded into a series of foothills, including the Toledo Foothills to the south and the Central Foothills in the north (King et al. 1992:36–37). The Western Uplands land region is another area of limestone located between the Maya Mountains to the south and east and the Central Foothills to the north. This region includes the Vaca Plateau (see Figure 5.1). Although the area has steep-sided eastern scarps (Wright et al. 1959:28), it is also home to "some of the most impressive karst in the country, making the term 'plateau' inappropriate" (King et al. 1992:36). The Vaca Plateau comprises numerous dry karst valleys and residual limestone hills punctuated by sinkholes, solution fissures, and caves (Reeder et al. 1996:125).

Most of the streams responsible for carving valleys in the Maya Mountains and eroding the surrounding limestone drain east to the coastal plain, but the flow from a few western streams feeds the Macal and Mopan Rivers. The

Río Machaquilá in the southwestern part of the mountains and a few smaller streams drain west into Guatemala (Wright et al. 1959:24).

The rugged terrain has limited modern settlement of large areas of the region, and much of the Vaca Plateau and Maya Mountains are covered in broadleaf forest. The Mountain Pine Ridge area of the Vaca Plateau provides a startling contrast with its sandy soils, pine trees, and dramatic waterfalls.

The northern part of the plateau is home to the sites of Minanha, Waybil, Camp 6, Ix Chel, and Caledonia, among others. The central and southern plateau witnessed the development of small centers like Mountain Cow and Las Cuevas as well as the massive urban center of Caracol.

Minanha

Setting

Minanha is located in the sparsely settled northern part of the Vaca Plateau on a strategic hilltop overlooking the junction of four important valley passes leading in different directions—one north toward the Belize Valley, one northeast toward the Macal River, one west toward the Petén, and one south into the Maya Mountains and toward Caracol (Iannone 2005:27, 29, 2010:359). The larger cities of Naranjo and Caracol, two important Classic period antagonists on the political landscape of the region, are 25 km to the northwest and south, respectively (see Iannone 2010:Figure 1).

Investigations

While working at Lubaantun in 1927 with the British Museum Expedition to British Honduras, Thomas A. Joyce, Thomas Gann, and several workers from the project went to the Cayo District to investigate reports of a ruin south of the border town of Benque Viejo (Gann 1927:138; Joyce et al. 1927:295). After a grueling mule ride, the archaeologist and six *chicleros* reached the ruins, which they named Minanha, or "no water" (Joyce et al. 1927:319–320). During the short week-long visit, the archaeologists made a pace-and-compass map of the ruins and conducted limited excavations at the ball court and several other mounds. The account of the investigations repeatedly describes the results of the excavations as "disappointing," but the expedition did establish that Minanha was a large site (Joyce et al. 1927:320, 322; see also Gann 1927:155).

At the request of the Belizean government, Gyles Iannone of Trent University attempted to relocate Minanha in 1997, 70 years after the British Museum's Expedition had first mapped and tested the ruins (Iannone 2001:127). Iannone's initial trip was unsuccessful because the site's location was incorrectly plotted on government maps, but a second trip in 1998 succeeded in finding the ruins, approximately 3.4 km northeast of their reported position (Iannone 2001:127). The site proved to be larger than expected and seemed like a promising locale for a multiyear project (Schwake 2008:102).

Following the site's rediscovery, Trent University's Social Archaeology Research Program (SARP) investigated Minanha between 1999 and 2012 (Iannone and Schwake 2013; Schwake 2008:102). Much of the initial SARP work focused on the site's epicenter (Iannone 2005; Iannone and Reader 2011:3; Schwake 2008; Lamoureux St-Hilaire 2011), investigating the rise and fall of the royal court (Iannone 2005) and collective memory (Schwake and Iannone 2010), but SARP subsequently studied the city's support population, nearby minor centers, and surrounding cave systems (see Iannone and Reader 2011:3–4; Iannone and Schwake 2013; Longstaffe 2011).

Site Plan and Urban Features

The Minanha epicentral court complex, as Iannone (2010) describes it, covers 9.5 ha of a strategically located hilltop and comprises 2 large plazas and 12 courtyards or patios (Figure 6.1). The line of monumental architecture exhibits a strong north–south axis (Iannone 2005:30).

A large plaza (Plaza A) dominates the southern end of the epicenter and is the setting for most of the apparent civic-ceremonial structures and six of the site's eight known stelae (Iannone 2010:360). The plaza measures approximately 100 m north–south by 80 m east–west and is irregularly shaped, likely conforming in part to the configuration of the hilltop on which it is built. The southern edge of the plaza is bound by a long range building. Structure 12A, a 40-m-long, 6.5-m-high tandem range building, which fronts an elevated courtyard (Courtyard F), is on the western side of the plaza (Lamoureux St-Hilaire 2011:52). The southern face of a large acropolis group forms the northern end of Plaza A. Minanha's ball court on the north and the complex of Structures 3A, 4A, and 5A on the south mark the eastern edge of the plaza. Structures take up much of Plaza A's floor space: the Structure 7A temple-pyramid in the southeastern corner of the plaza faces west toward Structure 13C, another temple-pyramid in the southwestern corner of the plaza; and Structure 9A, a low platform supporting Stelae 1 and 2, is in the approximate center of the plaza.

Sonja Schwake (2008:114) classifies the Structure 3A complex on the east and Structure 9A on the west as an E-Group. Structure 3A within this complex was an eastern ancestral shrine (Iannone 2010:361; Schwake and Iannone

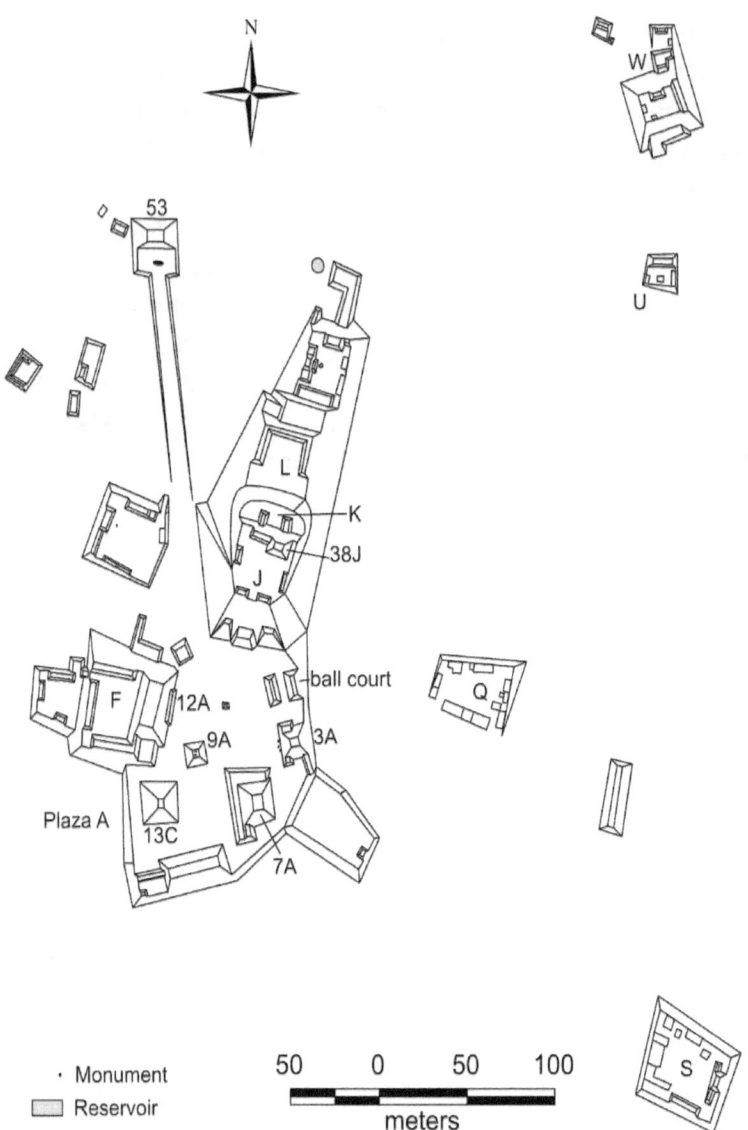

Figure 6.1. Map of Minanha, after Iannone (2010:Figure 3).

2010:334); at its western base excavators documented three stelae (two limestone and one slate) that were all broken in antiquity. Excavations along the primary axis of the mound encountered a series of three vertically aligned caches representing between 425 and 750 years of deposition between the first cache and the last (Schwake and Iannone 2010:335).

While many of the buildings in Plaza A share a common orientation (approximately 10° west of north), Courtyard F, the elevated and attached platform and supporting buildings on the western side of the plaza, the Stela 6 courtyard to the north, and the acropolis group are oriented 15° east of north. This contrasting alignment means that the eastern face of Structure 12A has an oblique view of the ball court, the possible E-Group, and Structure 7A.

Excavations at Structure 12A determined it to be one of the few vaulted buildings at the site (Lamoureux St-Hilaire 2011:52). It has eight masonry rooms divided by a central passageway that allowed access to Courtyard F from Plaza A, and Jeffrey Seibert's (2004:166) study of the building classified it as a "passageway range structure" and noted its dual public and private orientation. Similar structures are known at other sites in the Maya Mountains and Belize Valley including Caracol, Buenavista del Cayo, Las Ruinas de Arenal, El Pilar, and Cahal Pech (Seibert 2004:168–69).

To the north of Courtyard F, a *sacbe* exits Plaza A at an approximately 10° west of north orientation, terminating at a small platform supporting a south-facing temple-pyramid. With Stela 7 in front of it, Structure 53 is a terminus shrine and the farthest north building in the complex of civic-ceremonial structures. The *sacbe* shares the same orientation as most of the buildings in Plaza A and is aligned approximately 10° west of north, while the acropolis and Courtyard F are aligned 15° east of north. It is unclear if the differences in orientation reflect two different construction time frames and, thus, different planning agendas, or have some other significance. Drawing a line from the *sacbe* terminus shrine, down the center of the *sacbe*, to the southern end of the epicenter, highlights a possible ritual circuit or processional route involving the Structure 7A temple-pyramid, the small platform supporting Stelae 1 and 2, Stela 8, the *sacbe*, Stela 7, and the northern shrine. This possibility is explored more in chapter 11.

At the northern end of Plaza A rises the 13-m-high platform of the acropolis group, which includes a series of courtyards extending for nearly 200 m to the north. A formal vaulted entrance provided access to the southernmost courtyard in the acropolis from the south. The complex of structures, known as Group J, surrounding this courtyard included a vaulted throne room on the east, a performance platform on the west, and an 8.5-m-tall temple-pyramid with rounded corners on the north (Iannone 2005:30). Iannone (2010:360) believes all the buildings but the throne room were painted red, and the temple-pyramid was adorned with a stucco frieze; the throne room appears to have been painted red, blue-green, and white.

Immediately north of the royal courtyard is Group K, which Iannone (2010:36) refers to as a servants' area. To the north of that the acropolis drops in elevation into Group L, a U-shaped courtyard group, facing the Group J/K platform. Group L's buildings are low platforms with low masonry walls that presumably supported perishable superstructures (Lamoureux St-Hilaire 2001:55). Despite the unimposing nature of the buildings, they contained large masonry benches (Paauw 2007).

Controlling rainfall runoff and managing water at Minanha would have presumably been a concern for population, particularly after the rapid Late Classic expansion of the site that accompanied the establishment of the royal court, but the landscape does not appear to have been engineered for water management purposes to the degree seen at La Milpa, another hilltop city, in northwestern Belize (see chapter 8). Only a small reservoir near the northern end of the acropolis appears on maps of the epicenter, and the main water source for the city appears to have been an artificially modified *aguada* about 1 km to the northeast of the site core (Primrose 2003).

Thirty-nine smaller courtyards and isolated structures surround the epicenter on terraced platforms ringing the hill (Longstaffe 2011:8; Lamoureux St-Hilaire 2011:61). Among these is Group S to the southeast of the epicenter. This Plaza Plan 2–type courtyard (see Becker 2009) measures 50 × 50 m and has a tripartite temple on its eastern edge and nine residential structures on the other sides (Lamoureux St-Hilaire 2011:64).

Below this zone of settlement and farther from the epicenter are smaller residential groups and structures associated with extensive agricultural terracing (Longstaffe 2011:8). Iannone (2009:36) speculates that Minanha's settlement zone extends in a roughly 7-km radius, bound by the edge of the Vaca Plateau to the north, the Macal River to the east, and less firm frontiers to the south and west.

Recent settlement survey and reconnaissance by SARP have identified several secondary centers within the projected Minanha city-state territory. These include the sites of Waybil 1.92 km to the southwest and Martinez 5.8 km to the northeast of Minanha (Iannone 2011:24–25). Minanha is not connected to its secondary centers by *sacbeob*; this stands in stark contrast to the suburban landscape of the larger center of Caracol, discussed later.

Chronology

Minanha was settled by the late Middle Preclassic period, based on ceramics from fill contexts, and Iannone (2009:34) reports gradual growth in population through the Terminal Preclassic period. The earliest documented architecture at the site is from the Terminal Preclassic (Iannone 2005:29), and the modest Preclassic population was confined to the hilltop area that would become the Classic period site epicenter (Iannone et al. 2008:150).

Early and Middle Classic sherds have been found in fill deposits of later buildings in the epicenter, but no structures dating to these periods have been located in the epicenter of the site (Iannone 2005:29). The area around the hilltop, however, experienced moderate settlement growth (Iannone et al. 2008:150). In fact, the earliest version of the eastern shrine in the Group S courtyard dates to the Early Classic period (Lamoureux St-Hilaire 2011:65). The Early Classic buildings at Minanha were constructed in a consistent manner: small, dry-laid stone fill was overlain with a buff, or pinkish-orange, compact aggregate core, which was plastered, forming a thick and durable floor surface. The Early Classic platforms had faces constructed of cut blocks of limestone and supported perishable superstructures (Iannone et al. 2008:150; Longstaffe and Iannone 2011:49).

Although there is some evidence for ritual architecture in the area of the acropolis prior to 675 CE, it is after that date that Minanha's epicenter was transformed into the complex of plazas, courtyards, and monumental structures still visible on the landscape (Iannone et al. 2008:150). Between 675 and 810 CE, Minanha grew rapidly and became the largest and most important Maya city in the north Vaca Plateau (Iannone 2005:29). Concurrent with this growth, the new architecture at the site reflected the material trappings of divine kingship (Iannone 2005:29–30), best exemplified by the royal courtyard in Group J and its throne room. In the countryside, the number of rural household courtyards increased dramatically, and most of the mapped structures surrounding the epicenter date to the Late Classic period (Iannone et al. 2008:151–152). The Late Classic construction shows a decline in quality from the Early Classic, as builders relied on a mixture of cut stone and crudely shaped limestone blocks (Iannone et al. 2008:153).

The newly established royal court at Minanha prospered for several generations until dramatically failing at the beginning of the Terminal Classic period. In the early part of the ninth century, the rooms in the buildings surrounding Group J, the royal courtyard in the acropolis, and the courtyard itself were filled in a methodical, nonviolent manner. Floors were swept clean, and then the entire group was buried by 10–20 cm of fine matrix and then large boulders until only the top of Structure 38J was left uncovered. The new surface that resulted from the infilling of the Late Classic royal compound then served as a rather mundane Terminal Classic residential courtyard (Iannone 2005:34, 2006:156–157).

After this apparent termination event, the population in the epicenter and countryside declined (Iannone 2005:37; Iannone et al. 2008:155). Remnant populations, like the occupants of the courtyard built on top of Group J and those in Groups S and U outside the epicenter, continued to function and even engage in construction projects through the ninth century CE, but by the early tenth century Minanha was abandoned (Iannone et al. 2008:155–156). After this date, a few side-notched arrow points and Postclassic ceramics indicate subsequent visitations to the ruins or a very small Early Postclassic population at the site (see Iannone et al. 2008:157; Longstaffe 2011:209).

Political History

Although Minanha has eight stelae, none contain hieroglyphic texts and only two may have ever been carved (Iannone 2010:361). Therefore, reconstructing Minanha's political history is based on inferences from other lines of evidence. Situated in a buffer zone between Caracol and Naranjo, Minanha's political fortunes were undoubtedly tied to the actions of the kings and queens of those two long-time rival city-states. Despite their both being members of Calakmul's Early Classic alliance and its maneuvering against Tikal (discussed later), Caracol and Naranjo frequently warred against one another and each other's secondary centers (see Martin and Grube 2008).

Prior to the end of the seventh century or the beginning of the eighth century, Minanha was a small site with few civic-ceremonial structures. However, significant architectural construction in the epicenter accompanied the apparent establishment of a royal court at the site around 700 CE (Iannone 2005, 2010). Gyles Iannone (2010:365) uses multiple lines of evidence to conclude that nobles from the city of Caracol founded the royal court, albeit with the support and assistance of local agents. To briefly summarize his argument, the rise of Minanha's short-lived royal dynasty coincides with an apparent period of weakness at Caracol; between 680 and 798 CE, only one carved monument was erected and monumental construction ceased at Caracol, signaling a political crisis (Iannone 2010:365; Martin and Grube 2008:205). The founders of the royal court brought with them a host of Late Classic Caracol-style ritual and political practices, according to Iannone (2010:362) including:

> (1) a preference for caches and burials to be associated with eastern structures; (2) the construction and repeated use of multiple-entry grave chambers in both the epicenter and surrounding site core; (3) the construction of grave chambers long before they were actually used; (4) the use of slate capstones in graves; (5) the carving of slate monuments; (6) the practice of caching crude obsidian eccentrics, speleothems, and flanged effigy censers depicting the jaguar sun god of the underworld; (7) the smashing of flanged effigy censers as part of termination rituals associated with a royal funerary cult; (8) the caching of small ceramic

bowls with human finger bones inside; (9) the predominate use of Belize Red ceramic vessels in ritual contexts, particularly tripod plates with hollow oven feet with rattles; (10) the use of rounded corners on raised temples; (11) the widespread use of agricultural terracing; and, (12) the construction of an ancestor shrine complex comprising . . . an eastern structure fronted by a slate stela and two uncarved, compact limestone stelae and a western structure with two limestone stelae on its summit.

It appears that problems with Tikal kept Naranjo's rulers occupied during the period of Minanha's florescence. Tikal defeated Naranjo in battle in 744 CE, and only one new monument was erected at Naranjo between that defeat and 780 CE (Martin and Grube 2008:81–82). With both of its powerful neighbors weakened or distracted, Minanha's upstart royal court prospered (Iannone 2010:365).

Both Caracol and Naranjo enjoyed short-lived Terminal Classic revivals, which coincide with the sudden demise of Minanha's royal court and the infilling of the Group J courtyard. As a frontier kingdom between the two larger city-states, Minanha may have fallen victim to the Terminal Classic military campaigns Caracol and Naranjo launched against each other's frontier cities (see Iannone 2010:366). Iannone (2005:39–40) points to the care taken to fill the royal courtyard and the fact that it was not reused subsequently as a royal residence as evidence that sympathetic local agents performed the task, but they did so under the direction of an antagonistic party. The apparent intentional breaking of Stelae 3–5 in front of the eastern shrine in Plaza A around the same time may be evidence of outside forces directing the termination of the royal court (Iannone 2005:40).

Discussion

With apparently little antecedent construction in the area of the epicenter, the site plan of Minanha reflects fewer competing planning agendas than those at many cities in this volume. The epicenter has a strong north–south alignment, with the site's large public plaza at the southern end and the elite residential acropolis at the northern end. The city has a ball court, eight stelae, a possible E-Group, an intrasite *sacbe*, several palace-type structures, and five temple-pyramids in its epicenter.

Although Minanha demonstrates a long history of occupation, extensive excavations from a number of contexts demonstrate that the Late Classic period witnessed tremendous growth at the site accompanied by the establishment of a royal court. As a frontier kingdom on the buffer between two larger warring cities, Minanha's royal court was a short-lived experiment.

SARP's long-term research at Minanha is an excellent example of the type of analysis needed to reconstruct the political history of a site with no glyphic evidence for political connections. While speculative, the reconstruction of events put forth by Iannone and colleagues is based on multiple lines of evidence and links Minanha's construction history to the broader sequence of events taking place across the region.

Caracol

Setting

The massive city of Caracol developed in the contrasting and dramatic terrain of the southern Vaca Plateau and the foothills of the Maya Mountains. The site, named after the winding road that led there, is on the western edge of the Maya Mountains with the Macal River 15 km to the east and the Río Chiquibul 11 km to the west in Guatemala. The epicenter of the site is about 5 km from the border with Guatemala, on a high plateau 500 m above sea level (see A. Chase and D. Chase 1987:1). Mahogany logging in the early and middle twentieth century opened up a number of roads penetrating the plateau and making the ruins accessible. When sustained archaeological investigations began there in the 1980s, the site was largely covered in jungle consisting of mixed hardwood forest (A. Chase and D. Chase 1987:6; Healy et al. 1983:400).

Caracol, for a number of reasons highlighted in the following, is a remarkable Maya site and a unique expression of city building in the eastern lowlands. In terms of size, it dwarves the other cities in this book, and its large number of carved monuments and hieroglyphic texts provide more historical information than is available for all the other cities of the eastern lowlands combined. Beyond that, the city's planners used *sacbeob* to integrate the surrounding settlement more tightly than any other Maya site in the southern lowlands.

Investigations

A logger named Rosa Mai reportedly discovered Caracol in 1937. A. H. Anderson, the first commissioner of archaeology, visited in the ruins in 1938, making notes on structures, monuments, and reservoirs in the site core. He conducted limited excavations, discovering an intact doorway, complete with a wooden lintel, in a room in Structure A6 (A. Chase and D. Chase 1987:3).

In 1950 Linton Satterthwaite of the University Museum of the University of Pennsylvania—the same institution that would excavate Tikal beginning a few years later—visited the ruins for a period of two weeks. He returned for two additional seasons in 1951 and 1953 to document the carved monuments at the site, map the site core, and conduct limited structural excavations (Beetz and Satterthwaite 1981:1; A. Chase and D. Chase 1987:4–5). A significant component of the 1951 season was the removal of a number of monuments from the site; several whole monuments were moved to Belize City, but some broken stelae were shipped to Philadelphia (Beetz and Satterthwaite 1981:1). During the 1953 season, the investigations discovered two open tombs, which Anderson excavated (A. Chase and D. Chase 1987:5). After the University Museum's project ended, Anderson returned to the site over the next few years, excavating a rich tomb in the A Group and investigating the South Acropolis (A. Chase and D. Chase 1987:5).

Paul Healy of Trent University directed investigations of Maya agricultural terraces in the Maya Mountains, with visits to Caracol in 1978 and 1980 (Healy et al. 1983:401–2). Healy's team examined a group of hills about 2 km east of Caracol's epicenter, mapping and excavating terraces and house mounds and projecting high population estimates based on their results (Healy et al. 1983:402, 409).

The limited work at the site between its discovery and 1980 led Arlen Chase and Diane Chase of the University of Central Florida to conclude that the combination of epigraphy and archaeology at Caracol warranted intensive study. After two brief visits to the ruins to determine the feasibility of launching a project there, the Chases launched the Caracol Project (which was later renamed the Caracol Archaeological Project [CAP]) in 1985 (A. Chase and D. Chase 1987:6). Their advanced party of workers in 1985 found still-warm campfires in looters' camps around the site, and some of the earliest work by the project targeted recording and cleaning up many of the illegal excavations in the epicenter (A. Chase and D. Chase 1987:6, 8). The project has operated continuously since 1985, making it one of the longest sustained research projects ever in the Maya lowlands.

The Tourism Development Project (TDP), which worked at several sites in Belize from 2000 to 2004, conducted excavations and restoration at Caracol in the early 2000s (Trein 2007:29). That work resulted in the complete consolidation of the front of Caana, the largest structure at the site.

Site Plan and Urban Features

The epicenter of Caracol forms the center of a complex, dendritic system of *sacbeob* that includes both intersite *sacbeob* and less formal *vias* and intrasite *sacbeob* that connect to *sacbe* terminus groups, or termini (A. Chase and D.

Chase 2001a:274, 276). Within the epicenter are a number of large plazas and architectural groups generally arranged in a north–south alignment (Figure 6.2).

The B Plaza forms the northern end of the line of monumental architecture at the site (Figure 6.3). The plaza measures approximately 150 m east–west by 50 m north–south and is surrounded by large buildings. A massive building known as Caana (Figure 6.4) towers over the plaza on its northern side, rising 43.5 m above the floor of the B Plaza (A. Chase and D. Chase 2001b). Although its visible architecture is Late Classic in age, the architectural complex follows the Late Preclassic triadic temple form. Three temple-pyramids (Structures B18–B20) crown its summit, facing a central courtyard and concealing two smaller courtyards (called quadrangles) on the northwestern and northeastern corners of the summit of the complex. The tallest of the three temples is Structure B19, which faces south into the central courtyard and across the B Plaza. An earlier version of the building contained one of the largest tombs ever excavated at Caracol; the tomb's occupant was a woman, buried around 634 CE (A. Chase and D. Chase 1987:27).

The substructure that supports the summit architecture is massive, measuring over 100 m by 120 m at its base (A. Chase and D. Chase 1987:18). It sits on a low platform that extends out to the east, north, and west and supports smaller buildings. Caana's substructural platform rises in six tiers and possesses a wide

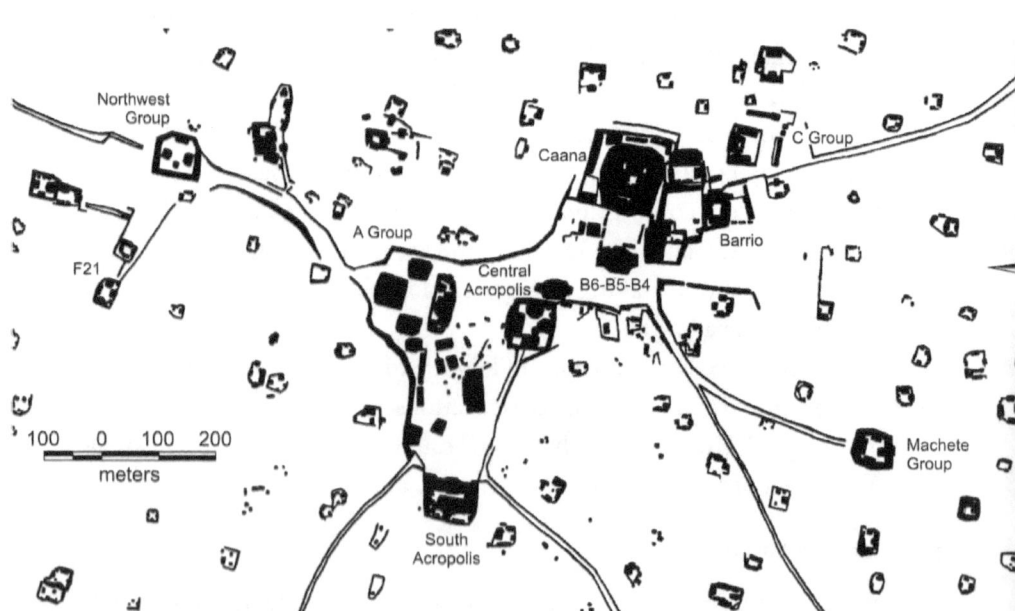

Figure 6.2. Map of Caracol's epicenter, after D. Chase and A. Chase (2004c:Figure 1). Used with permission of the Caracol Archaeological Project.

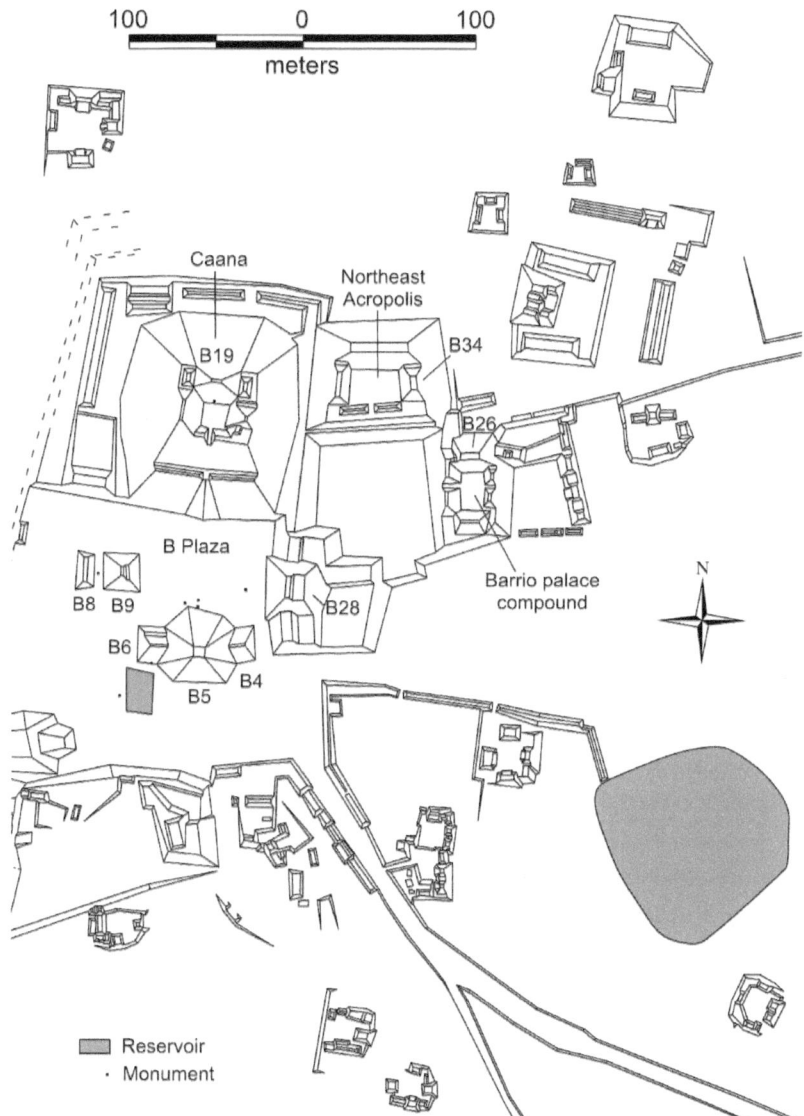

Figure 6.3. Map of B Group at Caracol, after A. Chase and D. Chase (1987:Figure 47).

central stairway on its southern face. Midway up the stairs, a tandem range building containing 24 once-vaulted rooms occupies a southern extension of the lower three tiers of the platform. Another tandem range building crowns the summit of the platform in front of the central courtyard.

When considered as a single unit, Caana is an elaborate palace compound comprising minimally 71 rooms, many with benches, grouped into four "palace units" and integrated with the three summit temples (A. Chase and D. Chase 2001b, 2001c:110). Extensive excavations by CAP established that con-

Figure 6.4. Photograph of Caana at Caracol, courtesy of the Caracol Archaeological Project (photograph by Diane Z. Chase).

struction post-680 CE raised the summit to its final level (A. Chase and D. Chase 2001b), and after this date, if not before, Caana functioned as the residential palace for the kings of Caracol (A. Chase and D. Chase 2001c:116).

Facing Caana from the south across B Plaza is the palace-temple compound of Structures B4–B6. Two palaces, Structures B4 and B6, flank a large temple-pyramid, Structure B5. The substructure for Structure B5 has distinctive rounded corners (Figure 6.5). The group dates to the Early Classic period, but Late Classic period construction significantly modified its appearance (A. Chase and D. Chase 2001c:117).

On the eastern side of the B Plaza is Structure B28, a small pyramid flanked by lower range buildings on its northern and southern sides. Inherently unstable construction matrix hampered excavations at Structure B28 in 2002, but excavations at the base of the building's stairway located fragments of a previously unknown carved stela (A. Chase and D. Chase 2002).

Structures B8 and B9 constitute a north–south oriented ball court occupying the western end of the B Plaza. The court's alleyway is approximately 5 m wide by 20 m long and is oriented on magnetic north. Excavations deter-

Figure 6.5. Photograph of Structures B4–B6 at Caracol, from left to right (photograph by the author).

mined the ball court was built in one construction episode. A centrally placed ball court marker found during those excavations is iconographically almost identical to a marker found near the A Group ball court, discussed below. Subsequent investigations discovered an additional marker at the northern end of the court in 1990 and another at the southern end of the court in 2004 (Helmke et al. 2006:1).

Two additional palace complexes complete the architectural inventory of the B Group. Immediately to the east of Caana is the Northeast Acropolis, a large complex built around a central courtyard with important Late Preclassic through Terminal Classic construction and deposits (A. Chase and D. Chase 2010:6). The group has an eastern temple-pyramid that rises 5 m above the courtyard and once contained a series of ritual deposits, burials, and tombs spanning the occupational history of the group.

Attached to the eastern side of the Northeast Acropolis is a group of buildings known as the Barrio palace compound. It comprises a series of once-vaulted structures facing a common courtyard. Three tandem range buildings bracket the southern, eastern, and western sides of the group, and Structure B26, an apparent temple-pyramid, borders the northern side (A. Chase and

D. Chase 2001b). Excavations revealed the remains of a series of deeply buried palaces under the latest version of this northern building, and determined that the final phase of the building was abandoned during a renovation project in the Terminal Classic period (A. Chase and D. Chase 2001b).

The A Plaza is situated approximately in the middle of the epicenter of the site, over 200 m to the southwest of the B Plaza, and is home to some of the largest structures at Caracol, including Structure A2, a 20-m-tall temple-pyramid (Figure 6.6). Three temples define the formal plaza area: Structure A2 on the west, Structure A1 on the south, and Structure A3 on the north. On the east is a long platform supporting Structures A4–A8, with Structure A6 in center and dominating the other buildings (Figure 6.7). Penetrating excavations determined that the eastern platform was first constructed in 70 CE during the Late Preclassic period as part of an early E-Group, which included the western temple, Structure A3 (A. Chase and D. Chase 2007a:63; D. Chase and A. Chase 2006:4). The earliest monuments at Caracol were cached in the platform close to Structure A5 during the Early Classic period (Martin and Grube 2008:87), and Structure A6 remained an important ceremonial building throughout Caracol's history (A. Chase and D. Chase 2007a:63).

On the eastern side of the Structure A6 platform is a broad open area that appears to share the same modified and built-up platform as the A Plaza. At the eastern edge of this surface is the Central Acropolis, a 5-m-high platform measuring 65 m east–west by 80 m north–south. Two temple-pyramids on the northern and eastern sides rise to 7 m above the plaza, while lower palace-type buildings mark the western, southern, and southeastern limits of the group. Excavations in the group encountered multiple tombs, including a royal tomb at the base of Structure A37, the eastern shrine (A. Chase and D. Chase 2001c:118–119; D. Chase and A. Chase 1996).

To the south of the open area between the Central Acropolis and Plaza A is a group of buildings not clearly organized around a common plaza. Among these buildings is the A Group ball court consisting of two parallel mounds oriented approximately 16° degrees west of north with an 8 m by 21 m alley between them. A large stone ball court marker was found east of the ball court, clearly out of context (A. Chase and D. Chase 1987:31), but excavations in the center of the alley discovered an in situ stone marker designated Altar 21 (A. Chase and D. Chase 1987:33). As discussed below, the 128 glyph blocks carved into the surface of the stone comprise one of the most important sources of political history in the Maya lowlands.

South of the ball court is Structure A13, a long range building with three stelae at its base that are all associated with an early Late Classic king named

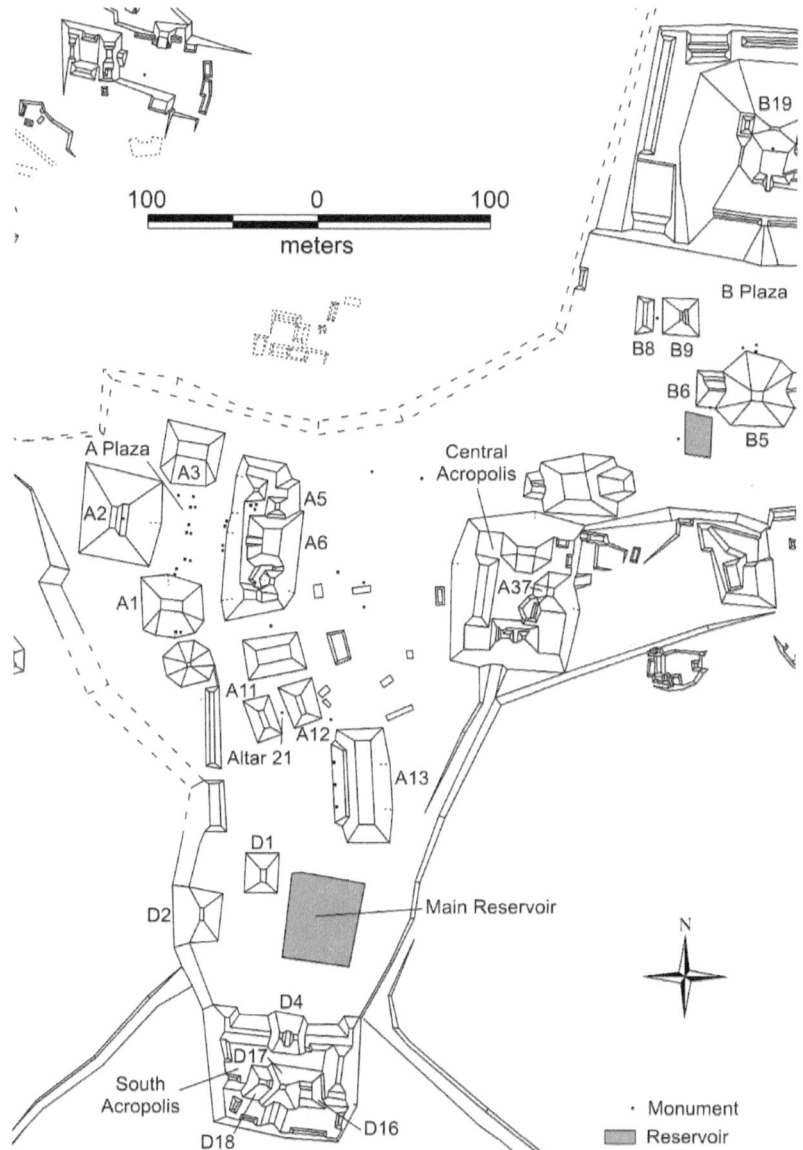

Figure 6.6. Map of A and D Groups at Caracol, after A. Chase and (D. Chase 1987:Figure 46, 47, and 50) and Martin and Grube (2008:84).

Knot Ajaw (Martin and Grube 2008:90). South of that structure is the Main Reservoir, which is fed by water draining off of the A Plaza and the platform in front of Structure A13 (see A. Chase and D. Chase 1987:31).

The South Acropolis anchors the southern end of Caracol's civic-ceremonial precinct. Three courtyards with over a dozen associated buildings all share a common elevated platform; the northern courtyard is the highest

Figure 6.7. Photograph of the eastern structures in Caracol's E-Group (photograph by the author).

of the three and is ringed by the largest structures (A. Chase and D. Chase 2003a). Structure D4, an approximately 80-m-long range building, fronts the South Acropolis and served as the formal entryway into the private northern courtyard behind it. Three heavily damaged buildings, Structures D16 through D18, from east to west, demarcate the southern side of the northern court and are the architectural focus of the entire South Acropolis. A. H. Anderson excavated these three buildings in the 1950s and encountered two tombs (A. Chase and D. Chase 2003a). More recent excavations by CAP determined the South Acropolis has a long construction sequence extending from the Late Preclassic through Late Classic, and the function of the group changed through time as its occupants modified and expanded it. During the Late Preclassic into the Early Classic, the South Acropolis was an elite residential unit, but its function shifted to a public one at the end of the Early Classic period. With the Late Classic construction of Structure D4, the northern courtyard retained a public function, but the southeastern courtyard functioned as residential space (A. Chase and D. Chase 2003a).

Surrounding the epicenter of Caracol is a heavily modified landscape of agricultural terraces, residential structures and courtyards, secondary centers, and causeways (Chase et al. 2011). Arlen Chase and Diane Chase (2001a:273)

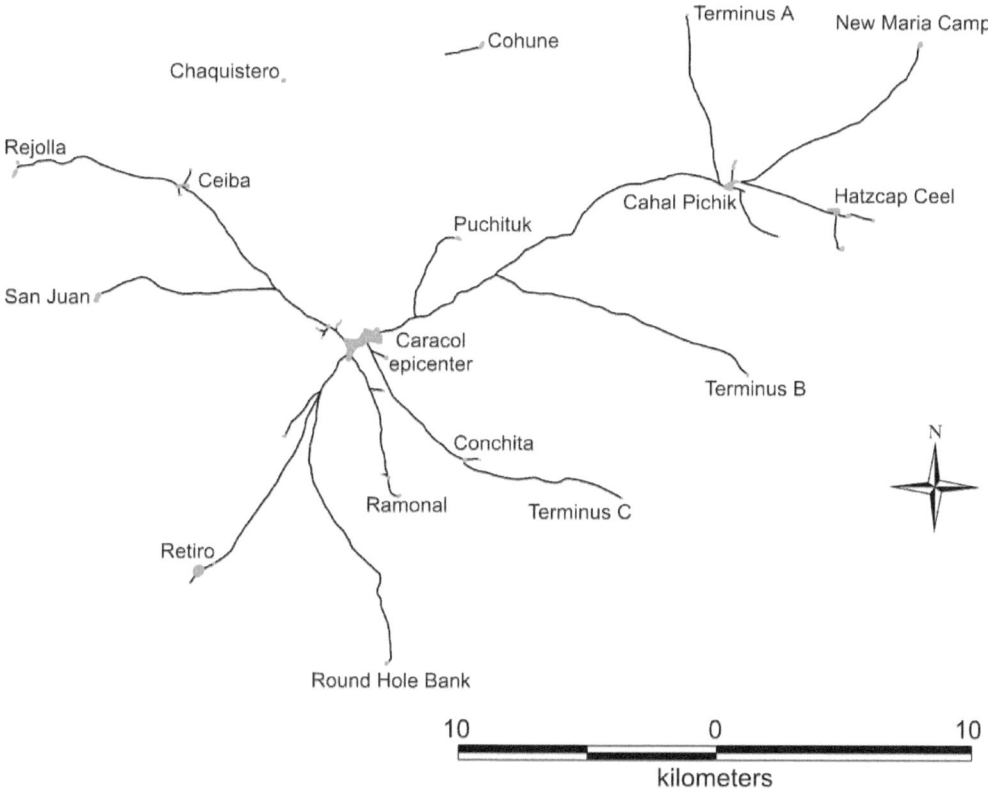

Figure 6.8. Map of the Caracol *sacbeob* network, after Chase et al. (2011:Figure 1).

estimate that Caracol's road system included up to 75 km of intrasite *sacbeob* and 85 km of intersite causeways that united an area covering 177 km² (Figure 6.8). The *sacbeob* vary in width from less than 3 m to as wide as 30 m and in height from ground level to as tall as 3 m, and many have parapets along their edges (A. Chase and D. Chase 2001a:273).

The intrasite causeways link Caracol to its surrounding settlement and terminate in two rings 2.7–3.0 km and 4.5–7.5 km from the epicenter. The Chases have concluded that architectural groups at the ends of the inner ring termini served administrative functions and helped integrate the rural settlement around the site core. These groups are characterized by plazas as large as those in the epicenter and may have served as areas for local exchange. Although the termini groups in the inner ring were not residential, shorter *sacbeob* connect them to elite residential groups (A. Chase and D. Chase 2001a:276).

As Caracol's suburban area sprawled, the city engulfed preexisting and once independent centers. City planners linked them to the epicenter by building long causeways; these groups constitute the outer ring of intrasite termini groups. There are examples in both rings of termini groups where the causeway running from the epicenter passes through a special-function plaza with low structures before connecting with the preexisting center. The Chases view these plazas as serving some "special control function" (A. Chase and D. Chase 2001a:276).

A particularly interesting characteristic of Caracol's road system is that the termini groups are for the most part only connected to the epicenter, rarely to another termini group. Less formal *vias* connect non-elite residential groups to various *sacbeob*, which would have presumably allowed people to move from one terminus to another without traveling as far as the epicenter, but formal communication links only existed between the epicenter and each of its termini groups (A. Chase and D. Chase 2001a:277).

Satellite imagery suggests that intersite causeways linked Caracol to other independent cities. One *sacbe* is projected to run 42 km to Naranjo in Guatemala, and two others appear to extend 24 km to the southeast (A. Chase and D. Chase 2001a:275).

Chronology

The first evidence for occupation around Caracol dates to the Middle Preclassic period and comes from a residential group 4.5 km away from the epicenter. At the Veracruz group, CAP excavated a burial beneath a residential building with Middle Preclassic ceramics. Another group nearby, nicknamed Monterey, yielded evidence for Late Preclassic occupation in the form of seven caches and four burials. Even farther afield, in the early twentieth century J. Eric Thompson excavated Late Preclassic construction marked by Late Preclassic caches at Cahal Pichik, a *sacbe* terminus group 7.9 km from the epicenter (A. Chase and D. Chase 2006:42, 46).

The origins of the civic-ceremonial core of Caracol lie in the Late Preclassic period. Although Caracol could not have been much more than a small village at the time, its leaders constructed the initial version of the E-Group in the A Plaza, and dedicated a renovation of the eastern building around 10 to 60 CE (A. Chase and D. Chase 2006:50–51, 53). Extremely elaborate caches accompanied the various construction phases of the E-Group during the Late Preclassic, including a geode containing liquid mercury, jadeite chips, *Spondylus* shells, malachite pieces, pumpkin seeds, and a jadeite mask (A. Chase and D. Chase 2006:51; D. Chase and A. Chase 1998:314–315).

Although the E-Group likely formed the ritual center of Caracol during the Late Preclassic period, excavations documented coeval construction in other areas of the epicenter as well, including the South Acropolis, the Northeast

Acropolis, and Caana (A. Chase and D. Chase 2006:47, 2010:6). In the Northeast Acropolis, excavations exposed refuse dating to about 100 BCE and two slightly later Late Preclassic buildings (A. Chase and D. Chase 2001b:11). By the end of the Late Preclassic period, it is possible that Caana began to replace the A Plaza as the focus of ritual life at Caracol. Excavations by CAP in 1995 determined that the Terminal Preclassic structure was 38 m tall, only about 5 m shorter than the Late Classic platform's summit (A. Chase and D. Chase 2006:47).

The Early Classic period's archaeological deposits remain somewhat elusive at Caracol, but it is clear that the site continued to grow and prosper after 250 CE. As discussed below, hieroglyphic texts attest to the site's power during the latter part of the period. A rich burial of a woman in the Northeast Acropolis, the architectural complex immediately east of Caana, in front of Structure B34 is one of several interments that mark the transition into the Classic period at Caracol. An elaborate mantle made of over 7,000 shell and jadeite beads and a fringe of dog teeth covered her remains in a cist containing 32 vessels spanning the Late Preclassic period to Early Classic period (A. Chase and D. Chase 2005:21). Excavations have also encountered caches dating to the first part of the Early Classic period from Structure A6 in the A Plaza, and it is clear that most of the A Plaza was constructed by end of the period (A. Chase and D. Chase 2005:25, 30). Outside the epicenter, Early Classic occupation around Caracol was sparse, but several architectural complexes enlarged older Preclassic constructions, creating a regularly spaced array of sizeable groups about 2 km from each other (A. Chase and D. Chase 2005:30).

Excavations in the Northeast Acropolis also encountered a rich offering buried in a pit over 2 m below the modern surface of the courtyard. The floor and walls of the pit were heavily burned, as were most of the artifacts within it. A 2–3 cm thick layer of carbon coated the floor, and a dense assemblage of artifacts that was covered in a thick layer of ash lay on the bed of carbon. The deposit appears to be a cremation, with the remains of at least three people evident. The offering included 20 ceramic vessels, only one of which had survived nearly whole, a broken mano and metate, 6 green obsidian points, 2 obsidian knives, 22 green obsidian blades and blade fragments, 7 gray obsidian blade fragments, slate backings for composite artifacts, and the shell tip of an atlatl, along with numerous other shell artifacts, specimens of worked bone, and stone, jade, and shell beads (A. Chase and D. Chase 2010:8–11). Based on the ceramics, several of which are Teotihuacan style, this deposit dates to approximately 330 CE, about the time Caracol's royal dynasty was founded, as discussed below (A. Chase and D. Chase 2010:10).

By the end of the Early Classic period in the early sixth century, the site was clearly well established. The earliest tomb from Structure B20 in Caana dates to 537 CE, and 40 years later, on the heels of a successful war against Tikal (discussed below), the rulers of Caracol substantially modified the building and constructed additional tomb chambers in it. Excavations in other parts of the site have documented similar intensification in construction around this time period and into the beginning of the Late Classic period (A. Chase and D. Chase 2005:32–33).

Both the archaeological and epigraphic records attest to Caracol's Late Classic florescence. Most of the rapid growth at the site appears to be related to a successful war against the rival city of Naranjo in the early- to mid-seventh century. The dendritic causeway system is a largely Late Classic addition to the city's plan, and it helped to foster a uniform "Caracol identity" (see A. Chase and D. Chase 2001a:280). This identity is expressed in commonalities across the Caracol community in ritual caches, burials, and residential architecture (D. Chase and A. Chase 2004b:142), and was part of a change in management strategy that characterized the Late Classic period. Arlen Chase and Diane Chase (2009:17–18) attribute Caracol's success in the Late Classic to an intentional policy on the part of the ruling elite to promote "symbolic egalitarianism"—the use of symbols to increase cooperation and minimize differences among a group of people.

In terms of epicenter architecture, the major plazas and surrounding structures achieved their basic final forms during the Late Classic period, although Terminal Classic construction and renovations reshaped a few complexes. The Central Acropolis was built in the early Late Classic and used through the end of the Late Classic (A. Chase and D. Chase 2001c:119). Caana was enlarged, and both ball courts at the site were constructed during the Late Classic. Most of the carved stelae, altars, and ball court markers, likewise, date to this period. Despite a break in the textual record between 680 and 800 CE, the archaeological data suggest that Caracol was stable and prosperous throughout the entire Late Classic period (D. Chase and A. Chase 2006).

Outside the epicenter, special-function plazas were constructed at the newly incorporated termini groups, and the suburban settlement density increased as the rural populace constructed thousands of agricultural terraces across the countryside (A. Chase and D. Chase 1998, 2001a, 2003b). This construction transformed Caracol into a "garden city," entirely dependent on terrace agriculture to feed its large population (A. Chase and D. Chase 1998:61).

Caracol's epicenter witnessed continued growth in several areas during the Terminal Classic period, including the Barrio palace group (A. Chase and D.

Chase 2007b:21) and the Northeast Acropolis (A. Chase and D. Chase 2010). The elite at the site, however, apparently rejected the successful Late Classic strategy of symbolic egalitarianism, based on differential ceramic assemblages between elite and non-elite residential groups (A. Chase and D. Chase 2009:21). This may have had a destabilizing effect on the non-elite population and ultimately contributed to the downfall of dynastic rule at the site. Some areas of the site with evidence for Terminal Classic occupation demonstrate stone robbing of some structures, perhaps to maintain others (see A. Chase and D. Chase 2010:15–16).

The abandonment of the epicenter occurred suddenly, slightly before 900 CE. Many buildings in the epicenter have artifacts left on their floors, apparently abandoned in situ, and unfinished building modifications exist in both the A and B Groups (A. Chase and D. Chase 2004a:349). The rural populace, too, abandoned their houses around this time, suggesting a complete breakdown of social and political order at Caracol prior to the tenth century CE. There is some evidence for Early Postclassic visitation to temples at the site, but no one ever reoccupied Caracol (A. Chase and D. Chase 2004a:350).

Political History

Caracol has two dozen known stelae, an equal number of altars, and four carved ball court markers. While not all of the stone monuments contain legible texts, many do, and numerous other texts from tomb walls and capstones as well as artifacts allow for a more detailed reconstruction of Caracol's political history than any other site's in the eastern lowlands. Simon Martin and Nikolai Grube (2008:86–99) present a comprehensive reconstruction of the known rulers of Caracol, which is summarized in Table 6.1.

Caracol's dynasty appears to have been founded in either 331 or 349 CE by a king named Te' K'ab Chaak (Martin and Grube 2008:86). The elaborate Teotihuacan-style cremation from the Northeast Acropolis dates to roughly this same time period, but the connection between Caracol and Teotihuacan is completely unknown. There is some suggestion, however, that Caracol may have played a role in the founding of Copán's ruling dynasty in 426 CE (see A. Chase and D. Chase 2011:15). The name of Copán's founder, K'inich Yax K'uk' Mo,' and a special title that names Uxwitza,' "Three-Hills-Water," identified as Caracol's place name, appear together on Stela 63 at Copán. David Stuart (2007) suggests that this indicates K'inich Yax K'uk' Mo' came from Caracol rather than Tikal, as long suspected. Recent isotopic studies of his bones lead Price and colleagues (2010:31) to conclude that K'inich Yax K'uk' Mo was a Caracol lord who grew up in Tikal's royal court.

Table 6.1. Political history of Caracol

Ruler	Long Count	Gregorian Date	Events and Notes
Te' K'ab Chaak (Founder?)		331–349>	Name mentioned in two Late Classic texts; likely dynastic founder (Martin and Grube 2008:86)
?		ca. 330	Teotihuacan-style cremation in Northeast Acropolis hints at connections with Central Mexico
?		400	Upper portion of Stela 20 gives likely accession date for unknown king (Martin and Grube 2008:86)
K'ahk' Ujol K'inich I (Ruler I)		ca. 470	Place in dynastic chronology uncertain; named on sixth century Stela 16 and on later Stela 6 in a belt device (Martin and Grube 2008:86)
Yajaw Te' K'inich I		484–514>	Stela 13 lists father as K'ahk' Ujol K'inich I? and mother as Lady Penis-head of Xultun. Son is K'an I (Martin and Grube 2008:86)
	9.2.9.0.16	April 11, 484	Accession
	9.4.0.0.0	October 16, 514	Celebrated period ending, Stela 13
K'an I (Ruler II)	9.5.0.0.0	July 3, 534	Celebrated period ending, Stela 16
Yajaw Te' K'inich II (Ruler III)	9.5.19.1.2	April 16, 553	Accession under the auspices of Tikal's king, Wak Chan K'awiil, Stela 21
	9.6.0.0.0	March 20, 554	Celebrated period ending, Stela 14
	9.6.2.1.1	March 30, 556	Defeated by Tikal, end of alliance with Tikal, Altar 21
	9.6.8.4.2	April 29, 562	Calakmul defeated Tikal, commemorated on Caracol Altar 21
	9.8.0.0.0	August 22, 593	Celebrated period ending, Altar 1, Stela 1
Knot Ajaw (Ruler IV)	9.8.5.16.12	June 24, 599	Accession, Stela 5
	9.9.0.0.0	May 10, 613	Celebrated period ending, Stela 6
K'an II (Ruler V)	9.9.4.16.2	March 7, 618	Accession
		619	Unknown event overseen by Calakmul's ruler, Yuknoom Chan
		626	Attacked Ko-Bent-Cauac, defeated Naranjo 40 days later
		629	Battle against Tzam
		658	Death
K'ahk' Ujol K'inich II (Ruler VI)	9.11.5.14.0	June 23, 658	Accession
		680	Defeated by Naranjo

Ruler	Long Count	Gregorian Date	Events and Notes
Ruler VII	9.13.0.0.0	March 16, 692	Celebrated period ending, Stela 21
Tum Yohl K'inich (Ruler VIII)		ca. 793	Involved in a fire-bearing ritual under supervision of ruler of Ixkun
K'inich Joy K'awiil (Ruler IX)		798	Dedicated B Group ball court
		799	Accession, ball court marker
	9.18.10.0.0	August 17, 800	Celebrated period ending, Stela 11
		800	Captured rulers of Ucanal and Bital, Altar 23
K'inich Toobil Yopaat (Ruler X)	9.18.13.10.19?	March 8, 804?	Accession
	9.19.0.0.0	June 26, 810	Celebrated period ending, Stela 18
		820	Alliance with Ucanal, Altars 12 and 13
	10.0.0.0	March 13, 830	Celebrated period ending?
K'an III (Ruler XII)	10.1.0.0.0	November 28, 849	Celebrated period ending with another lord, Stela 17
Ruler XIII	10.1.10.0.0	October 7, 859	Celebrated period ending, Stela 10

Sources: After Martin and Grube 2008; Sharer and Traxler 2006:Table 7.4.

Caracol's most important role in the political history of the southern lowlands swirls around the lifetime of Yajaw Te' K'inich II, a king who took the throne in 553 CE. Many of the following events were recorded on Altar 21 at Caracol, a Late Classic monument dedicated in 633 CE and used as the A Group ball court's marker. Yajaw Te' K'inich II was inaugurated under the sponsorship of Tikal's king, Wak Chan K'awiil, suggesting that Caracol was a client kingdom of its more powerful ally in the central Petén. Three years later Tikal attacked Caracol, implying that relations between the two kingdoms had soured. Six years after that, in 562 CE, Calakmul apparently attacked and defeated Wak Chan K'awiil at Tikal. Because this event is recorded on Altar 21 at Caracol, an early interpretation of the damaged hieroglyphic text was that Caracol was actually the conquering city, but recent studies suggest that Calakmul's king, Sky Witness, was really the victor (Martin 2005:4–5; Martin and Grube 2008:89–90). That the monument bearing this information is found at Caracol suggests Caracol had become an ally or vassal of Calakmul after the 556 CE defeat by Tikal.

K'an II, the second of two sons of Yajaw Te' K'inich II to take the throne at Caracol, apparently directed much of the Late Classic expansion of the kingdom and constructed the network of *sacbeob* during his 40-year reign between 618 and 658 CE (Martin and Grube 2008:91). Caracol remained allied with the more powerful state of Calakmul throughout his reign, and the two cities waged a coordinated military campaign against the site of Naranjo and its secondary centers between 626 and 631 CE.

Caracol's early Late Classic heyday ended in 680 CE when its next king, K'ahk' Ujol K'inich II fled the city following a battle with Naranjo and remained in exile for two months before it was safe to return. After this, the written record at Caracol fell silent until 798 CE, except for Stela 21, the only dated monument (702 CE) from this apparent hiatus (Martin and Grube 2008:95). However, the archaeological record suggests continued construction and stable populations at the city during this time. Gyles Iannone (2010:365) proposes that it was during this interval that nobles from Caracol founded the royal dynasty at Minanha.

Near the end of the Late Classic period, K'inich Joy K'awiil revived Caracol's royal traditions by embarking on a new construction campaign that included the B Group ball court and a number of new carved monuments around 800 CE. His successors continued to erect monuments in the site's epicenter as well as at a few of the secondary centers incorporated into the kingdom up until 859 CE, when a king known only as Ruler XIII dedicated Stela 10 in the A Plaza (Martin and Grube 2008:96–99).

Discussion

Caracol exceeds all the other cities of the eastern lowlands in terms of scale and complexity. With its massive monumental buildings, large paved plazas, expansive network of *sacbeob*, extensive agricultural terraces, and dense settlement, Caracol represents a heavily engineered built environment. Although the city grew incrementally, much of the Late Classic expression of the urban plan represents considerable planning, particularly with the use of *sacbeob* and the construction of water management features both within the epicenter, where two large reservoirs captured runoff from the paved plazas, and in the countryside, where settlement mapping has documented an average of five reservoirs per square kilometer (Chase et al. 2011:388).

The most striking feature of Caracol's urban setting is the monumentality of its structures, particularly Caana. The building is a magnificent display of wealth and power, and it recalls Late Preclassic architectural canons from centuries past. The E-Group assemblage of buildings around the A Plaza is another example of continuity between the Late Preclassic and Late Classic in Caracol's site plan.

The suite of common Maya city elements at Caracol includes temples, ball courts (two), palaces, acropoli, *sacbeob*, reservoirs, and stone monuments. What is remarkable about many of these elements is the accompanying wealth entombed within caches and burials associated with them. As a quick comparison, the large site of La Milpa in northwestern Belize has a comparable number of stone monuments and two ball courts, but the site's few known tombs and caches are impoverished when compared to Caracol's. While this difference clearly highlights disparities in wealth between the two cities, the disposal of tremendous numbers of high-status items in burials and caches, particularly the Early Classic Teotihuacan-style cremation that incinerated a great deal of material wealth, is appropriately interpreted as differences in power between the two cities as well (see A. Chase and D. Chase 2011:13).

Part of the common Caracol identity that emerged in the Late Classic period included a preference for *plazuela* organization following the Plaza Plan 2 arrangement first identified at Tikal by Marshall Becker (2004:128). At Tikal, 14 percent of the mapped courtyard groups follow this type of organization, characterized by a shrine on the eastern side of the courtyard, but at Caracol a staggering 80 percent of known courtyards follow this pattern (D. Chase and A. Chase 2004b:144). The result of this preference is a degree of standardization in household groups not found at any other Maya city.

From an archaeological perspective, Caracol's massive network of causeways is even more impressive than its monumental constructions. *Sacbeob* represent a tremendous labor investment and reflect strong central organization to oversee their planning, construction, and maintenance. They also indicate a completely different level of community integration at Caracol than is seen at any other eastern lowland city. While a number of cities, La Milpa included, have a ring of secondary centers approximately 3 km from their epicenters, only at Caracol are they physically connected by *sacbeob* to the center of the city. At other Maya cities in the eastern lowlands, including Dos Hombres and La Milpa, a radius of about 5 km established the limits of the city-state, but at Caracol a second ring of termini groups about 7 km from the site core reflects the integration of an atypically large area into the direct control of the kingdom.

Discussion and Concluding Remarks

Minanha and Caracol in many ways represent two extremes with respect to Maya urbanism given the disparities in the sizes of their epicenters. Minanha represents the vast majority of small kingdoms in the eastern lowlands, pushed and pulled by larger geopolitical players. Its short-lived royal court oversaw rapid and impressive growth of the site's modest epicenter before succumbing to outside pressures.

Caracol, on the other hand, is the city by which all others in the eastern lowlands are measured. Its rulers established Caracol as a ceremonial center as early as the Late Preclassic when they constructed an E-Group. By the Early Classic, the city may have been a direct participant in Tikal's expanding hegemony and was certainly an important eastern lowland ally. Most of Caracol's growth, however, can be attributed to the period following the defeat of Tikal. During the Late Classic, although part of Calakmul's alliance, Caracol enjoyed a high degree of autonomy as evidenced by its size and extent as well as the high degree of integration of the kingdom. The network of *sacbeob* linking the site core to its surrounding minor centers is an indication of unprecedented planning and political integration.

With the Maya Mountains acting as a natural barrier to the south, the rulers of Caracol and Minanha concerned themselves more frequently with developments to the north. There a number of important centers flourished in the fertile lands of the Belize Valley. Chapter 7 examines two of them: Xunantunich and El Pilar.

7

Belize Valley

A number of factors, including access to modern creature comforts, have made the Belize Valley the most intensively studied area in the country (see Garber 2004:12). During the summers it is impossible to throw a stick without hitting an archaeologist or archaeology student in San Ignacio. Since Gordon Willey and colleagues (1965) conducted their pioneering settlement pattern study at Barton Ramie in the mid-1950s, research in the Belize Valley has focused on a wide range of issues (from evidence for the earliest Maya to Classic period urbanism) and site types (from humble villages to urban centers like Xunantunich). James Garber (editor, 2004) synthesized the first 50 years of post–Barton Ramie archaeology in an edited volume.

The region is home to numerous Maya sites that have been studied to varying degrees (see Figure 5.1). Chapter 4 discussed the important Preclassic developments in the Belize Valley, and this chapter discusses two of the larger Classic period sites: Xunantunich and El Pilar. This discussion could have included any number of important sites, such as Pacbitun, Barton Ramie, and Buenavista del Cayo, but Xunantunich and El Pilar contrast in interesting ways. Archaeologists have been studying the former for nearly a century while the latter was first mapped in the 1980s. Both are large sites, but El Pilar strangely has no carved monuments while Xunantunich has nine stelae. Those stelae and other lines of evidence provide a little bit of political history for Xunantunich, but El Pilar, despite its size, remains a silent witness to the history of the Belize Valley.

Setting

The crystal clear Mopan River is one of the streams that drain the western side of the Maya Mountains. Its course begins in Guatemala as a northward flowing stream, and Río Chiquibul, which begins in Belize and flows west into Guatemala, joins it about 8 km southwest of the border town of Arenal. From the confluence, the Mopan River flows northeast, crossing into Belize to intersect the Macal River, which flows north and drains the Vaca Plateau. Where the Mopan and Macal meet, the Belize River begins, just north of the modern town of San Ignacio. From there it slices through Belize from west-southwest to east-northeast on its way to the Caribbean Sea, roughly dividing the country in half. The associated Belize Valley is divided into two subregions: upper and central. The upper Belize Valley includes the hilly terrain west of the confluence of the Macal and Mopan Rivers, and the central Belize Valley encompasses the area from the confluence east to the nation's capital of Belmopan. The central valley is wider and contains alluvial flatlands bordered by low hills. East of Belmopan the river descends into low-lying, marshy terrain that stretches for 30 km to the coast (Garber 2004:1, 3). King and colleagues (1992:35–37) include the entire valley from the coast to San Ignacio in the Northern Coastal Plain land region, noting that it is bounded by the Bravo Hills land region on the north and the Central Foothills land region on the south.

The Belize River and surrounding terrain had a tremendous effect on Maya settlement. East of the sites of Saturday Creek and Cocos Bank, the Maya found the swamps and savannas of the low coastal plain unsuitable for substantial settlement, but west of that point the remains of settlements are densely distributed along the banks of the Belize River (Garber 2004:3). In the central Belize Valley, seasonal flooding of the Belize River deposits alluvium across the floodplain and up onto the terraces of the river, allowing ancient and modern farmers to continuously crop fields in many areas of the valley.

Xunantunich

Setting

The epicenter of Xunantunich occupies a ridge on the north side the Mopan River in the upper Belize Valley. The river flows past the base of the ridge, 1 km southeast of the site's core, and the Guatemalan border is less than 1 km to the west. The monumental architecture occupies the top of the ridge above the 160–70-m contour lines, and the terrain drops steeply in all directions. With their largest structure, the Castillo, rising nearly 40 m above its plaza, Xunantunich's ruling elite enjoyed a dramatic view across the surrounding countryside. Today a mixture of secondary growth and broadleaf forest covers most of the site, although the monumental center has been cleared for tourism.

Investigations

Xunantunich, originally named Benque Viejo, has long been known to archaeologists. Early explorers, en route to the ruins of Guatemala, visited the site to document its carved monuments (Leventhal et al. 2010:3). Thomas Gann (1925) excavated some of the larger structures at the site in the late 1890s and again in the early 1920s (see also Leventhal et al. 2010:3). J. Eric Thompson (1942) conducted the first systematic excavations at the site in 1938 during his final field season in Belize and established the first ceramic chronology for the Belize Valley based on his data (Leventhal et al. 2010:4). World War II put an end to Thompson's career in the country (Pendergast 1993:6), although he returned to visit the ruins in 1959, noting that they had been "stupidly" renamed Xunantunich (Thompson 1963:271).

Following World War II, A. H. Anderson excavated at the Castillo in 1949 and encountered a stucco frieze first exposed by Gann. Linton Satterthwaite later worked on the frieze in 1950. From that point until the late 1970s, a number of researchers focused excavations on the larger structures in the epicenter and conducted structural consolidation (Leventhal et al. 2010:4–5).

In 1991 Richard Leventhal of UCLA began the Xunantunich Archaeological Project (XAP), focusing on the heart of the site in Group A, and two years later Wendy Ashmore launched the associated Xunantunich Settlement Survey to put the site in a larger regional context (Leventhal 1993:2–3; Leventhal et al. 2010:5, 7). Between 1991 and 1997, those two projects generated a wealth of new information about the site, which is compiled and synthesized in a superb volume entitled *Classic Maya Provincial Politics: Xunantunich and Its Hinterlands* (see LeCount and Yaeger, eds., 2010).

A significant focus of XAP's work involved developing the site for tourism (Leventhal et al. 2010:9), and collaboration between XAP, the Institute of Archaeology, and the Getty Conservation Institute resulted in a site management plan for Xunantunich (Trein 2007:19). The Tourism Development Project (TDP) selected Xunantunich as one of the sites to be enhanced between 2000 and 2004 (Leventhal et al. 2010:13; Trein 2007:29).

Following the TDP's work at the site, two regional projects began new investigations of the ruins. In 2005 Jason Yaeger (2007) began investigating Xunantunich as a component of his Mopan Valley Archaeological Project, and Mary Kathryn Brown's (2009) Mopan Valley Preclassic Project (MVPP) subsequently undertook a study of Group E at the site, specifically targeting the poorly understood Preclassic occupation near the epicenter.

Site Plan and Urban Features

The epicenter of Xunantunich has a distinctive north–south alignment with its major structures and plazas extending approximately 520 m from one end to the other (Figure 7.1). As Angela Keller (2010:187) observes, two east–west oriented causeways that exit from either side of the main plaza turn the site plan into a cruciform. The intersection of the north–south axis of major architecture and east–west line created by the two *sacbeob* falls in Plaza A-I, north of the Castillo. Plaza A-I measures approximately 50 m north–south by 65 m east–west. Plaza A-II to the north is of equal size, and, prior to the construction of Structure A-1 near the end of the Late Classic period, these two plazas formed one large public space measuring approximately 135 m long by 65 m wide.

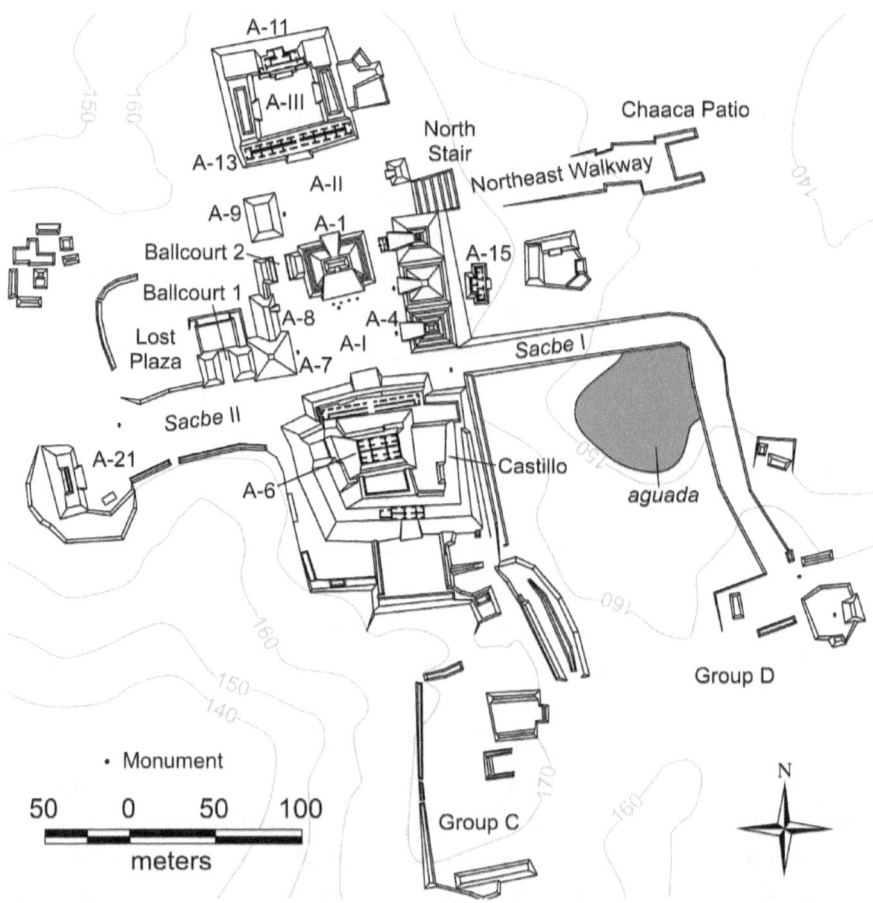

Figure 7.1. Map of Xunantunich, after LeCount and Yaeger (2010:Figure I.1). Contour interval is 10 m.

The Castillo dominates the entire site and is visible for miles around (Figure 7.2). Like Caana at Caracol, the Castillo is a massive architectural complex with a basal platform measuring approximately 100 m on a side. It consists of a central pyramidal structure (Structure A-6) that rises 39 m above Plaza A-I and is surrounded by smaller buildings occupying multiple terrace levels (Leventhal 2010:80–81). The Castillo served as the site's primary ritual building and the royal residence for at least part of its history (Leventhal 2010:81).

Structure A-6 was a large tandem range building with vaulted rooms and a roof comb that accentuated the height of the structure. During the Late Classic period, the penultimate version of the building had elaborate stucco friezes on all four sides of the upper portion of its superstructure. The northern and southern friezes are largely destroyed now, but the eastern and western friezes were protected by the final phase of the building (Fields 2004). The eastern frieze was discovered in the 1950s and has been reconstructed several times since then and is now covered by a fiberglass replica (Figure 7.3); the western frieze was excavated by XAP in 1993 (see Fields 2004; Leventhal et al. 2010) and was also recently consolidated.

Tucked behind the Castillo to the south, Group C spills down the gently sloping ridge top. This group contains two masonry buildings, one possible

Figure 7.2. Photograph of the Castillo from Structure A-1 (photograph by the author).

Figure 7.3. Photograph of the replica of the eastern frieze on Structure A-6 (photograph by the author).

residential patio, two nonresidential patios, and a sweat bath. Structure C-8 marks the southern end of the site core (LeCount and Yaeger 2010a:74).

The eastern side of Plazas A-I and A-II is dominated by three temple-pyramids that form a line with a slight deviation in orientation from the other monumental buildings around the two plazas. This arrangement of structures is reminiscent of an E-Group (Jamison 2010:124); however, Jaime Awe (2013) classifies the structures as "in-line triadic shrines," a possible variation on the triadic temple form.

The Plaza A-III palace, a quadrangle of buildings facing a small enclosed plaza, marks the northern end of Plaza A-II. A central passageway through Structure A-13 provided access to Plaza A-III from Plaza A-II (LeCount and Yaeger 2010a:73). Jason Yaeger (2010:150) identifies Structure A-11 in Plaza A-III as the Late Classic home of Xunantunich's ruling family and Plaza A-III as their royal court (Figure 7.4).

Two additional temple-pyramids, Structures A-7 and A-9, along with Structure A-8 form the western side of the Plazas A-I and A-II. Ballcourt 2, is lo-

Figure 7.4. Photograph of Structure A-11 (photograph by the author).

cated along the plaza's western edge between Structures A-8 and A-9 (LeCount and Yaeger 2010a:74).

Two prominent entrances provided access to the plaza from the east, and another entered from the west. Sacbe I enters between the Castillo and Structure A-4 on the southeastern corner of Plaza A-I. The causeway is a 15-m-wide, roughly 1-m-high platform that runs to the east for 140 m and then turns south for 150 m, ultimately connecting to Group D (Keller 2010). It once had a plaster surface, and its margins have low parapets (Keller 2010:Table 9.1). An uncarved stela marks the western end of the *sacbe*, and two uncarved stelae were found at the eastern end in Group D (Leventhal and Ashmore 2004:171; McCurdy et al. 2013).

Group D includes an elevated platform dominated by an eastern shrine structure (D-6) and an accompanying plain but large stela (LeCount and Yaeger 2010a:75) as well as another plain, small stela (McCurdy et al. 2013). The scattered buildings around the shrine's platform form an important elite residential area at the site where occupants crafted chert drills and carved slate artifacts (Braswell 2010:176).

Sacbe II connects Plaza A-I to Structure A-21, approximately 135 m to the west, and passes to the south of Ballcourt 1. This 40-m-wide causeway follows level terrain and is only elevated 0.5 m. Its surface was once plastered, and a low parapet wall marks its southern edge (Keller 2010:Table 9.1). The elevated area known as the Lost Plaza occupies the space west of the ball court and north of the causeway; it is a broad, gently sloping space devoid of internal features and structures. Based on high-density concentrations of lithic production debris, both obsidian and chert, Keller (2010:201–203) suggests the Lost Plaza may have been a marketplace.

The third formal access way is the North Stair and Northeast Walkway, which enter between Structures A-2 and A-14 near the northeastern corner of Plaza A-II. Unlike the other two *sacbeob*, the Northeast Walkway appears to be an externally focused connection, rather than an internal one, and it lacks parapets. From the base of the North Stair, the 20-m-wide, 0.4-m-tall walkway follows the slope of the hill for 140 m to a small U-shaped courtyard known as the Chaaca Patio. From this point Angela Keller (2010:191, 193) estimates a 1.3-km-long footpath followed the gentle grade down to another monumental stair built just above the river's floodplain.

Based on her study of the *sacbeob* at Xunantunich, Keller (2010:197–199) proposes that Sacbe I and Sacbe II likely served important ritual roles, specifically as routes for processions; she excavated broken musical instruments in a dump near Sacbe II and other ritual artifacts along the two causeways. The Northeast Walkway, on the other hand, served as a formal entrance to the city from the Mopan Valley, directing external traffic into Plaza A-II directly in front of the royal palace complex of Plaza A-III (Keller 2010:203).

Xunantunich faced the same challenge other hilltop cities had to confront with water management. Although no one has undertaken an explicit study of the water management system at the city, published maps identify an *aguada* on the eastern hill slope, southeast of Plaza A-I, nestled in the southern bend of Sacbe I. Shaw (2001:266) and others have commented on the use of *sacbeob* as dams in water management systems. Sacbe I may have operated in this fashion and effectively created a hilltop reservoir adjacent to the monumental core of the city.

Late in the history of the site, the rulers at Xunantunich commissioned Structure A-1, a large pyramid platform that may have supported a perishable superstructure (Figure 7.5). The building effectively divided the former large public plaza in half and radically changed the appearance and likely the function of the monumental core of the site (Jamison 2010:130; LeCount and Yaeger 2010a:76). The construction of Structure A-1 also disrupted the line of triadic shrines on the eastern side of the former plaza, and the construction of a wall between Structure A-1 and Structure A-3 completely removed the

Figure 7.5. Photograph of Structure A-1 (*center*), with Structure A-11 visible in the background (photograph by Vincent Sisneros).

northernmost temple-pyramid from the newly created Plaza A-I (see Jamison 2010:130).

One final note on the urban features of Xunantunich regards the ball courts at the site. Both courts are a rare form of "attached ball court," in which one of the ball court's structures is physically connected to another larger building. In both cases, however, the ball courts appear to be older than the structures to which they are attached. Rather than being an intentional design choice, the attached nature of the ball courts may be the result of later architects not having enough room to construct Structures A-1 and A-7 without impinging on the preexisting ball courts. This architectural style is restricted to a handful of nearby sites, including Chan Chich, Yalbac, Saturday Creek, and La Honradez.

Chronology

There is evidence of early Maya villagers living on the ridgetop during the Early Preclassic period. Excavations under the Castillo recovered Cunil ceramics, the oldest ceramic complex in Belize. The same tunnels beneath the

Castillo encountered two Early or Middle Preclassic platforms. Excavations in Plazas A-I and A-III and beneath Structure A-12 and Ballcourt 2 encountered Middle Preclassic deposits but almost no Late Preclassic material on the ridgetop (LeCount and Yaeger 2010a:70).

Group E, approximately 800 meters east of Group A, was the Middle Preclassic civic-ceremonial center for the general area (LeCount and Yaeger 2010a:70). The group includes two pyramids separated by a large, sloping plaza and a massive 13-m-high platform approximately 100 m northeast of the plaza. Excavations in Group E by the MVPP determined that the pyramids were built in the Middle Preclassic and enlarged in the Late Preclassic. The plaza covers likely Early Preclassic Cunil features and Preceramic materials, potentially pushing the occupation of this area back further in time (Brown et al. 2011).

With only minimal evidence for hilltop construction, the focus of activity appears to have shifted even farther away from Group A during the Early Classic, to the site of Actuncan, approximately 2 km to the north (LeCount and Yaeger 2010a:70). While the tunnel into the Castillo discovered a 2.2-m-high Early Classic platform, excavations in other areas of Group A have not located contemporary buildings (LeCount and Yaeger 2010a:70; Leventhal 2010:82), indicating the hilltop remained sparsely developed prior to the Late Classic.

The Early Classic platform beneath the Castillo, however, became the starting point for the subsequent construction of the complex during the Late Classic period. In its initial form, the Castillo served as the royal residence for the ruling family and doubled as the primary ritual building for the rapidly growing city (Leventhal 2010:84). Within the first 70 years of the Late Classic, during the Samal phase of the site's ceramic chronology, the builders expanded the Castillo's platform to about 100 m east-west by 75 m north–south. While the Castillo grew, the monumental core of the city took shape around a long plaza, bounded by the initial versions of the three temple-pyramids on the east and Ballcourt 2 on the west and likely open on the north (LeCount and Yaeger 2010a:71).

Xunantunich's apogee occurred during the end of the Late Classic period, as the site expanded rapidly over 75 years. It was during what is known as the Hats' Chaak ceramic phase, roughly equivalent to 675 to 775 CE, that most of the visible site plan took shape. In what must have been an impressive and carefully planned and scheduled construction campaign, the rulers of the city oversaw an expansion of the Castillo (Leventhal 2010:90), the construction of the intrasite causeways (Keller 2010:193–194), the creation of the Plaza A-III palace complex (Yaeger 2010:145), the elaboration of the structures around

Plazas A-I and A-II (Jamison 2010:123), and the establishment of Group C (LeCount and Yaeger 2010a:75).

During the beginning of the Hats' Chaak phase, even as Structure A-6-2nd with its stucco friezes was built in the center of the Castillo, the rulers moved from the Castillo to the new palace at the north end of the site (Leventhal 2010:90; Yaeger 2010:147). The move was short lived, however, as the central building in the palace, Structure A-11, was destroyed around 750–775 CE (Yeager 2010:156). Prior to its destruction, Structure A-11 had an upper and lower building, giving it the appearance of a two-story structure. In what Jason Yaeger (2010:156–157) interprets as an act of conquest, the buildings were dismantled and ceramic vessels smashed on their floors. An elaborate frieze on the building and a panel from one of its walls were both dismantled and scattered. Before the lower building was filled with marl, the body of an adult male was placed in a flexed position on the room's floor (Yaeger 2010:156–157).

Around this time Structure A-1 was built, dividing what had been one long plaza into two smaller ones and disrupting the earlier planning agenda (LeCount and Yaeger 2010a:76). The newly defined Plaza A-I between Structure A-1 and the Castillo became the focus of public ritual (Leventhal and Ashmore 2004:173), and the Castillo resumed its central role in the political and ritual life of the city (Leventhal 2010:84), although perhaps under new management (Yaeger 2010:157; see below).

During the end of the Late Classic period, population shrunk at the site, and Group C and most hinterland courtyards were abandoned (LeCount and Yaeger 2010a:75). In the site center, activity contracted farther to the Plaza A-I area, and even the south side of the Castillo fell into disrepair. Three early ninth-century stelae, all with militaristic imagery, were erected in front of Structure A-1, but by 849 CE monumental construction ceased, the rural population declined, and Xunantunich lay abandoned (LeCount and Yaeger 2010a:77). As was the case with many cities discussed in this book, the once-powerful center remained in the collective memory of later Postclassic peoples who placed offerings at the base of the stelae in Plaza A-I (LeCount and Yaeger 2010a:78).

Political History

Xunantunich has three carved stelae, a carved altar, and two hieroglyphic panels, which provide the basis for reconstructing the city's Late Classic political history (Helmke et al. 2010:98). When combined with other lines of evidence, it is possible to infer political relationships from even earlier time periods, and LeCount and Yaeger (2010b) present a well-argued reconstruction of events.

Prior to about 600 CE, Xunantunich was little more than a village with minor influence in the region. After that date, however, the city began to grow into a major center in the upper Belize Valley. Around the transition period from ca. 550 to 650 CE, the first evidence of contact with the city of Naranjo, only 13 km to the west in Guatemala, appears in the form of polychrome drinking vessels made in Naranjo style and with one bearing the Naranjo emblem glyph (LeCount and Yaeger 2010b:340). At the beginning of the Late Classic period, Naranjo became embroiled in conflicts with Caracol and withdrew its influence from the Belize Valley (LeCount and Yaeger 2010b:340).

By the end of the seventh century, however, Naranjo once again began to peddle influence in the region through gift giving, as evidenced by polychrome vases from Naranjo at a number of sites. Such an action would have created regional political tensions with Caracol (LeCount and Yaeger 2010b:342). This period of interest in the affairs of the Belize Valley fell during the reigns of Lady Six Sky and K'ahk' Tiliw Chan Chaak at Naranjo between 682 and 728 CE (Martin and Grube 2008:74).

Although a local dynasty arguably ruled Xunantunich during its initial Late Classic florescence, the construction of the Plaza A-III palace compound signals a takeover by Naranjo. Jason Yaeger (2010:152–154) calls the new authority at Xunantunich a "truncated court," noting that the complex housed fewer people than most Maya royal palaces and lacked a throne room. Carolyn Freiwald's (2011:94) study of strontium isotope values suggests the person buried in Structure A-11 within the palace compound was not from the Belize Valley; rather his strontium isotope values suggest he was raised in the central Petén.

Another line of evidence for political relationships comes in the form of architecture at the site. Wendy Ashmore (2010:57) has noted that the Late Classic site plan of Xunantunich has striking similarities to Group B at Naranjo, an apparent case of intentional emulation (see also Ashmore and Sabloff 2002:206), and other researchers have commented on other Petén-style characteristics present in architecture (LeCount and Yaeger 2010b; Keller 2010; Yaeger 2010), rulership (Yaeger 2010), and ceramics (LeCount 1999). All of these sources of evidence align with the conclusion that Naranjo controlled Xunantunich in the eighth century CE, either as a dependent ally or annexed province (LeCount and Yaeger 2010b:352).

The only glyphic monument from this period is Panel 1, which was later ripped down and broken during the termination of Structure A-11. The three surviving fragments, dated to 670–780 CE based on context and style, represent part of a glyphic rim band. Helmke et al. (2010:101) interpret the few partial glyphs as part of a parentage statement for a ruler at the site.

Naranjo sank into a state of decline following the death of Lady Six Sky in 741 CE (Martin and Grube 2008:77–78), setting the stage for expulsion of the ruling family at Xunantunich and the destruction of the royal palace at Structure A-11. By 780 CE, Xunantunich had new rulers who moved the seat of royal power back to the Castillo (Leventhal 2010:91; Yaeger 2010:157). Xunantunich's renewed independence is claimed on Panel 2, found at the Castillo by the TDP. Contextually and stylistically dated to 780–820 CE, Panel 2's fragmentary text contains the first instance of Xunantunich's emblem glyph and suggests a military alliance between the site's ruler and the lords of two unidentified sites (Helmke et al. 2010:105–107).

Structure A-1 was constructed as part of this renewed independence and was certainly completed by 820 CE, when an unknown ruler dedicated Stela 8 in front of it. This stela is one of three carved stelae (Stelae 1, 8, and 9) along with Altar 1 and an uncarved stela in a row on the north side of Plaza A-I. Stela 8 shows a royal male facing left and dressed as warrior with shield and spear. The heavily eroded text includes the Naranjo emblem glyph, a Calendar Round date, and the likely name of Naranjo's last known king, Waxaklajuun Ubaah K'awiil, commemorating a "stone-binding" event and dance (Helmke et al. 2010:109–110). Taken together, it seems as if the king of Naranjo witnessed the ritual performed by the king of Xunantunich (Helmke et al. 2010:110) on the same day that he performed a ceremony at Ucanal (see Helmke et al. 2010:110; Martin and Grube 2008:83). When this period-ending event took place at Xunantunich, the ruler portrayed on Stela 8 stood on equal royal footing as the visiting king from Naranjo (LeCount and Yaeger 2010b:364–365).

Stela 9 depicts a ruler attired in almost the same garb as the figure on Stela 8 but holding a K'awiil scepter in his right hand rather than a spear. Although it has the longest text of any monument at the site, the glyphs are heavily eroded. Helmke et al. (2010:112–113) suggest that the monument depicts the lord from Stela 8, 10 years later. The nearby Stela 1 is also heavily eroded and dates to the 10.1.0.0.0 k'atun ending in 849 CE (LeCount et al. 2002:55). Its iconography also conveys a militaristic theme.

Paired with Stela 1, Altar 1 completes the known corpus of hieroglyphic monuments at Xunantunich. Gann (1925:89–91) shipped the altar to the British Museum, trimming it to facilitate transport (see Helmke et al. 2010:117). The monument depicts a crouched skeletal figure next to a double column of glyphs, and, like Stela 1, dates to 10.1.0.0.0. It may commemorate a renovation of Structure A-1 (Helmke et al. 2010:119). The year 849 CE marks the end of recorded history at Xunantunich.

Considered as a group, the four carved monuments convey a martial tone and depict Xunantunich's king as a warrior. It is possible that one king erected all four monuments, but this cannot be confirmed because of erosion and damage to portions of the texts. The monuments also emphasize the importance of Plaza A-I during the Terminal Classic period and highlight the contraction of the kingdom prior to its abandonment in the middle of the ninth century.

Discussion

Although Xunantunich's ridgetop occupation extends back as far as the Early Preclassic period, most of the architecture at the city developed over a short span of time and represents two planning agendas, separable thanks to careful excavations and a well-defined chronology for the site. During the Samal phase, the epicenter included an early version of the Castillo at the south end of a long plaza, flanked by in-line triadic shrines and a ball court (Awe 2013; Jamison 2010:124–126; LeCount and Yaeger 2010b:344). During this time, the prominent north–south alignment of the site core was established.

Xunantunich's remarkable Hats' Chaak growth in the second part of the Late Classic period coincides with the apparent takeover of the city by Naranjo. Although previous construction draped the ridgetop, the new rulers found it possible to impose their own urban plan on the site through an ambitious building program. The new constructions, which included the Plaza A-III complex, the *sacbeob* and walkway, and Group C, along with renovations to the Castillo and other structures around the main plaza, enhanced the north–south axis of the city while transforming the overall plan into a cruciform. The new urban plan was a departure from the architectural standards of the Belize Valley (see LeCount and Yaeger 2010b:350) yet retained vernacular traits, particularly in the execution and iconography of the friezes on the Castillo (see Fields 2004:181). Ashmore (2010) and Ashmore and Sabloff (2002) point to political emulation of Group B at Naranjo, or perhaps Calakmul, as the inspiration for the Hats' Chaak urban plan at Xunantunich. Keller (2010:188–89) views the cruciform plan as "an image of the cosmos" and a symbolic statement on the part of the planners. Indeed, Ashmore and Sabloff (2002, 2003) argue that royal precinct planning can employ both cosmological symbolism and political emulation. The parapet-lined causeways and the unusual attached style of ball courts found at Xunantunich may argue for political emulation or ties to sites such as Chan Chich, El Pilar, or La Honradez, instead of or in addition to Naranjo.

El Pilar

Setting

El Pilar is in western Belize about 10 km north of the Belize River, straddling the modern border between Belize and Guatemala. In terms of physiography, the site occupies the rolling limestone uplands (or ridgelands) that flank the northern side of the river valley (Ford 2004:241), but Iannone and Morris (2009:3–4) argue that El Pilar, despite its peripheral setting, should be considered in discussions of the Belize Valley's political organization given its size. Despite its proximity to the Belize River and the strip of developed farming land that runs through the valley, the site is still shrouded in broadleaf forest and is currently protected by the El Pilar Archaeological Reserve for Maya Flora and Fauna, a unique binational preservation effort (Ford et al. 2005). El Pilar is approximately 34 km south of Chan Chich, 20 km northeast of Naranjo, and 16 km north of Xunantunich.

Investigations

First reported to the archaeological commissioner in the early 1970s, El Pilar did not receive much attention until 1983, when government archaeologists showed the site to Anabel Ford (Wernecke 1994:27). As an element of the Belize River Archaeological Settlement Survey (BRASS), Ford's teams mapped the site's epicenter in 1984 (Ford et al. 2001:11). BRASS conducted minimal excavation and salvage work at the site in 1986 (Wernecke 1994:27). The first full season of research devoted to El Pilar occurred in 1993 under the rebranded BRASS/El Pilar Program, and research continued through 2005. Ford has continued to be involved in the archaeological reserve and recently completed a LiDAR survey of the site (Ford and Bihr 2013).

Site Plan and Urban Features

Split by an international border, El Pilar is known primarily from the portion of its epicenter in Belize. According to Whittaker et al. (2009), the site consists of 25 mapped plazas, and Ford (2004:242) estimates the monumental precinct covers 50 hectares. The monumental architecture is split into three distinct groups: Xaman Pilar (north) and Nohol Pilar (south) in Belize and Pilar Poniente (west) in Guatemala (Figure 7.6). All three groups are aligned north–south, and the two groups in Belize form a nearly continuous north–south line, broken only by a 15-m gap between their basal platforms. The tallest buildings at the site are between 17 and 21 m high, and the architectural

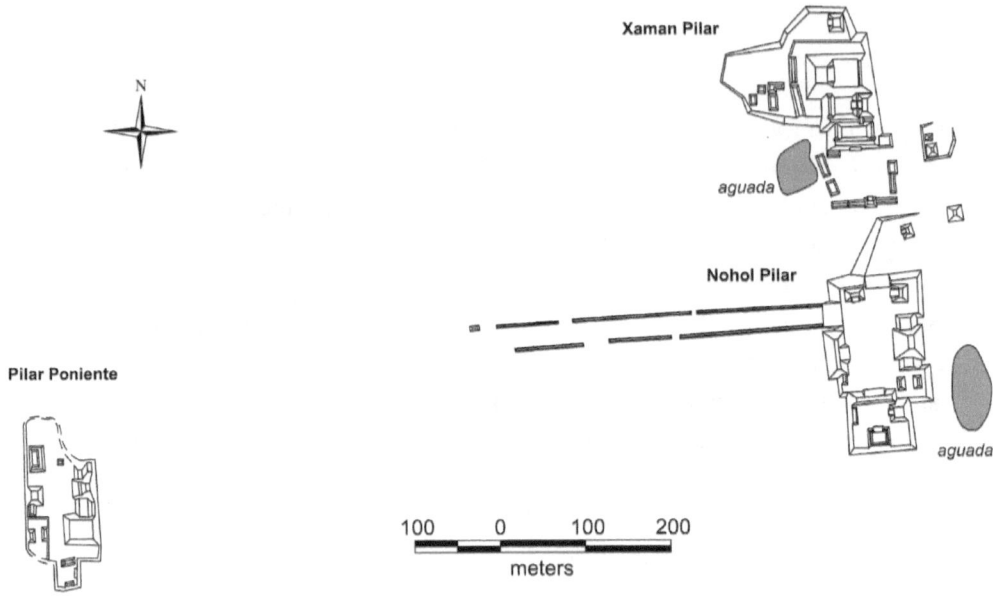

Figure 7.6. Map of El Pilar, after Ford (2004:Figure 15.2).

inventory includes "range-structures characterized by well-preserved standing room vaults, two ballcourts, a major acropolis with a labyrinth of palaces, and a system of causeways accessing the main open plaza, Plaza Copal" (Ford 2004a:250).

Plaza Copal is in Nohol Pilar, the southern group of monumental architecture, which also includes Plaza Axcanan and Plaza Duende (Figure 7.7). Plaza Axcanan, a 35 × 20–m plaza at the southern end of the group, follows a Plaza Plan 2 layout with an eastern temple-pyramid, another temple-pyramid on the south, and range structures around the northern and western edges. The primary entrance to the small, elevated plaza was through a central passageway in Structure EP3, a 50-m-long tandem range building on the northern side of Plaza Axcanan.

Plaza Copal, the main plaza at the site, measures approximately 55 m east–west by 115 m north–south and contains two of the largest structures at El Pilar as well as a ball court. Structure EP7 on the eastern side of the plaza comprises an approximately 60-m-long basal platform supporting a large central temple-pyramid flanked by two small foundation platforms on either side. From the adjacent plaza floor, the temple-pyramid is 17 m tall (Wernecke 1994:35, 37). Directly across the plaza is Structure EP10, a 12-m-tall, 60-m-long platform with one central stairway and a tandem range building on its summit. From plaza floor to the top of the mound, the structure is 17 m tall (Wernecke

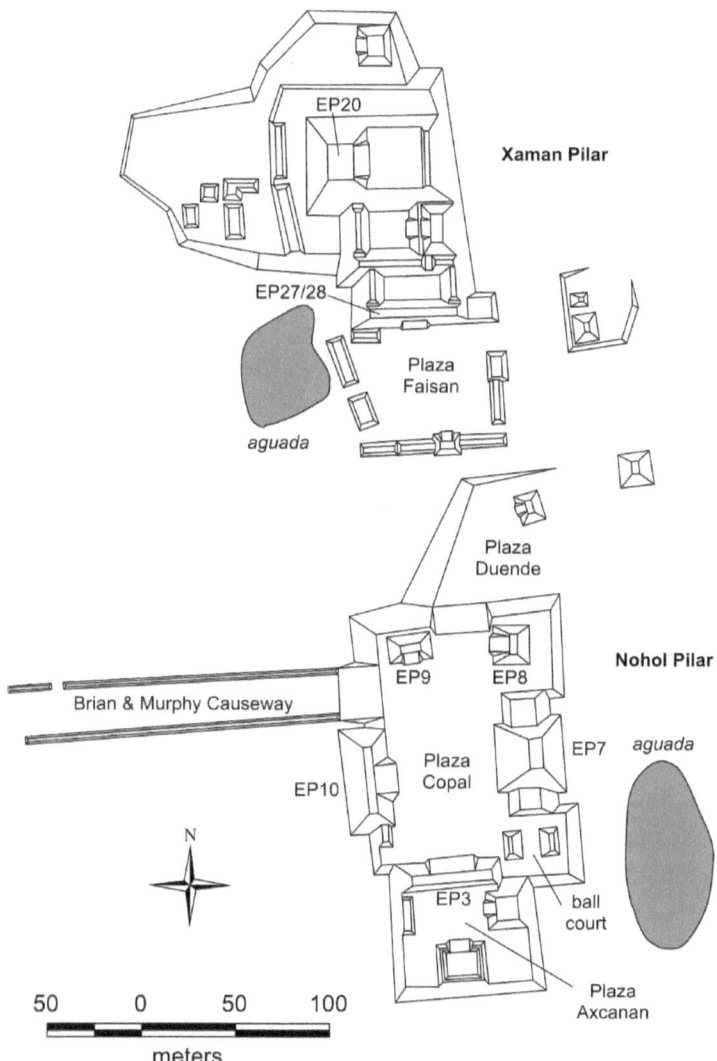

Figure 7.7. Map of the eastern groups at El Pilar, after Ford (2004:Figure 15.2).

1994:35). Together the complex constitutes an E-Group assemblage (Aimers and Rice 2006:Table 1; Wernecke 1994:57). Immediately south of Structure EP7 is a ball court (Structures EP3 and EP5), tucked into the southeastern corner of the plaza.

The northern end of the plaza features two smaller temple-pyramids that face access points into the plaza. Structure EP9 faces south, overlooking the point where a *sacbe* enters the plaza from the west, and Structure EP8 faces west and overlooks a monumental stairway that descends into the Plaza Duende (Wernecke 1994:35). Neither temple appears to have the plaza as its primary focus. Rather, one building faces where traffic would enter the plaza from the west, and the other faces where traffic would climb into the plaza on the monumental stairs leading from Plaza Duende. These two structures, then, appear to be more closely associated with the access ways than to the plaza itself. It is possible they served as viewing stands for processions entering the plaza.

Plaza Duende is an irregularly shaped platform measuring maximally 50 m east–west by 70 m north–south. The only structure in Plaza Duende is a 4-m-tall building with a single room.

The northern group of monumental architecture (Xaman Pilar) occupies a 235-m-long platform and comprises a plaza at its southern end and an acropolis group in its center. The platform extends north and west of the acropolis, where it supports at least seven additional structures.

Plaza Faisan, as it is known, likely served as the entrance to the acropolis. Low platforms flank the plaza to the west, south, and east, and a 15-m-wide gap on the eastern side of the plaza permitted access from Plaza Escoba. Structures EP27 and EP28, which appear to actually be one tandem range building, not two, form the northern edge of Plaza Faisan and the formal entrance into the acropolis group. The acropolis contains six additional courtyards, which are all referred to as plazas on site maps despite their small size and restricted access, flanked by a complicated arrangement of range buildings and temples. The architectural complex culminates at Structure EP20, a 19-m-tall structure supporting a number of rooms on its summit (Wernecke 1994:43).

According to Ford (2004:Figure 15.2), Pilar Poniente, the group of monumental architecture in Guatemala, is slightly over 700 m west-southwest of Plaza Copal. Little published information about this group is available, but from maps it appears to be a platform measuring 200 m north–south by 80 m east–west and supporting at least 13 structures. A ball court is located in the southwestern corner of the group, and four of the other mounds may comprise an E-Group.

A *sacbe* (dubbed the Bryan & Murphy Causeway), which begins at the northwestern corner of Plaza Copal, runs west-southwest for 390 m but does not extend all the way to Pilar Poniente. Johan Normark (2010) reports that the *sacbe* is 30 m wide and has low parapet walls with breaks in the northern wall to allow for water drainage. A map of settlement around the epicenter in the El Pilar Program's 2001 season report shows the *sacbe* terminating at a small hill (see Ford et al. 2001), and Normark (2010) reports a heavily looted mound there, roughly in line with the northern *sacbe* parapet. Although published maps of El Pilar (see Ford 2004:Figure 15.2) show a narrower *sacbe* offset nearly 90 m to the south of the Bryan & Murphy Causeway, this feature is reported to be a single parapet (Ford et al. 2001:18). It does not connect to Pilar Poniente, nor does it extend as far east as the termination of the Bryan & Murphy Causeway.

Wernecke (1994:35) reports a second causeway running east from Plaza Copal to a group of buildings to the west. The 2001 season report map depicts this causeway extending approximately 165 m. Like the feature described earlier, this is also only one parapet, which is more likely to be a wall or dam than a *sacbe* (see Normark 2010).

Chronology

Despite a sustained presence at the site by the BRASS/El Pilar Program, there are few specific published statements about the chronology of the site, so this section is necessarily brief. Ford (2004:242) reports that construction began at the site during the Middle Preclassic period, ca. 700 BCE, and continued unabated through the Terminal Classic period. The most intensively studied structure in terms of chronology is Structure EP7, the eastern temple-pyramid in Plaza Copal. Ford (2004:253) details initial construction and three remodeling episodes in the Middle Preclassic period, followed by a Late Preclassic reorientation of the building to face west. Based on tunneling excavations, at least nine major construction episodes took place at this structure from the Middle Preclassic period to the Terminal Classic period (Ford 2004:253). Structure EP7's Terminal Classic remodeling appears to have been left unfinished (Morris and Ford 2005:85). Ford (2004:251) also notes long occupation sequences for residential groups around the epicenter.

Late Preclassic construction is indicated in looters' trenches in Plaza Axcanan and in the acropolis, and excavations documented small Late Preclassic structures in Plaza Axcanan and Plaza Copal. Several major construction events took place at the very end of the Late Preclassic that established much of the southern plaza areas at the site (Morris and Ford 2005:84).

During the Early Classic period, construction may have shifted to focus on the northern group of architecture based on excavations in the acropolis. Late Classic construction took place across the site, and Morris and Ford (2005:85) observe that Terminal Classic construction ceased, unfinished, in several areas of the site, including Structure EP7.

No specific abandonment date for the site is given, other than the suggested date for construction cessation by 1000 CE. It is not clear exactly how the 1000

CE date was determined; if it is based purely on ceramic types, it seems about a century later than other site chronologies place the end of the Terminal Classic. Excavations encountered Postclassic ceramic debris on Late Classic floors in the northern part of the site (Morris and Ford 2005:85), but it is unclear if the debris represents monument veneration or some other post-abandonment activity.

Political History

There are no reported monuments from El Pilar, nor are any hieroglyphic texts mentioned in site reports or publications. Based on size and construction history alone, it is likely that El Pilar occupied an important political position in the region. The massive acropolis at the north end of the site argues for a long-lived royal dynasty, but we know nothing of it, or of its relationships with neighboring kingdoms. Ford (2004:249–250) argues that its size (which she calculates to be three times that of Xunantunich) and its location indicate that the site was "a major regional center of power" and that it had "clear regional ties with Maya lowlands."

Discussion

El Pilar's three major groups of architecture demonstrate strong north–south alignments, with the two Belizean groups forming a nearly continuous 530-m-strip of monumental architecture, and the site possesses many common urban features for a city of its size. Its largest public plaza boasts an E-Group and ball court—a combination possibly duplicated at Pilar Poniente to the west. The city has a Plaza Plan 2 palace compound anchoring one end of Nohol Pilar and a massive acropolis in the center of Xaman Pilar. The city has at least one intrasite causeway with parapets similar to examples at Caracol, Xunantunich, Chan Chich, and La Honradez. Ford et al. (2001:17) report water storage features dispersed across the landscape, including two large *aguadas* mapped immediately adjacent to the site's epicenter.

Most curiously, however, El Pilar has no known stone monuments and is, in fact, the largest site in the eastern lowlands other than Nohmul without a stela. With an apparent long construction history and significant investment in resources and labor in constructing a massive acropolis and large public plazas, the lack of stone monuments is puzzling given the site's geographic location. Perhaps looters removed stelae from the site, or perhaps none were ever present, which might suggest the royal family at El Pilar owed allegiance to another nearby polity.

Discussion and Concluding Remarks

As chapter 4 described, the Belize Valley contains the earliest evidence of settled villages in the eastern lowlands. By the Late Preclassic period, small settlements dotted the margins of the river's valley, and by the Late Classic period several major cities emerged. The two examples included in this chapter hardly paint a complete picture of the nature of Maya urbanism in the area, but they highlight the importance of long-term research and extensive excavations to reconstruct the chronology of an individual city in enough detail to begin to discuss its role in the political landscape in anything other than generalities. The comprehensive, multiproject investigations at Xunantunich allow for a plausible reconstruction of the political history of the site with only a handful of carved monuments and legible texts.

El Pilar remains an enigma; given its size and its location, the lack of stelae is puzzling. Smaller sites to its south, east, and west have stone monuments, and, as described in chapter 8, so too do La Milpa, Dos Hombres, and Chan Chich, to the north across the Yalbac Hills.

8

Northwestern Belize

Aside from perhaps the Belize Valley, no area of Belize has been as inundated by archaeologists as the northwestern corner of the country since 1992 (Figure 8.1). The Maya Research Program and the Programme for Belize Archaeological Project (PfBAP) have been conducting research in the area for over 20 years. Part of the appeal the area holds is that until about 1990 it was terra incognita and virtually nothing was known about the archaeological sites in northwestern Belize. With only one road providing access to the majority of the area, northwestern Belize is remote, and much of the area is inaccessible and shrouded in dense forest. The Programme for Belize's (PFB) Río Bravo Conservation and Management Area, Gallon Jug Ranch, and the Laguna Seca property account for approximately 390,000 acres of total land, of which about 360,000 acres are forested. Only the land north of PFB is developed; it is primarily agricultural land that has been largely cleared of forest by Mennonite farmers.

Surveying the forested terrain for undiscovered sites is difficult work, but without LiDAR, it is the only way to locate ruins beneath the canopy. Intrasite transects and settlement pattern studies initiated by the PfBAP (see Cortes-Rincon 2011; Hageman 2004; Lohse 2001; Robichaux 1995) and random sampling by the Belize Estates Archaeological Survey Team (BEAST) on the properties to the south of PFB (Houk et al. 2014; Sandrock 2013) are gradually filling in some of the blank areas on the map. BEAST, which began walking seismic survey lines cut through the Laguna Seca and Gallon Jug properties in 2013, is the first major survey effort attempted on the 130,000-acre swath of rain forest (Houk et al. 2014).

This chapter examines three of the larger cities in the area: La Milpa, Dos Hombres, and Chan Chich. La Milpa was discovered in the 1930s, but the other two sites were unknown until ca. 1990. Blue Creek is a fourth well-studied site in the area and the subject of two books (e.g., Guderjan 2007; Lohse 2013).

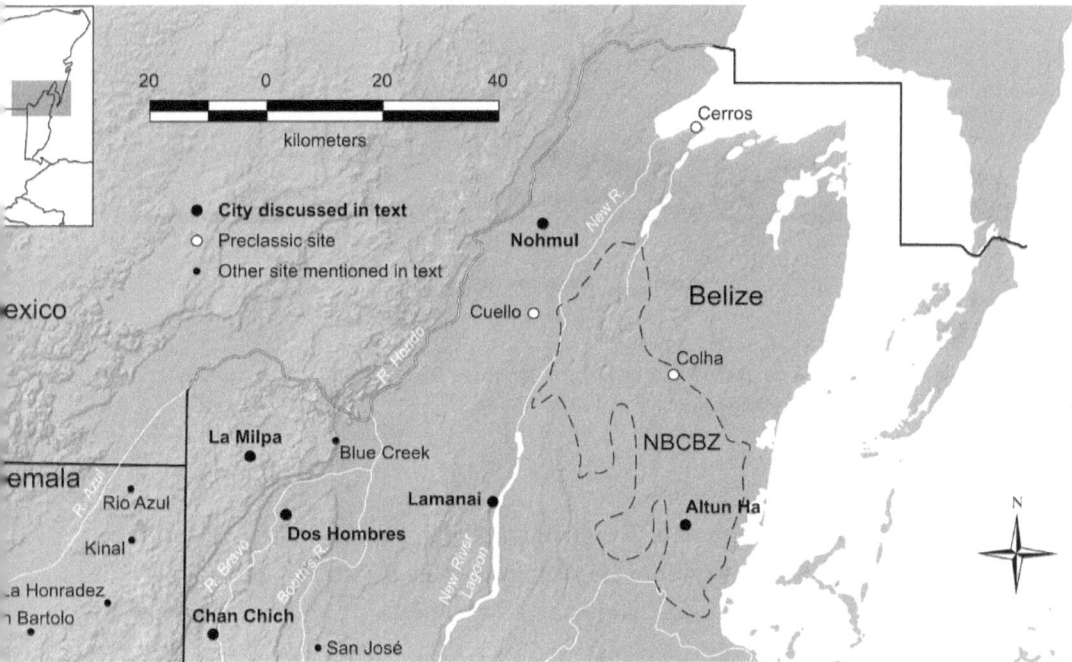

Figure 8.1. Map of northern Belize showing sites discussed in the text as well as the extent of the Northern Belize Chert Bearing Zone (NBCBZ). Base map courtesy NASA/JPL-Caltech, SRTM mission.

Setting

Northwestern Belize is part of the Three Rivers region, originally described by Richard E. W. Adams (1995) as a geographically defined study area and more recently redefined by Nicholas Dunning and colleagues as the Three Rivers adaptive region (Dunning et al. 1998; Garrison and Dunning 2009). The expanded boundaries of the region include the watersheds of the Río Bravo, Booth's River, and Río Azul / Río Hondo; this area covers parts of Mexico, northeastern Guatemala, and northwestern Belize and encompasses more than a dozen large Maya cities including Xultun, San Bartolo, La Honradez, and Río Azul in Guatemala, and Chan Chich, Punta de Cacao, Dos Hombres, Blue Creek, Gran Cacao, and La Milpa in Belize.

Faulting, slumping, and mass weathering, which have resulted in the formation of escarpments, uplands, and *bajos*, shape the karstic environment of the Three Rivers region, which straddles the eastern margin of the Petén Karst Plateau (Brokaw and Mallory 1993; Dunning et al. 1998:93). The eastern half of the region in Belize is dominated by a series of southwest-to-northeast fault lines that have produced three terrace uplands fronted by escarpments (Figure 8.2) of successively increasing east-to-west elevations (Brokaw and Mallory

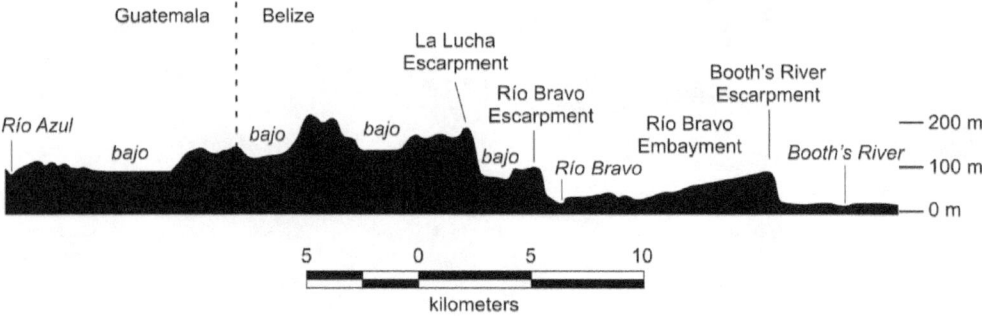

Figure 8.2. Generalized northern cross section of the Three Rivers region, based on Dunning et al. (2003:Figure 2.2). Vertical exaggeration is 20 times.

1993; Dunning et al. 2003). The terrain in the uplands from the edge of the La Lucha Escarpment west into Guatemala is characteristically undulating, with broadly rounded hills and stretches of level ground and *bajos* (Brokaw and Mallory 1993; Dunning et al. 2003).

King and colleagues (1992:35) include this area within the Bravo Hills land region. The Booth's River Escarpment, the easternmost and lowest of three escarpments in the area, is the eastern boundary of the region where it meets the Northern Coastal Plain land region (King et al. 1992:35). The change in elevation from the eastern edge of the region to its high point near the Guatemalan border is approximately 280 m (King et al. 1992:35). The most dramatic expression of this occurs near the site of Blue Creek, where the Río Bravo Escarpment rises abruptly over 100 m above the low-lying terrain to the east.

Three rivers drain the region. The Río Azul is the westernmost river, although most of the year and for most of its length it is a series of small pools that form in slumps along a fault line. During the wet season, however, it becomes an amorphous body of water as the *bajos* of the region flood. Its channel becomes more defined in Quintana Roo, where it follows a bedrock fracture (Dunning et al. 2003:14–15). Its course forms the border between Belize and Mexico, where it is known as Blue Creek and, farther downstream, the Río Hondo. The Río Bravo, which also begins in Guatemala as an intermittent stream, becomes a small perennial river near Chan Chich (Houk 2003). The river's flow is augmented by numerous small springs as it flows northward at the base of the Río Bravo Escarpment. Near the site of Gran Cacao, the Río Bravo meets the Booth's River and flows northward to join the Río Hondo southeast of the Mexican town of La Union.

La Milpa

Setting

La Milpa is the largest site in northwestern Belize. It is located on PFB property in the La Lucha uplands, situated on the highest hill in a 2-km radius. The topography around the site is rugged, particularly to the east (Scarborough et al. 1995:102). The monumental core of the site is built between 170 m to 190 m above sea level, with the Main Plaza occupying the highest position on the landscape.

Investigations

Although J. Eric Thompson first visited the site in 1938 (see Hammond 1990), no additional archaeological investigations were conducted for 50 years until PFB was established. Short mapping projects by Ford and Fedick (1988) and Guderjan (1991a) were followed by Boston University's La Milpa Archaeological Project (LaMAP), under the direction of Norman Hammond and Gair Tourtellot, which studied the site center and the surrounding 6-km-radius permit area between 1992 and 2002 (see Hammond and Tourtellot 2003, 2004; Hammond et al. 1996, 1998, 2000; Tourtellot and Rose 1993; Tourtellot, Everson, and Hammond 2003; Tourtellot, Estrada Belli et al. 2003). Vernon Scarborough and colleagues (1995) conducted a water-management study at the site in 1992 as part of a complementary but separate project. In 2007 the PfBAP took over the work at La Milpa (Houk and Valdez 2009), and since then various subprojects—including the La Milpa Core Project (LMCP), which I directed from 2007 to 2011—have studied different parts of the site (e.g., Heller 2011, 2012; Houk and Zaro 2011; Lewis and Me-Bar 2011; Martinez 2010; Trein 2011, 2012; Zaro and Houk 2012).

Site Plan and Urban Features

The epicenter of La Milpa, which LaMAP archaeologists dubbed La Milpa Centre (e.g., Tourtellot, Estrada Belli, et al. 2003), covers 650 by 400 m of the heavily modified hilltop (Hammond and Tourtellot 2004:290). The monumental architecture has a pronounced north–south arrangement, with the Great Plaza (Plaza A) at the north end and the Southern Acropolis at the south end (Figure 8.3). The Great Plaza is a massive public space covering 18,730 m^2 (Tourtellot and Rose 1993:14), second only to Plaza B at Xultun in terms of area in the Three Rivers adaptive region (Garrison 2007:Table 6.3). Three large temple-pyramids (Structures 1, 2, and 3, from north to south) are found side by side on the eastern side of the plaza, and a fourth (Structure 10) is set in the northwestern corner of the plaza, facing Structure 1. A fifth and smaller temple, Structure 5, is situated near the southwestern corner of Structure 1. Large range buildings border the southern and western margins of the plaza; the western structure fronts a small acropolis attached to the southwestern corner of the plaza. Two ball courts are located in the plaza: a north–south aligned group in the southeastern corner and an east–west aligned group in the northern part of the plaza (see Schultz et al. 1994). Seventeen of La Milpa's 23 known stelae are located in the Great Plaza, almost all on its eastern side in front of the row of temples, along with several unnumbered altars.

A *sacbe*, which exits the southeastern corner of Plaza A in front of Structure 3, runs south and then southeast, terminating in the northwestern corner of Plaza B (Hammond and Tourtellot 2004:292). The southern architecture at the site includes two plazas, linked together by two smaller courtyards, and the Southern Acropolis, a north–south aligned platform supporting a complex arrangement of buildings and courtyards. East and west of the Southern Acropolis are several large courtyard groups.

The largest freestanding structure in the southern part of the site is Structure 21, an 18-m-high, flat-topped mound on the eastern side of Plaza B (Zaro and Houk 2012:148). It is the fifth-largest pyramid at La Milpa (Hammond and Tourtellot 2004:292). Two small courtyards are located behind Structure 21, forming the northeastern edge of Plaza B.

One of La Milpa's key urban features is the local intrasite *sacbe* that integrates Plaza A with the southern plazas and the South Acropolis. The *sacbe* enters the southeastern corner of Plaza A as a steeply sloping ramp, and the southern ball court is situated directly north of this access point. The most unusual aspect of the *sacbe*, however, is its implied architectural association with Structure 3. The southernmost of the three large temples that define the eastern side of the plaza, Structure 3 is the most imposing building at any site in northwestern Belize. The southern half of the building actually extends beyond the limits of the plaza, meaning that the building, rather than facing the plaza or the southern ball court, overlooks the *sacbe* where it joins the plaza (Trein 2011). Trein's (2012) work on the structure has documented the stone armature for a now-destroyed stucco facade midway up the building (Figure 8.4). The structure also includes a curious square platform on its southwestern corner. During processions, the kings of La Milpa would have entered the Great Plaza via the *sacbe*, which was the physical connection with the royal court's palace in the Southern Acropolis, and Structure 3 was likely the stage for associated rituals and presumably served as the royal viewing stand for ball games in the southern court.

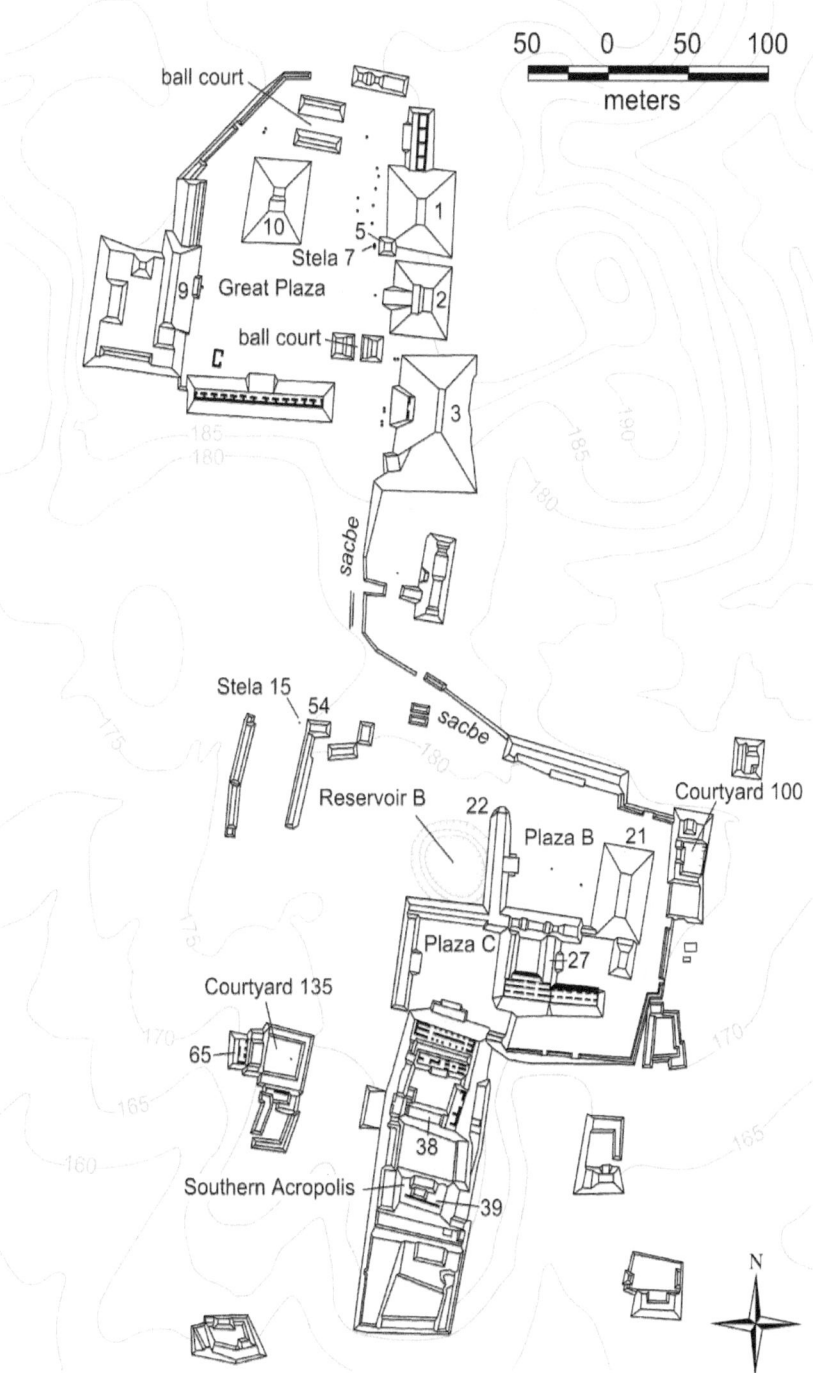

Figure 8.3. Map of La Milpa incorporating LMCP mapping and excavation data, adapted from Hammond and Tourtellot (2004:Figure 13.1) and Tourtellot and Rose (1993:Figure 1). Contour interval is 5 m.

Figure 8.4. Reconstruction drawing of the frieze on Structure 3 at La Milpa. Illustration by, and used with permission of, Debora Trein. Courtesy of the Programme for Belize Archaeological Project and University of Texas at Austin, Belize Program.

La Milpa's regal-ritual center developed incrementally and by the end of the Late Classic was a heavily engineered built environment. Scarborough et al. (1995) determined that the Maya created a microwatershed by directing the drainage of plazas, creating clay-lined reservoirs, and controlling runoff with check dams. Our understanding of exactly how the Maya managed and controlled the runoff from their plazas and courtyards is hampered by the fact that substructural drains are likely infilled and certainly buried by collapse debris, but Hammond et al. (2000:42) discovered a drain in the Southern Acropolis that would have alleviated the flooding of the interior courtyards, and Gregory Zaro and I concluded that a similar feature must be present under Structure 22 to drain Plaza B into its associated reservoir (Houk and Zaro 2012b:185). Our study of Plaza B also determined that the Late Classic builders practiced what we called ritual engineering by manipulating and integrating ritual or sacred features in the built environment as a form of symbolic communication (Houk and Zaro 2011:187).

Settlement surveys by LaMAP within a 6-km radius of the site center documented numerous residential groups surrounding La Milpa's core, including at least six outlying minor centers about 3–3.5 km from, and forming a ring around, the site center (Hammond et al. 2000; Houk and Hageman 2007; Robichaux 1995; Tourtellot et al. 2000). Four of these centers, La Milpa East, La Milpa West, La Milpa North, and La Milpa South, are located on the cardinal directions (Tourtellot et al. 2000). Say Ka and Thompson's Group are southeast and southwest of the site center, respectively, and both are positioned near large *bajos*. Studies by LaMAP (Hammond et al. 1996:86, 2000:40) and Hubert

Robichaux (1995:285) concluded that settlement density drops off significantly about 5 km from the site center.

Chronology

Current evidence points to La Milpa beginning as a village during the Late Preclassic period (Hammond and Tourtellot 2004:292; Sagebiel 2005:715; Zaro and Houk 2012:153). The size of the settlement at this time is difficult to estimate, but Late Preclassic floors and features are known from the Plazas A and B areas, and the first ritual structures were built during this period in early versions of Structure 1 on the eastern side of Plaza A (Sagebiel 2005:715–716) and Structure 27 on the western side of Courtyard D (Zaro and Houk 2012:148).

Data from looters' trenches and LaMAP excavations indicate that the Plaza A experienced modest to substantial growth during the Early Classic period, depending on whom you ask, and the earliest version of Structure 5 was built during this period (Hammond and Tourtellot 2004:292; Hammond et al. 1996:88; Sagebiel 2005:619). LMCP excavations at Structure 27 (Figure 8.5)

Figure 8.5. Photograph of Structure 27 at La Milpa with various construction phases spanning the Late Preclassic through Terminal Classic visible (photograph by the author).

and Courtyard 100 confirm Early Classic renovations and new construction, respectively (Moats et al. 2012:73; Zaro and Houk 2012:149). Based on plaza test pits, Sagebiel (2005:619) proposes that the earliest forms of the southern plazas were constructed during the Early Classic.

Six stelae in Plaza A appear to be Early Classic monuments, as does Stela 15 in front of Structure 54 to the south (Sagebiel 2005:776–778). Hammond and Bobo (1994) believe at least three of the six stelae were moved and reset in their current positions by Postclassic pilgrims to the city, and the Early Classic Stela 20 had been intentionally buried by the Maya, perhaps at the base of Structure 1 where it lay protected until looters removed it and tossed it in their back dirt (Hammond 2001:268).

Guderjan (1991a:12) hypothesizes that a looted chamber in Structure 1, which was capped by alternating layers of debitage and limestone aggregate, dates to the Early Classic period. LaMAP excavated a vaulted tomb in Plaza A near Structure 1 in 1996 (Hammond et al. 1996). This chamber was also capped with alternating layers of chert flakes and limestone slabs (Hammond et al. 1996:89). Ceramics from the tomb, which included a Paradero Fluted Teotihuacan-style tripod cylinder and mismatched lid, date to the end of the Early Classic period, ca. 450 CE (Hammond et al. 1996:90; Sagebiel 2005:728). Based on the associated grave goods and labor invested in the construction of the tomb, Hammond and colleagues (1996:90) concluded the occupant was a king of La Milpa.

Growth at the city accelerated in the Late Classic period, and Hammond and Tourtellot (2004:295) conclude that there are six Late Classic stelae in Plaza A in their original locations. As discussed below, the only stela with a still-legible Long Count date was erected to commemorate the Late Classic renovation of Structure 5 in 780 CE (Grube 1994:222; Sagebiel 2005:756). Four other stelae based on style may date to this same time frame (Sagebiel 2005:756).

Most of the visible architecture across the site dates to the Late Classic period, and several key elements of the site plan appear to have been constructed during this period, including the Southern Acropolis, the *sacbe*, and both ball courts (Hammond and Tourtellot 2004:293; Sagebiel 2005:653; Schultz et al. 1994:46). The structures surrounding Plaza B were all in use by the Late Classic (Zaro and Houk 2012).

The most complex architectural group at La Milpa is the Southern Acropolis. LaMAP investigated the area intensively and determined that the northern half of the group was built ca. 700 CE and underwent three construction phases, and the southern half was built about a century later in one phase (Sagebiel 2005:757). Structure 38 near the center of the group contained a succession of three thrones (Hammond and Tourtellot 2004:293); the last was a polychrome bench with fake, painted legs (Sagebiel 2005:758). Structure 38 was intentionally filled following a termination ritual in the ninth century, and the building's orientation was reversed to face a different courtyard to the south (Hammond and Tourtellot 2004:293). Renovations to Structure 39 on the southern side of the courtyard reversed its orientation to the south onto a new courtyard that was never finished.

The new south-facing Structure 39 contained a 7.4-m-long red bench, which may have been a throne (Hammond and Tourtellot 2004:293–294). Thrones at La Milpa are not confined to the Southern Acropolis, however. LaMAP excavated a polychrome throne, stylistically similar to the third throne in Structure 38, in Structure 65, an elite residential building west of the Southern Acropolis (Hammond and Thomas 1999). Although power sharing is one possibility to explain apparent royal thrones outside of the acropolis, another possibility is that different rulers used different palaces as the seat of their royal court, as Harrison (2003:117) documented at Tikal.

To return briefly to the notion of unfinished construction projects, like the expansion of the acropolis south of Structure 39, LMCP excavations determined the visible architecture on Structure 21 in Plaza B also represents an unfinished renovation to the building. Excavations on the summit of the mound revealed the truncated superstructure, platform summit, and central stairway to a partially demolished and buried building (Zaro and Houk 2012:151). Taken together, these abandoned renovations to the monumental core at the site likely speak to the royal family's declining power at the end of the Late Classic period.

Prior to that decline, as the built environment in the core of the city was remodeled and expanded during the Late Classic period, important architectural groups in the countryside also experienced significant growth. Older Late Preclassic and Early Classic structures were modified or buried under new construction at the minor center of Say Ka (Houk and Hageman 2007) and the outlying La Milpa East, La Milpa West, La Milpa South, and La Milpa North groups (Sagebiel 2005:604–605). All five of these groups are approximately 3.5 km away from the site's center. La Milpa East, La Milpa South, and La Milpa North each have one plain stela dating to the Late Classic period (Hammond et al. 2014).

Although it was previously believed that La Milpa succumbed to the Classic Maya collapse rather suddenly but without evidence of violence (e.g., Hammond and Tourtellot 2004; Hammond et al. 1998; Webster 2002:288–292), LMCP excavations documented apparent tenth-century construction at

Structure 27 and tenth-century occupation in Courtyard 100 (Zaro and Houk 2012:152–153).

It is unclear if the tenth-century occupation in the Plaza B area represents the last gasp for the city or if other parts of the epicenter were occupied as well. All of the buildings that have been excavated have clean rooms with no artifacts left behind that might shed light on the city's final abandonment (Hammond and Tourtellot 2004; Zaro and Houk 2012).

Once abandoned, however, the city was not forgotten. Researchers have found evidence for monument veneration beginning during the end of the Terminal Classic period and extending through the Late Postclassic period at a number of spots in the city. A complex and puzzling accumulation of artifacts along the eastern wall of Courtyard 100 began to form in the Terminal Classic as broken ceramics, lithics, figurine fragments, and even human bones were deposited. This practice continued into the fourteenth century (Houk and Zaro 2012b:10). In the Main Plaza, pilgrims placed offerings spanning the Late Postclassic to Historic periods at the base of stelae (Hammond and Bobo 1994) and left behind *incensarios* and other artifacts on the stairs and landing of Structure 3 (Trein 2011:49).

Political History

La Milpa, although it has 23 stelae, has only one recorded date and one named ruler; both bits of historical information are found on Stela 7 in front of Structure 5 in Plaza A. The stela apparently commemorates the dedication of the final version of the small temple on 9.17.0.0.0 (November 30, 780 CE) under the reign of a ruler identified by Nikolai Grube (1994) as Ukay. A colleague of mine, Hubert Robichaux, reads the text on Stela 7 differently and suggests that the ruler's name is actually "18-?" and not Ukay (Robichaux and Houk 2005). Stela 7 and Stela 12 include the La Milpa emblem glyph, a rare double-emblem glyph (Grube 1994:223). Other stelae at the site have partially preserved portraits of rulers, but we do not know their names or when they reigned.

It is possible to reconstruct a tentative political history for La Milpa based on fragmentary texts from elsewhere and from Kerry Sagebiel's (2005) detailed analysis of ceramics at the site. Tikal may have conquered the Three River region's greatest Early Classic city, Río Azul, in 385 CE, establishing a new dynasty in the process, one allied with Fire Is Born (Adams 1999:139). At La Milpa, two Early Classic stelae may date to this period of time; one, from ca. 406 CE, mentions a ruler named Bird-Jaguar, perhaps Yaxchilan's king who took the throne in 378 CE, and a second appears to mention the 426 CE founder of the Copán dynasty (Sagebiel 2005:731). Based on ceramic data from both elite and non-elite contexts, Sagebiel (2005:732) proposes that elites with strong ties to the Petén were in power. The transition in ceramics to Petén pottery was abrupt, suggesting new rulers may have come in and usurped the local elite, and some outlying settlements were abandoned after about 400 CE as the new rulers consolidated settlement into a 1.5-km zone around the city (Sagebiel 2005:732). The tomb in Plaza A, with its Teotihuacan-style vessel, dates to this general time period. All of this rather circumstantial evidence suggests La Milpa was brought into Tikal's sphere of influence, but exactly how La Milpa was related to the Tikal state and to Río Azul in the post-*entrada* period is still unclear.

Around 530 CE Río Azul was sacked (Adams 1999:144–145), and Tikal slipped into decline following its defeat by Calakmul in 562 CE (Martin and Grube 2008:39). Although there is no evidence for violence at La Milpa at the end of the Early Classic period, monumental construction activity ceased and the rulers apparently did not erect any stelae between about 500 and 670 CE (Hammond et al. 1996:90; Sagebiel 2005:738). This is more circumstantial evidence linking La Milpa to Tikal.

Río Azul never regained its former glory after it declined at the end of the Early Classic, and La Milpa may have emerged as the dominant site in the eastern part of Three Rivers region during the second century of the Late Classic period. Sagebiel (2005:750) suggests that an unnamed Late Classic king erected Stelae 11 and 12 around 672 CE; Stela 12 represents the earliest known use of the La Milpa emblem glyph. At Río Azul, Stela 2 possibly mentions a visit to Río Azul by a ruler from La Milpa sometime between 690 and 721 CE. Robichaux (2000a:41–43) suggests that two damaged glyphs on the monument may be La Milpa's double-emblem glyph.

La Milpa experienced significant growth between 650 and 800 CE. Most structures and plazas visible today were either built or refurbished during this period (Hammond and Tourtellot 2004; Sagebiel 2005; Schultz et al. 1994), and the rulers sponsored a significant renovation of Plaza B in the eighth or ninth century (Houk and Zaro 2011:190). The minor center of Say Ka was expanded (Houk and Hageman 2007), as were La Milpa North, La Milpa East, and La Milpa West (Sagebiel 2005:677). It is possible La Milpa's rulers established a client state at Dos Hombres about this time (Houk 2003; see below).

It is tempting to attribute much of the Late Classic growth to the reign of Ukay, but that is not possible with the kind of data available to us. The fact that the Southern Acropolis and surrounding groups have multiple throne rooms suggests that a number of powerful kings were responsible for La Milpa's Late Classic florescence. This dynasty's power peaked at the end of the Late Classic period before fading into obscurity (Zaro and Houk 2012).

Discussion

All of the standard forms of buildings one would expect to find at a Maya city are present at La Milpa. Plaza A, the largest public space in the eastern lowlands, includes four temple-pyramids, two ball courts, large range buildings, a small acropolis group, and numerous stone monuments. In fact, nearly all of the site's stelae and altars are in Plaza A. The exceptions are three stelae in groups south of Plaza A, three small stelae at outlying secondary centers (one each at La Milpa North, La Milpa South, and La Milpa East), a small altar in Plaza B, and another altar in Courtyard 135 (see Hammond and Tourtellot 2004:295–296; Heller 2012; Houk and Zaro 2011:185).

Like Caracol, La Milpa is surrounded by outlying residential and administrative groups. From an urban planning perspective, a significant difference between the two cities is that at La Milpa the outlying groups are not connected to the site core via *sacbeob* as they are at Caracol. La Milpa, though clearly a large site, does not exhibit the wealth evident at other large centers such as Caracol, or even smaller ones such as Altun Ha (discussed in the next chapter). The meager sample of burials known to date is unimpressive in terms of grave goods.

Regardless, a dynasty of divine kings ruled La Milpa beginning in the Early Classic period until the site was abandoned. They marshaled considerable resources to construct their royal precinct, even if their display of power was not matched by a similar display of wealth.

Dos Hombres

Setting

Dos Hombres is located in the Río Bravo Embayment, a low-lying structural trough between the Río Bravo Escarpment on the west and the Booth's River Escarpment on the east. The Río Bravo's channel and floodplain run along the base of the escarpment; the river's channel is usually no wider than 5 m, but during the rainy season it spills its banks and inundates its floodplain, which varies from 100 m to nearly 1 km wide (Dunning et al. 2003:17). In the vicinity of Dos Hombres, springs that emerge from the base of the escarpment form small streams that drain into the river and create large ponds along the river's channel. East of the Río Bravo floodplain, the embayment rises gradually as it ascends onto the Booth's River Upland. The site of Dos Hombres is approximately 1 km east of the Río Bravo and 13 km southeast of La Milpa. The major architectural groups at the site are built on low limestone hills surrounded by seasonally inundated *bajos*.

Investigations

When the PfBAP started in 1992, the expansive holdings of the PFB included vast areas of unexplored rain forest, a few known ruins (including La Milpa), and only one all-weather road crossing the property from north to south. Much of that first season was spent learning the terrain and relocating sites recorded by Guderjan et al. (1991) during an earlier reconnaissance. Peter Herrera, an employee of PFB, led a small team of archaeologists to visit a large, previously unrecorded ruin that he had come across. During that initial trip, the team designated a small courtyard group on a prominent hill RB-1, for Río Bravo 1, the first site officially recorded by the PfBAP, and a large plaza group nearby RB-2. Two of the team members rather arrogantly named the larger site after themselves, calling it Dos Hombres. Today, RB-1, RB-2, and RB-12 (a third group discovered later) are all known to be part of the large site of Dos Hombres (Houk 1996:107).

Behind only La Milpa, Dos Hombres is the second-most-studied ruin on PFB land. I conducted my dissertation research there in 1993 and 1994—the planned 1995 season was cancelled when we arrived at the base of the Río Bravo Escarpment in May to find that the river had crested its banks already and flooded our trail for the duration of the rainy season (Houk 1996). In those earlier years and subsequent seasons, other graduate students associated with the PfBAP conducted research projects at and around the site. These studies include Mary Kathryn Brown's (1995) thesis on the test pit program and buried Preclassic architecture at the site, Hubert Robichaux's (1995) and Jon Lohse's (2001) settlement surveys around the site core, Steven McDougal's (1997) study of a possible second ball court, Jeffrey Durst's (1998) excavations of a courtyard and Early Classic tomb near the site center, Jon Hageman's (2004) survey transect from Dos Hombres to the La Milpa suburban zone, Grant Aylesworth's (2005) investigations of two courtyards within 2 km of the site core, and Rissa Trachman's (2007) studies of residential groups near the site center. Additionally, Andrew Manning's (1997) neutron activation analysis of ceramics and Pamela Geller's (2004) study of burials from the region relied heavily on data collected by the students listed here.

In addition to graduate student research, professional archaeologists continue to investigate the site and its settlement area. Stan Walling (1995, 2005, 2011) has been investigating settlement along the Río Bravo Escarpment since the early days of the PfBAP. Rissa Trachman's Dos Hombres Archaeological Project recently began investigating the site center and peripheral household groups (Trachman et al. 2011), and Marisol Cortes-Rincon (2011) launched an ambitious 12-km survey transect to connect Dos Hombres to Gran Cacao that includes graduate student research (e.g. Boudreaux 2013).

Site Plan and Urban Features

The site core of Dos Hombres is built around four plazas arranged along a distinctive north–south axis (Figure 8.6). The Main Plaza (Plaza A-1) dominates the north end of this line of monumental architecture, covering approximately 13,000 m^2. An elevated quadrangle group is attached to the plaza's southwest corner, smaller than but reminiscent of the small acropolis in the same position at La Milpa. A heavily looted 12-m-high temple, Structure A-1, is slightly offset from the center of Plaza A-1 to the northwest. A massive platform supporting three small mounds on its summit occupies the eastern edge of the plaza (Houk 1996:131). Two low walls along the western side of the plaza connect otherwise separate buildings and block access to the plaza; the only unrestricted openings into the plaza are in its northeastern corner, southwestern corner, and southern side. The Main Plaza at Dos Hombres is curiously devoid of stone monuments.

A 100-m-long *sacbe* connects to a low platform in the center of plaza's southern edge, leading to a rectangular platform where the site's main ball court is found. The ball court and the buildings in Plaza A-1 are all aligned within 1° or 2° east of magnetic north (Houk 2003:56).

A wide sloping ramp connects the ball court platform to Plaza B-1, a small plaza on a limestone outcrop bordered by a small temple on the east and a range building on the west. This small plaza houses three plain stelae and an altar, the only known stone monuments at the site (Houk 1996:179). Beginning with Plaza B-1 and continuing to the southern end of the site core, the alignment of structures varies between 10° and 13° east of north, notably different from the alignments of the northern buildings. The Plaza B-1 platform drops down a steep ramp to connect to the large rectangular Plaza C-2 to the south. Tandem range buildings border the plaza on the east and west (Houk 1996:194).

The 28-m-high Structure C-1 faces into Plaza C-2 and forms the northern edge of the Acropolis (Houk 1996:194). Unfortunately, the mound is heavily looted, and no project to date has excavated the structure to determine if it faces north, south, or both, as I suspect it does.

The acropolis at Dos Hombres consists of three temples—Structure C-1 on the north and the paired temples, Structures C-2 and C-3, on the south—facing a small plaza surrounded by a complex of vaulted rooms and small

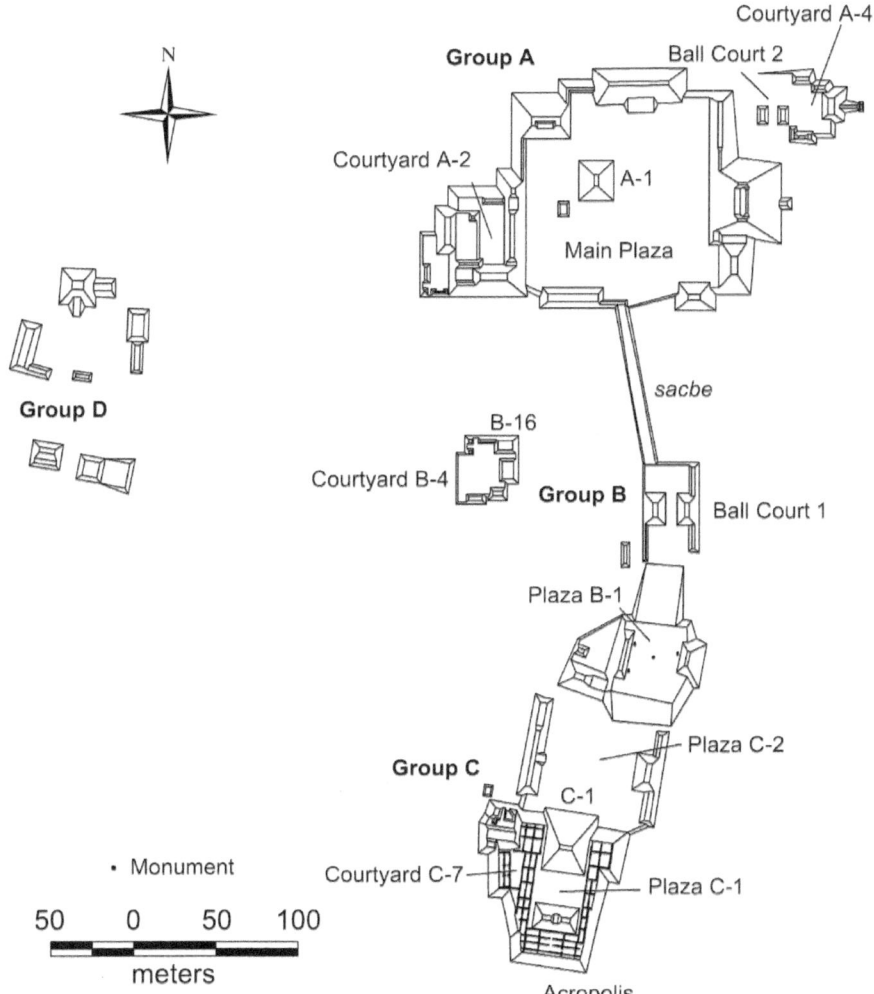

Figure 8.6. Map of Dos Hombres after Houk (1996:Figure 1.4) and Lohse (2001:Figure 3.2).

courtyards. The plaza is built on a natural outcrop, and the acropolis' platform drops steeply in all directions. The entrance to the acropolis is apparently through a series of climbing platforms at the complex's northwest corner (Houk 1996:197–199).

Within 200 m of the site core are three important courtyard groups. The largest is Group D, consisting of two courtyards and nine small structures on a prominent hill west of the Main Plaza (Lohse 2001). This is the group that was originally designated RB-1 during the first visit to Dos Hombres in 1992 (Houk 1996:107) and is notable for being perched on a 25-m-high hilltop overlooking the Main Plaza.

Courtyard A-4 is a smaller group of eight structures 25 m east of Plaza A-1 (Houk 1996:168). While the mounds in this group are all below 2 m in height, the group is interesting because it contains what is likely a small ball court with an 11-m-long, 3-m-wide alleyway flanked by 2-m-high mounds (McDougal 1997).

Courtyard B-4 is a small platform with seven low structures approximately 100 m west of the main ball court at the site (Houk 1996:191). As discussed in the following, this rather ordinary-looking group contained a very rich Early Classic tomb (Durst 1998; Robichaux and Durst 1999).

Chronology

Dos Hombres was first settled during the Middle Preclassic period, and, by the Late Preclassic period, a small village occupied the northern end of the site (Houk 1996:235). Kathryn Brown (1995) excavated a series of Late Preclassic platforms buried in Courtyard A-2, the small group attached to the southwestern corner of the Main Plaza. The oldest platform was a round structure, measuring approximately 6.25 m in diameter and 40 to 50 cm high (Brown 1995:72). The Late Preclassic occupation extended as far as Plaza B-1; foreshadowing a series of caches in the same location, Late Preclassic villagers placed a single Sierra Red bowl in the center of the Plaza B-1 platform.

The Early Classic occupation at the Dos Hombres site core remains poorly defined because little Early Classic material was found in plaza and courtyard test pits (Houk 1996:235). This is likely a result of sampling bias as excavations have not targeted the larger structures at the site, and, as Sullivan and Sagebiel (2003:28) and Sullivan and Valdez (2006) report, Late Preclassic ceramic styles in the area persisted into the Early Classic period, obscuring Early Classic occupations.

Chance discoveries of two Early Classic tombs in residential contexts demonstrate that growth did occur around the site center. Jeffrey Durst (1998) discovered a rich Early Classic tomb beneath Structure B-16 in 1997. In an ostentatious display of wealth, the Early Classic Maya interred a single adult with 11 *Spondylus* shells, 2 greenstone ear spools, 9 ceramic vessels, and hematite mirror fragments, and capped the tomb's chamber with over 23,000 obsidian artifacts, including blades, flakes, and cores (Houk and Valdez 2011:154; Robichaux and Durst 1999). The ceramic vessels (Figures 8.7 and 8.8) suggest the tomb was created ca. 350–500 CE (Houk and Valdez 2011:155).

As part of his Dos Hombres to La Milpa transect survey, Jon Hageman

(2004:353, 374) excavated a small Early Classic tomb at a residential courtyard dubbed the Barba Group, 2.5 km northwest of the site center. This tomb occupied an eastern shrine structure in the courtyard and contained a single adult male, five ceramic vessels, two shell beads, and one jade bead (Hageman 2004:374). Although smaller than the Structure B-16 tomb, the Barba Group tomb contained spectacular ceramics including a Teotihuacan-style tripod cylinder and matching lid, a small cup, and three effigy vessels: an ocellated turkey bowl, a bowl resembling a shell with a human head and arms along the rim, and a small polychrome jaguar bowl, complete with spots (Sullivan and Sagebiel 2003:29–30).

The Late Classic period is better documented in both residential contexts and the site center. The city's builders constructed essentially all of the visible architecture at the site during this period. The Main Plaza and its associated structures took shape during the Late Classic, burying the Late Preclassic village entirely. The construction boom included the main ball court, the buildings around Plaza B-1, Plaza C-2 and its structures, and the acropolis (Houk 1996:235–236). Test pitting in the acropolis' C-7 Courtyard documented a series of four floors, apparently all constructed between 700 and 850 CE (Houk 1996:202–209), suggesting that the presumed seat of royal power was built late in the history of the site and expanded regularly. The most significant expansion involved a ritual in Courtyard C-7 in which participants smashed a number of elite artifacts, including the Dos Hombres hieroglyphic plate, discussed below, on the second oldest floor before burying the courtyard in rubble fill and constructing a new courtyard 1 m higher than the previous one (Houk 1996:202–204).

Following this Late Classic boom, Dos Hombres experienced a dramatic reversal of fortunes in the Terminal Classic period. The site of the previous ritual that alluded to the Late Classic power of Dos Hombres' ruling family, Courtyard C-7, became the symbol for the demise of the royal family as thousands of ceramic vessels and other artifacts were smashed in the courtyard, and the acropolis was abandoned during the Terminal Classic period (Houk 2000a).

No construction occurred at the site after the Terminal Classic period, but Postclassic pilgrims visited the site at least once to deposit an *incensario* at the base of a stela in Plaza B-1, and it is possible that pilgrims reset all four monuments as well (Houk 1996:181, 190). Scattered finds of Postclassic arrow points attest to visits by small hunting parties who may have camped for short periods of time among the ruins (Houk et al. 2008:97).

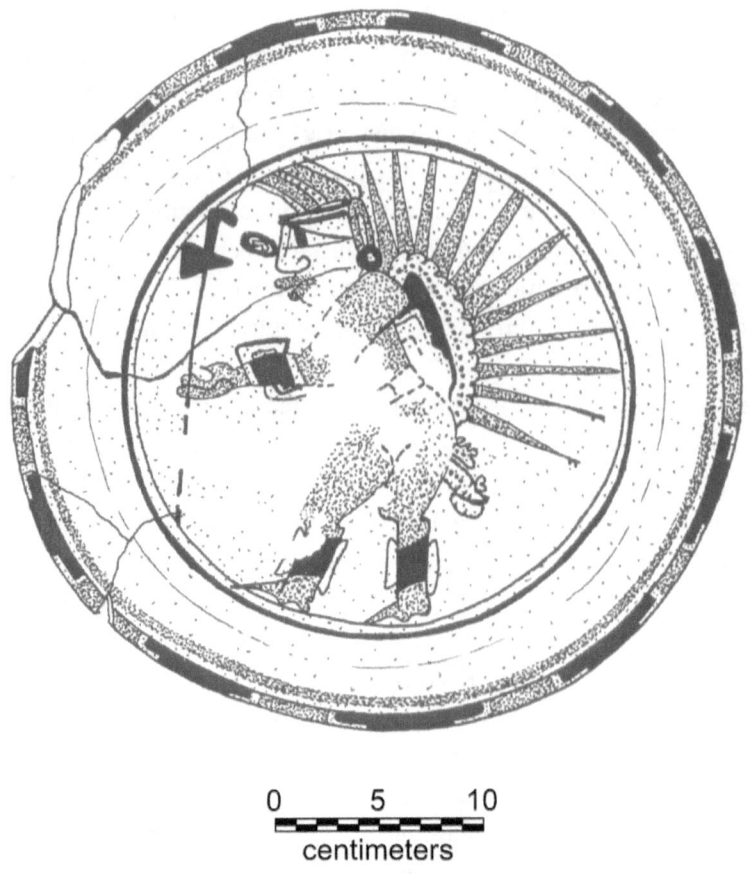

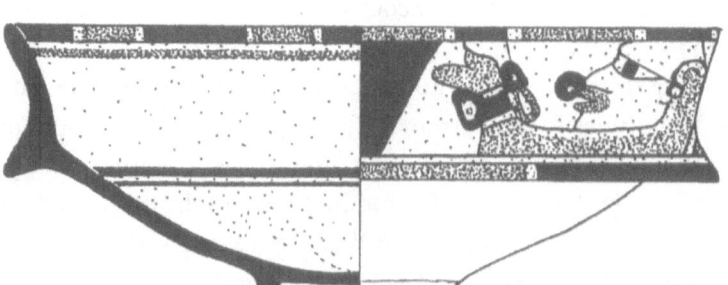

Figure 8.7. Illustrations of Yaloche Cream Polychrome lid with a macaw head from the Dos Hombres Structure B-16 tomb. Illustrations by Ashlyn Hoffman. Cross-section drawing after Sullivan (2002:Figure 7.8); from *Ancient Maya Political Economies*, edited by Marilyn A. Masson and David A. Freidel. Reprinted by permission Rowman & Littlefield Publishing Group. Plan drawing after Sullivan and Sagebiel (2003:Figure 3.3); from *Heterarchy, Political Economy, and the Ancient Maya*, edited by Vernon L. Scarborough, Fred Valdez Jr., and Nicholas Dunning. © 2003 The Arizona Board of Regents. Reprinted by permission of the University of Arizona Press.

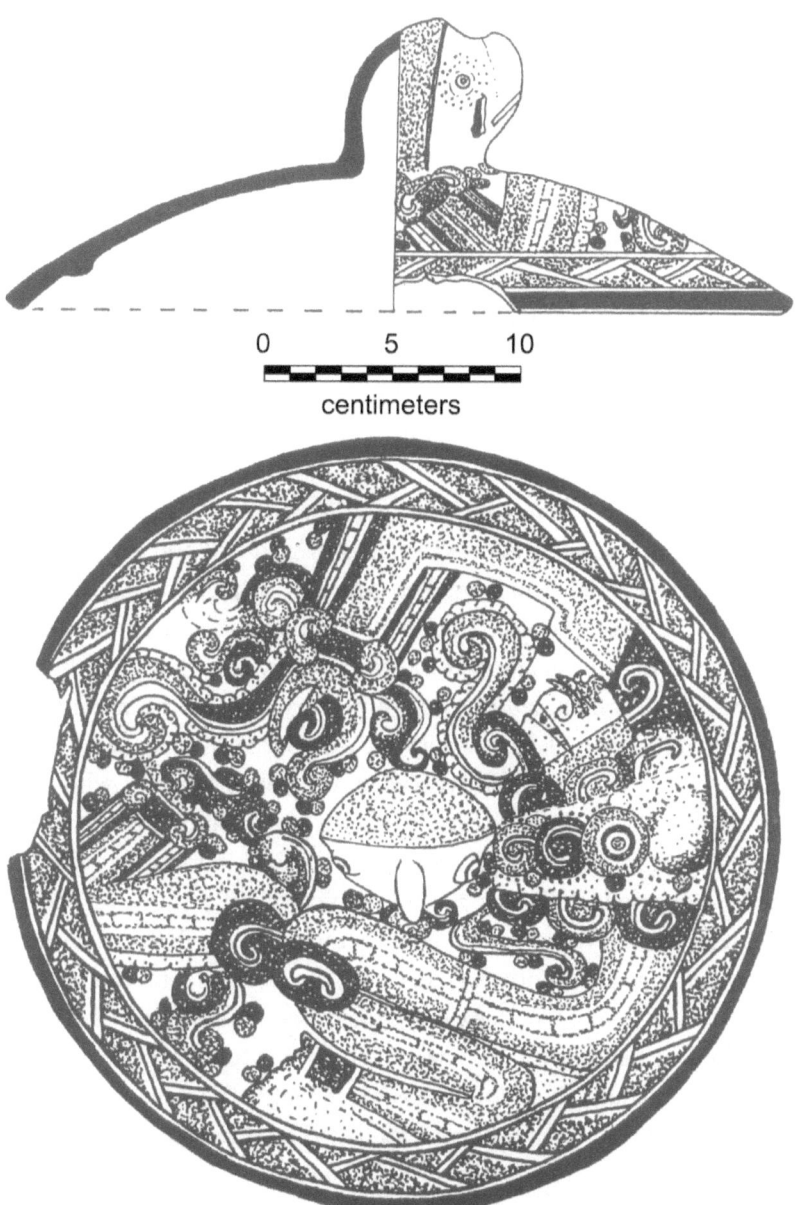

Figure 8.8. Illustrations of Dos Arroyos Orange Polychrome vessel from the Dos Hombres Structure B-16 tomb. Illustrations by Ashlyn Hoffman. Plan drawing after Sullivan (2002:Figure 7.4); from *Ancient Maya Political Economies*, edited by Marilyn A. Masson and David A. Freidel. Reprinted by permission Rowman & Littlefield Publishing Group. Profile drawing after Sullivan and Sagebiel (2003:Figure 3.2); from *Heterarchy, Political Economy, and the Ancient Maya* edited by Vernon L. Scarborough, Fred Valdez Jr., and Nicholas Dunning. © 2003 The Arizona Board of Regents. Reprinted by permission of the University of Arizona Press.

Political History

With no carved monuments, reconstructing the political history of Dos Hombres relies on other sources of data, including ceramics and construction sequences. Based on the grave goods in the two Early Classic tombs, we can infer that the Dos Hombres elite participated in Petén-based exchange networks perhaps mediated by Uaxactun initially and then Tikal after 378 CE. The Teotihuacan tripod in the Barba Group certainly suggests the elite had access to Tikal's trade network, and that is circumstantial evidence to suggest Dos Hombres was within Tikal's Early Classic political sphere.

Dos Hombres has yielded one short hieroglyphic text that provides tantalizing clues about its Late Classic political leanings. Excavations recovered a broken polychrome plate with a short hieroglyphic text from the Late Classic ritual deposit in the acropolis. Hubert Robichaux reads the incomplete text as referring to a *yajaw*—translated as "its/his/her lord" and implying subordinate status to another ruler—named Ah Muwaan, who was given the task of ruling a site named Bolon Tzuk Witz (Robichaux and Houk 2005:7–8). Ah Muwaan's superior is named on the plate as well, although only the first part of his name is included in the fragmentary text, the numeral 18 (Robichaux and Houk 2005:8). Rulers with the number 18 in their names are rare, although Naranjo's king 18 Jog (Waxaklajuun Ubaah K'awiil), who took the throne in 814 CE, is a possible candidate (see Martin and Grube 2008:83). In that scenario, it is possible that Naranjo's Late Classic foray into the eastern lowlands, discussed in Chapter 7 in the context of gifting polychrome vessels to elite in the Belize Valley, extended into northwestern Belize. Another possibility, one that is also controversial, is that the vessel's text refers to the ruler named on La Milpa's Stela 7. As mentioned previously, Robichaux suggests the only known Late Classic ruler from La Milpa is actually named "18-?" and not Ukay (Robichaux and Houk 2005:9). If that is the case, then the vessel not only provides a likely toponym for Dos Hombres but also gives us the name of a Late Classic king who must have ruled ca. 780 CE. As Jon Lohse and I have argued, this possibility is an appealing one, but it awaits verification; ceramics are portable artifacts, and the persons and places named in the text could be from just about anywhere in the southern lowlands (Houk and Lohse 2013).

Discussion

The site plan of Dos Hombres as we see it today took form in the Late Classic period and buried earlier Preclassic and likely Early Classic antecedent construction. Although Dos Hombres is smaller and is situated in a very different physiographic setting than is La Milpa, the two cities share important urban features. They both have a pronounced north–south alignment of the monumental architecture, a massive public plaza at the northern end of the site core, an elevated acropolis at the southern end, and a *sacbe* linking the architecture together (Houk 2003).

The site has three stelae and one altar. Although the number of monuments is small, only La Milpa has more stelae in northwestern Belize. Dos Hombres' massive Structure C-1 is also taller than any other buildings in northwestern Belize.

In the case of Dos Hombres, the approximately 10° variation in architectural orientation between the Main Plaza and the southern plazas is probably due to the differential construction histories of the two areas of the site. In the Main Plaza, the Late Classic architects likely copied an older Late Preclassic (or even Early Classic) pattern of aligning buildings. In the southern plazas, where there was no antecedent construction to restrict building orientation, the architects followed some other convention for orienting the architecture.

An important characteristic of Dos Hombres' site plan is its multiple ball courts. The main ball court is an important architectural link between the northern and southern ends of the site, and its placement echoes a key feature of Wendy Ashmore's (1991) Petén site-planning template. The second ball court at the site center is odd for its small size and its placement off of the platform supporting the monumental architecture at the site. There is an even more unusual ball court, which I have not previously mentioned, in the periphery of Dos Hombres. Stan Walling (2011) came across an incredibly unusual rural ball court built amidst the scattered settlement along the Río Bravo Escarpment's margins approximately 2.5 km east-southeast of the site core. This settlement area, named Chawak But'o'ob, has no other civic architecture and otherwise comprises modest house mounds (Scarborough and Valdez 2009:216).

Chan Chich

Setting

Chan Chich is located approximately 4.25 km east of the Guatemalan border in the Río Bravo Terrace Lowland on the western bank of Chan Chich Creek. Just north of the site, Chan Chich Creek and Little Chan Chich Creek join to form the Río Bravo, which flows northward through the Río Bravo Terrace Lowland before following the base of the Río Bravo Escarpment as it continues to drain northward. The terrain in the terrace lowland is marked by irregular *bajos* and hemispherical hills, particularly evident in the cleared pastures of nearby Gallon Jug Ranch.

The Main Plaza at Chan Chich is built on a broad hill at an elevation of 119 m above sea level (Houk 2012b:3). The imposing La Lucha Escarpment is visible approximately 3.75 km to the west, just inside the border with Guatemala. The small site of Kaxil Uinic is 2.6 km to the west of Chan Chich, with a large *bajo* lying between the two centers. The Yalbac Hills 18 km to the south create the divide between the Río Hondo and Belize River watersheds and mark the southern limit of the Three Rivers adaptive region, according to Garrison and Dunning (2009). As a result, Chan Chich is the southernmost city in the Belizean portion of the region.

Investigations

Chan Chich was first recorded in 1987, but the site had been looted in the 1970s or early 1980s (Guderjan 1991b:35). The initial investigations by the Río Bravo Archaeological Project were limited to mapping the core area of the site and profiling looters' trenches (Guderjan 1991b). In the late 1980s, the landowner constructed Chan Chich Lodge in and around the Main Plaza at the site. In preparation for construction, the builders hand-cleared the vegetation and filled the looters' trenches in the Main Plaza.

The Chan Chich Archaeological Project (CCAP) mapped 1.54 km^2 around the site in 1996 and conducted excavations in 1997–1999, 2001, and 2012–2014 (Herndon et al. 2014; Houk 1998a, 2000b, 2013a; Houk et al. 2010; Houk, Harris et al. 2013; Houk et al. 2014). For the most part, the early CCAP excavations were small-scale testing studies of various areas of the site. The discovery of a Terminal Preclassic tomb in the Upper Plaza, however, resulted in a large-scale excavation in that part of the site between 1997 and 1999 and prompted a more detailed study of the plaza's construction history in 2012–2014 (Herndon et al. 2014; Houk et al. 2010; Houk, Harris et al. 2013; Houk et al. 2014; Kelley 2014; Kelley et al. 2012). The 2012 season of the CCAP included a study of the historic Maya village and associated ruins of Kaxil Uinic (Harris and Sisneros 2012; Houk, Harris et al. 2013). As noted in Chapter 1, J. Eric Thompson (1963) had planned to excavate Kaxil Uinic back in 1931 but was forced to change his plans after the Belize Estate and Produce Company closed the nearby village (also see Houk 2012a).

Site Plan and Urban Features

The major architecture at the site (Figure 8.9), composed of the largest structures and plazas, is centered on the Main Plaza (Plaza A-1) and the Upper Plaza (Plaza A-2). The Main Plaza is square in plan, and at 13,080 m² is the third-largest plaza in the Three Rivers adaptive region (Garrison 2007:Table 6.3) and the second-largest in the eastern lowlands, behind only La Milpa's Great Plaza. Mounds border the plaza on all sides, but there are several important access points described below. A large, badly damaged range building, Structure A-2, is on the western side of the plaza. The only monument in the plaza is an eroded and burned stela at the base of this building; it shows no evidence of carving.

Two small and heavily looted temple-pyramids (Structures A-7 and A-9) linked by a low platform form the eastern side of the plaza. A low and very crudely built platform measuring approximately 4 × 6.5 m was located in the center of the plaza, but its age and function are unknown (see Houk 2000c). Guderjan (1991b:35) referred to this enigmatic pile of stones as an altar and speculated that it, along with the two temple-pyramids on the eastern side of the plaza, formed a "pseudo E-Group," which did not function as an astronomical observatory but was nonetheless viewed by the Maya "as necessary elements in public architecture" (Guderjan 2006:101).

An unusual 8-m-tall square-based platform, Structure A-4, occupies the northwestern corner of the plaza; it supports three low mounds on its northern, southern, and western sides. Structure A-5, a 64-m-long building, bounds the northern side of the Main Plaza. Investigations in 2013 determined that it is a 4.5-m-high platform that supported low walls and a perishable building on its summit (Figure 8.10). Importantly, the building has stairs on both the southern and northern faces, indicating that the space to the north of the mound was another functioning plaza, dubbed the North Plaza (Herndon et al. 2013; Houk et al. 2014). This space is bound on the east and west by Structures A-6 and A-4, respectively, but open to the north. It is unclear how much of the ground surface of the North Plaza is artificially elevated, but 70 m north of Structure A-5 the terrain drops steeply down to a spring-fed *aguada* that was likely an important water source for the city (Guderjan 1991b:45). Two openings between buildings at either end of Structure A-5 provide access to this area from the Main Plaza. To date, no excavations have been conducted in the North Plaza, but an apparent lithic workshop is visible on the surface near the northern end of Structure A-6, and it is tempting to hypothesize that the area was used for craft production or perhaps as a marketplace.

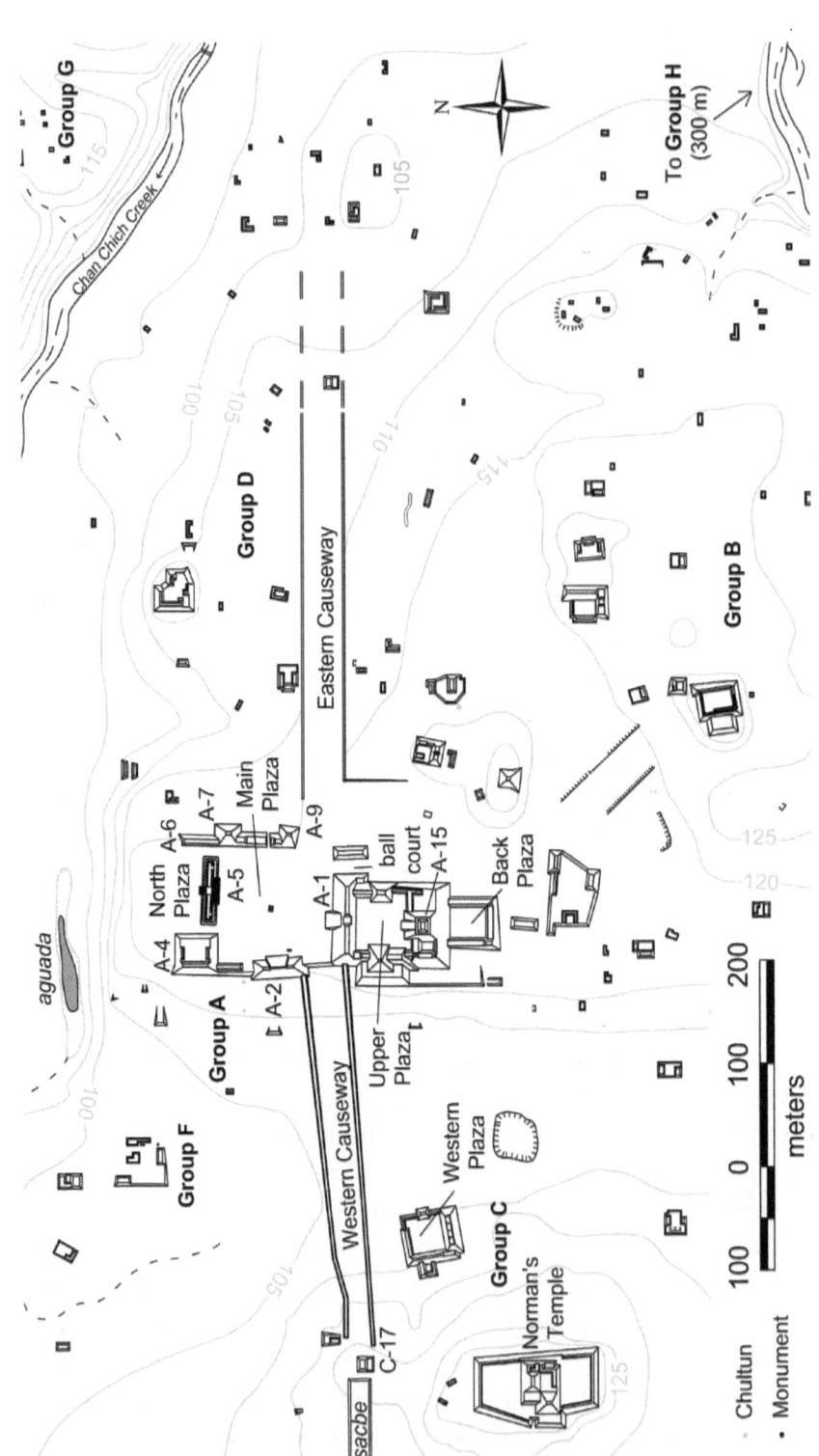

Figure 8.9. Map of Chan Chich, courtesy of Chan Chich Archaeological Project. Contour interval is 5 m.

Figure 8.10. Reconstruction drawing of Structure A-5 at Chan Chich. Illustration by Gary Smith, used with permission of the Chan Chich Archaeological Project.

The largest building at Chan Chich is the 70-m-long tandem range building that forms the southern side of the Main Plaza and the northern side of the Upper Plaza. A wide stairway leads up the northern face of Structure A-1 to a central landing that divides the superstructure in half and provided the sole means of access to the Upper Plaza when the site was occupied. The landing is 10 m higher than the Main Plaza and 3 m higher than the Upper Plaza. Excavations in 2014 on the structure determined that the large platform supported eight once-vaulted rooms on either side of the landing: on each side, four rooms faced the Main Plaza, and four faced the Upper Plaza (Herndon et al. 2014).

The site's ball court sits at the southeastern edge of the Main Plaza on a platform extending off the end of the eastern causeway, described below, at the same elevation as the plaza. The western structure is physically attached to the eastern end of Structure A-1, while the eastern structure is freestanding. Both buildings had tiered playing surfaces facing the alley (Ford 1998). While attached ball courts are not unknown, they are extremely rare, and the only other example in the Three Rivers adaptive region is found at La Honradez. The two ball courts at Xunanatunich, discussed in Chapter 7, are other examples of this attached style, and other examples are known from Yalbac and Saturday Creek. More unusual, however, are the tiered faces of the two mounds. The only other example of this style in the eastern lowlands comes from Lubaantun in southern Belize.

The Upper Plaza, with its tightly restricted access, is arguably the site's acropolis, but it lacks palace-type structures other than Structure A-1. Structure A-15, the tallest building at the site, dominates the southern side of the Upper Plaza. The Back Plaza is tucked behind Structure A-15 and is approximately 7–10 m lower in elevation.

Two causeways lead into the Main Plaza, entering it from the east and west in front of Structure A-1 and the ball court. The eastern causeway is a 40-m-wide elevated *sacbe* that extends for nearly 400 m before it becomes too poorly defined to follow. This causeway may actually terminate at a small shrine structure (Houk 2013b). The western causeway is composed of two parallel linear mounds defining a 40-m-wide space between them. Testing in 2014 determined the causeway is elevated at its eastern end where it enters the Main Plaza, but surface inspection suggests that for most of its length the causeway is a ground-level path defined by the flanking parapets. Thomas Garrison (2007:317) refers to these as "sunken" causeways. The causeway connects the Main Plaza to an isolated hilltop mound (Structure C-17), which is identical in form to the mound found at the end of the Eastern Causeway. It is possible that the two structures are shrines associated with a ritual function of the causeways (Houk 2013b). West of this mound another *sacbe* continues westward as an elevated surface (Houk et al. 1996). I suspect the *sacbe* at the western edge of the mapped area connects to the nearby site of Kaxil Uinic, but our 2012 attempt to verify that was thwarted by thick vegetation and downed trees—from the 2010 passage of Hurricane Richard—at Kaxil Uinic (Harris and Sisneros 2012; Houk, Harris, et al. 2013).

Chan Chich is the only site in northwestern Belize to have two causeways, and its western causeway is an extremely rare type. The only other "sunken" causeways in the region are found at La Honradez, where there are three equally wide causeways that radiate from the site center to the east, west, and north (see Von Euw and Graham 1984), and San Bartolo, where Garrison (2007:317) reports a Late Preclassic example. El Pilar's causeway also appears to conform to this type, and Keller (2010:Table 9.1) reports raised parapets on the two *sacbeob* at Xunantunich, which have the same type of radial arrangement as that seen at Chan Chich and La Honradez. Some causeways at Caracol have parapets as well (Chase and Chase 2001a:273).

When considered together, the two causeways, Structure A-1, and the ball court must have been important architectural elements of ritual processions entering the Main Plaza. Structure A-1 is similar to Structure 3 at La Milpa in this sense as both share a strong connection not only to their respective plazas but also to their ball courts and causeways.

The Western Plaza and its associated range buildings are approximately 250 m west of the Main Plaza at the base of a large hill. Another important architectural group, nicknamed Norman's Temple, crowns the top of this hill. The group includes a tightly enclosed courtyard with a small temple on its western edge and a range building on the north. Artificially leveled platforms extend north and south of the courtyard, and a low wall encircles the entire assemblage. Other smaller courtyard groups are located east of the Main Plaza.

The two causeways radiating out from the center of the site impart a cruciform shape to Chan Chich's plan. However, the North Plaza, Main Plaza, Upper Plaza, Back Plaza, and ball court stress the importance of the north–south orientation of the monumental heart of the city.

No settlement surveys have been conducted around Chan Chich beyond the limits of the 1996 mapping project (see Houk et al. 1996). However, using La Milpa as a model, Kaxil Uinic may be one of several minor centers associated with Chan Chich (Figure 8.11). The 2012 investigations determined the small site consists of 14 structures with one well-defined plaza (Harris and

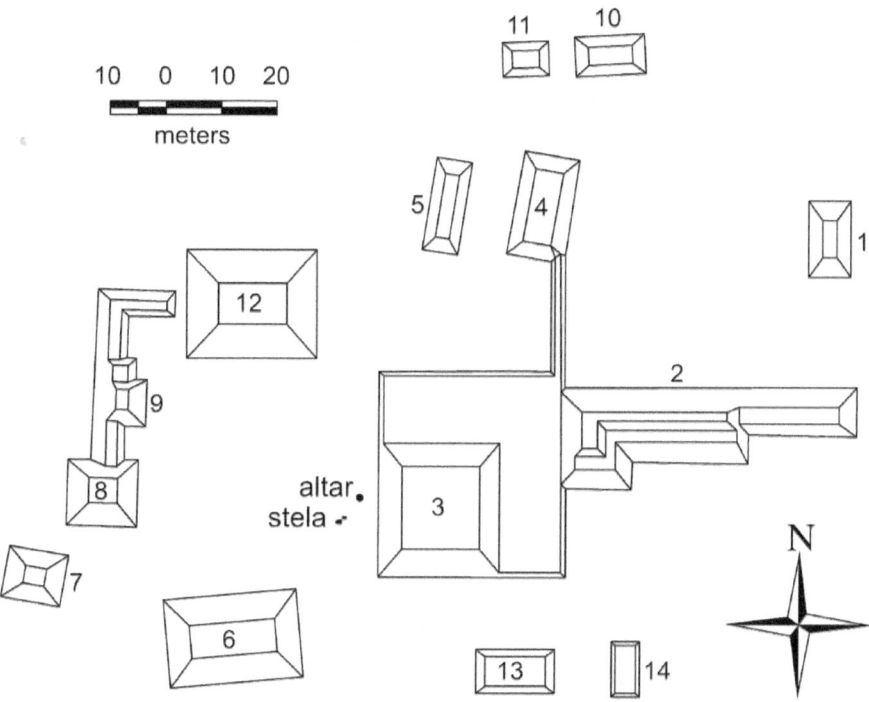

Figure 8.11. Map of Kaxil Uinic, courtesy of Chan Chich Archaeological Project.

Sisneros 2012). The plaza contains a large, uncarved altar and a broken and eroded, but once carved, stela. Hurricane Richard severely damaged the forest at the site in 2010, and massive fallen trees covered the area in 2012, preventing a systematic search for the *sacbe* believed to connect Kaxil Uinic to Chan Chich (Harris and Sisneros 2012; Houk, Harris, et al. 2013).

Chronology

Testing at the base of Structure 3 at Kaxil Uinic discovered an Early Preclassic sherd (ca. 1100 BCE) that is stylistically identical to Cunil ceramics, the earliest documented ceramics in Belize, from the Belize Valley (Harris and Sisneros 2012:56; Valdez and Houk 2012:68). Although in a mixed deposit, the sherd indicates that settlement began in the area near the end of the Early Preclassic period. Excavations into the Upper Plaza at Chan Chich discovered a buried midden deposit that dates to the Middle Preclassic period with a calibrated radiocarbon age of 770 BCE (Robichaux 1998:34), suggesting the site began as a small village in that area. The settlement expanded in the Late Preclassic as evidenced by floors and features in the Upper Plaza (Kelley et al. 2012; Robichaux et al. 2000), the Main Plaza (Houk 1998b; Houk 2000c), Structure C-8 in the Western Plaza (Guderjan 1991b:41), and Norman's Temple group (Meadows 1998). Structure A-15, the tallest mound at the site, began as a 3-m-high platform around this time (Guderjan 1991b:39).

The Upper Plaza underwent a number of replastering episodes in the Late Preclassic period before the builders cut through the floors and into bedrock to construct Tomb 2 in the Terminal Preclassic period (Houk et al. 2010). The tomb was a 3.25-m-long, 0.8-m-wide elliptical cut into bedrock that was sealed by 12 large capstones. The builders buried the tomb beneath fill to the level of the plaza floor and then capped it with a low shrine platform (Figure 8.12). The grave goods indicate the tomb contained an early king.

Although the evidence for Early Classic construction at the site is limited to inferences from looters' trenches and sporadic sherds in fill, two broken Early Classic polychrome bowls found in a looters' camp as reported by Guderjan (1991b:45) indicate continued construction and activity at the site in Early Classic period. It is possible that the major buildings on the southern and western sides of the Upper Plaza were expanded during this time, but their multiple construction phases are still poorly dated.

Chan Chich expanded greatly in the Late Classic period, and the final plan of the site took shape through renovations to existing buildings and the construction of new buildings and features. In the Upper Plaza a major construction event raised the plaza floor by 1 m and buried the Terminal Preclassic

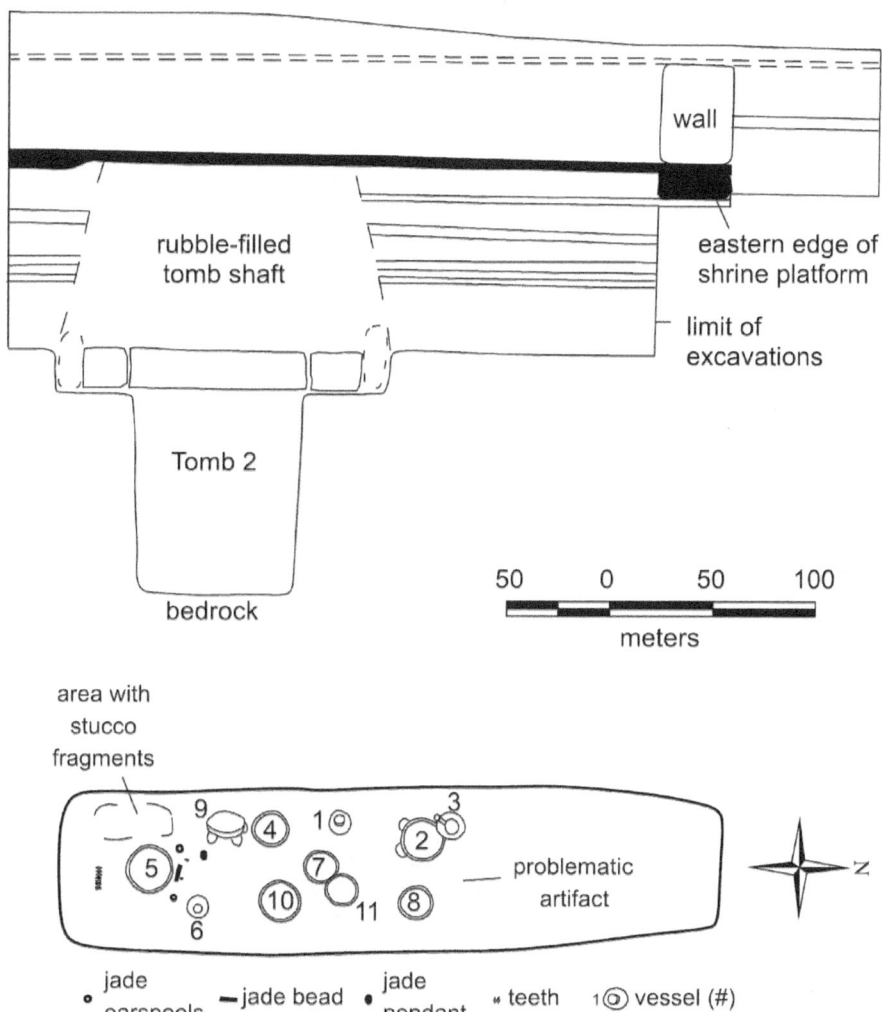

Figure 8.12. Tomb 2 at Chan Chich. Top is northern cross section of excavation area and tomb (after Houk et al. 2010:Figure 5). Bottom is plan of tomb's floor (after Houk et al. 2010:Figure 6).

shrine above Tomb 2 (Kelley 2014). Profiles in looters' trenches indicate the buildings around the Upper Plaza were expanded in the Late Classic period. The architectural renovation extended into the Main Plaza, where the builders elevated the plaza floor, completely burying older Late Preclassic features (Houk 1998b, 2000c). An examination of now-filled trenches in the structures around the Main Plaza by Guderjan's (1991b) teams suggest that Structures A-2, A-7, and A-9 were built in one phase during the Late Classic, although the 2013 excavations at Structure A-5 call this conclusion into question (Herndon et al. 2013; Houk et al. 2014). Though an earlier version may lie undiscovered, the visible version of the ball court dates to the Late Classic period (Ford 1998). The Western Plaza and Norman's Temple were both expanded (Ford and Rush 2000), and Richard Meadows and Kristen Hartnett (2000) determined that the lithic workshops in Group H date to the Late Classic as well.

The site apparently went into decline during the Terminal Classic period before being abandoned around 850–900 CE. Prior to abandonment, construction at the site reduced noticeably in quality. At Structure A-5, the final phase of the southern stairs included robbed vault stones in the construction (Houk et al. 2014), and Terminal Classic occupants of Structure C-6 in the Western Plaza also built a crude wall using robbed vault stones (Harrison 2000). That same structure included a Terminal Classic burial of a single adult male beneath an existing bench in the room. Grave goods included a black-slipped anthropomorphic bowl (Figure 8.13) and two shell discs (Harrison 2000:83).

Elite artifacts left broken on the steps of the largest structure in the Western Plaza and the range building in the Norman's Temple group date to the Terminal Classic period; they were likely deposited at or shortly after the time of the site's abandonment (Houk 2011). The site fell into ruin at that point, but Postclassic pilgrims made periodic visits to leave offerings, including an incense burner on the stairs to Structure A-5 (Houk et al. 2014:333) and another on the top of Structure A-4 (Guderjan 1991b:45). At Kaxil Uinic, during either the Late Postclassic period or Colonial period, pilgrims propped up half of the broken stela at the site and placed offerings of *incensarios* around its base (Houk, Harris, et al. 2013).

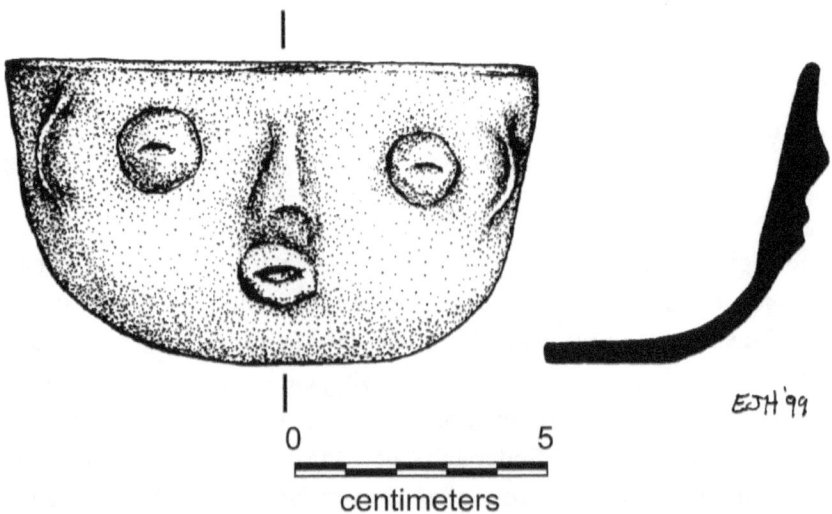

Figure 8.13. Illustration of Terminal Classic anthropomorphic bowl from Burial 8, Structure C-6, Chan Chich, after Harrison (2000:Figure 6.14). Illustration by Eleanor Harrison-Buck.

Political History

Chan Chich has no known emblem glyph, and the single stela at the site is too damaged to know if it was ever carved or not. While the stela at Kaxil Uinic was once carved, it is now too eroded to discern any details. Thus, what we can surmise of Chan Chich's political history is minimal. We do know that around the end of the Terminal Preclassic period or perhaps the beginning of the Early Classic period (around 200–350 CE), the Maya buried an early divine king beneath a small shrine in the Upper Plaza at the site (Houk et al. 2010:240). The jade helmet-bib head pendant included with the other grave offerings indicates the person buried in Tomb 2 was royalty; Linda Schele and David Freidel (1990:120) refer to these artifacts as "royal jewels," and they have been discovered in Late Preclassic contexts at sites like Cerros. Even though his kingdom was not very large at the time, the person buried in the Upper Plaza is the earliest divine king thus far discovered in the Belizean half of the Three Rivers region (Houk et al. 2010:240). William Saturno (2006:73) has reported an earlier royal tomb at San Bartolo in the western half of the region dating to around 150 BCE, and murals at that site show the coronation of another divine king about 50 years later.

Based on ceramics that have strong ties to Uaxactun, Chan Chich was likely participating in the Petén political sphere during the Early Classic period (Sullivan and Sagebiel 2003:29). By the Late Classic period, Chan Chich may have been politically tied to the larger city of La Honradez in the southwestern part of the Three Rivers adaptive region, or at least emulated aspects of that city's design in its urban expansion (see Garrison 2007:321; Houk 2003:60). Certain urban features at Chan Chich have analogs at La Honradez that are uncommon at other sites in the eastern lowlands.

In the late 1800s San Pedro Maya displaced from southern Quintana Roo, Mexico, settled around an *aguada* 500 m south of the ruins of Kaxil Uinic (see Houk 2012a). Grant Jones (1977:162) believes the settlers came from the village of Holuitz, which was abandoned sometime after 1868. The Belize Estate and Produce Company "closed" the historic village of Kaxil Uinic in 1931 and moved the inhabitants to San José (Houk 2012a).

Discussion

Although a large center during the Late Classic period, Chan Chich arguably had its heyday in the Terminal Preclassic period when the city's elite buried an early divine king in the Upper Plaza. Centuries later, during the Late Classic period, the rulers at the city established Chan Chich's visible site plan. The key urban features at the city are its massive Main Plaza, its east–west causeways (one of which is raised and one of which is "sunken"), its immense range building on the southern side of the Main Plaza, and its rare form of attached ball court.

The *sacbe* that exits the mapped limits of Chan Chich to the west provides an implied (if not actual) connection to the minor center of Kaxil Uinic, which is unusual in its own right for possessing a carved stela and one of the largest altars in the area. This connection stands in contrast to La Milpa's lack of physical ties to its minor centers.

Discussion and Concluding Remarks

The three cities presented in this chapter share key urban features, including prominent north–south orientations and massive public plazas. The main plazas at La Milpa and Dos Hombres have additional similarities, including temple-pyramids in their northwestern corners, quadrangle groups attached to and elevated above their southwestern corners, and *sacbeob* connecting to the southern parts of the two sites. The plan of Dos Hombres may be an example of political emulation. Chan Chich, though still in the Three Rivers adaptive region, shares more planning features with sites like La Honradez to the west and Xunantunich to the south than it does with Dos Hombres and La Milpa.

All three cities, however, share more in common with each other than do with the cities to the north and east in the last area of Belize to be discussed, northern Belize. The low and swampy terrain of northern Belize stretches from the Booth's River Escarpment to the coast and presents a radically different landscape than the rugged uplands of northwestern Belize. It is in that setting that the final three cities to be considered—Nohmul, Lamanai, and Altun Ha—arose.

Northern Belize

East and north of the Bravo Hills land region lie northern Belize and the Northern Coastal Plain land region (King et al. 1992:35). What northern Belize lacks in scenic beauty—unless you consider sugar cane fields, scrub forests, and swamps to be scenic—it makes up for in important archaeological discoveries. From the 1960s to early 1990s, northern Belize was one of the most intensively studied areas of the country, yielding discoveries like the stucco masks at Cerros, early ceramics at Cuello, stone tool workshops and a grisly pit of human skulls at Colha, spectacular architecture at Lamanai, and the famous jade head at Altun Ha. The three cities from the region discussed in this chapter are another study in diversity, and each brings something different to the table. Nohmul is by some measures the third-largest site in the eastern lowlands but has an atypical occupation history and, like El Pilar, lacks monuments. Lamanai represents a unique exercise in city building in which the New River Lagoon acted as a natural backdrop for the monumental architecture. Altun Ha is perhaps the oddest center discussed in this book; built on a bump in a coastal swamp, Altun Ha was a surprisingly wealthy place, but its rulers disregarded many basic standards for making a Maya city.

Setting

Although much lower in elevation than the northwestern corner of the country, the topography of northern Belize has been shaped by the same geological processes. Southwest to northeast trending fold and fault lines have produced low ridges and swampy swales in which a series of slow-moving rivers drain into the Caribbean Sea and Chetumal Bay (Johnson 1983:18). The Booth's River Escarpment extends from northwestern Belize into northern Belize, where it is sometimes referred to as the San Pablo Ridge, and passes west of the modern town of Orange Walk (McDonald and Hammond 1985:13). In general, elevation ranges from sea level to 20 m, with a few spots reaching 40 m above sea level (King et al. 1992:35).

From west to east, the major streams of northern Belize are the Río Hondo, which forms the modern border with Mexico, the New River, Freshwater Creek, and the Northern River (see Figure 8.1). The New River and Freshwater Creek both debouch in Chetumal Bay, flanking the narrow peninsula of land east of Lowry's Bight, where the ruins of Cerros are located. The Northern River feeds into Northern River Lagoon and eventually the Caribbean Sea.

At spots along these streams and in other synclines, inland and coastal lagoons dot the landscape. Ranging from freshwater to saltwater, these lagoons provided a range of natural resources to the Maya and became favored settlement areas during the Postclassic period (e.g., Masson 2000). The largest of these lagoons is the New River Lagoon, which stretches for 23 km. East of the New River, the low-lying coastal plain is also dotted with swamps, some of which are flooded for seven months out of the year (McDonald and Hammond 1985:14). The swampy terrain inhibited prehistoric settlement of the area east of Freshwater Creek (Hammond 1981:165).

As mentioned in chapters 3 and 4, there are important outcrops of chert and chalcedony in northern Belize. The fine-grained cherts occur in a zone between the site of Altun Ha on the south and the modern town of Orange Walk on the north (Shafer and Hester 1984:Figure 1). Chalcedonies occur along Freshwater Creek and the New River, north of this zone (Shafer and Hester 1984:158).

Nohmul

Setting

Nohmul is located on the east bank of the Río Hondo, straddling the modern border between the Corozal and Orange Walk districts of Belize (Hammond 1983c:245). The monumental precinct is approximately 4 km from the river, built on the low San Pablo Ridge about 20 m above sea level (Hammond 1985:43). The major mound groups are all built on the ridge, but settlement extends in all directions around the site center up to the river and margins of surrounding swamps (Hammond 1983c:245). The wetlands surrounding Nohmul on the west, north, and east show evidence of intensive agricultural systems of channeled and raised fields, the best documented being the fields at Pulltrouser Swamp to the east of the site (Hammond et al. 1985; Turner and Harrison 1983). In contrast to the ruins of northwestern Belize, which lie shrouded in rain forest, Nohmul is in an agriculture area "covered by patches of cane fields, corn fields, low bush, cow pastures, swamps, roads, and modern houses" (Pyburn 1988:14).

Investigations and Depredations

A number of archaeologists have detailed the history of research at Nohmul, including Norman Hammond (1983c, 1985), Anne Pyburn (1988), and Diane Chase (1982). Nohmul was one of the many sites subjected to Thomas Gann's rather destructive explorations. First known as Douglas, Thomas Gann changed the name of the site to Nohmul, meaning "great mound," after he visited the ruins in 1897 and again in 1908–1909, when he excavated four mounds (Hammond 1983c:247). His greatest impact to the site, however, came nearly 25 years later when he and his wife, Mary, excavated over 30 mounds at Nohmul and surrounding groups (Hammond 1983c:247).

Maya mounds in northern Belize are unfortunately frequent targets for quarrying, and government workers broke into a burial chamber in a large mound at Nohmul as they quarried the structure for road fill in 1940. Subsequent salvage work uncovered additional burial chambers with Terminal Preclassic ceramics (Chase 1982:28; Hammond 1983c:247).

Thirty years after that discovery, the Corozal Project, under the direction of Norman Hammond (1983c:247), conducted intensive survey, mapping, and excavations at Nohmul over the course of three seasons. Diane Chase's (1982) dissertation resulted from the 1978 field season, incorporating data from Nohmul and Santa Rita Corozal. Subsequently, the Nohmul Project studied the site for four seasons in 1982, 1983, 1985, and 1986 (Hammond 1983c; Hammond, ed. 1985; Hammond et al. 1985, 1987; Hammond, Pyburn et al. 1988) to investigate the development of the monumental architecture in the site core. Concurrently, Anne Pyburn (1988) directed the Nohmul Settlement Pattern Project in 1983, 1985, and 1986 for her dissertation research. The mapping at the site center and the settlement pattern work combined to produce one of the most extensive and detailed maps of a Maya city in Belize (see Hammond, Pyburn et al. 1988:Figure 3).

Between the writing of the first draft of this book and its publication, illegal quarrying activities devastated Nohmul in early 2013. A company from nearby Orange Walk Town quarried away nearly all of the largest structure in the western half of the site before the authorities shut down their operation. The depredations made international news, and criminal and civil legal proceedings were under way by July 2013.

Site Plan and Urban Features

Nohmul's site core consists of two large platforms about 400 m apart, connected by a southeast–northwest-aligned *sacbe* (Figure 9.1). The eastern group is the larger of the two, consisting of over 40 structures, and is dominated by the acropolis (Structure 1), a flat-topped platform covering 94 m² (Hammond 1985:45). The acropolis platform is 8 m higher than the plazas to its south and west and 12 m higher than the natural ground at the base of the eastern group. Structure 2, a 14-m-tall mound, occupies the southern edge of the acropolis

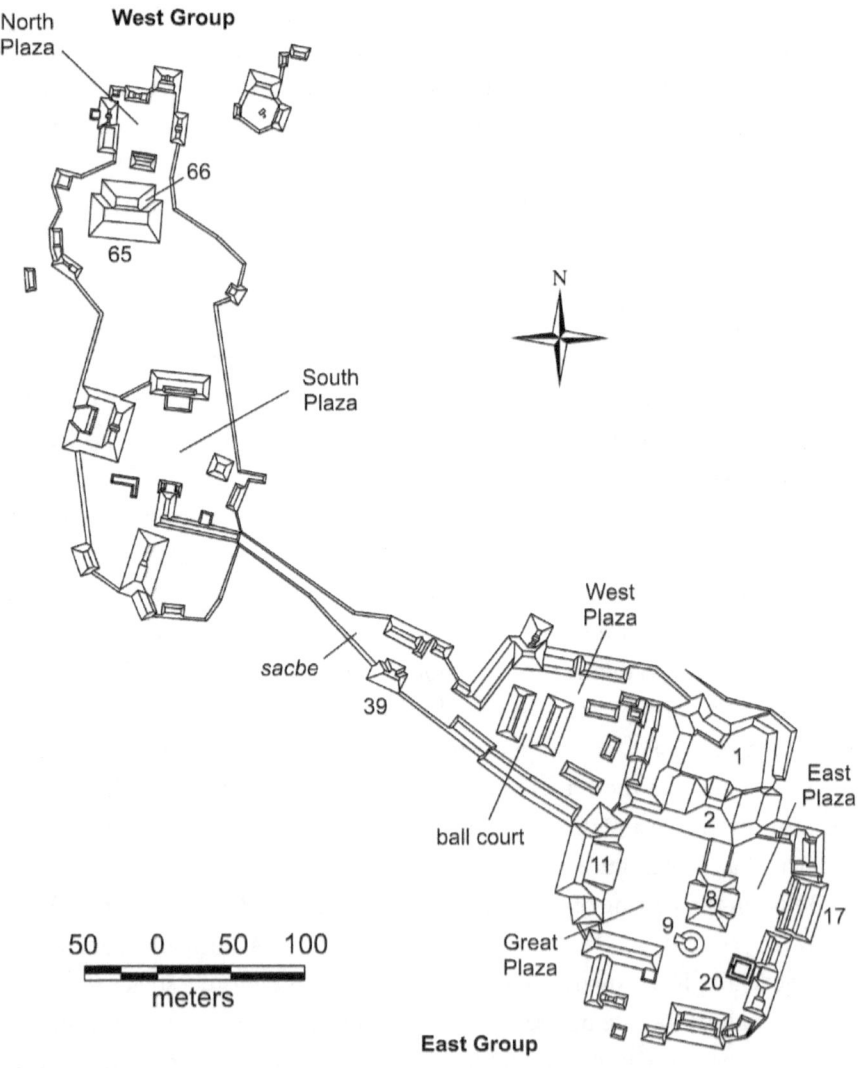

Figure 9.1. Map of Nohmul, after Hammond (1985:Figure 2.3) with Structure 9 data after D. Chase and A. Chase (1982:Figure 2).

(Hammond 1985:45); rising 26 m above the surrounding terrain, Structure 2 is visible for a great distance.

On the southern side of the acropolis, in the shadow of Structure 2, are the Great Plaza and the East Plaza, divided from each other by Structures 8 and 9. Prior to the Terminal Classic period, when Structures 8 and 9 were built, these two plazas formed one "giant plaza" measuring 125 m on each side (Hammond 1985:45; Hammond et al. 1985:189). As a point of comparison, Nohmul's Giant Plaza would have been about 75 percent the size of Plaza A at La Milpa. The Giant Plaza was built in the Terminal Preclassic or Early Classic and for six centuries or so was the heart of ancient Nohmul. The western side of the Giant Plaza is formed by a large range building, Structure 11, which is 80 m long and 10 m high. Prior to the Terminal Classic period, Structure 11 faced Structure 17, a smaller building sharing the same central axis (Hammond 1985:45).

Structure 8, a Terminal Classic period pyramid, disrupted the symmetry of the Giant Plaza and introduced, along with Structures 9 and 20, an exotic architectural style to the city (see Hammond et al. 1985:190). Excavations in 1983 uncovered vertically oriented slabs at the base of Structure 8, an architectural style not used at the site prior to the Terminal Classic period (Hammond et al. 1985:190). Hammond et al. (1987:262–263) interpret the poorly preserved remains of the superstructure—which had been excavated previously by Gann—to have been a west-facing building with two tandem chambers and three doorways. The single stairway led down the western face of the building into the Great Plaza.

Structure 9 is a round platform measuring nearly 15 m in diameter immediately south of Structure 8. Excavations in 1979 encountered the base of the superstructure's walls and determined the building on top of the platform was also circular, with a diameter of a little greater than 9 m and a single doorway that was 1.5 m wide (Figure 9.2). The doorway lined up with a frontal stair oriented about 17° north of west, facing the Great Plaza (D. Chase and A. Chase 1982:603). Diane Chase (1982:485) notes that this orientation was shared by the other Terminal Classic structures and differed by 5° farther east of north from the standard orientation of the earlier structures at the site. The Chases speculate that the walls of Structure 9 were never very tall and that they, along with a central masonry support, originally held a perishable superstructure (D. Chase and A. Chase 1982:603).

The third intrusive structure in the Terminal Classic group of buildings is Structure 20, a square building with low walls and a single 1.20-m-wide doorway on its western side (see Figure 9.2). The stone walls probably were about 1 m high originally, built on a 20-cm-high plinth or base, and once supported

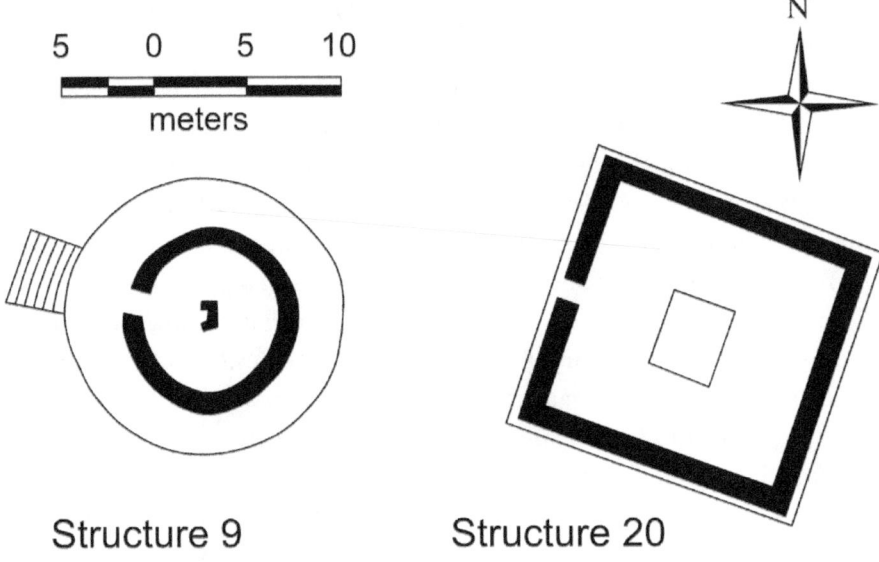

Figure 9.2. Plan maps of Structures 9 and 20, based on D. Chase and A. Chase (1982:Figure 2).

a perishable superstructure. The interior of the building measured 13 m on a side and contained a small sunken patio in its center (D. Chase and A. Chase 1982:598; Chase and Hammond 1982).

The West Plaza is an irregularly shaped platform that measures 105 m long by 94 m wide but actually contains little open space. Bound by low mounds on the north, west, and south, and by the base of the acropolis on the east, much of the West Plaza's floor space is taken up by Nohmul's ball court (Hammond 1985:46). With an alley measuring 7 m by 31 m, Nohmul's ball court is one of the largest in the southern lowlands (Scarborough 1991a:Figure 7.3) and dates to the Terminal Classic period (Hammond, Kosakowsky, et al. 1988:491).

A *sacbe* exits the northwestern corner of the West Plaza, passing between Structure 39 on the south and three low mounds on the north, and connects to the West Group approximately 100 m to the west-northwest. The West Group consists of two plazas and approximately 25 structures sharing a common platform. The *sacbe* enters the South Plaza, a loosely defined plaza with a small temple on its eastern side (Hammond 1985:46). A broad open space separates the structures of the South Plaza from the small North Plaza at the end of the ceremonial precinct. Structures 65 and 66, a large platform and attached temple, border the southern side of the North Plaza. Hammond (1985:47) speculates that this building, which is the largest free-standing pyramid at the site, was possibly the location for one of Gann's early excavations. This building is the one that was destroyed by quarrying in 2013. A small *plazuela* group to the east and the smaller mounds that border the North Plaza were likely residential buildings (Hammond 1985:47).

During the Corozal Project's 1974 season, Duncan Pring excavated a possible river port that included a small stone jetty extending into the river and a nearby mound (Pring and Hammond 1985). The jetty's age is unknown, but the mound was constructed in the Terminal Preclassic and reoccupied in the Late or Terminal Classic. Although the excavations did not find large quantities of imported materials, as would be expected at a port, they did yield numerous notched ceramic sherds used as net sinkers that suggest fishing or fish-drying were common activities at the mound (Pring and Hammond 1985:528).

Chronology

Nohmul had two important periods of occupation and construction separated by several centuries. The first occurred during the Late to Terminal Preclassic period, ca. 400 BCE to 250 CE, and the second during the Terminal Classic period, extending perhaps into the Early Postclassic, ca. 800 to 1100 CE (Hammond 1989:515). Although those two periods represent the intervals of major construction at the ceremonial precinct, which was largely deserted from about 400 to 800 CE, surface sampling of surrounding mound groups indicates the area around the ceremonial precinct was occupied from the Middle Preclassic into the Postclassic (Hammond, Pyburn, et al. 1988:3–4).

Large portions of both the West Group and East Group platforms as well as the *sacbe* were constructed during the Terminal Preclassic period (Hammond, Pyburn, et al. 1988:6). In the case of the East Group, constructing the platform was a massive undertaking in its own right as it required the quarrying, transportation, and deposition of enough earth and stone to cover nearly 60,000 m^2 in approximately 2 m of fill (see Pyburn 1988:63). The Structure 1 acropolis and Structure 2 are both of Terminal Preclassic age, and large-scale excavations of the summit of Structure 1 uncovered postholes left behind by massive wooden supports for a large building that once capped the platform (Hammond 1983c:250–251). The Terminal Preclassic burial chambers that were inadvertently discovered in the 1940s are further indication that the elite at Nohmul were both prosperous and powerful.

For reasons undetermined, the ceremonial precinct was apparently abandoned in the Early Classic about 400 CE, and the East Group was not wholly reoccupied until 800 CE. It is unclear if the West Group was reoccupied or not, but limited excavations there suggest no new construction took place

(Hammond, Pyburn, et al. 1988:6). Excavations in the West Plaza documented Terminal Preclassic and early Late Classic nonmonumental construction, but this area, too, was abandoned about 700 CE. About 100 years later, a workshop where craftsmen produced obsidian blades occupied this area, and shortly thereafter monumental construction resumed, culminating in the Terminal Classic ball court ca. 900 CE (Hammond, Pyburn, et al. 1988:7–8).

The cluster of Terminal Classic period structures noted earlier was also built after 800 CE. These buildings demonstrate clear Yucatán influences, and Nohmul's Terminal Classic resurgence is likely tied to contact with and influence from groups in the northern part of the peninsula. Extensive residential occupation accompanied this renewed construction in the ceremonial center during the Terminal Classic period, and Hammond, Pyburn, et al. (1988:12) characterize the community as "large and densely-settled" during this period. This late and curious occupation persisted into the Early Postclassic as late as 1100 CE, when the ceremonial precinct at Nohmul was finally abandoned. This stands in stark contrast to the population trends at most Maya cities in Belize.

Political History

Nohmul is the largest site in the eastern lowlands without stone monuments. However, stone monuments are generally rare in northern Belize, perhaps indicating a regional preference or a limitation imposed by the quality of limestone in the area. Reconstructing Nohmul's political history is, nonetheless, difficult. However, Nohmul's size and marked bimodal construction history suggests that it was a politically important center during two different time periods: the Terminal Preclassic / Early Classic and the Terminal Classic periods. The rich burials that road crews partially plundered in the 1940s produced an impressive assemblage of Terminal Preclassic ceramics (Hammond 1984), but due to the circumstances of their discovery it is unclear if any of the burials were royal or not. The presence of an early divine king at Nohmul is suggested, however, by a cache of four jade helmet-bib head pendants beneath a small pyramid (Structure 110) in the northern sector of the site, which was excavated in 1974 (Pyburn 1988:73). These jewels are similar to the one found in the early royal tomb at Chan Chich.

Kathryn Reese-Taylor and Debra Walker (2002:107) classify the Nohmul finds (and the Chan Chich royal tomb) as Holmul 1 burials, named after a site in Guatemala where this type of burial was first discovered. They suggest that the ceramics in these burials reflect ties to Tikal at the beginning of the Early Classic period (Reese-Taylor and Walker 2002:107).

During the Terminal Classic period the site experienced a resurgence, apparently due to beneficial interactions with Maya groups in the northern lowlands. As Eleanor Harrison-Buck (2012:114) has noted, at sites in the southern lowlands where elite occupation persists through the Terminal Classic, foreign traits suggesting contact with the northern lowlands show up in the archaeological record. New artifacts, new architectural styles—particularly the round structures, which may be imitations of the Caracol at the Terminal Classic metropolis of Chichén Itzá—and new forms of artistic expression all suggest foreign influence. The nature of this influence is debated, although trade or small-scale population movement are favored over large-scale migration and population replacement at the southern centers (Harrison-Buck 2012:114).

A rich burial found in Structure 8, one of the intrusive buildings at the site, may be that of a king of the site from the Terminal Classic period. The burial contained a single individual who was interred with two jade ear flares and two jade beads, four obsidian cores, a dozen obsidian blades, a large chert biface, and a chert eccentric (Hammond 1989:518; Hammond et al. 1987:265). Although the burial lacked ceramics, Hammond (1989:518) used obsidian hydration analysis to date the interment to 1050–1120 CE.

Discussion

Because Nohmul's site plan took shape in the Terminal Preclassic period, many of its urban features can be compared to the cities discussed in the Preclassic chapter of this book. However, Nohmul lacks certain Preclassic urban elements like an E-Group, ball court, or a triadic temple complex. Its most striking feature is what Norman Hammond (1981:165) described as its "contrasting structure," a trait observed at the northern Belize sites of Aventura and El Pozito as well. In all three cases, the ceremonial precinct is clearly split into two distinct groups. At Nohmul the two groups are connected by a *sacbe*, one of the earliest examples in the eastern lowlands.

Nohmul was undoubtedly involved in canoe-borne trade, located as it is on the banks of the Río Hondo, approximately 50 km from the Bay of Chetumal. Perhaps its strategic location along the river spurred interest from northern Maya during the Terminal Classic. The most atypical features of the site are its intrusive architectural elements that show northern Yucatán traits, including the round structure, which has counterparts at other Terminal Classic sites in the eastern lowlands. Nohmul's large ball court is coeval with the Yucatec-influenced revival of the site.

Lamanai

Setting

Lamanai is located on the west bank of the New River Lagoon, less than 2 km from the head of the New River. The lagoon is approximately 23 km long, but less than 1 km wide. Although the eastern side of the lagoon is relatively flat and subject to frequent flooding, on the western side the terrain is gently rolling and higher in elevation. The lower areas of the rolling terrain are punctuated by small *bajos* that dot the landscape (Powis 2002:48). The site occupies generally higher ground, covered in broadleaf forest, and extends to the shore of the lagoon on the east and to Barber Creek on the north. The southern and western limits of Lamanai's settlement are not well defined (Powis 2002:48).

In historic times, the river and lagoon served as an important transportation corridor for accessing the remote interior of northern and northwestern Belize. In 1623 Franciscan friars Bartolomé de Fuensalida and Juan de Orbita journeyed up the river and lagoon en route to the last free Maya kingdom of Tayasal on Lake Petén Itza, making passing mention of the Maya village of Lamayna. Three centuries later J. Eric Thompson (1963:225–228) took the flat-bottomed boat *Afrikola* from Belize City up the New River to Orange Walk, where he transferred his gear, his graduate assistant, and himself to a barge, which took them to Hill Bank at the southern end of the New River Lagoon prior to his 1931 season at San José. In his memoirs, he notes passing the ruins of Lamanai as the setting sun silhouetted them (Thompson 1963:227).

Investigations

Lamanai is an important site in large part because of its continuous occupation from the Middle Preclassic period through the Historic period. It is from a church list recorded in 1582 that we know the Maya name of the site (Roys 1957:163). Incorrectly recorded as Lamanai by the Spanish, the actual name was probably Lama'an/ayin, which appropriately translates as "submerged crocodile" (Pendergast 1981:32). Prior to the latter half of the twentieth century, the ruins were commonly referred to as "Indian Church," the name of the modern village immediately west of the site.

Thomas Gann (1926) conducted minor excavations at the site in 1917, and Pendergast (1981:32) makes mention of several archaeologists periodically visiting the ruins and making surface collections. Between 1974 and 1986, after the completion of his work at Altun Ha, David Pendergast directed extensive excavations and consolidation under the ROM Lamanai Project (Pendergast

1981; Powis 2002:52). Minor excavations took place after that as part of a small field school run through a nearby jungle lodge (Powis 2002:52). Beginning in 1997 Elizabeth Graham of University College London launched the Lamanai Archaeological Project (LAP), which was an interdisciplinary approach to studying the long-term occupation of the site (Graham 2004:224–228; Powis 2002:52). Scott Simmons joined the project in 1999 and became co-principal investigator in 2000. LAP terminated fieldwork at the end of the 2008 season, but artifact analysis is likely to continue for several more years (Scott Simmons, personal communication, 2013).

Site Plan and Urban Features

As Pendergast (1981:32) notes, Lamanai has a "decidedly non-standard settlement pattern" resulting from its placement along the banks of the lagoon (Figure 9.3). As he describes it, "the usual arrangement of one or more ceremonial precinct plaza groups, surrounded by zones of residential and other small structures, gives way to a sort of massive strip development with not a single ceremonial grouping resembling those generally encountered elsewhere" (Pendergast 1981:32). The site covers 4.5 km² and has eight major groups of monumental buildings in the Central Precinct. Altogether, Pendergast's (1981:32) project mapped 718 structures at the site.

Part of the uniqueness in Lamanai's site plan and settlement pattern undoubtedly stems from the city's exceptionally long occupation period. As Terry Powis (2002:51) notes, most of the Preclassic occupation is confined to a 2-km strip at the lagoon's edge in the northern part of the site. Through time, the focus of monumental construction in the ceremonial precinct shifted southward. The site always maintained a strong focus on the lagoon, however, which Powis (2002:51) suggests was due to an ongoing interest in easy access to canoe traffic.

At the northern end of the site, a large depression juts into the shoreline and possibly served as a harbor. However, excavations on an 100-m-long Late Preclassic range building, Structure P8-12, that overlooks the depression found no evidence to suggest that building was used as a storage or docking facility, and subsequent archaeological and geological investigations in the area cast doubt on the harbor hypothesis (Powis 2002:57). The range building is associated with a cluster of Preclassic constructions that formed the earliest monumental precinct at Lamanai. Directly west of the range building and across a small plaza is Structure P8-1, a large pyramid. South of the plaza is the largest platform at the site, Structure P9-25, which supports an acropolis-like group of buildings. The 18-m-high platform measures 90 m × 100 m on its

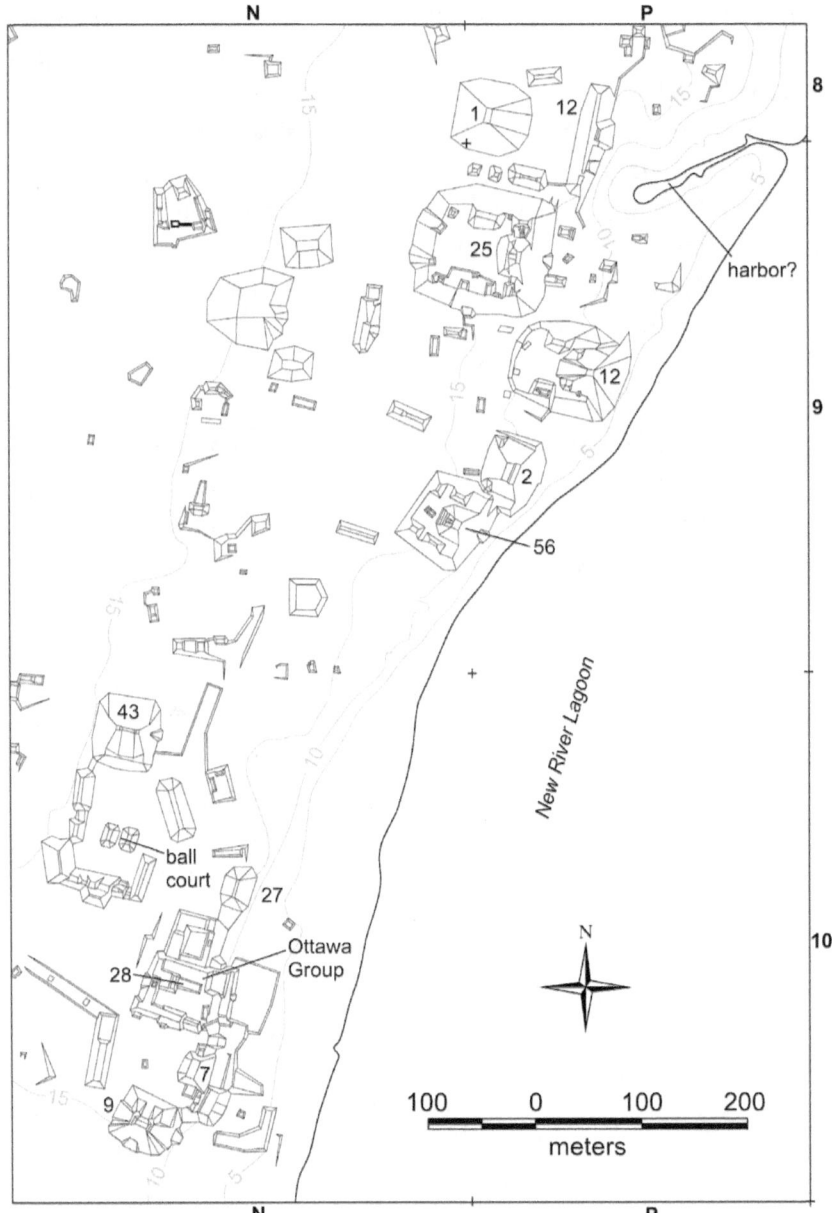

Figure 9.3. Map of Lamanai, after Pendergast (1981:Figure 3). Contour interval is 5 meters.

summit and supports over a dozen mounds, two of which are approximately 10 m tall (Pendergast 1981:34).

Southeast of the acropolis is a line of three large buildings, all with their backs facing the lagoon. Structure P9-12, flanked by smaller mounds on the northern and southern sides of a large platform, resembles a Late Preclassic triadic temple group. Structure P9-2, in the center of the line of three structures, is an isolated pyramid that never had a masonry superstructure on its summit (Pendergast 1981:40).

The third building in the line is Structure N9-56, the Mask Temple. Sitting on the lagoon side of a 50-m × 60-m platform and flanked by smaller mounds, the structure's summit is approximately 17 m higher than the ground at the base of the platform. The earliest incarnation of the building, which is of unknown age and form, was covered by a Late Preclassic structure, adorned with stucco masks similar to those at Cerros (Pendergast 1981:39). An Early Classic temple decorated with stone masks coated with stucco in turn buried this building. The exposed mask on the southern side of the temple's stairway (Figure 9.4) is of a human face with large ear spools and an elaborate, crocodile headdress (Pendergast 1981:38). Similar headdresses have been found on Postclassic *incensarios* at the site, suggesting a long-lived association between the people of Lama'anayin and crocodiles. Another renovation near the end of the Early Classic covered the masks and gave Structure N9-56 its final form as a terraced platform, with no superstructure on its summit but with a cham-

Figure 9.4. Photograph of fiberglass replica of Early Classic mask on Structure N9-56 at Lamanai (photograph by the author).

bered building set across the center stairway. This architectural style is known as the Lamanai Building Type, based on its ubiquity at the site.

The most impressive Late Preclassic structure at Lamanai is N10-43, known as the High Temple (Figure 9.5). The structure towers over the site at 33 m high; at the time Pendergast (1981:41) first excavated it, Structure N10-43 was the largest Late Preclassic building known in the Maya area. The Late Preclassic structure had a tripartite stair flanked by large stucco masks, and its summit supported two small chambered buildings facing inward toward a third platform with no building on its summit in a triadic arrangement. During the Late Classic the tripartite stairs were replaced by one broad stairway, and the summit structures were covered by a single platform with no superstructure. A long, single-room building was constructed across the full front of the structure, effectively transforming N10-43 into the Lamanai Building Type (Pendergast 1981:41).

Structure N10-43 marked the southern end of the ceremonial precinct during the Late Preclassic period. In the Classic period, the core of the city shifted south, extending in a line from N9-56, the Mask Temple, which was renovated in the Early and Late Classic periods, at the north to Structure N10-9 at the

Figure 9.5. The High Temple at Lamanai as it appears today (photograph by the author).

south. Structure N10-43 falls in the approximate middle of this reorganized ceremonial precinct, and during the Classic period it faced a large plaza to its south. Lamanai's only ball court occupies the southern end of this plaza. Its Terminal Classic construction was determined by an elaborate cache beneath a large, round stone marker in the center of the playing alley (Figure 9.6). A lidded vessel contained smaller vessels and small jade and shell objects, sitting in over 130 g of mercury (Pendergast 1981:41).

Southeast of the ball court plaza is Structure N10-27, a Late Classic Lamanai Building Type with its back to the New River Lagoon. Pendergast (1988:1, 4) excavated Stela 9 there in 1983, finding the butt of the stela in situ in the chamber built across the stairway and the upper part of the stela lying face down at the foot of the stairs. As discussed later, of Lamanai's nine known stelae, only three are carved, and Stela 9 is the only one with a legible text and Long Count date.

To the south of Structure N10-27 is the Ottawa Group, an elite place group on the northern side of a large plaza. Excavations encountered Early Classic construction beneath an extensive Late Classic assemblage of at least six buildings grouped around two courtyards. One of these Late Classic structures, N10-

Figure 9.6. Lamanai's Terminal Classic ball court (photograph by the author).

28, had an elaborate stucco frieze that was destroyed in a later renovation of the group. Excavations in 1981 recovered over 2,000 stucco fragments from the frieze (Graham 2004:224). Reconstruction of the fragments suggests the original theme of the frieze was rulership, and the composition contained a full-figure rendering of an apparent ruler of Lamanai (Graham 2004:224; Shelby 2000:71). A Terminal Classic expansion destroyed the frieze, razed the adjacent buildings, and buried the entire complex under distinctive dry-laid boulder fill. This construction event resulted in a larger platform, extending to the north. The new platform supported more buildings, and construction and use of the Ottawa Group continued into the Postclassic period (Graham 2004:232).

The structures surrounding the plaza to the south of the Ottawa Group demonstrate a similar construction sequence: Classic period antecedents were in use through the Terminal Classic period and extensively remodeled in the Postclassic (Pendergast 1981:43). Lamanai's builders constructed the bulk of Structure N10-7 on the eastern side of the plaza in single effort late in the ninth century CE, and people continued to use the structure until the fourteenth century (Pendergast 1981:43).

The most prominent structure in the group is Structure N10-9, known as the Temple of the Jaguar for the heavily stylized jaguar masks flanking the stairway on its lowest terrace. The structure began as a 19-m-tall pyramid in the Early Classic period. During the Late Classic period, extensive modifications to the structure included the addition of a chambered building across the stairway—this was the first example of the Lamanai Building Type identified at Lamanai (Powis 2002:57–58). In the Postclassic period, new stairside outsets were built that introduced a different architectural style to the building. Like Structure N10-7, the Temple of the Jaguar was abandoned by the fourteenth century (Pendergast 1981:43–44).

Between the Temple of the Jaguar and the lagoon is a small group of structures that became the focal point for Postclassic construction. Pendergast (1981:44) notes affinities with northern Yucatecan architecture, although the Lamanai architects relied on wood and wattle and daub rather than stone. The structures yielded a large number of burials with Postclassic chalices, copper and gold objects, shell artifacts, bone tubes, and pyrite mirrors (Pendergast 1981:44–48).

Chronology

David Pendergast (1998:56) points to a concentration of corn pollen in the suspected harbor as evidence for a possible Early Preclassic offering of whole corn plants ca. 1500 BCE. The first evidence for pottery and construction at

Lamanai, however, shows up in the late Middle Preclassic period around 600–400 BCE at five different areas in the northern part of the site (Powis 2002:54). The five locations extend from Structure N10-43 on the south to P8-108, which is north of the limits of the published site map. All the locations are within 200 m of the lagoon, suggesting that Lamanai's linear pattern of development and strong lagoon orientation were first established when it was a small Middle Preclassic village.

The site experienced significant growth in the Late Preclassic period. The Lamanai Project excavated Late Preclassic residential structures under the High Temple (Powis 2002:58) and the Cerros-like Late Preclassic version of the Mask Temple (Pendergast 1981:39). Another focus of much of the Late Preclassic construction was at the northern end of the site where the villagers built the acropolis-like platform P9-25 and the surrounding structures (Powis 2002:55). The crowning jewel, however, was undoubtedly the triadic temple, Structure N10-43, which buried the earlier residential platforms ca. 100 BCE (Pendergast 1981:41).

During the Early Classic period, the site experienced continued growth, and the gradual migration of the ceremonial precinct to the south began. The final modifications to the acropolis at the northern end of the site occurred about 400 CE (Pendergast 1981:40); the Early Classic Mask Temple was built about 500 CE or so (Pendergast 1981:38), as was the first version of the Temple of the Jaguar (Pendergast 1981:35).

Although less is known about the early part of the Late Classic period at Lamanai than any other period of occupation (see Graham 2004:Table 1; Pendergast 1981:42), it is clear that construction continued in the seventh and eighth centuries CE, although the pattern is one of renovation to existing buildings rather than new construction in most cases. Importantly, the Lamanai Building Type became the favored construction form at the beginning of the Late Classic (Pendergast 1981:42).

While many of the other cities of the eastern lowlands experienced dramatic declines in construction and population during the Terminal Classic, Lamanai continued to thrive. The elite palace group at the core of the city was actually expanded during the Terminal Classic, suggesting that royal authority was in no way diminished at the site, and the site acquired a ball court for the first time (Pendergast 1986). Caches and offerings from this period also reflect growing, not declining, prosperity; caches from the end of the Late Classic period were more opulent than those from earlier periods, and one of the largest offerings excavated at the site preceded a Terminal Classic construction effort (Pendergast 1998:58–59).

The city experienced a decline in population in the Middle and Late Postclassic periods, and settlement contracted to the southern part of the Central Precinct (Pendergast 1998:59). Elizabeth Graham (2004) notes that most activity around this time was focused along the lagoon's edge.

Lamanai was still occupied by the Maya when the Spanish arrived in Belize in the 1500s. The Spanish built the first of two churches south of the Central Precinct of the Maya city around 1544 CE and maintained a presence at the site until the seventeenth century (Graham 2011:204, 255). Several centuries later, a British company built a short-lived sugar mill near the site in the mid-nineteenth century. Like the earlier Spanish presence, the British enterprise failed, and the mill fell into ruin by the late-nineteenth century (Pendergast 1981).

Political History

Scarborough (1991b:Table 10) believes Lamanai was a primate center during the Late Preclassic period, on par with Colha and Nohmul, with a number of smaller villages likely under its control or influence. The ceramics at the site indicate ties to other northern Belize sites but also reflect a strong sense of community identity in the local production of most ceramics, including crocodile effigy pots (Powis 2002:520–521).

Circumstantial evidence in the form of Early Classic tombs at Structure N9-56 and the human mask portraits from that building's facade suggest that a royal dynasty was in place by 500 CE, if not earlier. It is unclear how Lamanai oriented itself on the political landscape during the Early Classic, but several Teotihuacan-style ceramics from the tomb of an apparent female ruler in Structure N9-56 (see Powis 2002:518) indicate ties to the trade in such vessels, likely facilitated by Tikal.

During the Late Classic period, Lamanai was active in trade and exchange with other cities in northern Belize and was providing architectural ideas to Altun Ha, as discussed in the following. The Late Classic Stela 9 from the front of Structure N10-27 provides the only written information on the political history of Lamanai. The stela has a Calendar Round date of 7 Ahau 3 Pop, marking the *tun* ending Long Count date of 9.9.12.0.0 and the dedication of the stela on March 7, 625. A second Calendar Round date and distance number falls 6,124 days earlier (9.8.14.17.16 6 Cib 4 Zec; May 31, 608 CE) and probably marks the day the ruler depicted on the monument took the throne (Closs 1988:9, 12). The ruler's name is glossed as "Smoking Shell" (Closs 1988:13). Although the stela is Late Classic age, certain aspects of the iconography recall the Early Classic period including Smoking Shell's elaborate serpent headdress, an emblematic head he holds in one hand, and the double-headed serpent bar in his other hand (Reents-Budet 1988:17). The monument also includes the emblem glyph for Lamanai (Closs 1988:11).

Lamanai's prospering in the Terminal Classic period was likely due to peaceful relations with Maya cities in the northern lowlands. Artifacts and architecture from the period clearly reflect cultural exchange but do not suggest population replacement (Aimers 2007a:344). Perhaps the Terminal Classic rulers simply relied on existing relationships built over centuries of canoe-borne contact with groups to the north to weather, and even prosper during, the Classic Maya collapse.

Who ruled the site through the Terminal Classic period and into the Postclassic period is unclear, but it is unlikely that the dynasty of Classic period divine kings was still in power after 1000 CE. Jim Aimers (2007b:47) posits that contact with northern sites like Tulum and Mayapan brought not only new artifact styles but also new religious ideas, which probably did not include continued worship of divine kings. Evidence suggests that Lamanai was part of Dzuluinicob, a Late Postclassic province apparently under the authority of the site of Tipu on the eve of the Spanish conquest (Graham 2011:47; Jones 1989:9).

Discussion

Largely due to its long history of occupation and strong association with the New River Lagoon, Lamanai's built environment is a unique expression of Maya urbanism. From its founding, the New River Lagoon shaped the development of the city and contributed to its linear appearance in plan view. It is probably worth noting that the site map exaggerates this linear arrangement because it presents a static composite of the end product of approximately 2,000 years of construction. At any given time over the city's long history, the ceremonial precinct was concentrated in part of the area ultimately encompassed by monumental buildings.

That many of the city's temples are oriented with their backs to the lagoon attests to the central importance of the lagoon in the mind of the city's planners; the lagoon would have formed the backdrop for any rituals conducted on the summits of the platforms. Of course, it probably helped that the lagoon's orientation meant that the temples along its edge would have the morning sun rising behind them as well. East, always an important direction in Maya cosmology, took on even more importance at Lamanai because of the lagoon.

The city contains many of the standard elements of Maya cities, including large plazas, elite palaces, temples, and a ball court, but it does not have any *sacbeob* or reservoirs. The lagoon likely alleviated the need for both. Lamanai has nine stelae, the second highest number for sites north of the Belize River. The possible harbor at the northern end of the city is another feature of the urban environment, and it is easy to picture numerous perishable docks and structures facilitating canoe traffic at the lagoon's edge.

The temples at Lamanai reflect an idiosyncratic architectural style and demonstrate the city's strong commitment to community identity (see Powis 2002:520) rather than a desire to emulate other Classic period centers. The Lamanai Building Type—a pyramid platform with no superstructure and a chambered building across its stairs—likely developed at the site and became widespread at Lamanai in the Late Classic. A contemporary example is known from Altun Ha, however, indicating the style is not unique to Lamanai (see Pendergast 1969:Figure 3, 1981:35).

Altun Ha

Setting

Altun Ha is the exception that proves the rule that no major sites are located in the coastal plain of Belize. The site's core is built only 5 m above sea level on at least two low rises in the gently rolling landscape. The ceremonial precinct is about 8 km west of Midwinters Lagoon and only 12 km from the Caribbean Sea. David Pendergast (1979:7) describes the setting as "effectively coastal," as the land between the site and the lagoon grades into mangrove swamp within just a few kilometers. To the west and southwest of the site is a sandy pine ridge devoid of Maya occupation. Between this pine ridge and the coast, the area around the site is dotted with numerous swamps (Pendergast 1979:8). This area is near the southern end of the Northern Belize Chert Bearing Zone (Shafer and Hester 1984), and Pendergast (1979:23) reports many small chert quarries within the site and to the west and southwest along the edge of the pine ridge.

Describing the vegetation that covers the coastal region of Belize to someone who has never attempted to walk through it is challenging because what sounds like hyperbole is actually understatement. When David Pendergast began his research there, the site was covered entirely in secondary growth; the forest's recovery from clearing by the ancient Maya had been interrupted by logging at the beginning of the twentieth century and milpa agriculture in the 1930s (Pendergast 1979:8). In his monograph on the excavations, Pendergast (1979:8–9) poetically and accurately describes the vegetation:

The understorey of Altun Ha bush beggars description. In a few areas untouched by recent milpa-cutting, a partly open understorey existed on occasion, but the site was almost entirely covered with a tangle of plant life which made even the most spirited cutters lose heart on occasion. An unidentified plant of the genus *Piper* was the most common enemy whenever cutting had occurred within 6 to 8 years, but it had numerous allies, including unidentified vines, *Heliconia* spp., *Philodendron* spp., *Mimosa* sp. . . . , ferns of delightful size and density, and the ever-present, always-unwelcome basket tie-tie. . . . Festoons of this last-named species provided more than sufficient needlelike spines to keep one from daydreaming during bush-cutting, and where they diminished in quantity their role was assumed by the pork-and-doughboy palm . . . armoured guardian of the swamps. . . . If the foregoing description of the environmental setting of Altun Ha makes the area sound ill suited to agriculture, pocked with swamps, choked in near-impenetrable forest, and otherwise unattractive, the lists and descriptions have accomplished their intended purpose.

Investigations

Altun Ha was originally named Rockstone Pond, after the nearby Creole village. Although known to archaeologists prior to 1963, the site had not been studied until local villagers uncovered a carved jade pendant while quarrying a mound for stone. The archaeological commissioner, A. H. Anderson, invited David Pendergast to examine the artifact and inspect the site that summer. That initial examination resulted in 3 weeks of text excavations and launched a 7-year project sponsored by ROM that began in 1964 and ended in 1970, logging 40 months of field time at the site (Pendergast 1979:1). The initial purpose of the project was to excavate a site in the Belizean coastal zone since literally nothing was known about Maya settlement in that setting at the time. Once the excavations began, however, "the archaeology of Altun Ha provided constant surprises," and Pendergast (1979:1) came to realize the site had far greater significance than he could have anticipated. Early on during the project, Pendergast (1979:1–2) changed the name of the site to Altun Ha, which is Mayan for "rockstone water." The ROM work has so far resulted in the publication of three volumes of a planned five-volume monograph set (Pendergast 1979, 1982, 1990a). The first three volumes are beautifully illustrated and include numerous foldout maps.

The ROM work included consolidation of several large structures at the site core, and Altun Ha became an archaeological park with limited visitor facilities in the 1970s (Pendergast 1976). It has the distinct advantage of being only 35 road miles north of Belize City, making it the closest tourist site to Belize's largest city. This fact led to Altun Ha's selection as one of five sites that were excavated and consolidated by the TDP between 2000 and 2004 (Trein 2007:29). Given its proximity to Belize City, Altun Ha is frequently inundated with cruise ship passengers (Trein 2007:41).

Site Plan and Urban Features

The densely settled portion of Altun Ha occupies about 2 km² of area confined between the sandy pine ridge to the west and low, swampy land in other directions (Figure 9.7). The Central Precinct comprises Groups A and B, which include 15 structures built around two plazas. Smaller structures are located on all sides of the Central Precinct; the greatest number and density of buildings occur in a loose north–south line south of Plaza B. Pendergast (1979:16) notes that the density of buildings in the mapped area is 85 percent higher than in residential areas of Tikal and speculates that Altun Ha's physical setting, on low rises surrounded by swamps, is to blame for unusually high structure density. Terrain, however, does not explain the lack of consistency in structure orientation, which Pendergast (1979:17) attributes to "an idiosyncrasy in local world view," rather than a lack of a central planning authority.

Plaza A forms the northern end of the Central Precinct and measures approximately 100 m north–south by 65 m east–west (Figure 9.8). Around it are grouped seven structures that range in height from 17 m (Structure A-6) to less than 2 m (Structure A-7). Structure A-6 is the most massive building at the site and forms the northern limits of Plaza A (Figure 9.9). It consisted of a three-tiered platform with a wide central stairway. On its summit the platform supported a tandem range building with 13 doorways in both the front and rear walls. The two parallel rooms each measured over 47 m long and would have had vaulted ceilings with wooden lintels above the doorways when the building was in use (Pendergast 1979:175).

The other large buildings in Plaza A include three temples (Structures A-1, A-3, and A-5), one on each side of the plaza. Of these, Structure A-1 has the most complicated construction history and longest history of excavations, which began on the first day of the 1964 field season and continued intermittently until the close of the 1970 season (Pendergast 1979:40, 42). The final form of the structure was a vaulted building with two parallel rooms oriented north–south and two small transverse rooms at each end sitting on top of a

Figure 9.7. Map of Altun Ha, redrawn from Pendergast (1979:Map 2). Contour interval is 1 m.

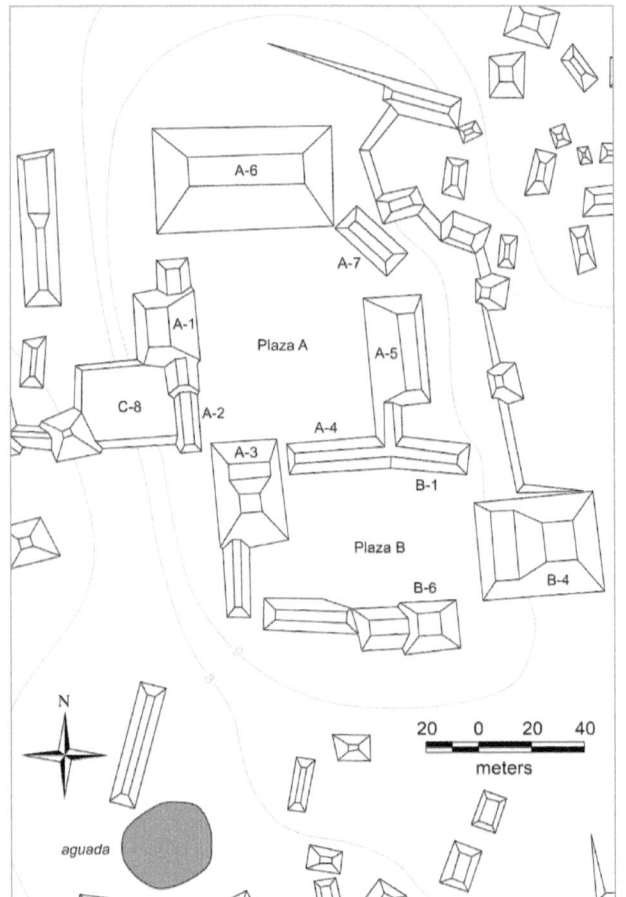

Figure 9.8. Map of Altun Ha Central Precinct, redrawn from Pendergast (1979:Map 2). Contour interval is 1 m.

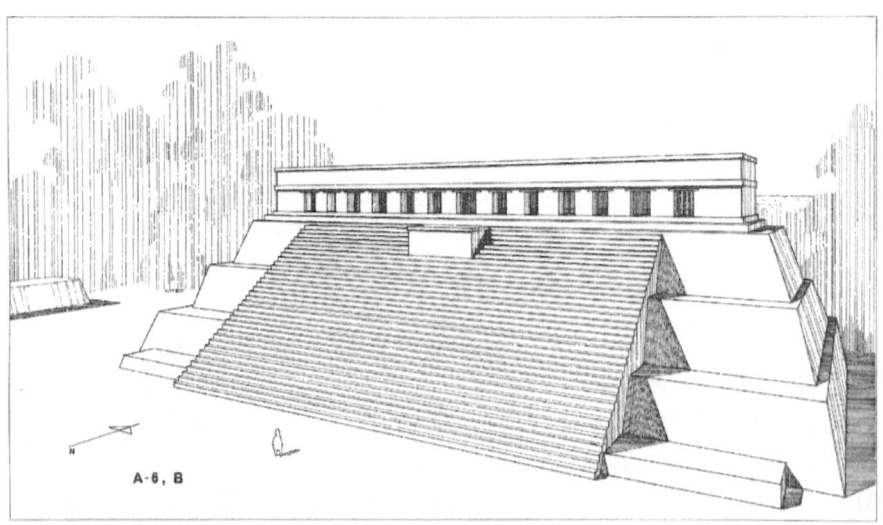

Figure 9.9. Perspective drawing of Structure A-6, B at Altun Ha, after Pendergast (1979:Figure 75). Courtesy of the Royal Ontario Museum.

terraced substructure with a broad stairway connecting it to the plaza. As noted in the following, the structure contained an amazingly rich tomb associated with the end of the Early Classic period, although the final phase of the building dates to Late Classic period (Pendergast 1979:92–93).

Plaza B is slightly smaller than Plaza A and measures 80 m east–west by 45 m north–south. It is framed by eight structures (two of which are also considered part of Plaza A) with highly inconsistent orientations. Unlike Plaza A, which follows the more "standard" plaza arrangement, as Pendergast (1982:144) describes it, Plaza B contains primarily residential structures and is dominated by a single ceremonial structure, Structure B-4, at its eastern end (Figure 9.10).

At 23 m tall, Structure B-4 is the tallest mound at Altun Ha. It is also distinguished by the facts that it was the most intensively studied structure at the site by the ROM project (Pendergast 1982:43), it contained the now famous jade head in one of its tombs, and its elevation drawing is part of the Belikin Beer logo. As it appears today, the structure is a massive tiered platform with a long, once-vaulted gallery near its base (Figure 9.11). A wide stairway summited the low platform supporting the vaulted building, and a second stairway behind led to the top of Structure B-4. Although Pendergast did not know it at the time, this style of building is common at Lamanai in the Late Classic period, where it is referred to as the Lamanai Building Type. The lower stairway

Figure 9.10. Perspective drawing of Group B at Altun Ha from the northwest with Structure B-4 on the left side of the illustration, after Pendergast (1982:Figure 85). Courtesy of the Royal Ontario Museum.

had a small stair block in the middle, the face of which was decorated with a stucco mask. Stucco masks also adorned two levels of outsets on either side of the stairs. The upper stairway was divided by a large stair block that begins about midway up its face. The platform did not have a building on its wide, flat summit. Rather, a round masonry altar sat along the primary axis of the mound.

ROM's excavations at Structure B-4 encountered seven royal tombs, and, beginning about 600 CE, each major modification to the building was associated with a new tomb (Pendergast 1982:134, 136). What is remarkable about these tombs is the staggering amount of wealth reflected in the grave goods. For example, Tomb 7 contained the jade head—a massive, 9.74-lb (4.42 kg) piece of jade carved in full-round into the head of K'inich Ahau, the Maya sun god—along with jade anklets, beads, and pendants, shell beads and pendants, antler pins, bone needles, fragments of hematite, the remains of a jaguar or

Figure 9.11. Photograph of Structure B-4 at Altun Ha. The version of the building that confronts visitors to Altun Ha today is an amalgamation of different phases of renovations and does not represent the structure as it looked at any point in its history. The final phase of the building had no altar, nor did it have the vaulted rooms at the base. It did, however, have the large stair block at the summit of the platform (photograph by the author).

puma and a smaller cat (ocelot, margay, or jaguarundi), and numerous other perishable items (Pendergast 1969:11–27, 1982:54–68). A cache below the floor of the tomb contained 13 chert eccentrics along with 2 ceramic vessels, charcoal, and jade beads (Pendergast 1969:27, 1982:68–70).

Outside the Central Precinct are scattered residential buildings and irregularly arranged courtyards (see Figure 9.7). Group E, with its 65 structures immediately south of Plaza B, is the most densely settled area of the site. At the southern end of the loose north–south alignment of the group is an approximately 200-m-long *sacbe* that connects to Group F at the southern end of the site.

Although a small group of only 19 structures, Group F is situated near the primary water source for the city, a large clay-lined pond, complete with a clay and stone dam west of Structure F-8 (Pendergast 1979:20–21). Excavations at Structure F-8 uncovered a square-based pyramid with five levels capped by a two-level platform, rather than a temple. The structure is architecturally unlike the temples of the Central Precinct, and the building contained an important Early Classic tomb and postinterment cache, discussed in the following.

The Central Precinct of Altun Ha was a heavily engineered landscape. Plaza A's final surface was canted slightly to direct runoff to the southwestern corner of the plaza, where it could drain into an *aguada* to the south (Pendergast 1979:39). Similarly, Plaza B's surface was engineered to keep runoff from Plaza A from entering Plaza B and to direct its own runoff to drain out of the southeastern corner of the plaza, ultimately into a depression east of Group E (Pendergast 1982:7).

Chronology

Altun Ha was initially settled in the Middle Preclassic period, about 800 BCE, and persisted as a small village through the Late Preclassic period (White et al. 2001:375–376). During these early centuries of the site's history, Altun Ha was not a major site; Vernon Scarborough (1991b:Table 10) suggests it was subordinate to Colha.

During the Early Classic period, Altun Ha experienced dramatic growth. The construction history of the plaza and buildings in Group A spans the Early Classic and early Late Classic periods (Pendergast 1979:199). In Group B, construction of the plaza probably began a little later than Group A but was certainly under way by the middle of the Early Classic period. By the close of the Early Classic, Plaza B contained early versions of several buildings, but traffic flow through the group would have been relatively unrestricted (Pendergast 1982:143). In the Central Precinct as a whole, by the end of the Early

Classic Plaza A had taken on its final form, and Plaza B's basic layout had been established.

About 700 m to the south, Early Classic construction at Group F is also apparent, and it is possible Structure F-8 was as important as any temple in the Central Precinct during the first part of the period. Construction at Structure F-8 began around 150 to 200 CE and ceased after 300 CE, although other buildings in the group continued to be modified into the Late Classic period (Pendergast 1990a:277).

During the Late Classic, Altun Ha continued to grow. The dense settlement in Group E began around 400 CE but witnessed a major burst of construction activity about 650 CE (Pendergast 1990a:243). The same pattern is also true of Group C, the cluster of mounds and courtyards west of the Central Precinct (Pendergast 1982:260).

In Group A major construction continued through the first century of the Late Classic, and tapered off to a period of building modification through the middle of the period. After that, the elite of Altun Ha continued to use the buildings around Plaza A until the end of the Late Classic, but they ceased to modify existing buildings or to construct new ones (Pendergast 1979:199). The focus of their building efforts shifted to Group B. The massive pyramid, Structure B-4, became the site of repeated expansions associated with a succession of Late Classic divine kings who used the pyramid as their funerary monument until the mid-ninth century (Pendergast 1982:138).

Occupation at Altun Ha persisted into the Terminal Classic, and Pendergast (1979, 1982, 1990a) documents what he calls "post-abandonment activity" at virtually every building in the Central Precinct. Early Postclassic pilgrims left Lamanai-style ceramic vessels on the tops of some mounds, and someone left behind shallow burials in the collapse debris on structures in the Central Precinct. The site was briefly and lightly reoccupied in the Late Postclassic period, in what was an obvious break with the Classic period population (Pendergast 1986:224).

Political History

Altun Ha began as a small village, below Colha, Cerros, and Nohmul in terms of size and presumably influence during the Late Preclassic period (Scarborough 1991b:Table 10). Stone tools made of Colha-like chert in Late Preclassic contexts at Altun Ha suggest the villagers imported tools from their neighbor to the north (Santone 1997:Table 2). However, the archaeological record hints at the stirrings of the site's political importance during the Early Classic period. The Early Classic tomb from Structure F-8 suggests that a king with connections to Teotihuacan ruled Altun Ha around 250 CE. The evidence for this claim comes from a cache placed on top of the tomb. The builders of the tomb capped the chamber with over 10,000 artifacts, mostly chert debitage, but also jade beads and pendants (whole and fragmented), slate laminae, shell, animal teeth, 248 pieces of green Pachuca obsidian, and 23 ceramic vessels from a Teotihuacan source (Pendergast 2003:238). The Pachuca obsidian artifacts constitute "all the elements of a Teotihuacan offering" and include eight humanoid eccentrics (Pendergast 2003:238–239). Isotope analysis determined the individual in the tomb was not from Teotihuacan (Pendergast 2003:243). Because no other Teotihuacan-related material has been found at Altun Ha, deciphering the significance and nature of the relationship between the two cities is difficult, but Pendergast (2003:246) interprets the offering as an attempt to honor the king in the tomb and not the polity at large.

The later tombs at Altun Ha attest to the tremendous wealth of the elite and particularly the rulers of the city. They all, with two exceptions, remain anonymous. The person buried in Tomb A-1/1 was likely a ruler of the site, given the tomb's wealth and placement in a temple in Group A. He was interred near the end of the Early Classic period with a large number of jade artifacts, ceramic vessels, and chert eccentrics (Pendergast 1979:61–82). Three glyph blocks adorned each of a pair of jade ear ornaments in the tomb, which Peter Mathews (1979:79–80) reads as identifying the owner with the name "? Bat ?."

A carved jade plaque from Tomb B-4/6 includes a portrait of a ruler on one side and a hieroglyphic text on the other. A plausible reading of the text indicates that a lord, whose name cannot be read, made a conquest in 569 CE and took the throne of Altun Ha in 584 CE with the royal name "Akbal Lord." The text names his mother as "Lady Sky" and his father as "Katun" (Pendergast 1982:85). Although the jade plaque is a portable object and could refer to another site, Pendergast (1982:85) is comfortable with concluding the ruler portrayed on the front of the plaque is "Akbal Lord" and that the emblem glyph presented in the text is Altun Ha's.

The introduction of a distinct building style from Lamanai during the Late Classic period at Structure B-4 may indicate ties between the two cities' ruling families. During the last two and a half centuries of Altun Ha's occupation, the ruling dynasty at Altun Ha used this temple to house a series of sumptuous royal tombs. They ruled over a wealthy kingdom on the very edge of the Maya lowlands from this rather atypical building.

While connections to Lamanai are not surprising, suspected ties to southern Belize are, at the very least, intriguing. Wanyerka's (2009:676) study of hieroglyphic texts from multiple sites indicates "Altun Ha was deeply involved in the Late Classic politics of southern Belize." Pusilhá Stela D may reference a battle at Altun Ha in 595 CE, although that interpretation is speculative (Wanyerka 2009:339). Nim Li Punit Stela 2 makes an apparent reference to an *ajaw* from Altun Ha who oversaw the accession of Nim Li Punit's king B'ahlam Te' alongside another foreign lord from Copán in 726 CE. The same stela records that an Altun Ha lord and Copán lord celebrated the 9.15.0.0.0 period ending at Nim Li Punit five years later (Wanyerka 2009:675–676).

Discussion

Altun Ha's near coastal setting in a low, swampy area affected its urban features and city planning. Despite being virtually surrounded by swamps, maintaining adequate supplies of potable water was clearly a concern for city planners. The city's setting also certainly affected the density of settlement, which is much higher than is found at most Classic period Maya cities. And, despite the previously noted haphazard arrangement of buildings and courtyards surrounding the Central Precinct, Pendergast (1990a:243) suggested that the residential structures might be organized into neighborhoods. If so, then Group E, 100–200 m southwest of Plaza B and built around an *aguada*, was apparently the wealthiest neighborhood at the site based on the quality of architecture and grave goods (Pendergast 1990a:243).

Despite the obvious wealth of Altun Ha's elite and ruling family, key features are missing from the city's architectural inventory. First, the site has no ball court. Second, it has no stone monuments. Third, it has few palaces and no acropolis. Other elements of the architectural inventory are present but differ dramatically from the norm. For example, Altun Ha's major temples are radically different from temples at other Maya cities, particularly Structure B-4, with its flat summit and masonry altar.

In a similar vein, while Altun Ha has two *sacbeob*, one of them appears to connect nothing to another group of nothing in the Group C area of the site. Pendergast (1979:19) suggests that the causeway is associated with Structure C-13, one of the largest and earliest buildings in that part of the site, but that building is over 60 m away from the northern end of the *sacbe*. The southern end terminates in an open area that is not associated with a plaza or structures.

Returning to the puzzling lack of stone monuments, it is possible that the quarries around the site were not capable of producing stones suitable for carving or large enough to serve as stelae. Transporting stela-sized stones from elsewhere would have been extremely difficult given the terrain around the site.

Discussion and Concluding Remarks

The three cities discussed in this chapter demonstrate the tremendous variety in Maya urbanism in northern Belize and the degree to which city plans were affected by location. Nohmul follows a minor regional pattern of city planning shared with Aventura and El Pozito, first noted by Norman Hammond (1981:165). In this site-planning scheme, the major architecture is split into two principal clusters of plazas separated by open ground or connected by a *sacbe*, as in the Nohmul case.

At Lamanai, the New River Lagoon affected urban growth and city planning for nearly 2,000 years. An apparent desire to incorporate the lagoon as a backdrop for many of the major structures at the site resulted in the linear growth of the site core, with the focal point of ceremonial life gradually moving through time from north to south.

At Altun Ha, city planners faced a harsh environment in which to build a large city. The loose arrangement of buildings and the lack of standard structure types and features would suggest the city's builders had less concern for such conventions than their peers. In stark contrast to this indifferent attitude toward urban design is the remarkable wealth evidenced in the tombs and caches at Altun Ha.

The following two chapters consider the Classic period cities from the five geographic areas of Belize together to look for patterns. Chapter 10 examines planning while chapter 11 considers meaning.

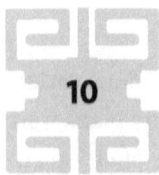

Comparisons and Urban Planning

This chapter treats the cities covered by this book as a group to highlight various aspects of urban planning in the eastern lowlands. The discussion begins by comparing the cities to illuminate similarities and differences. A major component of this is evaluating the sizes of sites, a task that is more difficult than might be imagined. A qualitative comparison of certain aspects of the cities in the sample follows. Rather than considering all the features of site plans described in chapters 5 through 9, the ones that highlight the most diversity are considered here: plazas, carved monuments, ball courts, and causeways. The chapter closes by applying Michael Smith's (2007) approach to studying ancient urban planning to the cities of the eastern lowlands. Described in more detail below, Smith (2007) proposes that planning can be examined by looking at the coordination of buildings within cities and the standardization of cities. The first approach is used to evaluate individual urban plans while the second looks at a group of cities to identify common planning characteristics.

Rank Ordering

As long as there have been debates about whether or not the Maya had cities, there has been disagreement between scholars about how to compare cities at the most basic level: size (see Adams and Jones 1981). How do you objectively measure the size of a Maya city? In the modern Western world, cities exist as political subdivisions with carefully surveyed limits, and, in the United States, every 10 years the federal government counts the number of citizens living in each city as part of the national census. With these kinds of data, it is quite easy to compare two cities by size, population, or population density. Imagine, however, if an archaeologist were to visit the ruins of an American city a thousand years from now, long after the printed and electronically stored data on city limits and population had turned to dust and electrons. How would he or she determine the size of cities? In many parts of the country, it would be fairly easy to establish boundaries around cities based on the limits of suburban settlement and adjacent farmland, but on the East Coast or along the I-35 corridor in Texas a future archaeologist might have trouble drawing accurate boundaries. Population would be even trickier. Which structures were residential? Were they all occupied at the same time? How many people lived in each house? Each apartment?

Archaeologists face the same problems when trying to determine the size and population of ancient cities. A compounding issue in the Maya area is the incomplete nature of the data on settlement distribution away from the epicenter of most sites. In most parts of the Maya world, archaeologists must physically walk survey transects to map and count ancient structures; therefore, only a small sample of the entire area of the lowlands has been carefully mapped, although the application of LiDAR promises to change that (e.g., Chase et al. 2012).

It is clear, however, that there is tremendous variation in the size of Maya cities based strictly on comparing their site cores. The average tourist who visits Caracol one day and Pusilhá the next can tell you that Caracol is larger—much larger, in fact—even though each city has an emblem glyph and impressive numbers of carved stone monuments, signaling a degree of political autonomy.

Richard E. W. Adams and Richard C. Jones (1981:303) proposed that an objective method of comparing Maya cities based strictly on published site maps was to quantify their paved areas by counting the number of courtyards. The reasoning behind this approach is that the monumental architecture at Maya cities is grouped around plazas and courtyards despite differences in the function of buildings (i.e., temples, palaces, ball courts, etc.). Adams and Jones (1981:304, 306) recognized problems in this system based on "sample quality and size" but still presented a rank ordering of Maya cities to look for evidence of hierarchical organization within various regions of the lowlands. Using their data as published in 1981, our hypothetical tourist could tell you that Caracol scored a 17 on the courtyard count, while Pusilhá only scored a 3, thus confirming in a quantifiable way the size difference between the two cities.

However, just as no two archaeologists will produce identical maps of a Maya site, no two archaeologists will count courtyards the same way. Thomas Garrison (2007:263) noted that, using the same map, one study counted 7 courtyards at the site of Xultun, while a second study listed 20 courtyards.

Turner et al. (1981) proposed a more sophisticated system to rank-order cities based on area and volume of construction, weighted based on other cultural features, but the method is difficult to employ and has not been widely adapted.

Thomas Guderjan (1991c:104) took the same conceptual approach—that "volume of construction . . . is directly related to political authority and power"—and modified Adams' and Jones' original courtyard counting system to include structures over 10 meters tall and "hallmarks of political power" like stelae and ball courts to compare Maya sites in northwestern Belize. Garrison (2007:267) later applied Guderjan's modified system to look at a larger sample of sites in northwestern Belize and northeastern Petén. Stated as an equation, the modified system proposed by Guderjan (1991c:104) looks like this:

(number of courtyards) + (number of ball courts) + (number of stelae) + (number of plazas × 2) + (number of 10-m-tall buildings × 0.5) = site score

While Adams (1999:195) praised the modifications to his system for its ability "to more clearly define ancient political and economic relationships among sites," it is not entirely evident that the arbitrary weights assigned to various categories are meaningful. Furthermore, the same difficulty in counting courtyards still exists but is now compounded by the fact that plazas carry additional weight. Another complication is that most published maps do not include the heights of structures, requiring supporting data to determine how many buildings are 10 m or taller. And why not give a higher score to buildings taller than 20 m, or 30 m?

In the original Adams and Jones (1981:303) study, counting courtyards was a proxy for making quantitative assessments of the paved areas at sites. Turning back to their original premise, this chapter uses a system for comparing the sizes of cities that measures the horizontal area covered by monumental architecture in the epicenter. The analytical foundation behind this approach is that the built environment of the civic-ceremonial architecture of a city's epicenter represents the end product of the labor and resources required for its construction. Therefore, a bigger plaza, for example, represents more labor and raw material than a smaller one and expresses a stronger statement about political power through its monumentality—consider that artificially constructed horizontal spaces and not just tall buildings make such statements. This is an example of middle-level meaning, which was discussed in chapter 2, and is the reason why our hypothetical tourist is likely more awestruck by the towering buildings and broad plazas at Caracol than she is by the smaller ones at Pusilhá.

The process of comparing cities using this method is rather straightforward but not entirely without problems. For example, what is considered part of the epicenter and what is not? The litmus test is function and scale: if a group of architecture appears to have a public function, like a big plaza with stelae, temples, and ball courts, or if it clearly required community participation in its construction, such as an acropolis or elite palace, I include it in the calculation. In this manner, *sacbeob*, which are not considered in the models described earlier, contribute to the equation because they represent important elements of the built environment. The volume of construction mass is lost, however, in this system of comparison. The sheer mass of the largest Maya buildings communicated much about the political power of the ruling families to citizens of and visitors to their cities. As a result, some cities, like Caracol and Xunantunich, may not score as high in this system as they would in another because the monumentality of very tall buildings like Caana and the Castillo is minimized. Other cities, however, such as those in southern Belize with their "Hollywood Set" style of construction, may be ranked higher in this system than they would be in one that included construction volume as a variable.

Even though my method of comparing core areas is rather simple to do, problems arise from inconsistencies in how sites have been mapped. For example, the published maps of Uxbenka are topographic maps with prismatic structure outlines superimposed on them. They do not include prismatic outlines of plaza platforms, and the system used here includes plazas and platforms in its calculations. To calculate site core area, a computer drafting program is used to create polygons representing the areas of monumental architecture. By scaling the drawings, it is possible to calculate the surface area of each polygon. These areas are added together for each site to derive the monumental core area. Table 10.1 lists the areas, data sources, and technical issues with each site, and Figure 10.1 shows the monumental areas of the sites used in the calculations at the same scale.

To flesh out the context for the cities discussed in this volume, Table 10.1 includes an arbitrary sample of other Classic period cities. By no means is the list intended to be complete or even representative, but it includes a number of additional sites with published site maps. The table includes regions so that the cities can be compared to one another in terms of proximity, and, even though not all sites are listed, the largest sites from each region appear on the table, which allows for comparisons across regions.

Table 10.1. Site core area calculations

City	Region[a]	Monumental Area (m²)	Map Source	Issues (see notes)
Caracol	VP	236,955	D. Chase and A. Chase 2004c:Figure 1	1, 2
Lamanai	NB	109,385	Pendergast 1981:Figure 3	3
Nohmul	NB	86,393	Hammond 1981:Figure 7.2A	
La Milpa	NWB	82,156	Hammond and Tourtellot 2004:Figure 31.1	4
El Pilar	BV	74,206	Ford 2004:Figure 15.2	5
Xunantunich	BV	73,690	LeCount and Yaeger 2010a:Figure 1.1	
Chan Chich	NWB	68,469	Houk 2012b:Figure 1.3	6
Buenavista del Cayo	BV	65,407	Yaeger et al. 2009:Figure 3	3
Ka'Kabish	NB	62,159	Haines 2011:Figure 2	
Gran Cacao	NWB	57,201	Lohse 1995:Figure 2	
Baking Pot	BV	56,249	Audet 2006:Figure 3.5	1
Maax Na	NWB	53,778	King et al. 2012:Figure 2	3, 7
Pusilhá	SB	51,741	Braswell, Prager, Bill, Schwake, and Braswell 2005:Figures 2–4; Pitcavage and Braswell 2010:Figure 1	3
Dos Hombres	NWB	47,014	Houk 2003:Figure 5.2	
Altun Ha	NB	46,423	Pendergast 1979:Map 2	1, 3
Tipan Chen Uitz	BV	41,316	Andres et al. 2011:Figure 2	
Pacbitun	BV	38,054	Healy, Hohmann, and Powis 2004:Figure 13.1	1, 8
Uxbenka	SB	35,855	Prufer 2007:Figure 2	3
Blue Creek	NWB	35,775	Driver 2002:Figure 4	
Minanha	VP	32,916	Iannone 2005:Figure 3	
Lubaantun	SB	32,306	Hammond 1975:Figure 21	
Yalbac	BV	29,409	Lucero 2007:Figure 2	3
Punta de Cacao	NWB	25,391	Guderjan et al. 1991:Figure 50	9
Nim Li Punit	SB	23,161	Leventhal 1990:Figure 8.2	3
San José	NWB	18,918	Thompson 1939:Figure 1	3

Notes: [a] Region Key: NB, northern Belize; NWB, northwestern Belize; BV, Belize Valley; VP, Vaca Plateau; and SB, southern Belize.

1. Intrasite causeway(s) add(s) to site core area.
2. Only area depicted on published figure included in calculation.
3. Edges of plazas and/or artificial platforms not consistently depicted on map.
4. Two elite courtyards included in calculation because they contain thrones.
5. Causeway's area calculated based only on parapets because the causeway itself is not elevated. Possible causeway in Guatemala not included in calculations.
6. Large eastern intrasite causeway adds to site core area. Western causeway's area calculated based only on parapets because the causeway itself is not elevated for its entire length.
7. Large open areas with few structures; score is probably inflated.
8. "Tzul Causeway" not included in calculation.
9. Likely causeway (personal observation) linking ball court and two groups of architecture included in calculation, but feature does not appear on published maps.

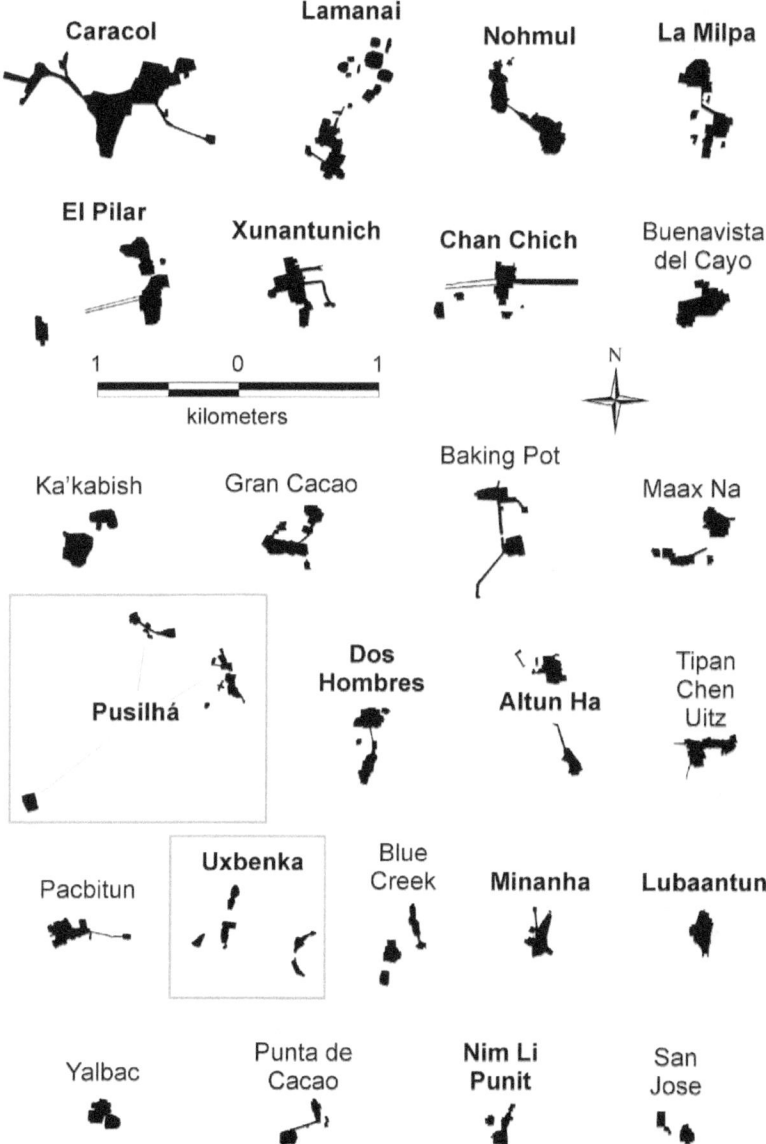

Figure 10.1. Site core areas shown at common scale.

In terms of monumental area within site cores, Caracol is over twice as large as the next largest city, Lamanai, and that is probably an understatement based on how Caracol's area was calculated. In northwestern Belize and the Belize Valley, the largest cities fall in the 74,000–87,000 m² range, approximately one-third the size of Caracol. The largest city in southern Belize, however, is less than 22 percent the size of Caracol. The differences in size are reflected on Figure 10.2.

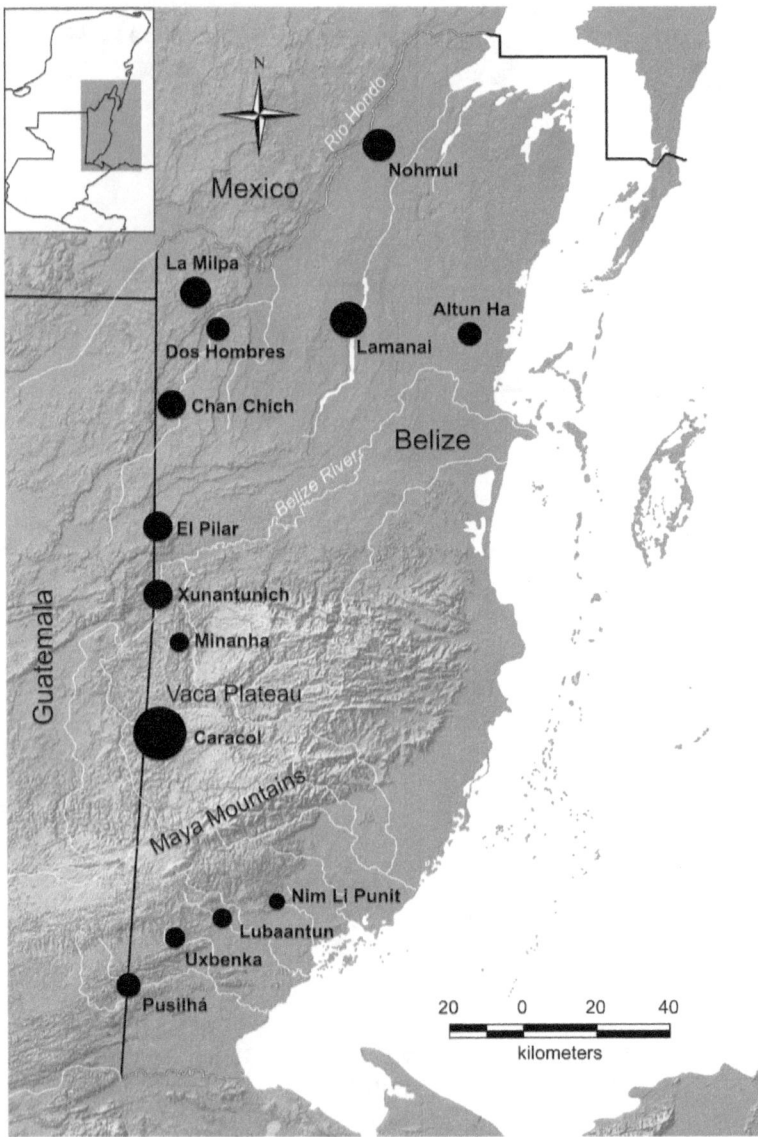

Figure 10.2. Cities in this volume presented at an exaggerated, but common, scale to illustrate size differences in monumental cores. Base map courtesy NASA/JPL-Caltech, SRTM mission.

Patterns, Trends, and Observations

Size alone is not the only useful way to compare Maya cities. The tables in this section include only the cities discussed in this book to highlight a number of points. Although the discussion is subdivided into topics, there is a tremendous amount of overlap because so many of the urban features are interrelated. By necessity, some observations are more involved than others.

Emblem Glyphs

Most but not all of the cities have known emblem glyphs (Table 10.2); those that do not have emblem glyphs include sites with either no stelae (El Pilar and Nohmul) or with stelae lacking texts (plain or eroded). As Altun Ha and Lubaantun demonstrate, stelae are not a requirement for possessing an emblem glyph. I would also argue that the old adage that "absence of evidence is not evidence of absence" applies in this case. Because an emblem glyph has not been discovered does not mean that a city did not at one time possess one; therefore, that El Pilar, Nohmul, or Chan Chich do not have emblem glyphs should not be used to make arguments that those cities were by default always politically subordinate to one of their neighbors or did not have their own royal families.

Plazas

Plazas are "owed primacy in understanding site layouts" because they are the central organizing unit in Maya cities (Ringle and Bey 2001). Maya plazas served a range of functions, as described in chapter 2, and represented sizeable construction projects in their own right. This section is more concerned with plaza form, size, and variability than it is with function because the goal is to highlight similarities and differences in city plans. Table 10.2 contains information on the largest plazas at the cities covered in this book. The open plaza area is defined as the space between the front bases of buildings around the plaza minus the footprint of any structures within the plaza. In the case of a ball court in a plaza, the area taken up by both structures and the playing alley between them was subtracted from the plaza area. Archaeologists often refer to the "main plaza" at a site so definitively and confidently that the uninformed visitor might assume the Maya left a sign that designated it as such. The term, however, is a descriptive construct that archaeologists impose on the data. In a city with more than one plaza, one of them usually stands out as the largest, as the one surrounded by the biggest buildings, and as the location of the majority of the stone monuments at the site. In this case, the label is not likely to cause confusion and is probably an accurate reflection of the importance of that plaza as an urban feature at that particular city. Plaza A, also known as the Great Plaza, at La Milpa is an example of this type of plaza: it is by far the largest space at the site, and it contains four of the five largest structures at the site, the city's two ball courts, and easily more than 90 percent of the stone monuments in the site core.

As Table 10.2 demonstrates, it is not always clear which plaza is the main

Table 10.2. Comparisons of cities

City	Region[1]	Monumental Area (meters²)	Emblem Glyph	Stelae Stela	Stela Density[2]	Period of Stela Use (k'atuns)
Altun Ha	NB	46,423	Yes	0	0.0	0.0
Caracol	VP	236,955	Yes	24	1.0	23.3
Chan Chich	NWB	68,469	No	1	0.1	?
Dos Hombres	NWB	47,014	No	3	0.6	?
El Pilar	BV	74,206	No	0	0.0	0.0
La Milpa	NWB	82,156	Yes	23	2.8	19.3
Lamanai	NB	109,385	Yes	9	0.8	?
Lubaantun	SB	32,306	Yes	0	0.0	0
Minanha	VP	32,916	No	8	2.4	?
Nim Li Punit	SB	23,161	Yes	21	9.1	3.9
Nohmul	NB	86,393	No	0	0.0	0.0
Pusilhá	SB	51,741	Yes	22	4.3	9.0
Uxbenka	SB	35,855	Yes	23	6.4	20.4
Xunantunich	BV	73,690	Yes	9	1.2	?

Notes: 1. Region Key: NB, northern Belize; NWB, northwestern Belize; BV, Belize Valley; VP, Vaca Plateau; and SB, southern Belize.
2. Stela density is number of stelae per 10,000 m² of monumental area.
3. Stela frequency is the number of stelae erected per *k'atun* for cities with estimated beginning and ending dates of stelae use.
4. Percentage of monumental area by plaza is calculated by dividing open plaza area (the space between the front bases of buildings around the plaza, minus the footprint of any structures within the plaza) by monumental area.

plaza. This is particularly true at the cities in southern Belize, where the largest plaza is not necessarily the stela plaza at the site. In fact, Uxbenka's stela plaza is the smallest plaza at the site, and at Pusilhá the stela plaza is nearly one-third the size of the Moho Plaza. This pattern contrasts sharply with La Milpa, which has a comparable number of stela but a truly massive main plaza. In fact, the Great Plaza at La Milpa could accommodate the stela plazas at Uxbenka, Pusilhá, and Nim Li Punit and still have over 11,000 m² of open space to spare.

Stela Frequency[3]	Ball Courts	Causeways	Plazas		
			Main Plazas	Open Plaza Area (m²)	Percentage of Monumental Area[4]
0.00	0	2	Plaza A	5,390	11.6%
1.03	2	36	B (Caana plaza)	8,220	3.5%
?	1	2	Plaza A-1	12,490	18.2%
?	2	1	Plaza A-1	11,650	24.8%
0.00	2	1	Plaza Copal	12,240	16.5%
1.04	2	1	Great Plaza	17,710	21.6%
?	1	0	High Temple plaza	6,600	6.0%
0.00	3	0	Plaza V	1,950	6.0%
?	1	1	Plaza A	6,700	20.4%
5.45	1	0	Stela Plaza	1,840	7.9%
0.00	1	1	"Giant Plaza"	13,460	15.6%
			Great Plaza	4,540	5.3%
2.44	3 or 4	1	Moho Plaza	7,050	13.6%
			Stela Plaza	2,560	5.0%
1.13	2	1	Group E Plaza	3,700	10.3%
			Group B Plaza	2,260	6.3%
			Group C Plaza	2,120	5.9%
			Stela Plaza	1,930	5.4%
?	2	3	Plazas A-I and A-II	9,550	13.0%
			Plaza A-I	5,010	6.8%

La Milpa's Great Plaza is over 130 percent larger than the next largest plaza in the sample, the "Giant Plaza" at Nohmul (the space that existed prior to about 800 CE), and is nearly 150 percent larger than the Plaza Copal at El Pilar. While La Milpa's main plaza is the largest, other cities in northwestern Belize also have unusually expansive plazas, a pattern I noted in an earlier study of cities in the region (Houk 1996:315). To gauge just how large these plazas are, Table 10.2 includes a column that expresses open plaza area as a percentage of the monumental area of each site. In northwestern Belize, Dos Hombres tops the list at 25 percent, followed by La Milpa (22 percent) and Chan Chich (18 percent). The only other site with a plaza larger than 18 percent of its monumental area is Minanha (20 percent), a much smaller city than the other three. In contrast, the stela plazas at the cities in southern Belize all account for less than 8 percent of their respective site's monumental area, and the plaza in front of Caana at Caracol comprises only 3.5 percent of that great city's monumental area.

Carved Monuments

Many of the sites in this study have stone monuments, including stelae and altars. Pusilhá has four zoomorphic altars, which are unique in the eastern lowlands. Their closest counterparts are at Quiriguá, Guatemala. Stelae, however, are the most common kind of stone monument and the most consistently documented in archaeological reports. They are, thus, the focus of this section.

From the outset, however, be aware that the following discussion is fraught with unavoidable problems that render these comparisons little more than a thought experiment. These problems fall into two general categories: counting stelae and preference for stelae.

A number of factors have the potential to throw off our counts of stelae at Maya sites. First, the Maya sometimes buried stelae during the renovations of major buildings. Second, stelae have the tendency to walk off, as they say. In particular, carved stelae are sometimes looted from sites because of their high values on the art market. Third, the Maya occasionally destroyed stelae when they conquered another city-state. Therefore, the numbers of stelae presented for each city are really an approximate count and are always a minimum number possible.

The second category of problem is related to the idiosyncratic displays of political power at sites. Not all Maya cities used stelae; some preferred other forms of artistic expression to convey the same kind of information. For example, at Palenque in Mexico, there is only one stela. Instead, rulers placed their portraits in stucco adornment directly on buildings (Sanchez 2005). Unfortunately, a stucco facade on a Maya building was the first thing to fall off following abandonment, making it difficult to infer even if one was present, much less interpret its iconography. This issue is not as significant as the question of missing stelae in the eastern lowlands because the regional trend appears to have been a preference for stelae when appropriate raw material was available.

The presence of stelae at a site is often considered an indication of some degree of political independence; one of the markers of Tikal's political weakness at the end of the Early Classic period is the fact that four consecutive kings did not—perhaps because Calakmul did not allow them to—erect any stelae in the 130-year period following the defeat of the city in 562 CE (Martin and Grube 2008:40; Sharer and Traxler 2006:377). That stelae were targets of desecration and destruction following a military defeat is another indication of their status as symbols of royal power (see Sharer and Traxler 2006:377).

As the data from the eastern lowlands demonstrate, the presence of stelae does not correspond to site size (i.e., not all large cities have stelae), nor are stelae necessary for a city to possess an emblem glyph. In some areas, the decision whether or not to erect stelae may have been affected by the available stone resources. Some areas, like southern Belize, have bedrock capable of producing large monuments that can be shaped and carved while other areas, like northern and northwestern Belize, have bedrock poorly suited to monument making. The limestone in northwestern Belize, for example, is coarse grained and often full of inclusions, which limits the size of stelae and makes them poorly suited for carving. Plain stelae may have once been decorated with stucco and painted, and it is possible Maya kings made do with wooden monuments in areas with poor stone resources. We know that some sites had carved wooden lintels, so the proposition that the Maya had wooden stelae is not far-fetched, but it is certainly unverified. If wooden monuments were ever used, the kings that dedicated them would have known they would not last long in the tropical climate of the lowlands and would therefore be a poor substitute for the long-lived stone stelae.

In our sample, only five cities have more than 21 stelae, and three of those are southern Belize cities (Table 10.2). La Milpa, with 23 (including 3 from its secondary centers), and Caracol with 24 are both situated close to the Petén, where there was a long-lived tradition of stelae use. Caracol boasts a large number of carved altars and ball court markers in addition to its stelae. While La Milpa has perhaps a dozen altars, none are carved.

Another way to compare stelae is to express them as a density, such as, in this case, the number of stelae per 10,000 m^2 of monumental area. Despite their high numbers of monuments, Caracol and La Milpa have stela densities of 1 and 2.4 per 10,000 m^2, respectively.

While high numbers of stone monuments at Caracol and La Milpa are not surprising given the sizes of those two cities, the southern Belize sites are remarkable because they are much smaller cities with equally high numbers of monuments and dramatically higher stela densities (4.3–9.1). Caracol, we know from multiple lines of evidence, exercised considerable political power over its smaller neighbors and was an important member of Calakmul's alliance; La Milpa was likely the dominant center in its corner of the world, at least during the Late Classic period. The southern Belize cities, however, never were able to dominate their neighbors, and they seem to have coexisted "as small regional polities" during the eighth century; their politically weak kings, who could not muster the force to dominate their neighbors, carved stelae (at Pusilhá, Uxbenka, and Nim Li Punit) and constructed elaborate hilltop acropoli (at Pusilhá and Lubaantun) to express their status (Braswell and Prufer 2009:51–52).

Another curious feature of the southern Belize cities with stelae is the manner in which they were displayed. In contrast to Caracol, where stelae are found across the site, or La Milpa, where most stelae are found in the largest plaza, the vast majority of stelae at the southern cities of Nim Li Punit, Uxbenka, and Pusilhá are grouped together in very small stela plazas. Perhaps Prufer and colleagues (2011:218) put it best when he described the stela plaza at Uxbenka as a "monument garden"; the phrase highlights the intimacy of the architectural setting for the royal monuments at the sites.

The lack of stelae at Nohmul is explained by its periods of florescence and at Altun Ha possibly explained by the city's geographic location, as is the slightly below-expected density at Lamanai (0.8). The complete lack of monuments at Lubaantun and El Pilar is harder to understand. To explain the lack of stelae at Lubaantun, Hammond (1981:179) speculated that perhaps Lubaantun and Nim Li Punit were dual capitals of the same polity, with the former serving a political and economic role and the latter acting as the "dynastic cult center" for the ruling dynasty. Braswell and Prufer (2009:46) conclude the sites are too far apart for that to be the case, and the 15-km distance between them is the typical spacing between major sites in the region and other parts of the eastern lowlands, including the Belize Valley and northwestern Belize. As noted in chapter 5, another possibility is that Lubaantun's rulers founded their city at a time when stelae use was waning, and they were simply not concerned with the practice.

The low stela density at Dos Hombres and Chan Chich may indicate very short spans of political independence for those two cities. However, the ages of the stelae are unknown, so their dedications cannot be tied into the cities' chronologies. This observation does bring up another important consideration: stela density is likely related to not only the size of a center but to time as well. Maya cities grew incrementally, and stelae are another component of the built environment that also accumulated incrementally. A city may have experienced architectural growth even during times of political subjugation, but rulers were unlikely to erect stelae during those periods.

To examine the temporal aspects of stela dedication, we can chart stela frequency by first estimating the duration of monument use (based on the oldest and youngest monument dates) and then dividing that age span by the number of monuments erected during that period. This method obscures punctuated flurries of monument dedication, assumes that we know the beginning and ending dates of stelae use, and is more subject to error than stela density, but it provides a composite picture. To estimate the period of monument dedication at a particular city, we need reasonable beginning and ending dates, and unfortunately we only have those data for La Milpa, Caracol, Uxbenka, Pusilhá, and Nim Li Punit.

At La Milpa, rulers were erecting stelae as early as about 400 CE (based on stylistic comparisons) and as late as 780 CE, a period of approximately 19.3 k'atuns. For reasons illuminated in the following, the k'atun—a period of 7,200 days—is more useful than a solar year when discussing stela frequency. The city has 20 known monuments within the site's epicenter (three at secondary centers are not considered in this analysis), which equates to a stela frequency of 1.04 stelae per k'atun (Table 10.2). At Caracol, monument dedication began about the same time but lasted to ca. 859 CE (23.3 k'atuns), and the stela frequency for Caracol is 1.03 stelae per k'atun.

Given the much higher stela density counts in southern Belize, one might expect the model to completely fall apart. However, it works surprisingly well at Uxbenka where, if we assume a period of stela dedication between roughly 378 and 780 CE (20.4 k'atuns), the stelae frequency is 1.13. Pusilhá, however, has a much higher frequency of 2.44, with 22 stelae erected in approximately 9 k'atuns. Nim Li Punit is the real curve buster, with a stela frequency of 5.45 between roughly 734 and 810 CE—this calculation does not include the strange Short Count monument that may date to 830 CE, nor does it consider the possibility that some undated stelae may actually be associated with the newly documented Early Classic occupation at the site.

This thought experiment suggests that during periods of stelae use—perhaps indicating political autonomy—rulers erected monuments at the pace of about one stela per k'atun, likely as part of a k'atun-ending celebration, with about one additional stela every 100 to 200 years or so to commemorate other important events. This is really not a surprising revelation, but it suggests that most plain or eroded stelae were likely erected as part of k'atun-ending celebrations as well.

As a test of the model, we can apply it to Minanha and Xunantunich, two cities for which we cannot calculate time spans for monument dedication. Both of these cities are located in areas where stela use at apparently independent centers was common, and both flourished over short spans of time. Minanha's eight stelae imply a period of monument use spanning 7.69 k'atuns, using an average stelae frequency of 1.04 stelae per k'atun. Counting back from 810 CE, when Minanha's royal court apparently fell from power (Iannone 2005:34), 7.69 k'atuns suggests an approximate beginning date of 658 CE, which is only 17 years earlier than the proposed founding of the dynasty based on other lines of evidence (e.g., Iannone et al. 2008:150).

At Xunantunich, we have an ending date for monument use, 849 CE, but not a beginning date. The nine stelae at the site suggest a period of monument use spanning 8.65 k'atuns, or almost 171 years. Working back from 849 CE, the proposed beginning date for monument use at Xunantunich is 678 CE, which is only 3 years later than the beginning of the Hats' Chaak phase, the period of growth when the visible plan at the site began to be constructed.

If accurate, this model can be applied to sites like Chan Chich and Dos Hombres, for which we have not established date ranges for monuments, to speculate perhaps about the duration of their periods of independence. In this case, the stela frequency approach suggests that Chan Chich's rulers were only independent for about a k'atun, while those at Dos Hombres may have enjoyed around three k'atuns of sovereignty.

Ball Courts

All of the cities in the sample have at least one ball court except for Altun Ha (Table 10.2). More than half of the sites have two or more ball courts. Possessing a ball court has long been considered an indication of the regional importance of a site (e.g., Garrison and Dunning 2009), and ball courts, perhaps more so than any other urban feature at Maya sites, served important social functions related to community integration, ritual, and political competition. As Jon Lohse and colleagues (2013:121) note, the ball game, its attendant public rituals, "and emphasis on performance, [indicate] a focus on individual rulers as ritual specialists." This is evident in ball game imagery on the markers at Lubaantun and Late Classic Stela 4 at La Milpa depicting a ruler with a dancing dwarf dressed as a ball player and holding a ball (see Grube and Hammond 1998:129; Lohse et al. 2013:106; Wanyerka 2003:18). As discussed in chapter 11, at several of the cities in our sample ball courts appear to be components of processional architecture.

There is a high degree of variation in ball court size and architecture. Most of the excavated examples have sloped aprons for playing surfaces, but the ball courts at Lubaantun and Chan Chich have tiered playing surfaces. Low walls surround most of the southern Belize courts, a trait not seen elsewhere in the eastern lowlands. Chan Chich and Xunantunich have ball courts physically attached to larger structures while the other cities have freestanding ball courts. Excavations in alleyways frequently, but not universally, encounter caches or markers. When present, ball court markers may convey important political information, such as the likely emblem glyph for Lubaantun (Wanyerka 2009:415) or the account of Tikal's defeat on Altar 21 at Caracol (Martin 2005).

The most obvious trend in the ball courts of the eastern lowlands is the overwhelming preference for north–south orientation. Of the 23 confirmed ball courts in Table 10.4, 21 are oriented north–south. The two exceptions are one of the ball courts in the Great Plaza at La Milpa and one in the Moho Plaza at Pusilhá. In a separate study of ball courts in northwestern Belize, Lohse et al. (2013:101) report 9 of 11 ball courts (or 6 of 7 ball courts that are not also included on Table 10.4) are oriented north–south, varying from 4.5° west of north to 17° east of north. The reason that some courts are oriented east–west is unclear, but Schultz et al. (1994:51) speculate that at La Milpa, where the two courts are morphologically dissimilar but coeval, the contrasting orientations reflect different "emphases for the ballgame," by which they mean perhaps the north–south-oriented South Ballcourt was used for a more ritualized or ceremonial version of the ball game.

In terms of placement on the urban landscape, ball courts are usually found in plazas or on separate platforms linked to a plaza by a *sacbe*. At Dos Hombres, the small second ball court is oddly placed outside of the main plaza, and the rural ball court 2.5 km from the site core is unique.

Causeways

All but three of the sites listed on Table 10.2 have at least one *sacbe*. When discussing *sacbeob*, Caracol is clearly the mountain cow in the room. The count of 36 causeways is based on an article by Arlen Chase and Diane Chase (2001a), which provides an excellent summary of and discussion about the variety and significance of the system of causeways at Caracol. As recently collected LiDAR data are fully analyzed (Chase et al. 2011), this count may increase. The site has both internal and external causeways, and, in nearly every case, all roads lead to Caracol. The intrasite network was built in the Late Classic and links both residential and nonresidential groups to the site's epicenter, and the intersite causeways—identified via satellite imagery—include two projected to extend 24 km to the southeast and a third projected to connect Caracol to Naranjo, 42 km to the northwest. Perhaps the most significant feature of the intrasite network is that it links termini groups to the site center but rarely to each other. As A. Chase and D. Chase (2001a:277) note, if you ignore the causeways and simply consider the placement of the causeway termini groups, then the secondary centers appear spaced almost equidistantly over the landscape. The causeway network, however, makes it apparent that the system is actually highly centralized, despite the equitable spacing of the termini groups. La Milpa, which occupies a similar landscape of rolling hills and flourished as Caracol did during the Late Classic period, has its own ring of secondary centers approximately 3.5 km from its epicenter, but none are linked to the site center by a causeway. Caracol's network is unique in the eastern lowlands and represents an unprecedented degree of political and economic integration for a major Classic period city.

Arlen Chase and Diane Chase (2001a:279) contrast Caracol's road system with that of Tikal, another major Late Classic city, to highlight the likely administrative function of Caracol's system. At Tikal, the causeways are much wider than those at Caracol, 21–70 m compared to 2.5–12 m, and architecturally connect ritual groups to one another. The longest causeway at Tikal, the approximately 750-m-long Mendez Causeway, connects the site center to the Temple of the Inscriptions, similar to other examples of *sacbe* termini at other cities (see Minanha, for example). This contrasts sharply with Caracol's special-function termini, which comprise small plazas with low range buildings and no temples.

Takeshi Inomata (2006:817) proposes that the construction of very wide causeways at Tikal during the Late Classic period was partially in response to the decreasing space available in plazas for mass spectacles and the increasing population of the city as a whole. The unusually wide causeways could accommodate large number of spectators, who likely lined the edges of the causeways during ritual processions by the elite. In this manner, more of the community could participate in the public spectacles put on by the king than would have been possible using only plazas as stages for ritual (Inomata 2006:817).

In the other cities considered here, variation in *sacbe* form is apparent. Most *sacbeob* are elevated platforms, and a distinction is made between elevated *sacbeob* with low parapets along their edges and what Garrison (2007:317) termed "sunken causeways" in which parapets bound a wide but not elevated corridor. The only examples of sunken causeways in the eastern and southern lowlands are known from Chan Chich, La Honradez, El Pilar, and San Bartolo, suggesting that this type of causeway is extremely rare and highly localized (see Garrison 2007:317).

The causeways listed in Table 10.2 at sites other than Caracol connect large groups of architecture together (at Nohmul, La Milpa, Dos Hombres, Altun Ha, and Pusilhá), connect to apparent termini shrines (at Xunantunich, Minanha, and possibly Chan Chich), radiate outward with no apparent connection (at El Pilar), or have absolutely no apparent connections (only at Altun Ha). At La Milpa, Dos Hombres, and Nohmul, the causeways provide direct architectural connections between the main plaza at the site and the rest of the monumental core, a pattern seen at other cities in northwestern and northern Belize and northeastern Petén (see Hammond 1981; Houk 2003).

The causeways at Chan Chich are unusual in two respects. First, they are both very wide (about 40 m), and, second, they are of contrasting form. The Western Causeway is of the rare sunken variety; it appears to terminate at a small hill top shrine structure approximately 390 m west of the main plaza. On the other side of the structure, a narrower, elevated *sacbe* continues west, beyond the mapped limits of the site core in the direction of the secondary center of Kaxil Uinic. The Eastern Causeway is elevated and extends for over 400 m from the site core before disappearing or possibly ending at a shrine structure (Houk 2013b). The Western Causeway may have an analog in the Bryan & Murphy Causeway at El Pilar, which is 30 m wide, sunken, and may connect to a small hilltop structure about 390 m to the west.

Causeways served multiple functions in Maya city planning, from utilitarian transportation corridors to routes for ritual processions. Additionally, studies have shown that causeways functioned as elements of water management systems at a number of Maya cities (Scarborough et al. 2012; Shaw 2001), and it is likely that many of the causeways in the eastern lowlands did so as well. However, water management studies require highly accurate topographic maps to identify drainage patterns, so in most cases it is not possible to do more than speculate on what role many of these causeways may have played as either dams or catchment surfaces. A likely example of a causeway doubling as a dam is Sacbe 1 at Xunantunich, which appears to have artificially impounded the *aguada* on the eastern side of the Castillo.

An Analysis of Urban Planning at Eastern Lowland Cities

This book looks at the cities of the eastern lowlands through two lenses: the built environment and ancient urban planning. Much of this book has relied on the former in its presentation and description of each city under consideration. The remainder of this chapter peers through the second lens to examine Maya city planning, saving a discussion of meaning behind the cities' plans for chapter 11.

Without ethnographic sources to indicate how and to what degree the Maya planned their cities, archaeologists must rely on other sources of information. This chapter relies on two approaches that focus on coordination of buildings within cities, which serves to organize space in a formal manner, and the standardization of cities (Smith 2007:6–7). Smith (2007:7) proposes using these two approaches in concert to examine the degree of planning evident in a particular city or group of cities, and he applied this approach to Aztec cities of central Mexico (Smith 2008). Following that model, this section applies Smith's (2007) approach to studying urban planning by examining coordination among buildings and spaces and standardization among cities to the Classic period cities discussed in this book. This is a really a test of the approach, one that Smith (2007:41) called for when he outlined the methods, noting "its validity and usefulness can only be established through confrontation with the archaeological and historical records—the messy empirical reality—of specific ancient cities."

Coordination

Under the rubric of coordination, Smith (2007:8–25) considers coordinated arrangement of buildings and spaces, formality and monumentality, orthogonal layouts, other forms of geometric order, and access and visibility. Each term is briefly defined in Table 10.3, even those that do not apply in the Maya area. Assessing many of the criteria in Table 10.3 is an exercise in subjectivity, although it does attempt to impose a degree of rigor on the analysis. Because the point of this exercise is to assess the degree of planning evident in each city, I have ranked each city for the various categories in comparison to the other cities in the sample.

Coordinated Arrangement of Buildings and Spaces

Table 10.4 presents data on coordinated arrangement of buildings and spaces. The data are organized by descending size of monumental precincts—those areas used to determine rank ordering and expressed here as a percentage of the largest city's monumental core. I also examined published maps and identified the one or two most common structure and feature orientations at each site and then calculated the percentage of structures and features following these orientations (within 1° either way). All structures have a primary

Table 10.3. Definitions of terms used to study coordination among buildings and spaces

Category	Definition	Method
Coordinated Arrangement of Buildings and Spaces	Degree to which buildings and feature share a common orientation and are coordinated with respect to each other. Smith (2007:8) points out that in some cases the common orientation may reflect something other than central planning, such as topography and shorelines.	Percentage of buildings and features in monumental precinct sharing a common orientation, and subjective assessment of coordination (low, medium, high).
Formality and Monumentality	Formality refers to the arrangement of buildings in an orderly fashion, and monumentality refers to buildings that are larger than needed for utilitarian purposes. The two are often combined in ancient cities.	Monumental area expressed as a percentage of largest city in the sample (Caracol).
Orthogonal Layouts	Use of grid patterns to arrange buildings and spaces. Orthogonal layouts do not occur in the Maya area and are rare in Mesoamerica.	Not applicable.
Other Forms of Geometric Order	Cities following a strict geometric layout that may orthogonal or non-orthogonal (such as circles), although this form of planning is rare in ancient cities and not documented in the Maya area.	Not applicable.
Access and Visibility	Access refers to features, such as walls, that limit access. Visibility refers to viewshed and includes the area that can be seen from a point as well as the areas from which a given point can be seen. Assessing visibility requires the use of a GIS loaded with three-dimensional mapping data.	Qualitative assessment based on formal entrances and walls within the monumental area.

Source: Smith 2007:8–29.

axis, which runs through the center of the building from front to rear, and a transverse axis, which is almost always perpendicular to the primary axis. For the sake of comparison and simplicity, orientation in Table 10.4 refers to whichever axis is oriented generally north–south because a structure with a primary axis of 0° and one with a transverse axis of 0° share the same orientation; it does not imply that most structures are oriented north–south. These calculations only consider buildings and features included within the monumental core area of each site. Additionally, most published site maps include magnetic north, without giving the year the data were collected, and not true north. Therefore, while the orientations and calculations are internally consistent within each site, there is an unknown degree of error in each orientation, which makes comparisons between sites more difficult. I have also ranked the degree to which buildings are coordinated with respect to each other for each site as low, medium, or high. This is a qualitative and subjective assessment, and other analysts might disagree with these scores. As with structure orientation, different levels of mapping precision may affect how building coordination is scored. Finally, Table 10.4 lists the number of causeways per site as an access-related factor.

At most of the cities included in Table 10.4, more than one common structure orientation is evident in the published maps of epicenters. In some cases, the competing orientations occur in the same plaza or courtyard, which suggests a lower level of coordination between buildings, but in other cases the different orientations occur in different areas of the site. A good example of the latter is Dos Hombres, where the structures in the northern plaza and the ball court share a 0° alignment, while most of the structures south of the ball court are oriented 9° east of north. The degree to which buildings are coordinated with respect to each other in each area of the site is high, despite the competing orientations in the overall site plan.

The sites with the most structures sharing a common orientation include El Pilar (82 percent), Chan Chich (64 percent), Dos Hombres (62 percent), Pusilhá (59 percent), and Caracol (51 percent). In all other cases, fewer than 50 percent of the buildings share a common orientation. The sites with the most inconsistent orientations include Nim Li Punit (13 percent), Lubaantun (21 percent), Altun Ha (25 percent), and Nohmul (27 percent). Not surprisingly, these four sites show low degrees of coordination between structures. Lamanai is an interesting case; although it is the second-largest city in the sample, only 32 percent of its structures share a common orientation, and the degree to which buildings are coordinated with respect to one another is low. In this case, however, the city planners appear to have been more concerned with coordinating structures with the New River Lagoon rather than with each other.

Formality and Monumentality

Table 10.4 considers monumentality as a measure of the horizontal size of the monumental architecture at the site because structure height or construction mass is not available for each structure at every site. In general, however, monumental area and size of structures correlate closely: Caracol is the largest site and has the tallest and most massive structure (Caana), Lamanai is the second-largest site and has the second-tallest building (High Temple), while the smallest sites have smaller structures—the tallest building at Nim Li Punit, for example, is only 11 m tall. All of the sites exhibit formality in their architecture, and in all cases plazas serve as the formal organizing unit for

Table 10.4. Measures of coordination among buildings

City	Area[1]	Core Area Rank	Primary Orientation (Degrees East of North)	Secondary Orientation (Degrees West of North)	% of Buildings Following Primary Orientation	% of Buildings Following Secondary Orientation	Coordination	Monumentality	Formality	Causeways
Caracol	VP	100.00%	7	0	51%	34%	Medium	High	High	36
Lamanai	NB	46.16%	19		32%		Low	High	Medium	0
Nohmul	NB	36.46%	13	3	27%	10%	Low	High	Medium	1
La Milpa	NWB	34.64%	1	16	33%	23%	Medium	High	High	1
El Pilar	BV	31.31%	-3.5		82%		High	High	High	1
Xunantunich	BV	31.10%	-8	-14	37%	13%	Medium	High	High	3
Chan Chich	NWB	28.90%	1		64%		High	Medium	High	2
Pusilhá	SB	21.81%	-16	-8	59%	10%	Medium	Medium	Medium	1
Dos Hombres	NWB	19.83%	0	9	62%	32%	High	Medium	High	1
Altun Ha	NB	19.58%	-6	-18	25%	14%	Low	Medium	Low	2
Uxbenka	SB	15.15%	10		36%		Low	Low	Medium	1
Minanha	VP	13.88%	15	-10	45%	19%	Medium	Low	High	1
Lubaantun	SB	13.63%	0	8	21%	21%	Medium	Low	Medium	0
Nim Li Punit	SB	9.79%	-3	-7	13%	7%	Low	Low	Medium	0

Note: 1. Region Key: NB, northern Belize; NWB, northwestern Belize; BV, Belize Valley; VP, Vaca Plateau; and SB, southern Belize.

most of the monumental architecture at the sites. While monumentality can be quantified in a number of ways, formality is more subjective. However, sites with higher degrees of coordination between structures and those that have *sacbeob* physically linking different groups of architecture arguably also have a higher degree of formality than those with inconsistent structure alignments within plazas and dispersed architectural groups.

Access

Without geographic information system (GIS) data on each city, assessing visibility is not possible, but some subjective statements on access can be made. The two features most related to access are causeways, which direct the flow of traffic, and walls or structures, which restrict the flow of traffic. Both types of features reflect urban planning (Smith 2007:24). Caracol, with its 36 causeways, shows the highest degree of concern with controlling access. Arlen Chase and Diane Chase (2001a:279) interpret the causeway system at Caracol as having an administrative function within the economic and political systems of the kingdom. Many of the *sacbeob* terminate in special-function plazas directly related to the causeways and apparently built at the same time, suggesting a high degree of planning went into their design and construction (A. Chase and D. Chase 2001a:278).

Other sites in the sample used causeways to apparently direct access into particular areas of the site, as seen clearly at Xunantunich, El Pilar, and Chan Chich. At other sites with causeways, the primary function was likely ritual or symbolic (although traffic flow would have also been a factor) because the causeways link distinctive groups of architecture.

A number of sites demonstrated features designed to control or restrict access to elite or royal residential groups. At Caracol, for example, once a visitor entered the monumental precinct, he or she would have found vast areas of the city open. Access between plazas does not appear to have been restricted, but the palaces and acropoli at Caracol demonstrate an abiding concern for limiting and controlling access to elite space. Caana best demonstrates this; access to the summit required a visitor to climb dozens of meters and pass through two buildings before reaching the small courtyard on the structure's summit.

Walls are less common but are found at Pusilhá, Lubaantun, and Nim Li Punit around the ball courts. At Xunantunich a wall constructed between Structure A-1 and Structure A-3 restricted access to Plaza A-I. At Dos Hombres two low walls on the margin of Plaza A-1 restricted access. The most extensive wall is the low feature that encircles the modified hilltop at Chan Chich where the Norman's Temple group is located. This wall may be defensive in nature, but it has not been formally investigated.

Standardization

Standardization includes architectural inventories, spatial patterns, and orientation and metrology (Smith 2007:25–29). Table 10.5 defines each term, and Table 10.6 presents criteria used to assess standardization between cities. The data are organized by descending size (core area as a percentage of Caracol's size). The table includes either counts or presence/absence for certain building types and features common at Maya sites. Note that counting plazas is a tricky thing; I counted large, accessible, bounded or clearly defined areas onto which monumental structures face as plazas, and indicted a "+" in cases where additional spaces may or may not be considered plazas. I did not count tightly enclosed or private spaces as plazas. Determining what may or may not constitute formal processional architecture is also subjective, and I indicated those cities with possible routes as "X?" and those with likely routes with an "X." That topic is explored more in chapter 11. Reservoir presence or absence should be considered preliminary data; formal water management studies have not been undertaken at most cities in the sample; therefore, additional reservoirs may await discovery.

For each site, I have classified the site core type as dispersed (D), moderately integrated (MI), or integrated (I). In a dispersed city, the groups of architecture comprising the monumental center are not necessarily proximate

Table 10.5. Definitions of terms used to assess standardization among cities

Category	Definition	Method
Architectural Inventories	Basic inventory of public buildings, spaces, and features.	Presence/absence and numerical counts of specified features and building types.
Spatial Patterns	While difficult to objectively document, common spatial patterns at a series of cities provide evidence for urban planning.	Qualitative assessment of published maps.
Orientation and Metrology	Orientation refers to similarities in orientation among cities, and metrology is the identification of standard units of measurement or the use of symbolically significant numbers in building plans.	Comparison of primary orientation of monumental architecture.

Source: Smith 2007:8–29.

Table 10.6. Measures of standardization between cities

City	Area[1]	Core Area Rank	Causeways	Sunken/Parapet Causeways	Stelae	Ball Courts	Plazas	Stela Plaza	E-Group
Caracol	VP	100.00%	36		24	2	4+		X
Lamanai	NB	46.16%	0		9	1	4+		
Nohmul	NB	36.46%	1		0	1	4+		X?
La Milpa	NWB	34.64%	1		23	2	3		
El Pilar	BRV	31.31%	1	X	0	2	4+		X
Xunantunich	BRV	31.10%	3	X	9	2	3		X?
Chan Chich	NWB	28.90%	2	X	1	1	4		
Pusilhá	SB	21.81%	1		22	3 or 4	3+	X	
Dos Hombres	NWB	19.83%	1		3	2	3+		
Altun Ha	NB	19.58%	2		0	0	2+		
Uxbenka	SB	15.15%	1		23	2	4+	X	
Minanha	VP	13.88%	1		8	1	1+		X
Lubaantun	SB	13.63%	0		0	3	4+		
Nim Li Punit	SB	9.79%	0		21	1	3+	X	

Notes: 1. Region Key: NB, northern Belize; NWB, northwestern Belize; BV, Belize Valley; VP, Vaca Plateau; and SB, southern Belize.
2. Site core types are dispersed (D), moderately integrated (MI), or integrated (I). See text for definitions.
3. Primary site axis is based on the generalized alignment of the monumental architecture from one end of the site to the other, and not necessarily on the primary orientation of structures. In the case of moderately integrated and dispersed cities, the primary axis reflects the general trend in the different groups of architecture and is expressed as approximately north–south (~N-S).

to each other and are not connected by *sacbeob*. In a moderately integrated city, most of the monumental architecture is connected together, but one or more groups may be disconnected from the rest of the site, as is the case with Chan Chich's Western Plaza and Norman's Temple group. In an integrated city, most or all of the monumental architecture is linked by *sacbeob*, connected platforms, or a combination of the two, such as at La Milpa and Dos Hombres. The primary axis for each site core is based on the generalized alignment of the monumental architecture from one end of the site to the other and not necessarily on the primary orientation of structures. In the case of moderately integrated and dispersed cities, the primary axis reflects the general trend in the different groups of architecture and is expressed as approximately north–south (~N-S). The methods used to identify the primary axis of a site are more fully described below.

Triadic Temple	Acropolis	Palaces	Reservoirs	Processional Architecture	Core Type[2]	Primary Site Axis[3]	Primary Orientation (Degrees East of North)
X	X	X	X	X?	I	N-S	7
X	X	X			D	N-S	19
	X	X		X?	I	~N-S	13
	X	X	X	X	I	N-S	1
	X	X	X?	X?	MI	~N-S	-3.5
	X	X	X	X	I	N-S	-8
	X	X	X?	X	MI	~N-S	1
	X			X?	D	~N-S	-16
X?	X	X		X	I	N-S	0
			X	X?	D	~N-S	-6
					D	~N-S	10
	X	X		X	I	N-S	15
	X?	X			I	N-S	0
		X			MI	~N-S	-3

Architectural Inventories

As is the case with all Mesoamerican civilizations, the plaza is the central focus of monumental architecture, and all of the cities in the sample have at least one clearly defined plaza. Most have at least three public plazas. All sites in the sample, except for Altun Ha, have at least one ball court. Most cities have an acropolis and at least one palace-type group, but not all do. In fact, Altun Ha has neither.

Other architectural assemblages are rare, including E-Groups and Triadic Temples. Both assemblages first appeared at Maya cities in the Late Preclassic period, although in some cases versions were constructed during the Classic period. The possible E-Groups in the sample include one initially constructed during the Late Preclassic period, at Caracol, and three Late Classic assemblages. Caracol's E-Group was used throughout the Classic period as well. The three sites with well-documented E-Groups cluster in western Belize. Aimers (1993) and Aimers and Rice (2006:Table 1) list Nohmul as having an E-Group, but Hammond (1985) does not mention one at the site.

The only two clearly defined triadic temples in Table 10.6 include the Late Preclassic High Temple at Lamanai and the Late Classic Caana at Caracol. A structure at Dos Hombres may be a smaller Classic period version of this architectural type, but the identification is uncertain (Houk 1996:136).

Spatial Patterns

The architectural inventories themselves are not as interesting as the ways in which the various elements were combined to create each city. Ashmore and Sabloff (2002:204) note that Maya city planners had an architectural lexicon with which to convey political or ideational messages, "but the choice of specific components varies from place to place and through time." Equally important is not only which components of city building were chosen but how they were arranged. It is in common spatial patterns that evidence for sources of planning ideas begins to emerge.

As Michael Smith (2007:26) notes, "common spatial patterns at a series of cities provides stronger evidence for urban planning than architectural inventories" but "are more difficult to document objectively." As examples of common spatial patterns among Maya cities, Smith (2007:27) observes that (1) the public architecture is concentrated in the epicenter of a site and planning is limited to the epicenter (i.e., the surrounding residential zones are unplanned) and (2) monumental buildings and temples are arranged around plazas. These two patterns are largely true of the cities under consideration here, although there are a couple of exceptions. Two of the southern Belize cities have more than one node of monumental architecture, and at Caracol the evidence for central planning in the form of the elaborate road system extends far from the epicenter, although individual residential structures surrounding the site core and its secondary centers may still be considered unplanned, in Smith's (2007) view.

A number of common spatial patterns are present in the sample of cities that are not as universal as the two previous examples. For example, although the core of each city is centered on at least one plaza, the size of plazas is highly variable. One common pattern highlighted in Table 10.2 is that the sites with the largest plazas (over 10,000 m^2) occur north of the Belize River, primarily in northwestern Belize. As Garrison's (2007:Table 6.3) research demonstrates, the pattern of large plazas extends across the border into northeastern Guatemala to include Xultun, San Bartolo, and Kinal as well. These exceptionally large plazas account for significant percentages of the monumental precincts at these sites, particularly at La Milpa and Dos Hombres, where the main plazas comprise over 20 percent of the monumental areas.

These large plazas contrast with the small stela plazas found at the southern Belize sites of Uxbenka, Nim Li Punit, and Pusilhá. These stela plazas are another common spatial pattern with a geographically restricted distribution. Stela plazas are small, even by southern Belize standards: they comprise between approximately 5 and 8 percent of the monumental area of their sites. While other sites have comparable numbers of stelae, their monuments are displayed very differently.

Another spatial pattern with a restricted geographic range are radial causeways connected to the main plaza at sites. Three sites in a roughly north–south line—Chan Chich, El Pilar, and Xunantunich—all have wide causeways that extending east–west from their main plazas; each site also includes at least one sunken or parapet-lined *sacbe*.

Orientation

In the site-planning debate mentioned in chapter 2 that played out primarily on the pages of *Latin American Antiquity* between 2002 and 2007, Ashmore and Sabloff (2002) contended that Maya kings and city builders during the Classic period favored a north–south orientation for the monumental precincts of their kingdoms. This "dynastic axis" replaced a Preclassic preference for a "solar axis," or east–west alignment, in city planning (Ashmore and Sabloff 2002:210). Michael Smith (2003:224) was critical of the basic premise that the north–south axis is even an empirical phenomenon. While it is certainly true that all of the cities included in this study have complicated site plans with east–west elements, I would argue—and do below with actual data—that most, if not all, display a pronounced north–south orientation, although the precise orientation varies from city to city and even within the same city (i.e., Minanha and Dos Hombres). In some cases the orientation applies to the entire monumental core; in others the preference for a north–south alignment is reflected in individual architectural groups.

Michael Smith (2003) challenges Maya archaeologists to be explicit in their methods and procedures in determining the primary axis of a site's orientation. In this study, I calculated the primary axis by examining the maps of the site core areas used in the rank ordering calculations and drew a line from one end of the monumental architecture to the other along the longest axis. In the case of dispersed site cores, I drew multiple lines and identified the most common orientation. Because of the importance of plazas in Mesoamerican urban traditions (e.g., Smith 2008:127), I considered the primary axis to be based on the arrangement of plazas, not secondary urban features like *sacbeob*. This is not to say that *sacbeob* were not critical elements of Maya cities but rather that the core of a city was defined by plazas and the buildings and platforms connected to them. By masking out the *sacbeob* on the maps of cities, which have been simplified to only show their monumental cores, the primary axis becomes easier to identify (Figure 10.3). In some cases I have drawn more than one axis, anticipating situations where reasonable people might quibble over one choice or another.

One of the most consistent features of the epicenters of the sites in this sample is that their monumental cores are oriented north–south or, in the case of dispersed epicenters, trend toward north–south orientation of individual groups. In all cases but two, the dominant orientation is within 20 degrees of north. The two most problematic sites for this exercise are Caracol, where the monumental core arcs from south to northeast (note, however, that the dominant structure orientation is north–south) and Nohmul. In the latter example one-half of the site forms a north–south line of plazas and buildings, but the other half has a pronounced northwest–southeast axis. Even in that case, however, the primary structure orientation is 13 degrees east of north.

In some cases *sacbeob* that link groups of architecture together emphasize (but do not define) the north–south orientation, such as at La Milpa and Dos Hombres. In other cases the north–south orientation of the major elements of the site core competes—at least visually on maps—with prominent east–west *sacbeob*, as is the case at Chan Chich and Xunantunich. In both cases, however, the major buildings face north–south, and contiguous plazas and acropoli or palaces reinforce the north–south orientation. Even in dispersed site cores, such as Uxbenka and Pusilhá, most of the individual plazas or connected groups of plazas clearly have north–south primary axes.

As is discussed in chapter 11, the north–south axis is an important element of Ashmore's (1991) site-planning study. Individual building assemblages and important structures may have east–west orientations, and in some cases the addition of *sacbeob* overlays an east–west axis—or, in the case of Caracol, multiple axes in various directions—on a city's plan. However, in all cases the plazas or linked groups of plazas that constitute the bulk of the site core are aligned north–south. I am not claiming that this is the case for all Maya sites in the eastern lowlands, but only for those in this study. This conclusion supports Ashmore's and Sabloff's (2003:230–231) assertion "that disposition of prominent construction along a north-south line *does* dominate parts or all of many Maya civic precincts in Classic times" (emphasis original).

There is tremendous variation in not only primary axis orientation but also

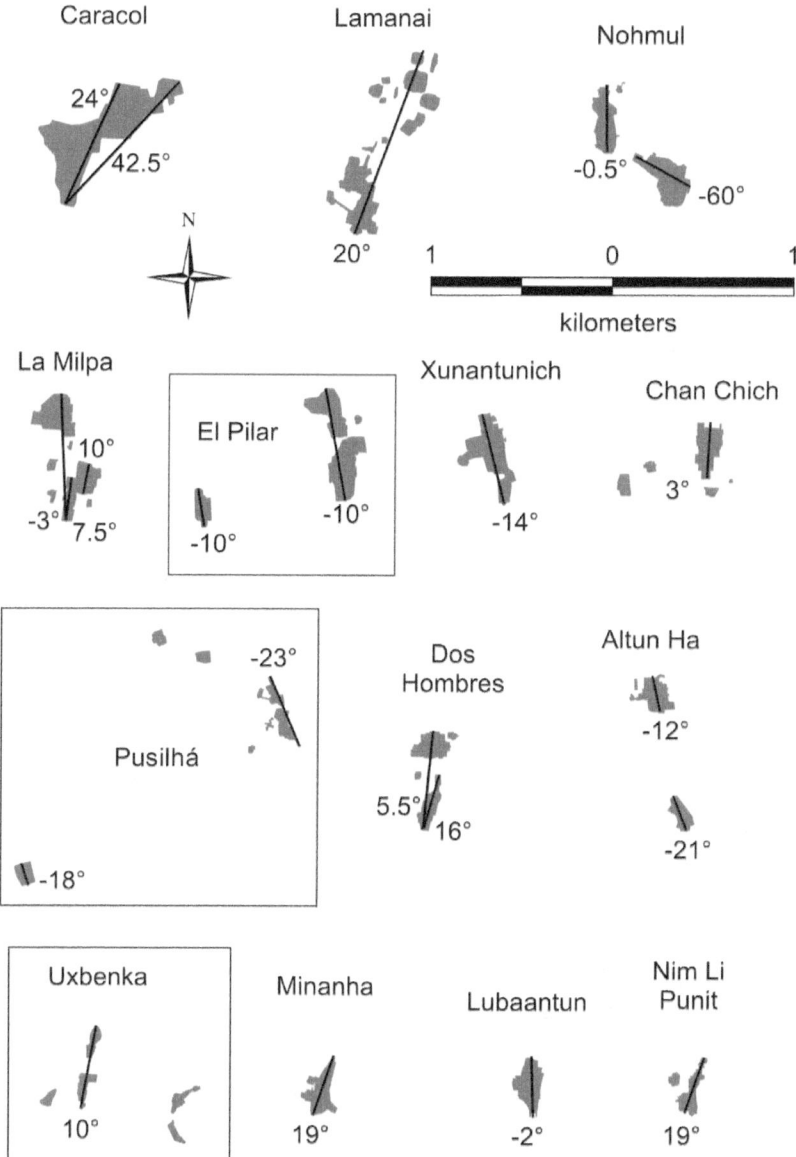

Figure 10.3. Simplified site maps used to calculate orientation.

the primary structure orientation in the cities in the sample. In the case of Lamanai both site and structure orientations were clearly influenced by the shape of the New River Lagoon. In other cases local topography constrained or affected plaza orientations, and Maya planners and builders were clearly willing to accept some degree of deviation from the norm in the construction of their cities.

Comparisons and Urban Planning   261

Discussion: Degrees of Planning

Michael Smith (2007:29) contends that by thinking of ancient urban planning as an ordinal scale, rather than stepping into the old debate of planned versus unplanned, it is possible to compare cities and classify them as more planned or less planned. At the same time, however, he acknowledges that "the planning scale is not simple" and that, other than quantifying the extent of planned area, comparing cities relies on "subjective judgments that are difficult to quantify."

While all of the cities in the sample were planned, it is evident from the application of this approach that stronger levels of centralized planning were involved at some cities than at others. At either end of the spectrum are Caracol and Altun Ha. On most scales under consideration here, Caracol demonstrates the highest degree of urban planning in the sample of cities we have examined. Not only does it have the largest monumental core but it also has *sacbeob* with specialized plazas that physically and symbolically link the epicenter to the surrounding secondary centers. Caracol also scores highest on monumentality in terms of number of large structures and size of structures, and it has the most complete architectural inventory of cities in the sample, including an E-Group and a triadic temple.

Altun Ha, on the other hand, evidences the lowest level of centralized planning. Although it is not the smallest city, its architectural inventory is the most incomplete in the sample, missing common things like carved monuments, a ball court, an acropolis, and clearly defined palaces. Furthermore, it demonstrates a low degree of coordination between buildings; only 25 percent of the structures and features in the epicenter follow the primary structural orientation. Despite the lack of evidence for strong urban planning based on the application of this approach, Altun Ha was a tremendously wealthy city, as evidenced by the quantity and quality of goods in caches and tombs. Power, it would seem, is not necessarily a prerequisite for wealth. And, as noted at the close of this chapter, other lines of evidence suggest centralized planning was stronger at Altun Ha than the preceding analysis suggests.

Despite its large size, Lamanai ranks lower on the planning scale than smaller sites. The New River Lagoon was clearly a major factor affecting the design of the city, and the pattern of urban growth was one of linear sprawl. The site map, in this case, is likely exaggerating the core area rank as the focus of occupation and construction moved from north to south along the shoreline through time. The city demonstrates a low degree of coordination between structures, and only 32 percent of buildings and features adhere to the most common orientation.

Ranking the remaining cities is not an easy task because, not only is the planning scale subjective, it appears as if different planning agendas or concepts were at play in the eastern lowlands. Therefore, what may seem less planned—such as the lack of rigid coordination between buildings within a plaza—may actually be "differently planned." I suspect, too, my own Western conceptions about what represents well planned, such as right angles and symmetry between buildings, is strongly affecting my subjective assessments of degrees of planning. For example, in my opinion, a number of cities demonstrate high—but not as high as Caracol—levels of planning, including Xunantunich, La Milpa, El Pilar, Chan Chich, and Dos Hombres. The first, while only demonstrating a medium level of coordination of structures and features and having fewer than 40 percent of its buildings following the primary structure orientation, nevertheless has very large monumental structures, *sacbeob* physically linking disparate groups of architecture, strong evidence for procession ways, and rich architectural inventories. The latter three all have high levels of structure coordination and high percentages of buildings complying with the primary structure orientation.

In contrast, in my view the southern Belize cities generally appear less planned, but I am not sure that is an accurate characterization. For one, they are smaller than the other cities just described, and the dispersed nature of Pusilhá's and Uxebenka's site cores would seem to require less planning than La Milpa's tightly integrated epicenter. Three of the four southern Belize cities have low or medium levels of coordination between structures, and fewer than 36 percent of their structures follow the most common orientation. At Nim Li Punit, only 13 percent of the buildings and features share the same orientation, implying a rather callous disregard for symmetry and common Maya urban aesthetics. Only at Pusilhá, the largest of the southern Belize cities, was common structure orientation an apparent concern; there 59 percent of the structures share the same orientation. Is all of this evidence of less planning or different planning? Was the southern Belize approach to urban design more concerned with integrating architecture with the natural topography, for example, than it was with creating symmetrical plazas and parallel structures?

Thoughts on Analyzing Planning

How well this chapter succeeded in accomplishing its goal of determining the degrees to which the Maya cities of the eastern lowlands were planned is open to debate. However, the exercise is a useful one, similar in some ways to formal analysis in art history. In formal analysis, an art historian considers the various formal elements used in a work of art; when a number of related or contemporary artworks are analyzed, patterns may emerge.

The method for studying urbanism employed in this chapter works in the same way and is what in anthropology we would consider an etic approach to the issue, that is, studying the issue from an outsider's perspective. Even if the goal is to be subjective in such an analysis, the very analytical categories used potentially bias the conclusions. For example, the approach assumes that orthogonal layouts are more planned than non-orthogonal layouts, which is largely true in the modern Western world. However, it does not consider the emic view on planning—the insider's perspective. We cannot even be sure that planning, as we conceive of it, was important to Mesoamerican city builders. My colleague Dr. Carolyn Tate made this observation to me during a discussion in early 2014 about Elizabeth Boone's (2000) analysis of Mixtec codices. The Mixtec were a Postclassic (900 to 1500 CE) Mesoamerican group that lived west of the Maya area in northern and western Oaxaca (Coe and Koontz 2013). In what may be one of the few glimpses of Mesoamerican depictions of city building (see Boone 2000), the *Codex Vienna* shows rituals associated with the founding of Mixtec towns. This is a glimpse of an emic view of city building, and what was clearly important to the Mixtec were the rituals associated with founding a polity, not instructions on how to design the town.

Even if we cannot know exactly what the Maya thought was important about city planning, we can see the patterns that emerged from their planning decisions. Whether or not the issue of more planned versus less planned is significant, the similarities and differences highlighted here allow for an examination of what all of this means in chapter 11.

A final cautionary note on this type of planning analysis is that without very detailed topographic data for each city being examined, certain engineering aspects of urban planning may be lost. This is particularly true in the Maya area because of the overriding need to control and manage drinking water during the long dry season each year. Maya city builders effectively created large catchment basins with their plaster-covered buildings and plazas, and even at the seemingly less-planned center of Altun Ha they carefully constructed plazas to direct runoff in specific directions. This type of engineering is evidence for a higher level of centralized planning than the low degree of coordination between buildings and spaces would imply.

Deciphering Meaning in Maya Cities

An alternate title for this chapter could easily be "Why Do Maya Cities Look the Way They Look?," as the word "meaning" is vague and prone to multiple interpretations. Identifying planning principles in Maya cities is one thing, but understanding the meaning behind the plans is another. As will become evident in the examples included in this chapter, in previous studies "meaning" is most often equated with Rapoport's (1988:325) "high-level meaning," the most difficult type of symbolic communication for archaeologists to identify. High-level meaning communicates information about worldview and cosmology. For all the reasons mentioned previously, interpreting high-level meaning from architecture is one of the more difficult and speculative aspects of archaeology, particularly for cultures like the ancient Maya, for which we have no written records about how they planned their cities. This chapter takes a more basic and holistic approach to studying site planning by asking why a city looks the way it looks. In other words, what factors can we identify that affected the final plan of a particular city? This is in line with Wendy Ashmore's and Jeremy Sabloff's (2002:202) "contention that more research is needed to establish the *mix* of ideational, social, environmental, economic, engineering, historical, and other sources in observed architectural forms and arrangements" (emphasis original).

This chapter explores the topic of meaning in the cities of the eastern lowlands first by looking at the issue of cosmograms in Maya studies. The idea that the Maya encoded high-level meaning about their worldview into city plans was popularized by Wendy Ashmore's (1991) research into the topic in the late 1980s and early 1990s. A slew of studies followed in which researchers proposed that the plans of various sites represented microcosms of the Maya worldview.

An important component of Ashmore's (1991) article was the identification of a site-planning template, referred to here as the Petén template, after its apparent area of origin. The degree to which the eastern lowland cities fit that template is assessed in this chapter. Beyond that, the discussion examines the ideas of political emulation as sources of city planning as well as the concept of "build what you know"—the idea that Maya architects and city builders could only replicate what they had seen, suggesting that the rarest elements in city plans may be the best place to look for evidence of emulation. The chapter also considers that even though deciphering high-level meaning may be impossible, archaeologists can recognize when symbolic communication has taken place. Finally, to return to how Maya cities functioned in the context of divine kingship, this chapter looks at groups of buildings and structures at a number of sites that represent probable processional architecture.

The Cosmogram Conundrum

Back in chapter 2 I introduced Wendy Ashmore's (1991) compelling article on Maya site planning. Although she was certainly not the only scholar studying planning at Maya cities, her article had a profound impact on the field of Maya archaeology and is widely cited by scholars attempting to interpret high-level meaning in city plans. Ashmore's (1991) study had two major elements. First, she identified a common set of planning principles (i.e., the Petén template), and, second, she attempted to link those principles to Mesoamerican cosmological concepts to interpret the significance of the template. Essentially, the first part of her study identified standardization among Maya cities and the second attempted to identify high-level meaning in the built environment.

A key element of the Petén template, which is primarily a Classic period manifestation, is an apparent concern with directionality. The Classic period preference was to emphasize the north–south axis in city planning, a break from the Preclassic preference for the east–west axis, best exemplified by the plans of El Mirador and Nakbe (Ashmore and Sabloff 2002). This "emphatic reference to a north-south axis in site organization" was combined with "formal and functional complementarity or dualism between north and south," the placement of a ball court as a transitional element between north and south, and the use of causeways to connect the key elements of the city plan (Ashmore 1991:200). At the central precinct or epicenter scale of analysis, the northern group often includes public, open space while the southern group includes private, enclosed architecture—hence the notion of duality (Ashmore 1989:274). The model also includes "the addition of elements on east and west to form a triangle with the north, and frequent suppression of marking the southern position" (Ashmore 1991:200), although this component of the model is perhaps the most difficult (or subjective) to identify in site maps.

Ashmore (1991:201) first identified the pattern (or standardization between cities) and then tried to decipher its significance by linking the components listed earlier to cosmological concepts. Key among these concepts posited by Ashmore (Ashmore 1991:201, 1992:176) are the notions that (1) the heavens, which are up, are the home of the ancestors, and the underworld, which is down, is the site of the "primordial ordeals of mythological Hero Twins"; that (2) vertical connections exist between the natural world and the supernatural realms (via mountains, caves, the *axis mundi*, etc.); that (3) in Maya worldview "north" equates to "up"; and that (4) the world is divided into four parts corresponding to the cardinal directions, along with a central position. In applying these concepts to the set of planning principles outlined earlier, Ashmore (1991:201) linked the northern group of architecture to the heavens, the home of the ancestors, and the southern group to the underworld. Thus, she proposed that kings who employed the Petén template created "a map of the universe, a microcosm, with the ruler placed in a position of consummate power" (Ashmore 1991:201).

Archaeologists studying the cities described in this book have, to varying degrees, attempted to interpret meaning in the design of their cities. More often than not, they turned to Ashmore's (1991) study for inspiration. Of the cities covered in this book, researchers have attempted to interpret high-level meaning at La Milpa, Xunantunich, Minanha, and the four cities in southern Belize.

La Milpa

Tourtellot, Estrada Belli, and colleagues (2003:48) propose that "a vast physical cosmogram or quincunx surrounds La Milpa Centre," consisting of the epicenter and outlying minor centers at each cardinal direction, 3.5 km from the center. They interpret the cosmogram as part of a large-scale, coordinated construction plan conceived and imposed by the elite that transformed La Milpa's epicenter into its own cosmogram and extended the ritual area of the city out to encompass half of the settlement area in the larger cosmogram marked by the minor centers of La Milpa North, La Milpa South, La Milpa East, and La Milpa West (Tourtellot, Estrada Belli, et al. 2003:48–49). They view the construction plan as a reflection of "a new governing model of the universe that was not atavistic ancestor veneration but [was] based on an encompassing worldview" (Tourtellot, Estrada Belli, et al. 2003:49).

Xunantunich

Jason Yaeger (2003:132) and Angela Keller (2006:590) have similarly analyzed the site plan of Xunantunich, describing it as a cosmogram. Yaeger (2003:132–133) proposes that the cruciform pattern imposed on the site's plan by the *sacbeob* entering the site core from east and west and the north–south axis created by the alignment of three contiguous plazas and related structures "recreates the quadripartite Maya cosmos." Keller (2006:586) describes the cruciform plan of the major architecture as "a clear, regular, and intentional design." She also notes that before the two causeways were identified and the extent of architecture south of the Castillo was known, the cruciform nature of the city's plan was unrecognized (Keller 2006:585). Building on the concept of vertical connections between the natural world and the supernatural domains, Yaeger (2003:133) and Keller (2006:591) comment on the central position of the Castillo in the city's plan, and Yaeger (2003:133) suggests that the Castillo may represent "the World Tree" based on its central position in the cosmogram and the symbolism on its stucco friezes.

Minanha

Gyles Iannone (2010:363) has also applied Ashmore's model to Minanha, noting that the site's epicenter "mimics the cosmologically-based civic plan of more potent centers in that it exhibits a strong north-south axis and follows the pattern of placing the royal residential compound . . . in the north, in association with the heavens." This is not a strict application of Ashmore's (1991) model, however, which places the public-ritual plaza in the north and the residential compound in the south.

Southern Belize

Geoffrey Braswell and colleagues (2011:117), without directly citing Ashmore, apply her model to the ruins in southern Belize. In the case of Pusilhá, Braswell et al. (2011:117) note:

> As at many other Classic Maya sites, the direction north is associated with the heavens, ancestor worship, and the sun at noon. In contrast, ballcourts are found at low elevations. The largest ballcourt at Pusilhá is located at the southern end of a *sacbe*. This probably reflects an association with the underworld.

However, in the cases of Lubaantun and Nim Li Punit, which have strong north–south axes with the highest points in the north, Braswell et al. (2011:117) report "there is scant evidence . . . that north is associated exclusively with ancestor worship." At Lubaantun, Braswell et al. (2011:117) propose that another cosmologically based urban planning principle may have been employed. They identify two inscribed triangles in the plan of the city, a smaller one formed by three pyramidal platforms, and a larger one created by three ball courts. They suggest that the first three structures "represent the three hearthstones of Maya creation, thought to be in the constellation Orion, and for that reason are the tallest platforms built at the site." The ball courts, on the other hand, "occupy a much lower position . . . and are probably associated with the underworld" (Braswell et al. 2011:117). Braswell et al. (2011:117–18) go on to observe that:

> This precise pattern of two inscribed triangles is unique in the Maya world, but may serve to mark Lubaantun as an *ox te tun*, or three stone place, one of many in the Maya area. It is important to note that if our interpretation of site planning principles at Lubaantun is correct, this plan probably emerged late in the construction history of the site.

A Critique of Cosmograms

Michael Smith (2005:220) published a highly critical evaluation of what he called "the new cosmogram studies," noting that they often begin "with the assumption that directional cosmology must have been expressed in architectural settings" and ultimately "assert confidently that the building/compound/city/reservoir/stelae in question formed a cosmogram." At the heart of Smith's (2005:220) critique is the observation that there are no "explicit statements in the ethnohistoric or epigraphic sources for direct cosmological influences on Mesoamerican architecture or urbanism." In other parts of the world, such as China, India, and Cambodia, there are ancient texts that describe the layout of the ideal city and state that rulers employed cosmological models in designing their royal capitals (M. Smith 2003:222). Without similar sources for the Maya, Michael Smith (2003:220) cautions scholars to "approach this question cautiously with rigorous and explicit methods." Smith (2005:220) does not, however, dispute that "cosmology may have played a role in architectural symbolism and perhaps even in the design and layout of buildings and cities," and in another article he agrees "that cosmology must have played a role in generating the layouts of cities among the Maya" (M. Smith 2003:221).

On another cautionary note, it is important to consider that the static plan maps of the cities presented in this book are misleading in a couple of ways. First, they show the final plan of a city and do not represent the functioning elements of the city at any time in its history. Certainly, all of the buildings and features shown on a map represent things that were present prior to a city's abandonment, but without excavating every structure it is impossible to know which buildings were occupied or in use at a particular point in time. Second, and perhaps more important, our western method of presenting maps—essentially a bird's-eye-view with north at the top—is not how the Maya would have conceived of their cities. Indeed, it is a view that no occupant of the city would have ever seen.

To return to the Xunantunich example, the entire cruciform design would not have been visible from any point in the city, so it is uncertain if the residents of Xunantunich would have even conceived of their city in such a manner. However, it would have been perceptible, maybe, from someone with access to both sides of the Castillo, which is perhaps the point. If indeed the design of the city is meant to convey high-level meaning, the symbolic communication may have had a very narrow target audience—the elite of the city and perhaps their peers from other cities.

Applying the Petén Template

Most of the examples listed earlier follow the second part of Ashmore's (1991) model, the cosmological component, without critically examining how closely a particular site fits the proposed Petén site-planning template. Table 11.1 attempts to do that by identifying the degree to which each site plan meets the five criteria in the template. I have ranked somewhat subjectively the degree of fit as strong, medium, weak, none, or unclear. In testing the template, the comparison is based on the plan of the entire monumental core of each city, not isolated elements. Following Ashmore (1991:200), the criteria in the template and their abbreviations in Table 11.1 are (1) empathic reference to a north–south axis in site organization [North–South Axis]; (2) formal and functional complementarity or dualism between north–south [Dualism]; (3) the addition of elements on east and west to form a triangle with the north, and frequent suppression of marking the southern position [Triangle]; (4) the presence in many cases of a ball court as transition between north and south [Ball Court Transition]; and (5) the frequent use of causeways to emphasize connections among the cited elements, thereby underscoring the symbolic unity of the whole layout [Causeways].

To that list I have added a related criterion: location of the main public plaza relative to the rest of the site plan [Plaza]. An unstated component of the second criterion is that the public plaza is situated in the north where it is

Table 11.1. Comparison of cities to the Petén template

Site	Area[1]	Core Type[2]	North–South Axis	Plaza[3]	Dualism	Triangle	Ball Court Transition	Causeways	Fit
Caracol	VP	I	Strong	North	Strong	Unclear	Moderate	Strong	Strong
Lamanai	NB	D	Strong	South	Unclear	None	Unclear	None	Weak
Nohmul	NB	I	Moderate	South	Strong	None	Weak	Strong	Weak
La Milpa	NWB	I	Strong	North	Strong	None	Strong	Strong	Strong
El Pilar	BV	MI	Moderate	South	Strong	Unclear	Weak	Weak	Weak
Xunantunich	BV	I	Strong	Center	Moderate	Strong	Moderate	Strong	Moderate
Chan Chich	NWB	MI	Moderate	North	Strong	Moderate	Strong	Unclear	Strong
Pusilhá	SB	D	Moderate	North	Strong	Unclear	Strong	Strong	Weak[4]
Dos Hombres	NWB	I	Strong	North	Strong	None	Strong	Strong	Strong
Altun Ha	NB	D	Moderate	North	Moderate	Moderate	None	Moderate	Moderate
Uxbenka	SB	D	Moderate	Unclear	Unclear	Unclear	Unclear	Unclear	Weak
Minanha	VP	I	Strong	South	Strong	Unclear	Moderate	Strong	Weak
Lubaantun	SB	I	Strong	South	Strong	Moderate	Unclear	None	Weak
Nim Li Punit	SB	MI	Moderate	South	Strong	Unclear	Strong	None	Weak

Notes: 1. Region Key: NB, northern Belize; NWB, northwestern Belize; BV, Belize Valley; VP, Vaca Plateau; and SB, southern Belize.
2. Site core types are dispersed (D), moderately integrated (MI), or integrated (I). See text for definitions.
3. Location of main public plaza relative to rest of site core.
4. See discussion later in the text regarding the Moho Plaza.

associated with ancestors and the heavens, which is the primary cosmological concept employed in most of the case studies previously discussed. In fact, I consider the relationship between north and south and public versus private to be the most diagnostic element of the Petén template (e.g., Ashmore 1989:274).

As the previous chapter concluded, all of the cities in the sample have north–south axes, so all score as moderate or strong for that criterion. Applying the other criteria to cities with dispersed site cores (per Table 10.6) becomes problematic, particularly for Pusilhá and Uxbenka, where the site cores are widely dispersed across the landscape. For those two cities, because of the subjectivity of applying the criteria to such disparate architectural groups, I classified the fit to the template as weak. However, if the Moho Plaza, which is several kilometers away from the rest of the site core, were removed from the equation, Pusilhá actually would be considered a strong fit for the Petén template.

The most difficult criterion to apply is the third one in Ashmore's (1991:200) description of the template. My attempt to apply it to the site plans is largely guesswork, and I did not consider that category an overriding factor in determining fit.

The cities that fit the template best are Caracol, La Milpa, Dos Hombres, and Chan Chich. In all cases, there is a strong formal and functional contrast between north and south, with the main public plaza at the north, an acropolis at the south, and a ball court serving as a transitional element. Xunantunich is a moderate fit; however, if an earlier version of the site plan were considered—prior to the construction of the palace at the north end of the site core—the fit would have been strong. Altun Ha scores as a moderate fit, although in terms of overall planning, it seems to be the least planned city in the batch.

Most cities are weak fits for the model primarily because they have their public plazas at the southern end of their site cores. Minanha falls into this category, as does El Pilar. This is not to say that the cities are unplanned or that they do not include symbolic communication in their plans; it simply means that the Petén template does not seem to be the source for their planning ideas.

Sources of Meaning and Planning

Although most cities are not a good fit for the Petén template, the three cities from northwestern Belize are all strong fits. I previously suggested that the eastern extent of sites fitting the template was northwestern Belize (Houk

1996). A different idea about site planning seems to have been in use to the east and north, in which the public plaza occurs at the southern end of the site and monumental architecture seems to have more variation in structure orientation (Houk 1996). Nohmul and several sites not included in this book—Blue Creek, Punta de Cacao, Gran Cacao, Aventura, and El Pozito—all fit this second pattern (Houk 1996:285, 289). My earlier research concluded that the two patterns did not geographically overlap: the eastern extent of the Petén template is the Río Bravo Embayment, no more than a few kilometers east of the river. The second pattern occurs along a line paralleling the Booth's River extending north along the Río Hondo into northern Belize (Houk 1996:285). While the two patterns or templates seem geographically distinct, not all sites within each area necessarily follow the dominant regional template.

The same observation about a geographic distribution of a planning template can be made for southern Belize. As noted earlier, Leventhal (1990) described southern Belize as "an ancient Maya region" based on a number of similarities between sites. Although he never fully investigated it before moving on to work at Xunantunich, he asked the question of whether or not "it is possible to argue that this same geographic area has any meaning within the cultural sphere" (Leventhal 1990:137). Leventhal (1990:138) proposed that if southern Belize truly constituted a geographic region, then "there should be greater homogeneity of cultural features among the centers within the region than among the centers outside the region." Specifically, a particular combination of features (architectural, urban planning, material culture, and hieroglyphic data) defines the region; it does not suggest that the same features would not be expected at sites outside the region (Leventhal 1990:138).

In general, his work, which built on the previous research by Hammond (1975), and the more recent investigations by Braswell and Prufer (2009; see also Braswell 2007; Braswell et al. 2011; Braswell, Prager, and Bill 2005; Braswell, Prager, Bill, et al. 2005; Prufer 2005, 2007; Prufer et al. 2011) do indicate a remarkable degree of homogeneity among the four major southern Belize sites, despite important differences between them. For example, the ball courts at Nim Li Punit, Pusilhá, and Lubaantun "are centrally located and mediate between two sections of the different sites" and have the unique walled enclosures (Leventhal 1990:138). The "Hollywood set" style of construction, which integrates the natural terrain into the architecture to create an illusion of great monumentality, sequentially entered tombs, the lack of vaulted architecture, and rather inconsistent lunar series content in Long Count dates are other commonalities in the cities of southern Belize (Leventhal 1990; Braswell and Prufer 2009:45). Other important traits are the high frequency of carved monuments and the small stela plazas in which they are displayed. The source of city planning in southern Belize appears to have been a shared regional template, and the use of that template explains why the cities look the way they do. Beyond that, however, higher-level meaning in the individual city plans is not clear.

Beyond Templates: Political Emulation

Although 14 Maya cities is a small sample, the data in this study support previous research that has identified urban planning templates with restricted geographic ranges (e.g., Ashmore 1991; Coggins 1967; Hammond 1981; Houk 1996; Leventhal 1990). To say that a group of sites seems to follow one particular site-planning template is not to say that the sites are identical to one another. The templates, which do seem to be valid constructs, represent a set of rules some builders apparently chose to follow, but no two sites are identical, nor do any share the exact same construction or occupation history. In fact, as seems clear at Xunantunich, different planning agendas overlap on the urban landscape as new rulers imposed their own stamp on the urban landscape. And, despite basing a design on an apparent set of planning rules, ancient architects freely employed styles and arrangements of structures likely borrowed from other cities, some of which may not have followed the same planning template.

For example, La Milpa, Dos Hombres, and Chan Chich all adhere strongly to the Petén template, and all three have massive plazas, a trait apparently common in the Three Rivers adaptive region (e.g., Garrison 2007:Table 6.3). In plan, however, Chan Chich looks very different from La Milpa and Dos Hombres, which share many similarities (see Houk 2003). In particular, the builders of Chan Chich chose to construct radial causeways extending east and west from the Main Plaza. Not only are these causeways up to four times wider than the north–south causeways at La Milpa and Dos Hombres, one of them is the rare sunken causeway type in which low parapets create a corridor, but the causeway itself is apparently not elevated for its entire length, although excavations in 2014 determined it is elevated near the Main Plaza. The sunken causeway style may have been borrowed from La Honradez or San Bartolo, approximately 19 and 31 km to west, respectively. At La Honradez, three radial sunken causeways enter the site core from the west, the north, and the northeast. As an aside, Chan Chich's ball court is also atypical in that the playing surface comprised three tiers rather than a sloping face; you have to look far to Lubaantun in southern Belize for another published example of that style. But it is also an attached ball court with one structure physically integrated into a completely separate building. This rare style is not seen elsewhere in Belize except at Xunantunich and the nearby smaller sites of Yalbac and Saturday Creek, but is found at La Honradez.

Returning to causeways, El Pilar, which does not follow the Petén template (based on the placement of the main plaza relative to the elite acropolis) also has a sunken causeway very similar to the western causeway at Chan Chich. The only other causeways with parapets in the sample of sites occur at Caracol and Xunantunich.

Other examples can be drawn from the cities under consideration, but these serve to illustrate two forces at work in city planning: political emulation and what I call "build what you know." Political emulation is likely responsible for many similarities in site plans. Ashmore and Sabloff (2002:203) note that an "important means of enhancing the political aura of a place is by constructing it to resemble locales of established stature: If a place looks like a recognized seat of authority, people behave there accordingly." In other words, rulers expressed their affiliation with executors of like projects and their political authority by commissioning monumental constructions that emulate powerful sites (e.g., Houk 2010:178). This type of urban planning was clearly exploited in multiple instances (Ashmore 1989:273).

Ashmore and Sabloff (2002:207) suggest that the planners at Xunantunich emulated the established city of Naranjo in their Late Classic design of the city, and that Naranjo and Xunantunich both may have copied the design of the older and more powerful city of Calakmul. Gyles Iannone (2005:31) similarly proposes that Minanha's Late Classic elite adopted the Calakmul-style civic plan to solidify their rulership.

In another example of this type of analysis, Ashmore and Sabloff (2002:207–208) compare the site plan of Labná to its larger neighbor, Sayil, noting a number of similarities. Both sites have residential palaces at their northern ends and nonresidential complexes at their southern ends, joined by causeways. The two cities are not identical, however, as Labná's central causeway is much shorter than Sayil's, and the smaller city lacks a ball court. However, the "orientations of the principal buildings at each end of the causeway are similar at the two centers, and . . . the observed buildings and spaces are broadly parallel in form and array." If the similarities are due to emulation, then "comparison of spatial order in the two places yields clues to political dynamics of founding order and hierarchical relations" (Ashmore and Sabloff 2002:208).

I have made a similar argument for a political relationship between Dos Hombres and La Milpa in northwestern Belize (Houk 1996, 2003). Although 43 percent smaller than La Milpa, the two sites share a number of similarities in their plans and are archetypal examples of the Petén template. Each site has (1) strong north–south orientation of the monumental precinct, (2) a massive public plaza in the north, (3) an isolated temple in the main plaza slightly offset from the center to the northwest, (4) an elevated quadrangle group attached to the southwestern corner of the main plaza, (5) a *sacbe* connecting the northern plaza to the southern part of the site, and (6) an acropolis at the southern end of the site core.

Arguments for political emulation are strongest when there are other lines of evidence connecting two sites such as artifact assemblages or hieroglyphic texts. In the case of Xunantunich, Naranjo's emblem glyph appears on Stela 8, which provides another data point to support the emulation hypothesis. In the Dos Hombres and La Milpa example, Hubert Robichaux and I (2005; see also Houk and Lohse 2013) have proposed that a fragmentary hieroglyphic text from Dos Hombres mentions a ruler at La Milpa, but our argument has not been well received, to put it mildly. Regardless, the emulation argument is not unreasonable given the construction history at the two sites and their proximity.

Build What You Know

When the political emulation approach is extended over tremendous distances, it becomes more problematic. Doing so, however, is a tempting proposition; finding similarities between eastern lowland cities and the distant Late Classic powers of Tikal and Calakmul would suggest that some rulers may have expressed their affiliation with one of the two Late Classic powers through architectural emulation. If true, this approach would hold tremendous potential for drawing Late Classic versions of political maps across the lowlands as Tikal's allies could be identified from Calakmul's allies based strictly on site plans.

The danger in this logic is that it does not take into consideration who planned and built Maya cities or how they went about it. It is most likely that planning, engineering, and architectural design were elite vocations, comparable to scribes or sculptors. But we really do not know anything about how planning or engineering know-how was spread from city to city. It does not appear likely that the Maya had the equivalent of architectural plans, because the surviving Postclassic codices and Classic texts do not make mention of such matters. Certainly, some polychrome vases and incised graffiti (at sites like Tikal) depict temples and palaces, but the images could hardly be considered construction plans. Furthermore, no scale models of cities or buildings have been found at Maya sites. As noted earlier, the types of maps we have of Maya cities are based on western conventions for displaying spatial information. Not only would the Maya at a particular site not have had a map of Calakmul, should they have desired to replicate its site plan, they would not have even had a map of their own city. While we do not know exactly how the Maya stored or transmitted planning and engineering information, it seems that for an architect to actually copy a building from another site or the plan of another site, he or she most likely would have to physically visit that site. Maya planners could only build what they knew, meaning they personally had to see a plaza's layout or building's plan to replicate it. Although we know that powerful kings frequently visited distant kingdoms (and perhaps they took along architects or engineers as part of their entourages), making the case for direct emulation of a site's plan becomes more difficult the greater the distance involved and the greater the disparity in power between the two centers.

What is possible, however, is a sort of trickle-down effect of traits and planning preferences from the "style centers" (e.g., Wheatley 1967) of Tikal and Calakmul, first to their closest neighbors, and then to their neighbors' neighbors, and so on. Maya builders only could build what they had seen, and probably only the architects from the most important cities traveled to see other major Maya cities. At smaller cities, the planners probably never went very far from home, meaning their sources of inspiration would be nearby centers within a few days' walking distance. If this scenario is accurate, then an idea might start at one city and then trickle outward, becoming constantly modified by memory. An apt analogy is to the children's game where a bit of information is whispered from one person to the next; invariably the information that reaches the last child in line is much different than the original statement.

If the "build what you know" concept is appropriate, then identifying the rare elements, or rare arrangement of elements, that co-occur at nearby sites may provide the best evidence for emulation or affiliation. An example from the cities discussed in this book is the limited use of sunken causeways or causeways with parapets. This type of causeway is found at four cities in western Belize (Caracol, Xunantunich, El Pilar, and Chan Chich) and two cities in the northeastern Petén (San Bartolo and La Honradez), but the ultimate source for the concept maybe the style center of Tikal, where the Mendez Causeway has 1.5–2-m-high mounds flanking its margins.

Deciphering Meaning

Political emulation is a form of symbolic communication through architecture, and it communicates middle-level meaning about identity and political relationships. Similarly, the use of a particular site-planning template, regardless of any high-level meaning that may be involved in the template, communicates middle-level meaning about political, social, or cultural ties. However, it is likely that only the elite would be aware of this symbolic communication (e.g., Smith 2008:145).

It is also likely that cosmology played a role in shaping the designs of Maya cities (e.g., Ashmore and Sabloff 2002; M. Smith 2003:221), but identifying the message that is the symbolic communication is especially difficult for archaeologists (M. Smith 2003:221). However, Gregory Zaro and I have suggested that a useful first step is recognizing when such symbolic communication has taken place (Houk and Zaro 2011:196).

As mentioned previously, our work at La Milpa investigated Plaza B and the surrounding courtyards from 2007 to 2011 (Houk and Zaro 2011, 2012b; Zaro and Houk 2012). We concluded that—concurrent with more mundane planning and civil engineering concerns, such as artificially building up the plaza with boulder and cobble fill and canting its surface to create an internal drainage feature (a curious planning choice that would have necessitated the construction of a drain beneath an adjacent range building)—the planners also considered the creation and placement of ritual deposits. Two spatially discrete caches, one at the base of the western range building and one beneath a small altar in the center of the plaza, contained similar materials and nearly identical ceramic vessels. Deposited as part of the same construction event, the two caches "provide evidence for a coherent royal precinct plan" (Houk and Zaro 2011:187). Although much of the meaning of the cosmological symbolism suggested by the artifacts in the caches is unclear, the stylistically similar ceramic lids decorated with incised mat designs suggest a connection to the ruling family of the site and likely to royal sponsorship of or participation in the design and construction of the Late Classic plaza. Plaza B, in other words, was not only an example of civil planning and engineering; it was also a ritually engineered landscape with special deposits that communicated political and cosmological messages (Houk and Zaro 2011:196). We may not be able to fully read the symbolic content of the messages, but it is important that we recognize that some kind of statement was made.

Processional Architecture in the Eastern Lowlands

Returning to the premise at the beginning of this book, that Maya cities were essential trappings of rulership, the architectural plan of Maya cities should reflect functions related to kingship. Stated another way, how did the design of a city complement or enhance certain aspects of divine kingship? Such a question is another approach to understanding why particular cities look the way they do by attempting to understand how architecture functioned within the context of Maya political systems.

Maya kings undoubtedly had many responsibilities, not all of which involved public events in public places. For example, there are numerous Late Classic codex-style vessels with depictions of royal persons doing things inside palaces—conducting private rituals, greeting visitors, giving and accepting gifts, dressing for ritual dances, feasting, and even negotiating marriage arrangements (Reents-Budet 2001:213). When kings are shown inside buildings, they are dressed rather simply with modest headdresses. Some things rulers did involved either lots of other people or lots of witnesses. Other ceramic vessels and the murals at Bonampak depict kings holding court on the steps or terraces of their royal palaces. Presumably, greater numbers of people could witness the events that took place outside of palace buildings rather than within them. Reents-Budet (2001:197, 202) notes that the types of activities depicted in such settings include the public presentation of prisoners, prisoner sacrifice, and official court visits by other elite. In these settings, the king is often seated on a wooden, presumably movable, throne, and wearing more elaborate attire than in the interior scenes.

In some instances the king apparently participated in even larger public events, or mass spectacles, and dressed for the part. As Inomata (2006:810) argues, the massive headdresses and elaborate backracks worn by kings as depicted on stelae were designed to be highly visible during mass spectacles. Kings not only sponsored elaborate public spectacles but also in many cases were the key performers in them, and Inomata (2006) contends that one function of public plazas was to accommodate large audiences to witness such events. Depictions of kings being carried on litters or palanquins bedecked with images of giants or animals suggest that some mass spectacles involved processions in which the king was carried along a prescribed route in front of the spectators. The murals at Bonampak depict a possible procession in which people wearing special costumes and carrying ritual paraphernalia walk in a single-file line. Among the participants are banner carriers, musicians, and dancers (Miller and Brittenham 2013:115–116). These spectacles and processions were important for community identity and "were probably the occasions on which people felt their ties with the ruler most strongly" (Inomata 2006:818).

From a functional perspective, then, Maya city planning likely took into consideration the need for city architecture to serve as a stage for performances from time to time. In our culture, regular city streets serve as routes for parades, but parades are not the overarching concern in street design. For the ancient Maya, however, the inverse may have been true; the need for processions, mass spectacles, and elaborate rituals may have been the primary concern in the arrangement of certain urban design elements. From this perspective, it is possible to examine city plans for architectural elements that likely functioned together as platforms for rituals, spectacles, and processions. Strong cases for processional architecture can be made for Chan Chich, Xunantunich, La Milpa, El Pilar, Dos Hombres, and Minanha.

At Chan Chich the Eastern and Western Causeways, which are both larger than required for simple transportation routes, enter the Main Plaza in front of Structure A-1, a massive structure with a broad stairway and central summit landing flanked by tandem range buildings. Attached to the eastern side of Structure A-1 is the site's ball court, which sits on the platform created by the Eastern Causeway. These four elements, along with the Main Plaza itself, likely constituted the stage for a variety of performances involving processions along the causeways, spectacles on the stairs and landing of Structure A-1, and ball games. The two structures at either end of the causeways may have been shrines and part of the processional architecture (Houk 2013b).

In a similar arrangement to Chan Chich, Sacbeob I and II at Xunantunich enter Plaza A-1 from the east and west at the base of the Castillo. While Sacbe I is only 19 m wide, Sacbe II is 40 m wide, comparable to the two causeways at Chan Chich. Angela Keller's (2006:610) dissertation research recovered artifacts from these two *sacbeob* that appear to be associated with processions—a broken ceramic drum and bits of jewelry that likely fell off of costumes, for example. These artifactual data support the architectural evidence for ritually focused groups of buildings and features that include not only the causeways and the Castillo but also Ballcourt 1, which is associated with Sacbe II, and the structures at the *sacbe* termini.

La Milpa is another example of a city with an apparent association between a *sacbe*, a large structure, and a ball court. In this example, however, the arrangement of the elements is different. The *sacbe* that connects Plaza B and the rest of the southern monumental architecture to the Great Plaza enters the Great Plaza's southeast corner via a steeply sloping ramp. As noted in chapter 8, Structure 3, the most massive temple-pyramid at La Milpa, does not face into the plaza but appears to face the eastern end of Structure 8. This rather unusual orientation suggests that the building is functionally more associated with the *sacbe* than it is with the Great Plaza. Debora Trein's (2012) excavations have uncovered evidence that Structure 3 once had an elaborate stucco frieze approximately midway up the building. Completing this architectural assemblage is the Southern Ballcourt, situated northwest of Structure 3 and in direct line with the *sacbe*. Schultz et al. (1994:51) proposed that, of the two ball courts at La Milpa, this one was likely more ritual in function.

The placement and orientations of two small temples at El Pilar are best explained by considering them in association with entrances to the Plaza Copal rather than with the plaza itself. Structure EP8 faces west, toward the eastern end of Structure EP9. Similar to Structure 3 at La Milpa, the real focus of Structure EP8 is likely the ramp or staircase that enters Plaza Copal's northern edge from Plaza Duende. Similarly, Structure EP9 faces the area in Plaza Copal where the Bryan & Murphy Causeway enters. The two structures likely functioned in the context of processions entering or exiting the plaza through those two routes.

At Dos Hombres, the main ball court at the site sits at the southern end of a narrow *sacbe* that leads to the main plaza. In this case there is no large building associated with the *sacbe*'s entrance, and it is not entirely clear that the causeway functioned as a processional route. However, it is possible that the *sacbe*'s only function was ritual, as people moving down it would have to pass through the ball court alley to access the southern architecture at the site— perhaps regular traffic entered and exited the main plaza through the wide gap in structures to the east of the *sacbe* and bypassed the ball court entirely. Immediately south of the ball court, the sloping ramp to Plaza B-1 could have served as a viewing stand for the ball court. As the location of the only carved monuments at Dos Hombres (three plain stela and an altar), Plaza B-1 could have been part of a processional route.

At Minanha a possible processional route is indicated by the contrasting structure orientations in the site's epicenter. While most of the structures at the site are oriented 15° east of north, a handful of buildings and the site's only *sacbe* are oriented 10° west of north. The *sacbe* exits from the main plaza's northwest corner and terminates at the shrine-like Structure 53 and Stela 7. In the main plaza, the Structure 7A temple-pyramid, the E-Group (Structure 3A), the ball court, the small platform supporting Stelae 1 and 2, and Structure 14C share the same orientation as the *sacbe*. A line drawn from Structure 14C at the south to Structure 53 at the north passes in front of Structure 7A and past four of the site's stelae, suggesting a relationship between these otherwise spatially disparate elements of the site plan.

At this point the proposed processional architecture at these sites represents hypotheses to be tested. However, taking processions and rituals into consideration as a primary concern in Maya city design makes nagging questions seem less puzzling. For example, processions could explain why the causeways at Chan Chich are so wide and why Structure 3 at La Milpa appears to face the end of a range building. If these special assemblages of buildings and features functioned together as the stages for processions and rituals, seemingly random structure placement or orientation makes sense. The assemblages highlighted include *sacbeob*, ball courts, plazas, and sometimes the largest structures at these sites, which likely served as viewing stands in some cases and as stages for rituals in other cases. When these sites were in use, elaborate stucco friezes and facades adorned many of these buildings, including the Castillo at Xunantunich and Structure 3 at La Milpa. These friezes would have acted as the backdrop for rituals performed on the steps of the buildings.

Obviously, proving that these groups functioned together as the stages for processions and rituals is difficult, but Angela Keller's (2006) work at Xunantunich gives us a starting point. Keller excavated what she called "clearing units" along the edges of the causeways where she thought trash might accumulate. Importantly, she found sherds from ceramic drums along both causeways and a concentration of them near Structure A-21 and the western end of Sacbe II. She also found sherds from censers in the same area and concluded that "the rituals enacted on Structure A-21 were directly associated with musical performance along the causeways" (Keller 2006:452). She also found other types of artifacts along the causeways, including a chert eccentric, a pyrite mirror fragment, a marine shell pendant, a jade bead, portions of ceramic bowls, and obsidian blades. Some of this debris she interprets as bits of costume lost during processions, but some she interprets as the remnants of rituals conducted along the procession route (Keller 2006:610). Perhaps by stopping the procession along its route to perform some offering or ritual, the participants could engage an even larger number of spectators.

The possibility that architectural features are functionally linked as elements for processions and mass spectacles raises another pitfall in assessing planning. Minanha, for example, scored in the middle of the scale for "coordinated arrangement of buildings and spaces," but perhaps that is not really accurate if significant numbers of buildings and features are actually coordinated to function together as processional architecture.

Final Thoughts

The cities of the eastern lowlands demonstrate the tremendous complexity and variety of Maya urbanism. Of course, such variation is not surprising given the long time frame and geographic distances in question. Through the lenses of the built environment and ancient urban planning, the case studies presented in this book highlight important concepts related to the development of Maya urbanism during the Late Preclassic period, at which time the link between monumental architecture and the institution of divine kingship was first established, through the elaboration and expansion of kingdoms large and small across the eastern lowlands by the end of the Classic period. Beyond that, they align what we know about the political history of these cities with the larger developments that occurred in the Maya world during the Classic period.

Hopefully archaeologists investigating ancient urbanism, regardless of geographic area, will find the application of Smith's (2007) approach to studying planning useful. The same concepts can be applied to other parts of the Maya world as easily as they can to ancient cities in Africa. The true utility of the method may not be that it identifies more-planned cities versus less-planned cities particularly well but rather that it identifies and highlights differences in planning. For example, the cities of southern Belize generally appear less planned than Caracol. And, while it is true that Caracol represents a significant planning accomplishment with its extensive network of causeways, it might be more accurate to say that southern Belize cities follow a different idea about planning and are not necessarily less planned. The kings of southern Belize were clearly concerned with creating small plazas for displaying their royal monuments and integrating the natural topography into their structures. It may be that their preference for dispersed epicenters is part of a regional template for city building and not an indication of a low degree of central planning. The application of Smith's (2007) approach, however, is the very tool that highlights these differences.

There are other ideas about city building apparent in the data. In northwestern Belize, the Petén template identified by Ashmore (1991) guided the general design of cities, but the rulers in the region put their own stamp on it by creating massive plazas. Along the western edge of the region, wide causeways defined by parapets suggest common planning concepts at Caracol, Chan Chich, Xunantunich, and El Pilar.

Chan Chich, in particular, is an interesting application of the "build what you know" idea because it incorporates the massive large plaza plan of northwestern Belize with the parapet-lined causeways and the rare form of attached ball court found primarily in the Belize Valley at places like Xunantunich, Yalbac, and Saturday Creek. Chan Chich, based on a site-planning analysis, may have been more closely affiliated with kingdoms to its south rather than with Dos Hombres and La Milpa to its north.

The variability in site plans and the implied ability of city planners to pick and choose from contemporary and even historical architectural design concepts is a fascinating aspect of Maya urbanism, one that scholars in other parts of the world may find to be a useful contrast. Smith (2007:25) proposes that "the presence of similar buildings, layouts, and other urban features in a series of related cities suggests adherence to a common plan or idea of city planning." Aztec city-state capitals in the state of Morelos, for example, follow a "highly standardized pattern" in which "the plazas are quite formal, the major temple-pyramid is always on the east side of the plaza, and other sides of the plaza are typically occupied by one or more of the following features: a palace, a ballcourt, or a row of small altars" (Smith 2007:27). This standardization could be interpreted to represent a higher level of planning than in typical Mesoamerican cities (Smith 2007).

I would suggest, however, that the variability seen in Maya cities, which nonetheless all draw on a standard inventory of urban forms—plazas, ball courts, temples, causeways, palaces, and so on—has more to do with the nature of Maya kingship than it does with a lack of common ideas about how to build a city. In a culture that stressed the achievements of individual kings and their ancestors and was never united under one political yoke, perhaps the common idea about urban planning was flexibility: the freedom to combine the building blocks of a Maya city in unique ways. One concern for Maya kings and city planners appears to have been the need to create within the layout of their centers routes for processions and stages for mass spectacles. How they did this, however, highlights the flexible nature of Maya urban planning as common architectural elements were combined in ways that highlighted each kingdom's unique design and reflected, perhaps, subtle relationships between peers and neighboring kingdoms.

The cities of the eastern lowlands—from tiny Minanha to sprawling Caracol, from swampy Altun Ha to hilltop Xunantunich—are unique variations on a theme, or perhaps variations on a related set of themes, despite their differences in setting, size, and design. Similarities between cities point to sources of planning like political emulation and previously recognized site-planning templates, including the pervasive Petén template recognized by Wendy Ashmore (1991). Differences between cities highlight the flexibility of the complicated and long-lived tradition that was ancient Maya urbanism in the eastern lowlands.

References Cited

Adams, Richard E. W.
1986   Rio Azul. *National Geographic* 169:420–451.
1991   *Ancient Mesoamerica*, rev. ed. University of Oklahoma Press, Norman.
1995   Introduction. In *The Programme for Belize Regional Archaeological Project: 1994 Interim Report*, edited by Richard E. W. Adams and Fred Valdez Jr., pp. 1–15. Center for Archaeology and Tropical Studies and the University of Texas at San Antonio.
1999   *Río Azul: An Ancient Maya City*. University of Oklahoma Press, Norman.

Adams, R. E. W., and Richard C. Jones
1981   Spatial Patterns and Regional Growth Among Maya Cities. *American Antiquity* 46:301–322.

Aimers, James J.
1993   Messages from the Gods: An Hermeneutic Analysis of the Maya E-Group Complex. Unpublished M.A. thesis, Department of Anthropology, Trent University, Peterborough, Ontario.
2007a What Maya Collapse? Terminal Classic Variation in the Maya Lowlands. *Journal of Archaeological Research* 15:329–377.
2007b Anti-Apocalypse: The Postclassic Period at Lamanai, Belize. *Archaeology International* 10:45–48.

Aimers, James J., Terry G. Powis, and Jaime J. Awe
2000   Preclassic Round Structures of the Upper Belize River Valley. *Latin American Antiquity* 11:71–86.

Aimers, James J., and Prudence M. Rice
2006   Astronomy, Ritual, and the Interpretation of Maya "E-Group" Architectural Assemblages. *Ancient Mesoamerica* 17:79–96.

Andres, Christopher R., Gabriel D. Wrobel, Jason J. Gonzalez, Shawn G. Morton, and Rebecca Shelton
2011   Power and Status in Central Belize: Insights from the Caves Branch Archaeological Survey Project's 2010 Field Season. *Research Reports in Belizean Archaeology* 8:101–113.

Andrews, George F.
1975   *Maya Cities: Placemaking and Urbanization*. University of Oklahoma Press, Norman.

Anthony, Dana, and Stephen L. Black
1994   Operation 2031: The 1983 Main Plaza Investigations. In *Continuing Archeology at Colha, Belize*, edited by Thomas R. Hester, Harry J. Shafer, and Jack D. Eaton, pp. 39–58. Studies in Archeology 16. Texas Archeological Research Laboratory, University of Texas at Austin.

Aquino, Valorie V., Keith M. Prufer, Clayton Meredith, Brendan J. Culleton, and Douglas J. Kennett
2013   Constraining the Age of Abandonment of Uxbenka Site Core Using Archaeological Stratigraphy and AMS^{14}C Dates. *Research Reports in Belizean Archaeology* 10:269–279.

Ashmore, Wendy
1989   Construction and Cosmology: Politics and Ideology in Lowland Maya Settlement Patterns. In *Word and Image in Maya Culture: Explorations in Language, Writing, and Representation*, edited by W. F. Hanks and Don S. Rice, pp. 272–286. University of Utah Press, Salt Lake City.
1991   Site-Planning Principles and Concepts of Directionality among the Ancient Maya. *Latin American Antiquity* 2:199–226.
1992   Deciphering Maya Architectural Plans. In *New Theories on the Ancient Maya*, edited by Elin C. Danien and Robert J. Sharer, pp. 173–184. Museum Monographs. University of Pennsylvania Museum, Philadelphia.
2010   Antecedents, Allies, Antagonists: Xunantunich and Its Neighbors. In *Classic Maya Provincial Politics: Xunantunich and Its Hinterlands*, edited by Lisa J. LeCount and Jason Yaeger, pp. 46–64. University of Arizona Press, Tucson.

Ashmore, Wendy, and Jeremy A. Sabloff
2002   Spatial Orders in Maya Civic Plans. *Latin American Antiquity* 13:201–215.
2003   Interpreting Ancient Maya Civic Plans: Reply to Smith. *Latin American Antiquity* 14:229–236.

Ashmore, Wendy, Jason Yaeger, and Cynthia Robin
2004   Commoner Sense: Late and Terminal Classic Social Strategies in the Xunantunich Area. In *The Terminal Classic in the Maya Lowlands: Collapse, Transition, and Transformation*, edited by Arthur A. Demarest, Prudence M. Rice, and Don S. Rice, pp. 303–323. University Press of Colorado, Boulder.

Audet, Carolyn M.
2006   Political Organization in the Belize Valley: Excavations at Baking Pot, Cahal Pech, and Xunantunich. Unpublished Ph.D. dissertation, Vanderbilt University, Nashville, Tennessee.

Aveni, Anthony
2009   *The End of Time: The Maya Mystery of 2012*. University Press of Colorado, Boulder.

Aveni, Anthony F., Anne S. Dowd, and Benjamin Vining
2003 Maya Calendar Reform? Evidence from Orientations of Specialized Architectural Assemblages. *Latin American Antiquity* 14:159–178.

Awe, Jaime J.
1992 Dawn in the Land between the Rivers: Formative Occupation at Cahal Pech, Belize and Its Implications for Preclassic Development in the Maya Lowlands. Unpublished Ph.D. dissertation, Institute of Archaeology, University of London.
2012 The Archaeology of Belize in the Twenty-First Century. In *The Oxford Handbook of Mesoamerican Archaeology*, edited by Deborah L. Nichols and Christopher A. Pool, pp. 69–82. Oxford University Press, Oxford, England.
2013 Was There a Prehistoric Dzuluinicob? Examining the Archaeological Evidence for a Belize Valley Identity. Paper presented at the Eleventh Annual Belize Archaeology and Anthropology Symposium, San Ignacio.

Awe, Jaime J., and Paul F. Healy
1994 Flakes to Blades? Middle Formative Development of Obsidian Artifacts in the Upper Belize River Valley. *Latin American Antiquity* 5:193–205.

Aylesworth, Grant R.
2005 A Science of Networks Approach to Ancient Maya Sociopolitical Organization. Unpublished Ph.D. dissertation, Department of Anthropology, University of Texas at Austin.

Bair, Daniel A., and Richard E. Terry
2012 In Search of Markets and Fields: Soil Chemical Investigations at Motul de San José. In *Motul de San José: Politics, History, and Economy in a Maya Polity*, edited by Antonia E. Foias and Kitty F. Emery, pp. 357–385. University Press of Florida, Gainesville.

Becker, Marshall J.
2004 Maya Heterarchy as Inferred from Classic-Period Plaza Plans. *Ancient Mesoamerica* 15:127–138.
2009 Tikal: Evidence for Ethnic Diversity in a Prehispanic Lowland Maya State Capital. In *Domestic Life in Prehispanic Capitals: A Study of Specialization, Hierarchy, and Ethnicity*, edited by Linda R. Manzanilla and Claude Chapdelaine, pp. 69–84. Memoirs of the Museum of Anthropology. University of Michigan, Ann Arbor.

Beetz, Carl P., and Linton Satterthwaite
1981 *The Monuments and Inscriptions of Caracol, Belize*. University Museum Monograph 45. University of Pennsylvania Museum of Archaeology and Anthropology, Philadelphia.

Berlin, Heinrich
1958 El glifo "emblem" en las inscripciones mayas. *Journal de la Sociéte de Américanistes* n.s. 47:111–119.

Bill, Cassandra R., and Geoffrey E. Braswell
2005   Life at the Crossroads: New Data from Pusilhá, Belize. *Research Reports in Belizean Archaeology* 2:301–312.

Black, Stephen L.
1990   Field Methods and Methodologies in Lowland Maya Archaeology. Unpublished Ph.D. thesis, Department of Anthropology, Harvard University, Cambridge, Massachusetts.

Blom, Franz
1924   Report on the Preliminary Work at Uaxactun, Guatemala. *Carnegie Institution of Washington Year Book* 23:217–219.

Boone, Elizabeth Hill
2000   *Stories in Red and Black: Pictorial Histories of the Aztecs and Mixtecs*. University of Texas Press, Austin.

Boudreaux, Sarah N.
2013   Life on the Edge: Investigating Maya Hinterland Settlements in Northwestern Belize. Unpublished M.A. thesis, Department of Sociology, Anthropology, and Social Work, Texas Tech University, Lubbock.

Braswell, Geoffrey E.
2002   Pusilhá Archaeological Project. Report submitted to the Foundation for the Advancement of Mesoamerican Studies, Crystal River, Florida.
2003   Introduction: Reinterpreting Early Classic Interaction. In *The Maya and Teotihuacan: Reinterpreting Early Classic Interaction*, edited by Geoffrey E. Braswell, pp. 1–43. University of Texas Press, Austin.
2007   Late and Terminal Classic Occupation at Pusilhá, Toledo District, Belize: Site Planning, Burial Patterns, and Cosmology. *Research Reports in Belizean Archaeology* 4:67–77.

Braswell, Geoffrey E. (editor)
2003   *The Maya and Teotihuacan: Reinterpreting Early Classic Interaction*. University of Texas Press, Austin.

Braswell, Geoffrey E., Cassandra R. Bill, and Christian M. Prager
2008   Exchange, Political Relations, and Regional Interaction: The Ancient City of Pusilhá in the Late Classic Maya World. *Research Reports in Belizean Archaeology* 5:51–62.

Braswell, Geoffrey E., Nancy Peniche May, Megan R. Pitcavage, and Kiri L. Hagerman
2011   Revisiting the Kingdom of the Crystal Skull: New Investigations at Lubaantun. *Research Reports in Belizean Archaeology* 8:115–126.

Braswell, Geoffrey E., Megan R. Pitcavage, and Andrew Somerville
2009   Toledo Regional Interaction Project: 2008–2009 Annual Report. Report submitted to the Belize Institute of Archaeology, Belmopan.

Braswell, Geoffrey E., Christian M. Prager, and Cassandra R. Bill
2005   The Kingdom of the Avocado: Recent Investigations at Pusilhá, a Classic Maya City of Southern Belize. *Anthropological Notebooks* 11:60–88.

Braswell, Geoffrey E., Christian M. Prager, Cassandra R. Bill, and Sonja A. Schwake
2004   Recent Archaeological and Epigraphic Research at Pusilhá, Belize: Report on the 2001 and 2002 Field Seasons. *Research Reports in Belizean Archaeology* 1:333–345.
Braswell, Geoffrey E., Christian M. Prager, Cassandra R. Bill, Sonja A. Schwake, and Jennifer B. Braswell
2005   The Rise of Secondary States in the Southeastern Periphery of the Maya World: A Report on Recent Archaeological and Epigraphic Research at Pusilhá, Belize. *Ancient Mesoamerica* 15:219–233.
Braswell, Geoffrey E., and Keith M. Prufer
2009   Political Organization and Interaction in Southern Belize. *Research Reports in Belizean Archaeology* 8:43–54.
Braswell, Jennifer B.
2010   Elite Craft Production of Stone Drills and Slate at Group D, Xunantunich. In *Classic Maya Provincial Politics: Xunantunich and Its Hinterlands*, edited by Lisa J. LeCount and Jason Yaeger, pp. 161–183. University of Arizona Press, Tucson.
Brokaw, Nicholas V. L., and Elizabeth P. Mallory
1993   *Vegetation of the Rio Bravo Conservation and Management Area, Belize*. Manomet Bird Observatory, Manomet, Massachusetts.
Brown, Mary Kathryn
1995   Test Pit Program and Preclassic Investigations at the Site of Dos Hombres, Belize. Unpublished M.A. thesis, University of Texas at San Antonio.
2009   The Preclassic in the Mopan River Valley: Preliminary Investigations at Nohoch Ek and Xunantunich. *Research Reports in Belizean Archaeology* 6:63–71.
Brown, M. Kathryn, Jennifer Cochran, Leah McCurdy, and David Mixter
2011   Preceramic to Postclassic: A Brief Synthesis of the Occupation History of Group E, Xunantunich. *Research Reports in Belizean Archaeology* 8:209–219.
Brown, M. Kathryn, and James F. Garber
2005   The Role of Public Architecture and Ritual in the Rise of Complexity: An Example from Blackman Eddy, Belize. *Research Reports in Belizean Archaeology* 2:53–65.
2008   Establishing and Reusing Sacred Space: A Diachronic Perspective from Blackman Eddy, Belize. In *Ruins of the Past: The Use and Perception of Abandoned Structures in the Maya Lowlands*, edited by Travis W. Stanton and Aline Magnoni, pp. 147–170. University of Colorado Press, Boulder.
Bueche, Paulo
2012   Maya Scholar Deciphers Meaning of Newly Discovered Monument That Refers to 2012. Electronic document, http://www.utexas.edu/know/2012/06/28/la-corona/, accessed August 18, 2013.
Bullard, William R., Jr.
1965   *Stratigraphic Excavations at San Estevan, Northern British Honduras*. Occasional Paper 9. Royal Ontario Museum, Toronto.

Bullard, William R., Jr., and Mary Ricketson Bullard
1965   *Late Classic Finds at Baking Pot, British Honduras*. Occasional Paper 8. Royal Ontario Museum, Toronto.

Carmean, Kelli, Nicholas Dunning, and Jeff Karl Kowalski
2004   High Times in the Hill Country: A Perspective from the Terminal Classic Puuc Region. In *The Terminal Classic in the Maya Lowlands: Collapse, Transition, and Transformation*, edited by Arthur A. Demarest, Prudence M. Rice, and Don S. Rice, pp. 424–449. University Press of Colorado, Boulder.

Carrasco Vargas, Ramón, Verónica A. Vázquez López, and Simon Martin
2009   Daily Life of the Ancient Maya Recorded on Murals at Calakmul, Mexico. *PNAS* 196(46):19,245–19,249.

Chase, Arlen F., and Diane Z. Chase
1987   *Investigations at the Classic Maya City of Caracol, Belize: 1985–1987.* Monograph 3. Pre-Columbian Art Research Institute, San Francisco, California.
1996   More Than Kin and King: Centralized Political Organization among the Late Classic Maya. *Current Anthropology* 37:803–810.
1998   Scale and Intensity in Classic Period Maya Agriculture: Terracing and Settlement at the "Garden City" of Caracol, Belize. *Culture & Agriculture* 20:60–77.
2001a   Ancient Maya Causeways and Site Organization at Caracol, Belize. *Ancient Mesoamerica* 12:273–281.
2001b   Continued Investigation into Epicentral Palaces: Report of the 2001 Field Season at Caracol, Belize. Electronic document, http://caracol.org/reports/2001.php, accessed February 20, 2013.
2001c   The Royal Court of Caracol, Belize: Its Palaces and People. In *Royal Courts of the Ancient Maya*, Vol. 2, edited by Takeshi Inomata and Stephen D. Houston, pp. 102–137. Westview Press, Boulder, Colorado.
2002   Continued Investigation of Caracol's Social Organization: Report of the Spring 2002 Field Season at Caracol, Belize. Electronic document, http://caracol.org/reports/2002.php, accessed February 20, 2013.
2003a   At Home in the South: Investigations in the Vicinity of Caracol's South Acropolis: 2003 Field Report of the Caracol Archaeological Project. Electronic document, http://caracol.org/reports/2003.php, accessed February 20, 2013.
2003b   Minor Centers, Complexity, and Scale in Lowland Maya Settlement Archaeology. In *Perspectives on Ancient Maya Rural Complexity*, edited by Gyles Iannone and Samuel Connell, pp. 108–118. Monograph 49. The Cotsen Institute of Archaeology, University of California, Los Angeles.
2004a   Terminal Classic Status-Linked Ceramics and the Maya "Collapse": De Facto Refuse at Caracol, Belize. In *The Terminal Classic in the Maya Lowlands: Collapse, Transition, and Transformation*, edited by in Arthur Demarest, Prudence Rice, and Don S. Rice, pp. 342–366. University of Colorado Press, Boulder.
2004b   Exploring Ancient Economic Relationships at Caracol, Belize. *Research Reports in Belizean Archaeology* 1:115–127.

2005   The Early Classic Period at Caracol, Belize: Transitions, Complexity, and Methodological Issues in Maya Archaeology. *Research Reports in Belizean Archaeology* 2:17–38.
2006   Before the Boom: Caracol's Preclassic Era. *Research Reports in Belizean Archaeology* 3:41–57.
2007a   Ancient Maya Urban Development: Insights from the Archaeology of Caracol, Belize. *Belizean Studies* 29(2):60–72.
2007b   "This is the End": Archaeological Transitions and the Terminal Classic Period at Caracol, Belize. *Research Reports in Belizean Archaeology* 4:13–27.
2009   Symbolic Egalitarianism and Homogenized Distributions in the Archaeological Record at Caracol, Belize: Method, Theory, and Complexity. *Research Reports in Belizean Archaeology* 6:15–24.
2010   Household Patterning, the "Collapse," and LiDAR Ground-Checks: Continued Investigation in and near Caracol's Epicenter: 2010 Field Report of the Caracol Archaeological Project. Report submitted to the Belize Institute of Archaeology. Department of Anthropology, University of Central Florida, Orlando.
2011   Status and Power: Caracol, Teotihuacan, and the Early Classic Maya World. *Research Reports in Belizean Archaeology* 8:3–18.

Chase, Arlen F., Diane Z. Chase, Christopher T. Fisher, Stephen J. Leisz, and John F. Wieshampel
2012   Geospatial Revolution and Remote Sensing LiDAR in Mesoamerican Archaeology. *PNAS* 109(32):12,916–12,921.

Chase, Arlen F., Diane Z. Chase, John F. Weishampel, Jason B. Drake, Ramesh L. Shrestha, K. Clint Slatton, Jaime J. Awe, and William E. Carter
2011   Airborne LiDAR, Archaeology, and the Ancient Maya Landscape at Caracol, Belize. *Journal of Archaeological Science* 38:387–398.

Chase, Diane Z.
1982   Spatial and Temporal Variability in Postclassic Northern Belize. Unpublished Ph.D. dissertation, Department of Anthropology, University of Pennsylvania, Philadelphia.

Chase, Diane Z., and Arlen F. Chase
1982   Yucatec Influence in Terminal Classic Northern Belize. *American Antiquity* 47:596–614.
1996   Maya Multiples: Individuals, Entries, and Tombs in Structure A34 of Caracol, Belize. *Latin American Antiquity* 7:61–79.
1998   The Architectural Context of Caches, Burials, and Other Ritual Activities for the Classic Period Maya (as Reflected at Caracol, Belize). In *Function and Meaning in Classic Maya Architecture*, edited by S. D. Houston, pp. 299–332. Dumbarton Oaks Research Library and Collection, Washington, D.C.
2004a   Santa Rita Corozal: Twenty Years Later. *Research Reports in Belizean Archaeology* 1:243–255.

2004b   Archaeological Perspectives on Classic Maya Social Organization from Caracol, Belize. *Ancient Mesoamerica* 15:139–147.
2004c   Exploring Ancient Economic Relationships at Caracol, Belize. *Research Reports in Belizean Archaeology* 1:115–127.
2006   What the Hieroglyphs Don't Tell You: Archaeology and History at Caracol, Belize. Paper presented at the International Congress of Americanists, Seville, Spain.

Chase, Diane Z., and Norman Hammond
1982   Excavation of Nohmul Structure 20. *Mexican* 4(1): 7–12.

Cheetham, David
2004   The Role of "Terminus Groups" in Lowland Maya Site Planning. In *The Ancient Maya of the Belize Valley, Half a Century of Research*, edited by James F. Garber, pp. 125–148. University Press of Florida, Gainesville.

Christie, Jessica Joyce
2003   Introduction. In *Maya Palaces and Elite Residences: An Interdisciplinary Approach*, edited by Jessica Joyce Christie, pp. 1–12. University of Texas Press, Austin.

Cliff, Maynard B.
1986   Excavations in the Late Preclassic Nucleated Village. In *Archaeology at Cerros, Belize, Central America*, Vol. 1, edited by Robin A. Robertson and David A. Freidel, pp. 45–64. Southern Methodist University Press, Dallas, Texas.

Closs, Michael P.
1988   *The Hieroglyphic Text of Stela 9, Lamanai, Belize*. Research Reports on Ancient Maya Writing 21. Center for Maya Research, Washington, D.C.

Cobos, Rafael
2004   Chichén Itzá: Settlement and Hegemony during the Terminal Classic Period. In *The Terminal Classic in the Maya Lowlands: Collapse, Transition, and Transformation*, edited by Arthur A. Demarest, Prudence M. Rice, and Don S. Rice, pp. 517–544. University Press of Colorado, Boulder.

Coe, Michael D.
2011   *The Maya*. 8th ed. Thames and Hudson, New York.

Coe, Michael D., and Rex Koontz
2013   *Mexico: From the Olmecs to the Aztecs*. 7th ed. Thames and Hudson, New York.

Coe, Michael D., and Mark Van Stone
2005   *Reading the Maya Glyphs*. 2nd ed. Thames & Hudson, London.

Coggins, Clemency C.
1967   Palaces and the Planning of Ceremonial Centers in the Maya Lowlands. Manuscript on file, Tozzer Library, Peabody Museum, Harvard University, Cambridge.

Cortes-Rincon, Marisol
2011   Dos Hombres to Gran Cacao Settlement Survey Project: 2010 Field Season.

In *Research Reports from the Programme for Belize Archaeological Project*, Vol. 5, edited by Brett A. Houk and Fred Valdez Jr., pp. 243–250. Occasional Papers, No. 12. Mesoamerican Archaeological Research Laboratory, University of Texas at Austin.

Culbert, T. Patrick (editor)

1973 *The Classic Maya Collapse*. School for American Research and University of New Mexico Press, Albuquerque.

Dahlin, Bruce H., Christopher T. Jensen, Richard E. Terry, David R. Wright, and Timothy Beach

2007 In Search of an Ancient Maya Market. *Latin American Antiquity* 18:363–384.

Demarest, Arthur A.

2004a After the Maelstrom: Collapse of the Classic Maya Kingdoms and the Terminal Classic in Western Petén. In *The Terminal Classic in the Maya Lowlands: Collapse. Transition, and Transformation*, edited by Arthur A. Demarest, Prudence M. Rice, and Don S. Rice, pp. 102–124. University Press of Colorado, Boulder.

2004b *Ancient Maya: The Rise and Fall of a Rainforest Civilization*. Cambridge University Press, Cambridge, England.

Demarest, Arthur A., Prudence M. Rice, and Don S. Rice

2004 The Terminal Classic in the Maya Lowlands: Assessing Collapses, Terminations, and Transformations. In *The Terminal Classic in the Maya Lowlands: Collapse. Transition, and Transformation*, edited by Arthur A. Demarest, Prudence M. Rice, and Don S. Rice, pp. 545–572. University Press of Colorado, Boulder.

Demarest, Arthur A., Prudence M. Rice, and Don S. Rice (editors)

2004 *The Terminal Classic in the Maya Lowlands: Collapse. Transition, and Transformation*. University Press of Colorado, Boulder.

Doyle, James A.

2012 Regroup on "E-Groups": Monumentality and Early Centers in the Middle Preclassic Maya Lowlands. *Latin American Antiquity* 23:355–379.

Driver, W. David

2002 An Early Classic Colonnaded Building at the Maya Site of Blue Creek, Belize. *Latin American Antiquity* 13:63–84.

Dunham, Peter S.

1990 Coming Apart at the Seams: The Classic Development and Demise of Maya Civilization (a Segmentary View from Xnaheb, Belize). Unpublished Ph.D. dissertation, State University of New York at Albany.

Dunning, Nicholas P., Timothy Beach, Pat Farrell, and Sheryl Luzzadder-Beach

1998 Prehispanic Agrosystems and Adaptive Regions in the Maya Lowlands. *Culture & Agriculture* 20:87–101.

Dunning, Nicholas P., John G. Jones, Timothy Beach, and Sheryl Luzzadder-Beach

2003   Physiography, Habitats, and Landscapes of the Three Rivers Region. In *Heterarchy, Political Economy, and the Ancient Maya*, edited by Vernon L. Scarborough, Fred Valdez Jr., and Nicholas P. Dunning, pp. 14–24. University of Arizona Press, Tucson.

Dunning, Nicholas P., Sheryl Luzzadder-Beach, Timothy Beach, John G. Jones, Vernon Scarborough, and T. Patrick Culbert

2002   Arising from the Bajos: The Evolution of a Neotropical Landscape and the Rise of Maya Civilization. *Annals of the Association of American Geographers* 92:267–283.

Dunning, Nicholas P., Timothy P. Beach, and Sheryl Luzzadder-Beach

2012   Kax and Kol: Collapse and Resilience in Lowland Maya Civilization. *PNAS* 109(10):3652–3657.

Durst, Jeffrey J.

1998   Early Classic Maya Tomb in Northwestern Belize. Paper presented at the 63rd Annual Meeting of the Society for American Archaeology, Seattle, Washington.

Eaton, Jack D., and Barton Kunstler

1980   Excavations at Operation 2009: A Maya Ball Court. In *The Colha Project, Second Season, 1980 Interim Report*, edited by Thomas R. Hester, Jack D. Eaton, and Harry J. Shafer, pp. 121–132. The Center for Archaeological Research, University of Texas at San Antonio.

Estrada-Belli, Francisco

2006   Lightning Sky, Rain, and the Maize God: The Ideology of Preclassic Maya Rulers at Cival, Peten, Guatemala. *Ancient Mesoamerica* 17:57–78.

2011   *The First Maya Civilization: Ritual and Power Before the Classic Period*. Routledge, New York.

Estrada-Belli, Francisco, Nikolai Grube, Marc Wolf, Kristen Gardella, and Claudio Lozano Guerra-Librero

2003   Preclassic Maya Monuments and Temples at Cival, Petén, Guatemala. *Antiquity* 77(296). Electronic document, http://www.antiquity.ac.uk/projgall/belli296/, accessed March 15, 2014.

Fauvelle, Mikael, Chelsea R. Fisher, and Geoffrey E. Braswell

2013   Return to the Kingdom of the Eagle: Archaeological Investigations at Nim Li Punit, Belize. *Research Reports in Belizean Archaeology* 10:241–251.

Fedick, Scott L.

1996   *The Managed Mosaic: Ancient Maya Agriculture and Resource Use*. University of Utah Press, Salt Lake City.

Fields, Virginia M.

2004   The Royal Charter at Xunantunich. In *The Ancient Maya of the Belize Valley, Half a Century of Research*, edited by James F. Garber, pp. 180–190. University Press of Florida, Gainesville.

Foias, Antonia E.
2013 *Ancient Maya Political Dynamics*. University Press of Florida, Gainesville.
Ford, Anabel
2004 Integration among Communities, Center, and Region: The Case from El Pilar. In *The Ancient Maya of the Belize Valley, Half a Century of Research*, edited by James F. Garber, pp. 238–256. University Press of Florida, Gainesville.
Ford, Anabel, and Hugo Bihr
2013 Using Cutting-Edge LiDAR Technology at El Pilar to Discover Ancient Maya House Sites. Paper presented at the Eleventh Annual Belize Archaeology and Anthropology Symposium, San Ignacio.
Ford, Anabel, and Scott Fedick
1988 Draft Report on the Archaeological Resource Potential and Management of the Programme for Belize Lands, Orange Walk, Belize. Manuscript on file, Mesoamerican Research Center, Social Process Research Institute, University of California, Santa Barbara.
Ford, Anabel, Rudy Larios, Johan Normark, Paulino Morales, and Carmen Ramos
2001 Influence of Ancient Settlement in the Contemporary Maya Forest: Investigating Land Use at El Pilar. BRASS/El Pilar 2001 Field Season. Report submitted to the Belize Department of Archaeology. Mesoamerican Research Center, University of California, Santa Barbara.
Ford, Anabel, Melanie C. Santiago Smith, and John M. Morris
2005 Community Integration and Adaptive Management at El Pilar. *Research Reports in Belizean Archaeology* 2:459–470.
Ford, Owen
1998 Excavations at the Ballcourt. In *The 1997 Season of the Chan Chich Archaeological Project*, edited by Brett A. Houk, pp. 53–58. Papers of the Chan Chich Archaeological Project, No. 3. Center for Maya Studies, San Antonio, Texas.
Ford, Owen, and Amy E. Rush
2000 1998 Excavations at the Western Groups. In *The 1998 and 1999 Season of the Chan Chich Archaeological Project*, edited by Brett A. Houk, pp. 41–48. Papers of the Chan Chich Archaeological Project, No. 4. Mesoamerican Archaeological Research Laboratory, University of Texas at Austin.
Fox, Richard
1977 *Urban Anthropology*. Prentice Hall, Englewood Cliffs, New Jersey.
Freidel, David A.
1986a Introduction. In *Archaeology at Cerros, Belize, Central America*, Vol. 1, edited by Robin A. Robertson and David A. Freidel, pp. xiii–xxiii. Southern Methodist University Press, Dallas, Texas.
1986b The Monumental Architecture. In *Archaeology at Cerros, Belize, Central America*, Vol. 1, edited by Robin A. Robertson and David A. Freidel, pp. 1–22. Southern Methodist University Press, Dallas, Texas.

Freidel, David A., and Linda Schele
1988a Symbol and Power: A History of the Lowland Maya Cosmogram. In *Maya Iconography*, edited by Elizabeth P. Benson and Gillette Griffin, pp. 44–93. Princeton University Press, Princeton.
1988b Kingship in the Late Preclassic Maya Lowlands: The Instruments and Places of Ritual Power. *American Anthropologist* 90:547–567.

Freiwald, Carolyn
2011 Patterns of Population Movement at Xunantunich, Cahal Pech, and Baking Pot during the Late and Terminal Classic (AD 600–900). *Research Reports in Belizean Archaeology* 8:89–100.

Gann, Thomas W. F.
1925 *Mystery Cities: Exploration and Adventure in Lubaantun*. Duckworth, London.
1926 *Ancient Cities and Modern Tribes: Exploration and Adventure in Maya Lands*. Charles Scribner's Sons, New York.
1927 *Maya Cities: A Record of Exploration and Adventure in Middle America*. Duckworth, London.

Garber, James F.
2004 The Archaeology of the Belize Valley in Historical Perspective. In *The Ancient Maya of the Belize Valley, Half a Century of Research*, edited by James F. Garber, pp. 1–14. University Press of Florida, Gainesville.

Garber, James F. (editor)
2004 *The Ancient Maya of the Belize Valley, Half a Century of Research*. University Press of Florida, Gainesville.

Garber, James F., and Jaime J. Awe
2008 Middle Formative Architecture and Ritual at Cahal Pech. *Research Reports in Belizean Archaeology* 5:185–190.
2009 A Terminal Early Formative Symbol System in the Maya Lowlands: The Iconography of the Cunil Phase (1100–900 BC) at Cahal Pech. *Research Reports in Belizean Archaeology* 6:151–159.

Garber, James F., M. Kathryn Brown, Jaime J. Awe, and Christopher J. Hartman
2004a Middle Formative Prehistory of the Central Belize Valley: An Examination of Architecture, Material Culture, and Sociopolitical Change at Blackman Eddy. In *The Ancient Maya of the Belize Valley: Half a Century of Archaeological Research*, edited by James F. Garber, pp. 25–47. University Press of Florida, Gainesville.
2004b The Terminal Early Formative Kanocha Phase (1100–900 B.C.) at Blackman Eddy. *Research Reports in Belizean Archaeology* 1:13–25.

Garber, James F., M. Kathryn Brown, W. David Driver, David M. Glassman, Christopher J. Hartman, F. Kent Reilly III, and Lauren A. Sullivan
2004 Archaeological Investigations at Blackman Eddy. In *The Ancient Maya of the Belize Valley: Half a Century of Archaeological Research*, edited by James F. Garber, pp. 48–69. University Press of Florida, Gainesville.

Garber, James F., Jennifer L. Cochran, and Jaime J. Awe

2007 The Middle Formative Ideological Foundations of Kingship: The Case from Cahal Pech, Belize. *Research Reports in Belizean Archaeology* 4:169–175.

Garrison, Thomas G.

2007 Ancient Maya Territories, Adaptive Regions, and Alliances: Contextualizing the San Bartolo-Xultun Intersite Survey. Unpublished Ph.D. dissertation, Department of Anthropology, Harvard University, Cambridge, Massachusetts.

Garrison, Thomas G., and Nicholas P. Dunning

2009 Settlement, Environment, and Politics in the San Bartolo-Xultun Territory, El Peten, Guatemala. *Latin American Antiquity* 20:525–552.

Geller, Pamela L.

2004 Transforming Bodies, Transforming Identities: A Consideration of Pre-Columbian Maya Corporeal Beliefs and Practices. Unpublished Ph.D. dissertation, University of Pennsylvania.

Gill, Richardson B.

2001 *The Great Maya Droughts: Water, Life, and Death.* University of New Mexico Press, Albuquerque.

Glover, Jeffrey B., and Travis W. Stanton

2010 Assessing the Role of Preclassic Traditions in the Formation of Early Classic Yucatec Cultures, México. *Journal of Field Archaeology* 35:58–77.

Graham, Elizabeth A.

1987 Resource Diversity in Belize and Its Implications for Models of Lowland Trade. *American Antiquity* 52:753–767.

1994 *The Highlands of the Lowlands: Environment and Archaeology in the Stann Creek District, Belize, Central America.* Monographs in World Archaeology No. 19. Prehistory Press, Madison, Wisconsin.

2004 Lamanai Reloaded: Alive and Well in the Early Postclassic. *Research Reports in Belizean Archaeology* 1:223–241.

2011 *Maya Christians and Their Churches in Sixteenth-Century Belize.* University Press of Florida, Gainesville.

Grube, Nikolai

1994 A Preliminary Report on the Monuments and Inscriptions of La Milpa, Orange Walk, Belize. *Baessler-Archiv* n.s. 42:217–238.

2000 The City-States of the Maya. In *A Comparative Study of Thirty City-State Cultures*, edited by Mogens Herman Hansen, pp. 547–566. The Royal Danish Academy of Sciences and Letters, Copenhagen.

Grube, Nikolai, and Norman Hammond

1998 Rediscovery of La Milpa Stela 4. *Mexicon* 20:129–132.

Guderjan, Thomas H.

1991a Investigations at La Milpa. In *Maya Settlement in Northwestern Belize: The 1988 and 1990 Seasons of the Río Bravo Archaeological Project*, edited by Thomas H. Guderjan, pp. 7–34. Labyrinthos, Culver City, California.

1991b Chan Chich. In *Maya Settlement in Northwestern Belize: The 1988 and 1990*

Seasons of the Río Bravo Archaeological Project, edited by Thomas H. Guderjan, pp. 35–57. Labyrinthos, Culver City, California.
1991c Aspects of Maya Settlement in the Río Bravo Area. In *Maya Settlement in Northwestern Belize: The 1988 and 1990 Seasons of the Río Bravo Archaeological Project*, edited by Thomas H. Guderjan, pp. 103–113. Labyrinthos, Culver City, California.
2006 E-Groups, Pseudo E-Groups, and the Development of Classic Maya Identity in the Eastern Peten. *Ancient Mesoamerica* 17:97–104.
2007 *The Nature of an Ancient Maya City: Resources, Interaction, and Power at Blue Creek, Belize*. University of Alabama Press, Tuscaloosa.

Guderjan, Thomas H., Michael Lindeman, Ellen Ruble, Froyla Salam, and Jason Yaeger
1991 Archaeological Sites in the Rio Bravo area. In *Maya Settlement in Northwestern Belize*, edited by Thomas H. Guderjan, pp. 55–88. Labyrinthos, Culver City, California.

Hageman, Jon B.
2004 Late Classic Maya Social Organization: A Perspective from Northwestern Belize. Unpublished Ph.D. dissertation, Department of Anthropology, Southern Illinois University, Carbondale.

Haines, Helen R.
2011 How the Other-Half Lived: Continuing Discussions of the Enigma That Is Ka'Kabish, Belize. *Research Reports in Belizean Archaeology* 8:137–150.

Hammond, Norman
1970 Excavations at Lubaantun, 1970. *Antiquity* 44:216–223.
1975 *Lubaantun: A Classic Maya Realm*. Peabody Museum of Archaeology and Ethnology Monograph, 2 vols. Harvard University, Cambridge, Massachusetts.
1978 Crystal Skull to Cuello. *Brukdown* 8:4–5, 30.
1981 Settlement Patterns in Belize. In *Lowland Maya Settlement Patterns*, edited by Wendy Ashmore, pp. 157–186. School of American Research Advanced Seminar Series. University of New Mexico Press, Albuquerque.
1983a The Development of Belizean Archaeology. *Antiquity* 57:19–27.
1983b Lords of the Jungle: A Prosopography of Maya Archaeology. In *Civilization in the Ancient Americas*, edited by Richard M. Leventhal and Alan L. Kolata, pp. 3–32. University of New Mexico Press, Albuquerque.
1983c Nohmul, Belize: 1982 Investigations. *Journal of Field Archaeology* 10:245–254.
1984 Holmul and Nohmul: A Comparison and Assessment of Two Lowland Maya Protoclassic Sites. *Cerámica de Cultura Maya* 13:1–17.
1985 The Site of Nohmul. In *Nohmul: A Prehistoric Maya Community in Belize, Excavations 1973–1983*, Part i, edited by Norman Hammond, pp. 45–166. BAR International Series 250(i). British Archaeological Reports, Oxford, England.
1989 Obsidian Hydration Dating of Tecep Phase Occupation at Nohmul, Belize. *American Antiquity* 54:513–521.
1990 The Discovery of La Milpa. *Mexicon* 13:46–51.

1991   Archaeological Investigations at Cuello, 1975–1987. In *Cuello: An Early Maya Community in Belize*, edited by Norman Hammond, pp. 8–22. Cambridge University Press, Cambridge, England.

2001   A New Maya Stela from La Milpa, Belize. *Antiquity* 75:267–268.

2005   The Dawn and the Dusk: Beginning and Ending a Long-Term Research Program at the Preclassic Maya Site of Cuello, Belize. *Anthropological Notebooks* 11:45–60.

Hammond, Norman (editor)

1985   *Nohmul: A Prehistoric Maya Community in Belize, Excavations 1973–1983*. 2 volumes. BAR International Series 250. British Archaeological Reports, Oxford.

1991   *Cuello: An Early Maya Community in Belize*. Cambridge University Press, Cambridge, England.

Hammond, Norman, and Matthew R. Bobo

1994   Pilgrimage's Last Mile—Late Maya Monument Veneration at La Milpa, Belize. *World Archaeology* 26:19–34.

Hammond, Norman, Catherine Clark, Mark Horton, Mark Hodges, Logan McNatt, Laura J. Kosakowsky, and Anne Pyburn

1985   Excavation and Survey at Nohmul, Belize, 1983. *Journal of Field Archaeology* 12:177–200.

Hammond, Norman, Amanda Clarke, and Sara Donaghey

1995   The Long Goodbye: Middle Preclassic Maya Archaeology at Cuello, Belize. *Latin American Antiquity* 6:120–128.

Hammond, Norman, Amanda Clarke, and Cynthia Robin

1991   Middle Preclassic Buildings and Burials at Cuello, Belize: 1990. *Latin American Antiquity* 4:352–363.

Hammond, Norman, Sara Donaghey, Colleen Gleason, J. C. Staneko, Dirk Van Tuerenhout, and Laura J. Kosakowsky

1987   Excavations at Nohmul, Belize, 1985. *Journal of Field Archaeology* 14:257–281.

Hammond, Norman, and Juliette Cartwright Gerhardt

1990   Early Maya Architectural Innovation at Cuello, Belize. *World Archaeology* 21:461–481.

Hammond, Norman, Juliette Cartwright Gerhardt, and Sara Donaghey

1991   Stratigraphy and Chronology in the Reconstruction of Preclassic Developments at Cuello. In *Cuello: An Early Maya Community in Belize*, edited by Norman Hammond, pp. 23–60. Cambridge University Press, Cambridge, England.

Hammond, Norman, Eric Heller, Brett A. Houk, and Gair Tourtellot, III

2014   Three New Stelae at La Milpa, Belize? *Mexicon* 36:88–93.

Hammond, Norman, Sheena Howarth, and Richard R. Wilk

1999   *The Discovery, Exploration, and Monuments of Nim Li Punit, Belize*. Research Reports on Ancient Maya Writing 40. Center for Maya Research, Washington, D.C.

Hammond, Norman, Laura J. Kosakowsky, K. Anne Pyburn, John R. Rose, J. C. Staneko, Sara Donaghey, C. M. Clark, Mark Horton, Colleen Gleason, Deborah Muyskens, and Thomas Addyman
1988   The Evolution of an Ancient Maya City: Nohmul. *National Geographic Research* 4:474–495.

Hammond, Norman, K. Anne Pyburn, John Rose, J. C. Staneko, and Deborah Muyskens
1988   Excavation and Survey at Nohmul, Belize, 1986. *Journal of Field Archaeology* 15:1–15.

Hammond, Norman, and Ben Thomas
1999   Another Maya Throne Room. *Context* 14:15–16.

Hammond, Norman, and Gair Tourtellot III
2003   La Milpa. *Current World Archaeology* 1:36–43.
2004   Out with a Whimper: La Milpa in the Terminal Classic. In *The Terminal Classic in the Maya Lowlands: Collapse, Transition, and Transformation*, edited by Arthur A. Demarest, Prudence M. Rice, and Don S. Rice, pp. 288–301. University Press of Colorado, Boulder.

Hammond, Norman, Gair Tourtellot III, Sara Donaghey, and Amanda Clarke
1996   Survey and Excavation at La Milpa, Belize, 1996. *Mexicon* 18:86–91.
1998   No Slow Dusk: Maya Urban Development and Decline at La Milpa, Belize. *Antiquity* 72:831–837.

Hammond, Norman, Gair Tourtellot III, Gloria Everson, Kerry L. Sagebiel, Ben Thomas, and Marc Wolf
2000   Survey and Excavation at La Milpa, Belize, 1998. *Mexicon* 22(2):38–45.

Hansen, Mogens Herman
2000   The Concepts of City-State and City-State Culture. In *A Comparative Study of Thirty City-State Cultures*, edited by Mogens Herman Hansen, pp. 11–34 The Royal Danish Academy of Sciences and Letters, Copenhagen.
2008   Analyzing Cities. In *The Ancient City: New Perspectives on Urbanism in the Old and New World*, edited by Joyce Marcus and Jeremy A. Sabloff, pp. 67–76. Resident Scholar Series. School for Advanced Research, Santa Fe, New Mexico.

Hansen, Richard D.
1990   *Excavations in the Tigre Complex, El Mirador, Petén, Guatemala*. New World Archaeological Foundation, Brigham Young University, Provo, Utah.
1991   The Road to Nakbe. *Natural History* 100(5):8–14.
1998   Continuity and Disjunction: Preclassic Antecedents of Classic Maya Architecture. In *Function and Meaning in Classic Maya Architecture*, edited by Stephen D. Houston, pp. 49–122. Dumbarton Oaks Research and Library Collection, Washington, D.C.
2001   The First Cities: The Beginnings of Urbanization and State Formation in the Maya Lowlands. In *Maya, Divine Kings of the Rainforest*, edited by Nikolai Grube, pp. 51–64. Konemann Verlagsgesellschaft mbH.

Harris, Matthew C., and Vincent M. Sisneros

2012   Results of the 2012 Excavations at Kaxil Uinic Ruins. In *The 2012 Season of the Chan Chich Archaeological Project*, edited by Brett A. Houk, pp. 45–64. Papers of the Chan Chich Archaeological Project, No. 6. Department of Sociology, Anthropology, and Social Work, Texas Tech University, Lubbock.

Harrison, Ellie

2000   Structure C-6: Excavation of an Elite Compound. In *The 1998 and 1999 Season of the Chan Chich Archaeological Project*, edited by Brett A. Houk, pp. 71–94. Papers of the Chan Chich Archaeological Project, No. 4. Mesoamerican Archaeological Research Laboratory, University of Texas at Austin.

Harrison, Peter D.

2001a   Maya Architecture at Tikal. In *Maya, Divine Kings of the Rainforest*, edited by Nikolai Grube, pp. 218–231. Konemann Verlagsgesellschaft mbH.

2001b   Thrones and Throne Structures in the Central Acropolis of Tikal as an Expression of the Royal Court. In *Royal Courts of the Ancient Maya*, Vol. 2, edited by Takeshi Inomata and Stephen D. Houston, pp. 74–101. Westview Press, Boulder, Colorado.

2003   Palaces of the Royal Court at Tikal. In *Maya Palaces and Elite Residences: An Interdisciplinary Approach*, edited by Jessica Joyce Christie, pp. 98–119. University of Texas Press, Austin.

Harrison, Peter D., and B. L. Turner (editors)

1978   *Pre-Hispanic Maya Agriculture*. University of New Mexico Press, Albuquerque.

Harrison-Buck, Eleanor

2012   Rituals of Death and Disempowerment among the Maya. In *Power & Identity in Archaeological Theory and Practice: Case Studies from Ancient Mesoamerica*, edited by Eleanor Harrison-Buck, pp. 103–115. University of Utah Press, Salt Lake City.

Harrison-Buck, Eleanor, Marieka Brouwer Burg, Mark Willis, Chet Walker, Satoru Murata, Brett A. Houk, and Astrid Runggaldier

2014   Drones, Mapping, and Excavations in the Middle Belize Valley: Research Investigations of the Belize River East Archaeology (BREA) Project. Paper presented at the Twelfth Annual Belize Archaeology Symposium, San Ignacio, Belize.

Harrison-Buck, Eleanor, and Patricia M. McAnany

2006   Terminal Classic Circular Shrines and Ceramic Material in the Sibun Valley, Belize: Evidence of Northern Yucatec Influence in the Eastern Maya Lowlands. *Research Reports in Belizean Archaeology* 3:287–299.

Healy, Paul F., David Cheetham, Terry G. Powis, and Jaime J. Awe

2004   Cahal Pech: The Middle Formative Period. In *The Ancient Maya of the Belize Valley, Half a Century of Research*, edited by James F. Garber, pp. 103–124. University of Press Florida, Gainesville.

Healy, Paul F., Bobbi Hohmann, and Terry G. Powis

2004   The Ancient Maya of Pacbitun. In *The Ancient Maya of the Belize Valley: Half a Century of Research*, edited by James F. Garber, pp. 207–227. University Press of Florida, Gainesville.

Healy, Paul F., John D. H. Lambert, J. T. Arnason, and Richard J. Hebda

1983   Caracol, Belize: Evidence of Ancient Maya Agricultural Terraces. *Journal of Field Archaeology* 10:397–410.

Heller, Eric J.

2011   The 2010 Season of Survey and Excavation at La Milpa North. In *Research Reports from the Programme for Belize Archaeological Project*, Vol. 5, edited by Brett A. Houk and Fred Valdez Jr., pp. 109–122. Occasional Papers, No. 12. Mesoamerican Archaeological Research Laboratory, University of Texas at Austin.

2012   Set in Stone: The Importance of Sociality and Materiality in the Placement of Stela 1, La Milpa North, Belize. Paper presented at the 77th Annual Meeting of the Society for American Archaeology, Memphis, Tennessee.

Helmke, Cristophe, Jaime Awe, and Nikolai Grube

2010   The Carved Monuments and Inscriptions of Xunantunich. In *Classic Maya Provincial Politics: Xunantunich and Its Hinterlands*, edited by Lisa J. LeCount and Jason Yaeger, pp. 97–121. University of Arizona Press, Tucson.

Helmke, Cristophe, Harri Kettunen, and Stanley Guenter

2006   Comments on the Hieroglyphic Texts of the B-Group Ballcourt Markers at Caracol, Belize. *Wayeb Notes* 23:1–27.

Hendon, Julia A., and Rosemary Joyce

2004   Glossary. In *Mesoamerican Archaeology: Theory and Practice*, edited by Julia A. Hendon and Rosemary Joyce, pp. 323–331. Blackwell, Oxford.

Herndon, Kelsey E., Ashley Booher, and Brett A. Houk

2013   Results of Excavations at Structure A-5 at Chan Chich. In *The 2013 Season of the Chan Chich Archaeological Project*, edited by Brett A. Houk, pp. 39–62. Papers of the Chan Chich Archaeological Project, No. 7. Department of Sociology, Anthropology, and Social Work, Texas Tech University, Lubbock.

Herndon, Kelsey E., Brett A. Houk, and David Sandrock

2014   The 2014 Season of the Chan Chich Archaeological Project. Paper presented at the 12th Annual Belize Archaeology Symposium, San Ignacio, Belize.

Houk, Brett A.

1996   The Archaeology of Site Planning: An Example from the Maya Site of Dos Hombres, Belize. Unpublished Ph.D. dissertation, Department of Anthropology, University of Texas at Austin.

1998a   An Introduction to the 1997 Season. In *The 1997 Season of the Chan Chich Archaeological Project*, edited by Brett A. Houk, pp. 1–14. Papers of the Chan Chich Archaeological Project, No. 3. Center for Maya Studies, San Antonio, Texas.

1998b   Excavations at Structure A-1. In *The 1997 Season of the Chan Chich Archaeo-*

logical Project, edited by Brett A. Houk, pp. 25–30. Papers of the Chan Chich Archaeological Project, No. 3. Center for Maya Studies, San Antonio, Texas.

2000a Life, the Universe, and Everything: Re-Evaluating Problematic Deposit 2 from Dos Hombres, Belize. In *The 1998 and 1999 Season of the Chan Chich Archaeological Project*, edited by Brett A. Houk, pp. 141–150. Papers of the Chan Chich Archaeological Project, No. 4. Mesoamerican Archaeological Research Laboratory, University of Texas at Austin.

2000b An Introduction to the 1998 and 1999 Seasons. In *The 1998 and 1999 Season of the Chan Chich Archaeological Project*, edited by Brett A. Houk, pp. 1–14. Papers of the Chan Chich Archaeological Project, No. 4. Mesoamerican Archaeological Research Laboratory, University of Texas at Austin.

2000c Excavations at the Temple of the Jaguar Skull. In *The 1998 and 1999 Season of the Chan Chich Archaeological Project*, edited by Brett A. Houk, pp. 101–104. Papers of the Chan Chich Archaeological Project, No. 4. Mesoamerican Archaeological Research Laboratory, University of Texas at Austin.

2003 The Ties That Bind: Site Planning in the Three Rivers Region. In *Heterarchy, Political Economy, and the Ancient Maya: The Three Rivers Region of the East-Central Yucatán Peninsula*, edited by Vernon L. Scarborough, Fred Valdez Jr., and Nicholas P. Dunning, pp. 52–63. University of Arizona Press, Tucson.

2010 A Site-Planning Analysis of Historic Downtown Austin. *Bulletin of the Texas Archeological Society* 81:177–190.

2011 The Deadly Years: Terminal Classic Problematic Deposits and the Fates of Dos Hombres and Chan Chich, Belize. Paper presented at the 76th Annual Meeting of the Society for American Archaeology, Sacramento, California.

2012a Kaxil Uinic: A Report on Archival Investigations and Reconnaissance of the Historic Maya Village. In *The 2012 Season of the Chan Chich Archaeological Project*, edited by Brett A. Houk, pp. 31–44. Papers of the Chan Chich Archaeological Project, No. 6. Department of Sociology, Anthropology, and Social Work, Texas Tech University, Lubbock.

2012b Return to Paradise: An Introduction to the 2012 Chan Chich Archaeological Project. In *The 2012 Season of the Chan Chich Archaeological Project*, edited by Brett A. Houk, pp. 1–6. Papers of the Chan Chich Archaeological Project, No. 6. Department of Sociology, Anthropology, and Social Work, Texas Tech University, Lubbock.

2013a An Introduction to the 2013 Season of the Chan Chich Archaeological Project. In *The 2013 Season of the Chan Chich Archaeological Project*, edited by Brett A. Houk, pp. 1–14. Papers of the Chan Chich Archaeological Project, No. 7. Department of Sociology, Anthropology, and Social Work, Texas Tech University, Lubbock.

2013b Pomp and Circumstance in the Eastern Maya Lowlands. Paper presented at the 4th Annual South-Central Conference on Mesoamerica, Houston, Texas.

Houk, Brett A., and Jon B. Hageman
2007   Lost and Found: (Re)-Placing Say Ka in the La Milpa Suburban Settlement Pattern. *Mexicon* 29:152–156.

Houk, Brett A., Matthew C. Harris, Krystle Kelley, and Vincent Sisneros
2013   The 2012 Investigations at Chan Chich and Kaxil Uinic. *Research Reports in Belizean Archaeology* 10:179–186.

Houk, Brett A., Krystle Kelley, David Sandrock, and Kelsey E. Herndon
2014   The Chan Chich Archaeological Project and the Belize Estates Archaeological Survey Team, 2013 Season. *Research Reports in Belizean Archaeology* 11:327–336.

Houk, Brett A., and Jon C. Lohse
2013   Northwestern Belize and the Central Lowland Classic World. In *Classic Maya Political Ecology: Resource Management, Class Histories, and Political Change in Northwestern Belize*, edited by Jon C. Lohse, pp. 25–41. Ideas, Debates, and Perspectives 6. Cotsen Institute of Archaeology Press, University of California, Los Angeles.

Houk, Brett A., Hubert R. Robichaux, and Jeffrey Durst
1996   Results of the 1996 Season. In *The 1996 Season of the Chan Chich Archaeological Project*, edited by Brett A. Houk and Hubert R. Robichaux, pp. 21–30. Papers of the Chan Chich Archaeological Project, No. 1. Center for Maya Studies, San Antonio, Texas.

Houk, Brett A., Hubert R. Robichaux, and Fred Valdez Jr.
2010   An Early Royal Maya Tomb from Chan Chich, Belize. *Ancient Mesoamerica* 21:229–248.

Houk, Brett A., Lauren A. Sullivan, and Fred Valdez Jr.
2008   Rethinking the Postclassic in Northwest Belize. *Research Reports in Belizean Archaeology* 5:93–102.

Houk, Brett A., and Fred Valdez Jr.
2009   La Milpa and the Programme for Belize Archaeological Project. *Research Reports in Belizean Archaeology* 6:227–233.
2011   The Precocious Dead: Status, Power, and Early Tombs in the Eastern Three Rivers Region. *Research Reports in Belizean Archaeology* 8:151–158.

Houk, Brett A., Chester P. Walker, Mark D. Willis, and Kelsey E. Herndon
2013   Structure from Motion Mapping and Remote Sensing at Structure A-5, Chan Chich, Belize. In *The 2013 Season of the Chan Chich Archaeological Project*, edited by Brett A. Houk, pp. 27–38. Papers of the Chan Chich Archaeological Project, No. 7. Department of Sociology, Anthropology, and Social Work, Texas Tech University, Lubbock.

Houk, Brett A., and Gregory Zaro
2011   Evidence for Ritual Engineering in the Late/Terminal Classic Site Plan of La Milpa, Belize. *Latin American Antiquity* 22:178–198.

2012a The Cities on the Edge of History. Paper presented at the 77th Annual Meeting of the Society for American Archaeology, April 18–22. Memphis, Tennessee.

2012b The 2011 La Milpa Core Project Season Summary. In *The 2011 Season of the La Milpa Core Project*, edited by Brett A. Houk, pp. 1–14. Occasional Paper, No. 13. Mesoamerican Archaeological Research Laboratory, University of Texas at Austin.

Houston, Stephen, John Robertson, and David Stuart

2000 The Language of Classic Maya Inscriptions. *Current Anthropology* 41:321–338.

Hutson, Scott R.

2012 "Unavoidable Imperfections": Historical Contexts for Representing Ruined Maya Buildings. In *Past Presented: Archaeological Illustration and the Ancient Americas*, edited by Joanne Pillsbury, pp. 282–316. Dumbarton Oaks, Washington, D.C.

Iannone, Gyles

2001 Rediscovery of the Ancient Maya Center of Minanha, Belize: Background, Description and Future Prospects. *Mexicon* 23:125–129.

2005 The Rise and Fall of an Ancient Maya Petty Royal Court. *Latin American Antiquity* 16:26–44.

2006 Investigations in the Buried Royal Residential Courtyard at Minanha, Belize. *Research Reports in Belizean Archaeology* 3:149–160.

2009 The Jungle Kings of Minanha: Constellations of Authority and the Ancient Maya Socio-Political Landscape. *Research Reports in Belizean Archaeology* 6:33–41.

2010 Collective Memory in the Frontiers: A Case Study from the Ancient Maya Center of Minanha, Belize. *Ancient Mesoamerica* 21:353–371.

2011 Archaeological Research in the North Vaca Plateau: Summary of the 2011 Investigations. In *Archaeological Investigations in the North Vaca Plateau, Belize: Progress Report of the Thirteenth (2011) Field Season*, edited by Gyles Iannone, Sonja A. Schwake, Jaime J. Awe, and Philip P. Reader, pp. 23–29. Social Archaeology Research Program, Department of Anthropology, Trent University, Peterborough, Ontario.

Iannone, Gyles (editor)

2013 *The Great Maya Droughts in Cultural Context*. University Press of Colorado, Boulder.

Iannone, Gyles, Carmen McCormick, and James Conolly

2008 Community Archaeology at Minanha: Some Preliminary Insights from the Phase II Settlement Study. *Research Reports in Belizean Archaeology* 5:149–158.

Iannone, Gyles, and John Morris

2009 Ancient Maya Socio-Political Organization: Perspectives from Belizean Archaeology. *Research Reports in Belizean Archaeology* 6:3–14.

Iannone, Gyles, and Philip P. Reader

2011 Socio-Environmental Dynamics in the North Vaca Plateau, Belize: A Long Term Perspective (Phase III, Part 2). In *Archaeological Investigations in the North Vaca Plateau, Belize: Progress Report of the Thirteenth (2011) Field Season*, edited by Gyles Iannone, Sonja A. Schwake, Jaime J. Awe, and Philip P. Reader, pp. 1–22. Social Archaeology Research Program, Department of Anthropology, Trent University, Peterborough, Ontario.

Iannone, Gyles, and Sonja Schwake

2013 Alternative Approaches to Socio-Ecological Crisis: Perspectives from Belize's North Vaca Plateau. *Research Reports in Belizean Archaeology* 10:3–11.

Inomata, Takeshi

1997 The Last Day of a Fortified Classic Maya Center: Archaeological Investigations at Aguateca, Guatemala. *Ancient Mesoamerica* 8:337–351.

2001 King's People: Classic Maya Courtiers in a Comparative Perspective. In *Royal Courts of the Ancient Maya*, Vol. 1, edited by Takeshi Inomata and Stephen D. Houston, pp. 27–53. Westview Press, Boulder, Colorado.

2004 The Spatial Mobility of Non-Elite Populations in Classic Maya Society and Its Political Implications. In *Ancient Maya Commoners*, edited by Jon C. Lohse and Fred Valdez Jr., pp. 175–196. University of Texas Press, Austin.

2006 Plazas, Performers, and Spectators: Political Theaters of the Classic Maya. *Current Anthropology* 47:805–842.

Inomata, Takeshi, and Stephen D. Houston

2001 Opening the Royal Maya Court. In *Royal Courts of the Ancient Maya*, Vol. 1, edited by Takeshi Inomata and Stephen D. Houston, pp. 3–23. Westview Press, Boulder, Colorado.

Jackson, Sarah E.

2013 *Politics of the Maya Court: Hierarchy and Change in the Late Classic Period*. University of Oklahoma Press, Norman.

Jamison, Thomas R.

2010 Monumental Building Programs and Changing Political Strategies at Xunantunich. In *Classic Maya Provincial Politics: Xunantunich and Its Hinterlands*, edited by Lisa J. LeCount and Jason Yaeger, pp. 122–144. University of Arizona Press, Tucson.

Johnson, William C.

1983 The Physical Setting: Northern Belize and Pulltrouser Swamp. In *Pulltrouser Swamp: Ancient Maya Habitat, Agriculture, and Settlement in Northern Belize*, edited by B. L. Turner II and Peter D. Harrison, pp. 8–20. University of Texas Press, Austin.

Jones, Grant D.

1977 Levels of Settlement Alliance among the San Pedro Maya of Western Belize

and Eastern Petén, 1857–1936. In *Anthropology and History in Yucatán*, edited by Grant D. Jones, pp. 139–189. University of Texas Press, Austin.
1989   *Maya Resistance to Spanish Rule*. University of New Mexico Press, Albuquerque.

Joyce, T. A., J. Cooper Clark, and J. E. Thompson
1927   Report on the British Museum Expedition to British Honduras, 1927. *Journal of the Royal Anthropological Institute of Great Britain and Ireland* 57:295–323.

Joyce, T. A., T. Gann, E. L. Gruning, and R.C.E. Long
1928   Report on the British Museum Expedition to British Honduras, 1928. *Journal of the Royal Anthropological Institute of Great Britain and Ireland* 58:323–350.

Keller, Angela H.
2006   Roads to the Center: The Design, Use, and Meaning of the Roads at Xunantunich, Belize. Unpublished Ph.D. dissertation, University of Pennsylvania, Philadelphia.
2010   The Social Construction of Roads at Xunantunich, from Design to Abandonment. In *Classic Maya Provincial Politics: Xunantunich and Its Hinterlands*, edited by Lisa J. LeCount and Jason Yaeger, pp. 184–208. University of Arizona Press, Tucson.

Kelley, Krystle
2014   Establishing the Acropolis: Two Seasons of Investigations in the Upper Plaza of Chan Chich, Belize. Unpublished M.A. thesis, Department of Sociology, Anthropology, and Social Work, Texas Tech University, Lubbock.

Kelley, Krystle, Kevin A. Miller, and Ashley Booher
2012   Chan Chich: 2012 Investigations of the Upper Plaza. In *The 2012 Season of the Chan Chich Archaeological Project*, edited by Brett A. Houk, pp. 19–30. Papers of the Chan Chich Archaeological Project, No. 6. Department of Sociology, Anthropology, and Social Work, Texas Tech University, Lubbock.

Kennett, Douglas J., Sebastian F. M. Breitenbach, Valorie V. Aquino, Yemane Asmerom, Jaime Awe, James U. L. Baldini, Patrick Bartlein, Brendan J. Culleton, Claire Ebert, Christopher Jazwa, Martha J. Macri, Norbert Marwan, Victor Polyak, Keith M. Prufer, Harriet E. Ridley, Harald Sodemann, Bruce Winterhalder, and Gerald H. Haug
2012   Development and Disintegration of Maya Political Systems in Response to Climate Change. *Science* 338:788–791.

King, Eleanor M., James E. Brady, Leslie C. Shaw, Allan B. Cobb, C. L. Kieffer, Michael L. Brennan, and Chandra L. Harris
2012   Small Caves and Sacred Geography: A Case Study from the Prehispanic Maya Site of Maax Na, Belize. *Latin American Antiquity* 23:611–628.

King, R. B., I. C. Baillie, T.M.B. Abell, J. R. Dunsmore, D. A. Gray, J. H. Pratt, H. R. Versey, A.C.S. Wright, and S. A. Zisman

1992   *Land Resource Assessment of Northern Belize.* 2 vols. Bulletin 43. Natural Resources Institute, United Kingdom.

Lamoureux St-Hilaire, Maxime

2011   The Last Inhabitants of Minanha: Examining the Differential Abandonment of an Ancient Maya Community. Unpublished M.A. thesis, Department of Anthropology, Trent University, Peterborough, Ontario.

Laporte, Juan Pedro

2003   Architectural Aspects of Interaction between Tikal and Teotihuacan during the Early Classic Period. In *The Maya and Teotihuacan: Reinterpreting Early Classic Interaction*, edited by Geoffrey E. Braswell, pp. 199–216. University of Texas Press, Austin.

Laporte, Juan Pedro, and Vilma Fialko

1990   New Perspectives on Old Problems: Dynastic References for the Early Classic at Tikal. In *Vision and Revision in Maya Studies*, edited by Flora Clancy and Peter Harrison, pp. 33–66. University of New Mexico Press, Albuquerque.

LeCount, Lisa J.

1999   Polychrome Pottery and Political Strategies in Late and Terminal Classic Lowland Maya Society. *Latin American Antiquity* 10:239–258.

LeCount, Lisa J., and Jason Yaeger

2010a   A Brief Description of Xunantunich. In *Classic Maya Provincial Politics: Xunantunich and Its Hinterlands*, edited by Lisa J. LeCount and Jason Yaeger, pp. 67–78. University of Arizona Press, Tucson.

2010b   Placing Xunantunich and Its Hinterlands Settlements in Perspective. In *Classic Maya Provincial Politics: Xunantunich and Its Hinterlands*, edited by Lisa J. LeCount and Jason Yaeger, pp. 337–369. University of Arizona Press, Tucson.

LeCount, Lisa J., and Jason Yaeger (editors)

2010   *Classic Maya Provincial Politics: Xunantunich and Its Hinterlands.* University of Arizona Press, Tucson.

LeCount, Lisa J., Jason Yaeger, Richard M. Leventhal, and Wendy Ashmore

2002   Dating the Rise and Fall of Xunantunich, Belize. *Ancient Mesoamerica* 13:41–63.

Leventhal, Richard M.

1990   Southern Belize: An Ancient Maya Region. In *Vision and Revision in Maya Studies*, edited by Flora S. Clancy and Peter D. Harrison, pp. 124–141. University of New Mexico, Albuquerque.

1992   The Development of a Regional Tradition in Southern Belize. In *New Theories on the Ancient Maya*, edited by Elin C. Danien and Robert J. Sharer, pp. 145–153. University Museum Symposium, Vol. 3. University of Pennsylvania Museum of Archaeology and Anthropology, Philadelphia.

1993   Introduction. In *Xunantunich Archaeological Project, 1993 Field Season*, edited by Richard M. Leventhal, pp. 1–6. Report on file, Institute of Archaeology, Belmopan, Belize.

2010 Changing Places: The Castillo and the Structure of Power at Xunantunich. In *Classic Maya Provincial Politics: Xunantunich and Its Hinterlands*, edited by Lisa J. LeCount and Jason Yaeger, pp. 79–96. University of Arizona Press, Tucson.

Leventhal, Richard M., and Wendy Ashmore

2004 Xunantunich in a Belize Valley Context. In *The Ancient Maya of the Belize Valley: Half a Century of Research*, edited by James F. Garber, pp. 168–190. University Press of Florida, Gainesville.

Leventhal, Richard M., Wendy Ashmore, Lisa J. LeCount, and Jason Yaeger

2010 The Xunantunich Archaeological Project, 1991–1997. In *Classic Maya Provincial Politics: Xunantunich and Its Hinterlands*, edited by Lisa J. LeCount and Jason Yaeger, pp. 1–19. University of Arizona Press, Tucson.

Lewis, Brandon S., and Yoav Me-Bar

2011 Examination of Tow Extended Elite Lineages: The 2010 La Milpa Archaeological Field Season. In *Research Reports from the Programme for Belize Archaeological Project*, Vol. 5, edited by Brett A. Houk and Fred Valdez Jr., pp. 67–92. Occasional Papers, No. 12. Mesoamerican Archaeological Research Laboratory, University of Texas at Austin.

Lohse, Jon C.

1993 Operation 4046 Colha, Belize: A Reconsideration of a Lowland Archaic Deposit. Unpublished M.A. thesis, Department of Anthropology, University of Texas at Austin.

1995 Results of Survey and Mapping during the 1994 PfB Season at Gran Cacao. In *The Programme for Belize Archaeological Project: 1994 Interim Report*, edited by Richard E. W. Adams and Fred Valdez Jr., pp. 106–114. The Center for Archaeology and Tropical Studies and University of Texas at San Antonio.

2001 The Social Organization of a Late Classic Maya Community: Dos Hombres, Northwestern Belize. Unpublished Ph.D. dissertation, Department of Anthropology, University of Texas at Austin.

2004 Intra-Site Settlement Signatures and Implications for Late Classic Maya Commoner Organization at Dos Hombres, Belize. In *Ancient Maya Commoners*, edited by Jon C. Lohse and Fred Valdez Jr., pp. 117–145. University of Texas Press, Austin.

2010 Archaic Origins of the Ancient Maya. *Latin American Antiquity* 21:312–352.

Lohse, Jon C. (editor)

2013 *Classic Maya Political Ecology: Resource Management, Class Histories, and Political Change in Northwestern Belize*. Ideas, Debates, and Perspectives 6. Cotsen Institute of Archaeology Press, University of California, Los Angeles.

Lohse, Jon C., Jaime Awe, Cameron Griffith, Robert M. Rosenswig, and Fred Valdez Jr.

2006 Preceramic Occupations in Belize: Updating the Paleoindian and Archaic Record. *Latin American Antiquity* 17:209–226.

Lohse, Jon C., Kerry L. Sagebiel, and Joanne P. Baron
2013 The Ball Game, Community Ceremony, and Political Development in Northwestern Belize. In *Classic Maya Political Ecology: Resource Management, Class Histories, and Political Change in Northwestern Belize*, edited by Jon C. Lohse, pp. 99–125. Ideas, Debates, and Perspectives 6. Cotsen Institute of Archaeology Press, University of California, Los Angeles.

Lohse, Jon C., and Fred Valdez Jr.
2004 Examining Ancient Maya Commoners Anew. In *Ancient Maya Commoners*, edited by Jon C. Lohse and Fred Valdez Jr., pp. 1–21. University of Texas Press, Austin.

Longstaffe, Matthew
2011 Ancient Maya Site Core Settlement at Minanha, Belize: Development, Integration, and Community Dynamics. Unpublished M.A. thesis, Department of Anthropology, Trent University, Peterborough, Ontario.

Longstaffe, Matthew, and Gyles Iannone
2011 Households and Social Trajectories: The Site Core Community at Minanha, Belize. *Research Reports in Belizean Archaeology* 8:45–59.

Loten, H. Stanley
2003 The North Acropolis: Monumentality, Function, and Architectural Development. In *Tikal: Dynasties, Foreigners, and Affairs of State*, edited by Jeremy A. Sabloff, pp. 227–252. School of American Research Press, Santa Fe, New Mexico.

Loten, H. Stanley, and David M. Pendergast
1984 *A Lexicon for Maya Architecture*. Archaeology Monograph 8. Royal Ontario Museum, Toronto.

Lucero, Lisa J.
2002 The Collapse of the Classic Maya: A Case for the Role of Water Control. *American Anthropologist* 104:814–826.
2006 *Water and Ritual: The Rise and Fall of Classic Maya Rulers*. University of Texas Press, Austin.
2007 Classic Maya Temples, Politics, and the Voice of the People. *Latin American Antiquity* 18:407–427.

Lucero, Lisa J., Joel D. Gunn, and Vernon L. Scarborough
2011 Climate Change and Classic Maya Water Management. *Water* 3:479–494.

Lund, Laura D., and Jennifer Weber
2013 Scanning the Jungle—The 2012 LiDAR Project at Pacbitun, Belize. In *Pacbitun Regional Archaeological Project (PRAP): Report on the 2012 Field Season*, edited by Terry G. Powis, pp. 32–48. Department of Geography and Anthropology, Kennesaw State University, Kennesaw, Georgia.

Lundell, Cyrus L.

1945 The Vegetation and Natural Resources of British Honduras. In *Plants and Plant Science in Latin America*, edited by Frans Verdoorn, pp. 270–273. Chronica Botanica, Waltham, Massachusetts.

MacNeish, Richard. S., S. Jeffrey Wilkerson, and Antoinette Nelken-Turner

1980 *First Annual Report on the Belize Archaic Archaeological Reconnaissance*. R. S. Peabody Foundation, Andover, Massachusetts.

Manning, Andrew P.

1997 The Assessment of Urban Cultural Roles from the Archaeological Record: A Ceramic Perspective. Unpublished Ph.D. dissertation, Department of Anthropology, University of Texas at Austin.

Marcus, Joyce

1973 Territorial Organization of the Lowland Classic Maya. *Science* 180:911–916.

1993 Ancient Maya Political Organization. In *Lowland Maya Civilization in the Eighth Century A.D.*, edited by Jeremy A. Sabloff and John S. Henderson, pp. 111–183. Dumbarton Oaks, Washington, D.C.

Martin, Simon

2001 Court and Realm: Architectural Signatures in the Classic Maya Southern Lowlands. In *Royal Courts of the Ancient Maya*, Vol. 1, edited by Takeshi Inomata and Stephen D. Houston, pp. 168–194. Westview Press, Boulder, Colorado.

2003 In Line of the Founder: A View of Dynastic Politics at Tikal. In *Tikal: Dynasties, Foreigners, and Affairs of State*, edited by Jeremy A. Sabloff, pp. 3–46. School of American Research Press, Santa Fe, New Mexico.

2005 Caracol Altar 21 Revisited: More Data on Double-Bird and Tikal's Wars of the Mid-Sixth Century. *The PARI Journal* 6(1):1–9.

Martin, Simon, and Nikolai Grube

2008 *Chronicle of the Maya Kings and Queens*. 2nd ed. Thames & Hudson, London.

Martinez, Maria

2010 Power, Memory, and Community: Defining the Development and Function of a Quadrangle Group, La Milpa, Belize. In *Research Reports from the Programme for Belize Archaeological Project*, Vol. 4, edited by David M. Hyde and Fred Valdez Jr., pp. 97–132. Occasional Papers, No. 11. Mesoamerican Archaeological Research Laboratory, University of Texas at Austin.

Masson, Marilyn A.

2000 *In the Realm of Nachan Kan: Postclassic Maya Archaeology at Laguna de On, Belize*. University Press of Colorado, Boulder.

2001 The Dynamics of Maturing Statehood in Postclassic Maya Civilization. In *Maya, Divine Kings of the Rainforest*, edited by Nikolai Grube, pp. 340–353. Konemann Verlagsgesellschaft mbH.

Masson, Marilyn A., Maxine H. Oland, and Josalyn M. Ferguson

2004 Late Maya Settlement at Progresso Lagoon: Terminal Classic Through Colonial Periods. *Research Reports in Belizean Archaeology* 1:257–266.

Masson, Marilyn A., Timothy S. Hare, and Carlos Peraza Lope

2006   Postclassic Maya Society Regenerated at Mayapán. In *After Collapse: The Regeneration of Complex Societies*, edited by Glenn M. Schwartz and John Nichols, pp. 188–207. University of Arizona Press, Tucson.

Mathews, Peter

1979   The Glyphs on the Ear Ornaments from Tomb A-1/1. In *Excavations at Altun Ha, Belize, 1964–1970*, Vol. 1, by David M. Pendergast, pp.79–80. Royal Ontario Museum, Toronto, Canada.

1991   Classic Maya Emblem Glyphs. In *Classic Maya Political History, Hieroglyphic and Archaeological Evidence*, edited by T. Patrick Culbert, pp. 19–29. Cambridge University Press, Cambridge, England.

Maya Research Program

2011   Purpose. Electronic document, http://www.mayaresearchprogram.org/webcontent/aboutus_purpose.html, accessed January 20, 2013.

McCurdy, Leah, Whitney Lytle, and M. Kathryn Brown

2013   Revisiting the Xunantunich Site Core. Paper presented at the Eleventh Annual Belize Archaeology and Anthropology Symposium, San Ignacio.

McDonald, Roy Charles, and Norman Hammond

1985   The Environment of Northern Belize. In *Nohmul: A Prehistoric Maya Community in Belize, Excavations 1973–1983*, Part i, edited by Norman Hammond, pp. 13–44. BAR International Series 250(i). British Archaeological Reports, Oxford, England.

McDougal, Steven R.

1997   Archaeological Investigations at Ballcourt 2, Dos Hombres, Belize. Unpublished M.A. thesis, University of Cincinnati, Ohio.

McKillop, Heather

2004   *The Ancient Maya: New Perspectives*. W. W. Norton & Company, New York.

2005   *In Search of Maya Sea Traders*. Texas A&M University Press, College Station.

Meadows, Richard K.

1998   Test Pit Program in Group C. In *The 1997 Season of the Chan Chich Archaeological Project*, edited by Brett A. Houk, pp. 59–66. Papers of the Chan Chich Archaeological Project, No. 3. Center for Maya Studies, San Antonio, Texas.

Meadows, Richard K., and Kristen M. Hartnett

2000   Archaeological Excavations at Group H: Investigating Craft Production and Domestic Architecture at Chan Chich, Belize. In *The 1998 and 1999 Season of the Chan Chich Archaeological Project*, edited by Brett A. Houk, pp. 15–40. Papers of the Chan Chich Archaeological Project, No. 4. Mesoamerican Archaeological Research Laboratory, University of Texas at Austin.

Medina-Elizalde, Martín, Stephen J. Burns, David W. Lea, Yemane Asmerom, Lucien von Gunten, Victor Polyak, Mathias Vuille, and Ambarish Karmalkar

2010   High Resolution Stalagmite Climate Record from the Yucatán Peninsula

Spanning the Maya Terminal Classic Period. *Earth and Planetary Science Letters* 298:255–262.

Milbrath, Susan, and Carlos Peraza Lope
2003   Revisiting Mayapan: Mexico's Last Maya Capital. *Ancient Mesoamerica* 14:1–46.

Miller, Mary Ellen
1999   *Maya Art and Architecture*. Thames and Hudson, London.

Miller, Mary, and Claudia Brittenham
2013   *The Spectacle of the Late Maya Court: Reflections on the Murals of Bonampak*. University of Texas Press, Austin.

Moats, Lindsey R., Walter Beckwith, and Gregory Zaro
2012   The 2011 Excavations at Courtyard 100. In *The 2011 Season of the La Milpa Core Project*, edited by Brett A. Houk, pp. 39–76. Occasional Paper, No. 13. Mesoamerican Archaeological Research Laboratory, University of Texas at Austin.

Mock, Shirley Boteler
2005   The Terminal Classic to Postclassic Ceramics from Saktunja, a Coastal Site in Northern Belize. *Research Reports in Belizean Archaeology* 2:425–440.

Morley, Sylvanus G.
1938   *The Inscriptions of Petén*, Vol. IV. Publication No. 347. Carnegie Institute of Washington, Washington, D.C.

Morris, John, and Anabel E. Ford
2005   Early Classic Manifestations at El Pilar and Mountain Cow. *Research Reports in Belizean Archaeology* 2:79–97.

Normark, Johan
2010   Causeway(s) at El Pilar. Electronic document, *http://haecceities.wordpress.com/2010/05/23/causeways-at-el-pilar/*, accessed February 28, 2013.

Oland, Maxine H., and Marilyn A. Masson
2005   Late Postclassic-Colonial Period Maya Settlement on the West Shore of Progresso Lagoon. *Research Reports in Belizean Archaeology* 2:223–230.

O'Mansky, Matt, and Nicholas P. Dunning
2004   Settlement and Late Classic Political Disintegration in the Petexbatun Region, Guatemala. In *The Terminal Classic in the Maya Lowlands: Collapse: Transition, and Transformation*, edited by Arthur A. Demarest, Prudence M. Rice, and Don S. Rice, pp. 83–101. University Press of Colorado, Boulder.

Paauw, Derek A. M.
2007   Archaeological Investigations in Group L at the Ancient Maya Centre of Minanha, Belize. Unpublished M.A. thesis, Department of Anthropology, Trent University, Peterborough, Ontario.

Pendergast, David M.
1969   *Altun Ha, British Honduras (Belize): The Sun God's Tomb*. Art and Archaeology Occasional Paper 19. Royal Ontario Museum, Toronto, Canada.

1976 *Altun Ha: A Guidebook to the Ancient Maya Ruins.* 2nd ed., rev. University of Toronto Press, Canada.

1979 *Excavations at Altun Ha, Belize, 1964–1970,* Vol. 1. Royal Ontario Museum, Toronto, Canada.

1981 Lamanai, Belize: Summary of Excavation Results, 1974–1980. *Journal of Field Archaeology* 8:29–53.

1982 *Excavations at Altun Ha, Belize, 1964–1970,* Vol. 2. Royal Ontario Museum, Toronto, Canada.

1986 Stability Through Change: Lamanai, Belize, from the Ninth to Seventeenth Century. In *Late Lowland Maya Civilization: Classic to Postclassic*, edited by Jeremy A. Sabloff and E. Wyllys Andrews V, pp. 223–249. University of New Mexico Press, Albuquerque.

1988 *Lamanai Stela 9: The Archaeological Context.* Research Reports on Ancient Maya Writing 20. Center for Maya Research, Washington, D.C.

1990a *Excavations at Altun Ha, Belize, 1964–1970,* Vol. 3. Royal Ontario Museum, Toronto, Canada.

1990b Engineering Problems in Ancient Maya Architecture: Past, Present, and Future. *Environmental Geology and Water Sciences* 16(1):67–73.

1993 The Center and the Edge: Archaeology in Belize, 1809–1992. *Journal of World Prehistory* 7:1–33.

1998 Intercessions with the Gods: Caches and Their Significance at Altun Ha and Lamanai, Belize. In *The Sowing and the Dawning: Termination, Dedication, and Transformation in the Archaeological and Ethnographic Record of Mesoamerica*, edited by Shirley Boteler Mock, pp. 55–63. University of New Mexico Press, Albuquerque.

2003 Teotihuacan at Altun Ha: Did It Make a Difference. In *The Maya and Teotihuacan: Reinterpreting Early Classic Interaction*, edited by Geoffrey E. Braswell, pp. 235–247. University of Texas Press, Austin.

Pitcavage, Megan R.

2008 Companion Burials in the Kingdom of the Avocado: Indirect Evidence of Human Sacrifice in Late and Terminal Classic Maya Society. Unpublished M.A. thesis, University of California, San Diego.

Pitcavage, Megan R., and Geoffrey E. Braswell

2010 Diet, Health, and Death at Pusilhá, Belize. *Research Reports in Belizean Archaeology* 7:65–72.

Pohl, Mary D. (editor)

1990 *Ancient Maya Wetland Agriculture: Excavations on Albion Island, Northern Belize.* Westview, Boulder, Colorado.

Powis, Terry G.

2002 An Integrative Approach to the Analysis of the Late Preclassic Ceramics at

Lamanai, Belize. Unpublished Ph.D. dissertation, Department of Anthropology, University of Texas at Austin.

Powis, Terry G., and David Cheetham
2007   From House to Holy: Formative Development of Civic-Ceremonial Architecture in the Maya Lowlands. *Research Reports in Belizean Archaeology* 4:177–186.

Prager, Christian M.
2002   Die Inschriften von Pusilhá: Epigraphische Analyse und Rekonstruktion der Geschichte einer klassischen Maya-Stätte. Unpublished M.A. thesis, Institut für Altamerikanistik und Ethnologie, Universität Bonn.

Prager, Christian M., Beniamino Volta, and Geoffrey E. Braswell
2014   The Dynastic History and Archaeology of Pusilhá, Belize. In *The Maya and Their Central American Neighbors*, edited by Geoffrey E. Braswell, pp. 245–307. Routledge, New York.

Price, T. Douglas, James H. Burton, Robert J. Sharer, Jane E. Buikstra, Lori E. Wright, and Loa P. Traxler
2010   Kings and Commoners at Copan: Isotopic Evidence for Origins and Movement in the Classic Maya Period. *Journal of Anthropological Archaeology* 29:15–32.

Primrose, Ryan
2003   The Ancient Maya Water Management System at Minanha, Belize. Unpublished M.A. thesis, Department of Anthropology, Trent University, Peterborough, Ontario.

Pring, Duncan, and Norman Hammond
1985   Investigation of a Possible River Port at Nohmul. In *Nohmul: A Prehistoric Maya Community in Belize, Excavations 1973–1983*, Part ii, edited by Norman Hammond, pp. 527–565. BAR International Series 250(i). British Archaeological Reports, Oxford, England.

Proskouriakoff, Tatiana
1960   Historical Implications of a Pattern of Dates at Piedras Negras, Guatemala. *American Antiquity* 25:454–475.

Prufer, Keith M.
2005   Report of the Uxbenka Archaeological Project (UAP)—2005 Field Season. Report submitted to the Foundation for the Advancement of Mesoamerican Studies, Crystal River, Florida.
2007   The Uxbenka Archaeological Project 2006 Field Season. Report submitted to the Foundation for the Advancement of Mesoamerican Studies, Crystal River, Florida.

Prufer, Keith M., Holley Moyes, Brendan J. Culleton, Andrew Kindon, and Douglas J. Kennett
2011   Formation of a Complex Polity on the Eastern Periphery of the Maya Lowlands. *Latin American Antiquity* 22:199–223.

Prufer, Keith M., and Amy E. Thompson

2013   Settlements as Neighborhoods and Districts at Uxbenka: The Social Landscape of Maya Community. Paper presented at the Eleventh Annual Belize Archaeology and Anthropology Symposium, San Ignacio.

Pyburn, K. Anne

1988   The Settlement of Nohmul: Development of a Prehispanic Maya Community in Northern Belize. Unpublished Ph.D. dissertation, Department of Anthropology, University of Arizona, Tucson.

Rapoport, Amos

1988   Levels of Meaning in the Built Environment. In *Cross-Cultural Perspectives in Non Verbal Communication*, edited by Fernando Poyatos, pp. 317–336. J. Hogrefe, Toronto.

Reeder, Philip, Robert Brinkmann, and Edward Alt

1996   Karstification on the Northern Vaca Plateau, Belize. *Journal of Cave and Karst Studies* 58(2):121–130.

Reents-Budet, Dorie

1988   *The Iconography of Lamanai Stela 9*. Research Reports on Ancient Maya Writing 22. Center for Maya Research, Washington, D.C.

2001   Classic Maya Concepts of the Royal Court: An Analysis of Renderings on Pictorial Ceramics. In *Royal Courts of the Ancient Maya*, Vol. 1, edited by Takeshi Inomata and Stephen D. Houston, pp. 195–233. Westview Press, Boulder, Colorado.

Reese-Taylor, Kathryn, and Debra S. Walker

2002   The Passage of the Late Preclassic into the Early Classic. In *Ancient Maya Political Economies*, edited by Marilyn A. Masson and David A. Freidel, pp. 87–122. AltaMira Press, Walnut Creek, California.

Rice, Don S.

1993   Eighth-Century Physical Geography, Environment, and Natural Resources in the Maya Lowlands. In *Lowland Maya Civilization in the Eighth Century A.D.*, edited by Jeremy A. Sabloff and John S. Henderson, pp. 11–63. Dumbarton Oaks, Washington, D.C.

Ricketson, Oliver G.

1924   Report on the Excavations at Baking Pot, British Honduras. *Carnegie Institution Year Book* 23:219–221.

Ricketson, Oliver G., and Edith B. Ricketson

1937   *Uaxactún, Guatemala: Group E 1926–1931*. Publication 477. Carnegie Institution of Washington, Washington, D.C.

Ringle, William M., and George J. Bey, III

2001   Post-Classic and Terminal Classic Courts in the Northern Maya Lowlands. In *Royal Courts of the Ancient Maya*, Vol. 2, edited by Takeshi Inomata and Stephen D. Houston, pp. 266–307. Westview Press, Boulder, Colorado.

Robichaux, Hubert R.

1995 Ancient Maya Community Patterns in Northwestern Belize: Peripheral Zone Survey at La Milpa and Dos Hombres. Unpublished Ph.D. dissertation, Department of Anthropology, University of Texas at Austin.

1998 Excavations at the Upper Plaza. In *The 1997 Season of the Chan Chich Archaeological Project*, edited by Brett A. Houk, pp. 31–52. Papers of the Chan Chich Archaeological Project, No. 3. Center for Maya Studies, San Antonio, Texas.

2000a The Stelae of Rio Azul, Guatemala. In *Rio Azul Reports Number 5, the 1987 Season*, edited by Richard E. W. Adams, pp. 35–53. University of Texas at San Antonio.

2000b Looking Down on the Public: The 1999 Excavations on the Upper Plaza. In *The 1998 and 1999 Season of the Chan Chich Archaeological Project*, edited by Brett A. Houk, pp. 57–70. Papers of the Chan Chich Archaeological Project, No. 4. Mesoamerican Archaeological Research Laboratory, University of Texas at Austin.

Robichaux, Hubert R., and Jeffrey J. Durst

1999 Aspects of Ancient Maya Ideology, as Derived from Two Recently Discovered Elite Tombs in Northwestern Belize. Paper presented at the 64th Annual Meeting of the Society for American Archaeology, Chicago, Illinois.

Robichaux, Hubert R., and Brett A. Houk

2005 A Hieroglyphic Plate Fragment from Dos Hombres, Belize: Epigraphic and Archaeological Evidence Relating to Political Organization in the Three Rivers Region of Northwestern Belize and Northeastern Guatemala. *Mono y Conejo* 3:4–12.

Robichaux, Hubert R., Jennifer Jellen, Alexandra Miller, and Jennifer Vander Galien

2000 Report on the 1998 Excavations on the Upper Plaza. In *The 1998 and 1999 Season of the Chan Chich Archaeological Project*, edited by Brett A. Houk, pp. 49–56. Papers of the Chan Chich Archaeological Project, No. 4. Mesoamerican Archaeological Research Laboratory, University of Texas at Austin.

Robin, Cynthia, and Norman Hammond

1991 Burial Practices. In *Cuello: An Early Maya Community in Belize*, edited by Norman Hammond, pp. 204–225. Cambridge University Press, Cambridge, England.

Rosenswig, Robert

2004 The Late Archaic Occupation of Northern Belize: New Archaeological Excavation Data. *Research Reports in Belizean Archaeology* 1:267–277.

Rothenberg, Kara

2014 Interpreting Plaza Spaces Using Soil Chemistry: The View from Honduras. In *Mesoamerican Plazas: Arenas of Community and Power*, edited by Kenichiro Tsukamoto and Takeshi Inomata, pp. 121–129. University of Arizona Press, Tucson.

Roys, Ralph L.
1957 *The Political Geography of the Yucatán Maya*. Publication 613. Carnegie Institution of Washington, Washington, D.C.

Ruppert, Karl
1940 A Special Assemblage of Maya Structures. In *The Maya and their Neighbors*, edited by Clarence L. Hay, Ralph L. Linton, Samuel K. Lothrop, Harry L. Shapiro, and George C. Vaillant, pp. 222–231. Appleton-Century, New York.

Sagebiel, Kerry L.
2005 Shifting Allegiances at La Milpa, Belize: A Typological, Chronological, and Formal Analysis of the Ceramics. Unpublished Ph.D. dissertation, Department of Anthropology, University of Arizona.

Sanchez, Julia L. J.
2005 Ancient Maya Royal Strategies: Crafting Power and Identity through Art. *Ancient Mesoamerica* 16:261–275.

Sanders, William T., and David Webster
1988 The Mesoamerican Urban Tradition. *American Anthropologist* 90:521–546.

Sandrock, David
2013 Preliminary Results of the 2013 Gallon Jug and Laguna Seca Survey and Reconnaissance. In *The 2013 Season of the Chan Chich Archaeological Project*, edited by Brett A. Houk, pp. 63–80. Papers of the Chan Chich Archaeological Project, No. 7. Department of Sociology, Anthropology, and Social Work, Texas Tech University, Lubbock.

Santone, Lenore
1997 Transport Costs, Consumer Demand, and Patterns of Intraregional Exchange: A Perspective on Commodity Production and Distribution from Northern Belize. *Latin American Antiquity* 8:71–88.

Saturno, William A.
2006 The Dawn of Maya Gods and Kings. *National Geographic* 209:68–77.
2009 Centering the Kingdom, Centering the King: Maya Creation and Legitimization at San Bartolo. In *The Art of Urbanism: How Mesoamerican Kingdoms Represented Themselves in Architecture and Imagery*, edited by William L. Fash and Leonardo López Luján, pp. 111–134. Dumbarton Oaks Research Library and Collection, Washington, D.C.

Saturno, William A., David Stuart, and Boris Beltrán
2006 Early Maya Writing at San Bartolo, Guatemala. *Science* 311(5795):1281–1283.

Sausnavar, Jose and Arthur Demarest
2011 Variability in the Violent Destruction of the Pasion Valley Cities and Cancuen: Implications for the Early Collapse of the West. Paper presented at the 76th Annual Meeting of the Society for American Archaeology, Sacramento, California.

Scarborough, Vernon L.
1991a Courting the Southern Maya Lowlands: A Study in Pre-Hispanic Ballgame

Architecture. In *The Mesoamerican Ballgame*, edited by Veron L. Scarborough and David R. Wilcox, pp. 129–144. University of Arizona Press, Tucson.

1991b   *The Settlement System in a Late Preclassic Maya Community*. Vol. 3 of *Archaeology at Cerros, Belize*. Series edited by David Freidel. Southern Methodist University Press, Dallas.

1998   Ecology and Ritual: Water Management and the Maya. *Latin American Antiquity* 9:135–159.

Scarborough, Vernon L., Mathew E. Becher, Jeffrey L. Baker, Gary Harris, and Fred Valdez Jr.

1995   Water and Land at the Ancient Maya Community of La Milpa. *Latin American Antiquity* 6:98–119.

Scarborough, Vernon L., Nicholas P. Dunning, Kenneth B. Tankersley, Christopher Carr, Eric Weaver, Liwy Grazioso, Brian Lane, John G. Jones, Palma Buttles, Fred Valdez, and David L. Lentz

2012   Water and Sustainable Land Use at the Ancient Tropical City of Tikal, Guatemala. *PNAS* 109(31):12,408–12,413.

Scarborough, Vernon L., and Gary G. Gallopin

1991   A Water Storage Adaptation in the Maya Lowlands. *Science* 251(4994):658–662.

Scarborough, Vernon L., and Robin A. Robertson

1986   Civic and Residential Settlement at a Late Preclassic Maya Center. *Journal of Field Archaeology* 13:155–175.

Scarborough, Vernon L., and Fred Valdez Jr.

2009   An Alternative Order: The Dualistic Economies of the Ancient Maya. *Latin American Antiquity* 20:207–227.

Schele, Linda, and David Freidel

1990   *A Forest of Kings: The Untold Story of the Ancient Maya*. William and Morrow, New York.

Schultz, Kevan C., Jason J. Gonzalez, and Norman Hammond

1994   Classic Maya Ballcourts at La Milpa, Belize. *Ancient Mesoamerica* 5:45–53.

Schwake, Sonja A.

2008   The Social Implications of Ritual Behavior in the Maya Lowlands: A Perspective from Minanha, Belize. Unpublished Ph.D. dissertation, Department of Anthropology, University of California at San Diego, San Diego.

Schwake, Sonja A., and Gyles Iannone

2010   Ritual Remains and Collective Memory: Maya Examples from West Central Belize. *Ancient Mesoamerica* 21:331–339.

Seibert, Jeffrey

2004   A Functional Analysis of Structure 12A, Minanha, Belize. *Research Reports in Belizean Archaeology* 1:165–171.

Shafer, Harry J., and Thomas R. Hester

1983 Ancient Maya Chert Workshops in Northern Belize, Central America. *American Antiquity* 48:519–543.

1984 Exploitation of Chert Resources by the Ancient Maya of Northern Belize, Central America. *World Archaeology* 16(2):157–173.

1991 Lithic Craft Specialization and Product Distribution at the Maya Site of Colha, Belize. *World Archaeology* 23:79–97.

Sharer, Robert

1994 *The Ancient Maya*, 5th ed. Stanford University Press, Stanford, California.

Sharer, Robert, and Loa P. Traxler

2006 *The Ancient Maya*, 6th ed. Stanford University Press, Stanford, California.

Shaw, Justine M.

2001 Maya *Sacbeob* Form and Function. *Ancient Mesoamerica* 12:261–272.

Shelby, Thomas M.

2000 Report of the 1998 and 1999 Investigations on the Archaeology and Iconography of the Polychrome Stucco Façade of Structure N10-28, Lamanai, Belize. Report submitted to the Foundation for the Advancement of Mesoamerican Studies, Crystal River, Florida.

Shook, Edwin M.

1998 *Incidents in the Life of a Maya Archaeologist*. Southwestern Academy Press, San Marino, California.

Smith, A. Ledyard

1962 Residential and Associated Structures at Mayapan. In *Mayapan, Yucatan, Mexico*, by H.E.D. Pollock, Ralph L. Roys, T. Proskouriakoff, and A. Ledyard Smith, pp. 165–318. Publication 619. Carnegie Institution of Washington, Washington, D.C.

Smith, Adam T.

2003 *The Political Landscape: Constellations of Authority in Early Complex Societies*. University of California Press, Berkeley.

Smith, Michael E.

2003 Can We Read Cosmology in Ancient Maya City Plans? Comment on Ashmore and Sabloff. *Latin American Antiquity* 14:221–228.

2005 Did the Maya Build Architectural Cosmograms? *Latin American Antiquity* 16:217–224.

2007 Form and Meaning in the Earliest Cities: A New Approach to Ancient Urban Planning. *Journal of Planning History* 6(1):3–47.

2008 *Aztec City-State Capitals*. University Press of Florida, Gainesville.

2011 Classic Maya Settlement Clusters as Urban Neighborhoods: A Comparative Perspective on Low-Density Urbanism. *Journal de la Société des Américanistes* 97(1):51–73.

Smith, Monica L.

2010 Introduction: The Social Construction of Ancient Cities. In *The Social Con-

struction of Ancient Cities, edited by Monica L. Smith, pp. 1–36. Smithsonian Institution, Washington, D.C.

Stephens, John Lloyd

1841   *Incidents of Travel in Central America, Chiapas, and Yucatan.* Harper, New York.

1843   *Incidents of Travel in Yucatan.* 2 vols. Harper, New York.

Stevens, Rayfred L.

1964   The Soils of Middle America and Their Relation to Indian Peoples and Cultures. In *Natural Environment and Early Cultures*, edited by Robert C. West, pp. 265–315. *Handbook of Middle American Indians*, Vol. 1. University of Texas Press, Austin.

Stuart, David

2000   "The Arrival of Strangers": Teotihuacan and Tollan in Classic Maya History. In *Mesoamerica's Classic Heritage: From Teotihuacan to the Aztecs*, edited by Davíd Carrasco, Lindsay Jones, and Scott Sessions, pp. 465–515. University Press of Colorado, Boulder.

2007   The Origin of Copan's Founder. Electronic document, http://decipherment.wordpress.com/2007/06/25/the-origin-of-copans-founder/, accessed February 21, 2013.

Stuart, David, and Stephen D. Houston

1994   *Classic Maya Place Names.* Studies in Pre-Columbian Art and Archaeology, 33. Dumbarton Oaks Research Library and Collection, Washington, D.C.

Suhler, Charles, Traci Arden, David Freidel, and Dave Johnstone

2004   The Rise and Fall of Terminal Classic Yaxuna, Yucatán, Mexico. In *The Terminal Classic in the Maya Lowlands: Collapse. Transition, and Transformation*, edited by Arthur A. Demarest, Prudence M. Rice, and Don S. Rice, pp. 450–484. University Press of Colorado, Boulder.

Sullivan, Lauren A.

1991   Preclassic Domestic Architecture at Colha, Belize. Unpublished M.A. thesis, Department of Anthropology, University of Texas at Austin.

2002   Evidence for Changing Dynamics in the Regional Integration of Northwestern Belize. In *Ancient Maya Political Economies*, edited by Marilyn A. Masson and David A. Freidel, pp. 197–222. AltaMira Press, Walnut Creek, California.

Sullivan, Lauren A., and Jaime J. Awe

2012   Establishing the Cunil Ceramic Complex at Cahal Pech, Belize. In *Ancient Maya Pottery: Classification, Analysis, and Interpretation*, edited by James John Aimers, pp. 107–120. University Press of Florida, Gainesville.

Sullivan, Lauren A., M. Kathryn Brown, and Jaime J. Awe

2009   Refining the Cunil Ceramic Complex at Cahal Pech, Belize. *Research Reports in Belizean Archaeology* 6:161–168.

Sullivan, Lauren A., and Kerry L. Sagebiel
2003   Changing Political Alliances in the Three Rivers Region. In *Heterarchy, Political Economy, and the Ancient Maya: The Three Rivers Region of the East-Central Yucatán Peninsula*, edited by Vernon L. Scarborough, Fred Valdez Jr., and Nicholas Dunning, pp. 25–36. University of Arizona Press, Tucson.

Sullivan, Lauren A., and Fred Valdez Jr.
2006   The Late Preclassic to Early Classic Transition in the Three Rivers Region. *Research Reports in Belizean Archaeology* 3:73–84.

Thompson, Amy E., Claire E. Ebert, and Keith M. Prufer
2013   Shifting Dynamics and Use of Space at Uxbenka. *Research Reports in Belizean Archaeology* 10:25–267.

Thompson, J. Eric S.
1938   Reconnaissance and Excavation in British Honduras. *Carnegie Institution Year Book* 37:152–153.
1939   *Excavations at San José, British Honduras*. Publication 506. Carnegie Institution, Washington, D.C.
1942   *Late Ceramic Horizons at Bauque Viejo, British Honduras*. Publication 528. Carnegie Institution, Washington, D.C.
1954   *The Rise and Fall of Maya Civilization*. University of Oklahoma Press, Norman.
1963   *Maya Archaeologist*. University of Oklahoma Press, Norman.

Tourtellot, Gair, III
1988   *Excavations at Seibal, Department of Peten, Guatemala: Peripheral Survey and Excavation, Settlement and Community Patterns*. Memoirs of the Peabody Museum of Archaeology and Ethnology, Vol. 16. Harvard University, Cambridge, Massachusetts.

Tourtellot, Gair, III, Francisco Estrada-Belli, John J. Rose, and Norman Hammond
2003   Late Classic Maya Heterarchy: Hierarchy, and Landscape at La Milpa, Belize. In *Heterarchy, Political Economy, and the Ancient Maya*, edited by Vernon L. Scarborough, Fred Valdez Jr., and Nicholas P. Dunning, pp. 37–51. University of Arizona Press, Tucson.

Tourtellot, Gair, III, Gloria Everson, and Norman Hammond
2003   Suburban Organization: Minor Centers at La Milpa, Belize. In *Perspectives on Ancient Maya Rural Complexity*, edited by G. Iannone and S. Connell, pp. 95–107. Monograph 49, Cotsen Institute of Archaeology, UCLA, Los Angeles.

Tourtellot, Gair, III, and John Rose
1993   *More Light on La Milpa Mapping: Interim Report on the 1993 Season*. La Milpa Archaeological Project, Boston University.

Tourtellot, Gair, III, Marc Wolf, Francisco Estrada-Belli, and Norman Hammond
2000   Discovery of Two Predicted Ancient Maya Sites in Belize. *Antiquity* 74:481–482.

Trachman, Clarissa M.

2007 Excavated Households Excavated Lives: Social Reproduction, Identity, and Everyday Life for the Ancient Maya in Northwestern Belize. Unpublished Ph.D. dissertation, Department of Anthropology, University of Texas at Austin.

Trachman, Rissa M., Kirby Farah, Thomas Ewing, and Jana Murdock

2011 Summary Report for Investigations at the Site of Dos Hombres and the Surrounding Settlement, Summer 2010. In *Research Reports from the Programme for Belize Archaeological Project*, Vol. 5, edited by Brett A. Houk and Fred Valdez Jr., pp. 235–242. Occasional Papers, No. 12. Mesoamerican Archaeological Research Laboratory, University of Texas at Austin.

Trein, Debora

2007 Current Issues in Site Management in Belize, Central America. Unpublished M.A. dissertation, University College London, England.

2011 Investigating Monumental Architecture at La Milpa: The 2010 Season. *Research Reports from the Programme for Belize Archaeological Project*, Vol. 5, edited by Brett A. Houk and Fred Valdez Jr., pp. 39–66. Occasional Papers, No. 12. Mesoamerican Archaeological Research Laboratory, University of Texas at Austin.

2012 Use and Access to a Monumental Structure at the Site of La Milpa, Belize. Paper presented at the Third Annual South-Central Conference on Mesoamerica, Lubbock, Texas.

Trigger, Bruce G.

1989 *A History of Archaeological Thought*. Cambridge University Press, Cambridge, England.

1990 Monumental Architecture: A Thermodynamic Explanation of Symbolic Behaviour. *World Archaeology* 22:119–132.

2003 *Understanding Early Civilizations: A Comparative Study*. Cambridge University Press, Cambridge, England.

Turner, B. L., II

1983 The Excavations of Raised and Channelized Fields at Pulltrouser Swamp. In *Pulltrouser Swamp: Ancient Maya Habitat, Agriculture, and Settlement in Northern Belize*, edited by B. L. Turner II and Peter D. Harrison, pp. 30–51. University of Texas Press, Austin.

Turner, B. L., II, and Peter D. Harrison (editors)

1983 *Pulltrouser Swamp: Ancient Maya Habitat, Agriculture, and Settlement in Northern Belize*. University of Texas Press, Austin.

Turner, Ellen Sue, Norman I. Turner, and R.E.W. Adams

1981 Volumetric Assessment, Rank Ordering, and Maya Civic Centers. In *Lowland Maya Settlement Patterns*, edited by Wendy Ashmore, pp. 71–88. School of American Research, Santa Fe, New Mexico.

UCF Anthropology

2013 Investigations at Caracol, Belize. Electronic document, http://www.caracol.org/dig/investigations/, accessed June 8, 2014.

Valdez, Fred, Jr.
2012 Three Decades of Research in the Three Rivers Region, NE Peten and NW Belize. Paper presented at the Third Annual South-Central Conference on Mesoamerica, Lubbock, Texas.

Valdez, Fred, Jr., and Brett A. Houk
2012 Preliminary Comments on the 2012 Ceramics Analysis. In *The 2012 Season of the Chan Chich Archaeological Project*, edited by Brett A. Houk, pp. 65–72. Papers of the Chan Chich Archaeological Project, No. 6. Department of Sociology, Anthropology, and Social Work, Texas Tech University, Lubbock.

Vivó Escoto, Jorge A.
1964 Weather and Climate of Mexico and Central America. In *Natural Environment and Early Cultures*, edited by Robert C. West, pp. 187–215. *Handbook of Middle American Indians*, Vol. 1. University of Texas Press, Austin.

Volta, Beniamino P.
2007 Archaeological Settlement Patterns in the Kingdom of the Avocado. Unpublished M.A. thesis, University of California, San Diego.

Von Euw, Eric, and Ian Graham
1984 *Corpus of Maya Hieroglyphic Inscriptions*, Vol. 5, Pt. 2. Peabody Museum of Archaeology and Ethnology, Harvard University, Cambridge, Massachusetts.

Walker, Debra S.
2005 Sampling Cerros' Demise: A Radiometric Check on the Elusive Protoclassic. Report submitted to the Foundation for the Advancement of Mesoamerican Studies, Inc., Crystal River, Florida.

Walling, Stanley
1995 Bajo and Floodplain Sites along the Rio Bravo: 1994 Survey and Excavations. In *The Programme for Belize Archaeological Project 1994 Interim Report*, edited by Richard E. W. Adams and Fred Valdez Jr., pp. 63–67. The Center for Archaeology and Tropical Studies, University of Texas at San Antonio.
2005 Archaeological Investigation of Prehispanic Maya Residential Terraces, Commoner Housing and Hydrology at Chawak But'o'ob, Belize. Electronic document, http://www.antiquity.ac.uk/projgall/walling/index.html, accessed February 5, 2013.
2011 Overview of Recent Ballcourt Complex Investigations at Chawak But'o'ob, Belize. In *Research Reports from the Programme for Belize Archaeological Project*, Vol. 5, edited by Brett A. Houk and Fred Valdez Jr., pp. 251–261. Occasional Papers, No. 12. Mesoamerican Archaeological Research Laboratory, University of Texas at Austin.

Wanyerka, Phillip J.
2003 The Southern Belize Epigraphic Project: The Hieroglyphic Inscriptions of

  Southern Belize. Report submitted to the Foundation for the Advancement of Mesoamerican Studies, Crystal River, Florida.

2005 Epigraphic Evidence of Macro-Political Organization in Southern Belize: A View from the Early Classic Period. *Research Reports in Belizean Archaeology* 2:179–191.

2009 Classic Maya Political Organization: Epigraphic Evidence of Hierarchical Organization in the Southern Maya Mountains Region of Belize. Unpublished Ph.D. dissertation, Department of Anthropology, Southern Illinois University, Carbondale.

Webster, David

1998 Classic Maya Architecture: Implications and Comparisons. In *Function and Meaning in Classic Maya Architecture*, edited by Stephen D. Houston, pp. 5–47. Dumbarton Oaks Research and Library Collection, Washington, D.C.

2002 *The Fall of the Ancient Maya*. Thames and Hudson, London.

Wernecke, D. Clark

1994 Aspects of Urban Design in an Ancient Maya Center: El Pilar, Belize. Unpublished M.A. thesis, Florida Atlantic University, Boca Raton, Florida.

West, Robert C.

1964 Surface Configuration and Associated Geology of Middle America. In *Natural Environment and Early Cultures*, edited by Robert C. West, pp. 33–83. Handbook of Middle American Indians, Vol. 1. University of Texas Press, Austin.

Wheatley, Paul

1967 *City as Symbol*. H. K. Lewis, London.

White, Christine D., David M. Pendergast, Fred J. Longstaffe, and Kimberley R. Law

2001 Social Complexity and Food Systems at Altun Ha, Belize: The Isotopic Evidence. *Latin American Antiquity* 12:371–393.

Whittaker, John C., Kathryn A. Kamp, Anabel Ford, Rafael Guerra, Peter Brands, Jose Guerra, Kim McLean, Alex Woods, Melissa Badillo, Jennifer Thornton, and Zerifeh Eiley

2009 Lithic Industry in a Maya Center: An Axe Workshop at El Pilar, Belize. *Latin American Antiquity* 20:134–156.

Willey, Gordon R., William R. Bullard Jr., John B. Glass, and James C. Gifford

1965 *Prehistoric Maya Settlements in the Belize Valley*. Papers of the Peabody Museum of Archaeology and Ethnology, Vol. XIV. Harvard University, Cambridge, Massachusetts.

Wood, Gregory P.

1990 Excavations at Op. 4046, Colha, Belize: A Buried Preceramic Lithic Deposit. Unpublished M.A. thesis, Department of Anthropology, University of Texas at San Antonio.

Wright, A.C.S., D. H. Romney, R. H. Arbuckle, and V. E. Vial

1959 *Land in British Honduras*. Report of the British Honduras Land Use Survey Team. Her Majesty's Stationery Office, London.

Yaeger, Jason
2003   Untangling the Ties that Bind: The City, the Countryside, and the Nature of Maya Urbanism at Xunantunich, Belize. In *The Social Construction of Cities*, edited by Monica L. Smith, pp. 121–155. Smithsonian Institution Press, Washington, D.C.
2010   Shifting Political Dynamics as Seen from the Xunantunich Palace. In *Classic Maya Provincial Politics: Xunantunich and Its Hinterlands*, edited by Lisa J. LeCount and Jason Yaeger, pp. 145–160. University of Arizona Press, Tucson.

Yaeger, Jason (editor)
2007   The Mopan Valley Archaeology Project: Results of the 2007 Season. Report on file, Institute of Archaeology, Belmopan, Belize.

Yaeger, Jason, Bernadette Cap, Meaghan Peuramaki-Brown
2009   The 2007 Field Season of the Mopan Valley Archaeological Project: Buenavista del Cayo's East Plaza and Near-Periphery Settlement. *Research Reports in Belizean Archaeology* 6:209–216.

Yaeger, Jason, and Cynthia Robin
2004   Heterogeneous Hinterlands: The Social and Political Organization of Commoner Settlements near Xunantunich, Belize. In *Ancient Maya Commoners*, edited by Jon C. Lohse and Fred Valdez Jr., pp. 147–173. University of Texas Press, Austin.

Zaro, Gregory, and Brett A. Houk
2012   The Growth and Decline of the Ancient Maya City of La Milpa, Belize: New Data and New Perspectives from the Southern Plazas. *Ancient Mesoamerica* 23:143–159.

Index

The letter *f* following a page number denotes a figure. The letter *t* following a page number denotes a table.

Abandoned projects, 134, 177; as subcategory of built environment, 14–15
Abandonment of Maya centers, 14–15, 46t, 56, 59–60, 64–65, 199; Caracol, 60, 141; Chan Chich, 198; Cobá, 69; Dos Hombres, 185; El Pilar, 165–66; La Milpa, 177–78, 179, 180; Lubaantun, 110; Minanha, 126; Nohmul, 207–8; Uxbenka, 100; Xunantunich, 60, 157, 160. *See also* Holuitz
Abbreviating Long Count dates, 62
Access and visibility, 250, 251t, 254–55
Acropoli, 37; Altun Ha, 230, 257, 262; Cahal Pech, 72f; Caracol, 129, 130f, 131f, 133, 134, 135f, 136, 138–39, 140, 141, 145; Chan Chich, 192f, 194; Dos Hombres, 182, 183f, 185, 188, 189; El Pilar, 162f, 163f, 164, 165, 166; Lamanai, 212f, 217; La Milpa, 171, 172f, 173f, 174, 176–77, 179, 180; Lubaantun, 105f, 109; Minanha, 121, 122f, 123, 125, 127; Nohmul, 204f, 205, 207, 211–12; Pusilhá, 87–89, 92, 93, 94, 244; Tikal, 55, 58, 62; Uxbenka, 96f, 98, 102
—comparisons, 235, 244, 254, 257t, 260, 272, 275, 276
Actuncan, 156
Adams, Richard E. W., 25, 169, 178, 233, 234
Agriculture, evidence of, 9, 23, 46t, 48, 50, 140, 202–3
Aguadas, 48, 79, 199; Altun Ha, 223f, 224f, 227, 230; Cerros, 81f; Chan Chich, 191, 192f; El Pilar, 162f, 163f, 166; Minanha, 124; Xunantunich, 150f, 154, 249
Ah Muwaan, 188

Aimers, Jim, 219, 258
AJAW glyph, 55
Albion Island, 9
Alleyways. *See* Ball courts
Altars, 38, 53, 71, 74, 89–90, 103, 141, 142t–43t, 242, 284; Altun Ha, 226, 230; Caracol, 134, 135f, 142t, 143, 243, 247; Chan Chich, 191; Dos Hombres, 182, 189, 281; Kaxil Uinic, 195f, 196, 200; La Milpa, 172, 180, 243, 278; Nohmul, 209; Xunantunich, 142t, 157, 159. *See also* Thrones
Alta Verapaz, 48
Altun Ha, xviii, 4f, 8, 21, 46t, 93, 116, 169f, 231; chronology and political history, 227–30; comparisons, 236t, 237f, 238f, 239, 240t, 241t, 244, 246, 249, 262, 264, 271t, 272; coordination, 252, 253t; jade head, 201, 225, 226; site description, 220–27, 230; standardization, 256–57t, 261f; ties to other cities, 225, 228–30; ties to Teotihuacan, 228–29
Analytical approaches, 13
Ancient Maya, The (McKillop), 51
Ancient urban planning analysis, 13, 15–19
Anderson, A. H., 128, 129, 136, 149, 221
Andrews, George, 19, 35, 37
Anthropomorphic bowls, 198f
Antillean orogenic belt, 48
Aquatic adaptions, 67, 76
Archaic period, 9–10, 52
Archaic states, 54, 56
Arch construction. *See* Corbeled vaults
Architectural components of Maya cities, 33–39

Architectural inventories, 13, 21, 255t, 257–58
Arenal, 148
Ashmore, Wendy, 15–17, 149, 158, 160, 258, 259, 260, 275; Petén template, 16, 38, 189, 265–67, 268, 270–72, 283, 284
Attached ball courts, 37, 155, 160, 193, 200, 247, 274–75, 280, 283
Aveni, Anthony, 53, 61
Aventura, 209, 231, 273
Awe, Jaime, 6, 53, 95, 152

Backracks, 279
B'ahlam Te', 230
Bajos, 48, 49, 56, 169, 170f, 174, 180, 190, 210
Baking Pot, Belize, 7, 8, 236t, 237f
Bak'tuns, 61, 62
B'alam, 94, 116
Ball court markers, 37, 38, 115, 215, 247; Caracol, 133, 134, 140, 141, 143t, 243; Lamanai, 215; Lubaantun, 103, 107, 108, 109, 110, 246; Nim Li Punit, 113f, 115; Uxbenka, 98f
Ball courts, 37–38; Altun Ha, 21, 230, 246; Blackman Eddy, 74; Cahal Pech, 71, 72f; Caracol, 132–33, 134, 140, 143t, 144–45; Cerros, 80, 81f, 82; Chan Chich, 108, 155, 192f, 193, 194–95, 197, 198, 200, 247; Chichén Itzá, 66; Colha, 78; Dos Hombres, 183f, 184, 185, 189; El Pilar, 162, 163f, 164, 166; Lamanai, 212f, 215f, 21, 247, 280–81; La Milpa, 172, 173f, 176, 180, 181, 182, 184, 185, 239, 247, 280–81; Lubaantun, 103, 106–7, 108, 110, 246–47, 273, 274; Minanha, 120, 121, 122f, 123, 127; Nakbe, 53; Nim Li Punit, 113f, 114, 115; Nohmul, 204f, 206, 208, 209; Pusilhá, 87, 88f, 89, 90, 92, 94, 247, 268, 273; Uxbenka, 98, 99f, 102; Xunantunich, 150f, 152–53, 155, 156, 160, 247
—as architectural transitions, 16, 38, 266, 270, 271t, 272
—comparisons, 239, 240t, 246–47, 268–69, 280, 283; coordination, 252, 254; standardization, 256t, 257; Petén template, 270, 271t, 272, 273, 274–75; of processional architecture, 280, 281, 282; rank ordering in, 233, 234–35
—as urban features, 246–47
Ball game imagery, 246
Barrio palace compound, 130f, 131f, 133–34, 140

Bars and dots, 61
Barton Ramie, 8, 85f, 147
Base-20 mathematical systems, 61
"Batter," 28, 29f
Beads, 139, 185, 197f, 209, 227, 282
BEAST (Belize Estates Archaeological Survey Team), 168
Becker, Marshall, 145
Belize. *See* Altun Ha; Barton Ramie; Blackman Eddy; Blue Creek; Buenavista del Cayo; Cahal Pech; Caracol; Chan Chich; Cuello; Dos Hombres; El Pilar; Gran Cacao; Kaxil Uinic; Lamanai; La Milpa; Lubaantun; Minanha; Nim Li Punit; Nohmul; Nohol Pilar; Pacbitun; Punta de Cacao; Pusilhá; Saktunja; San José; Saturday Creek; Uxbenka; Wild Cane Caye; Xaman Pilar; Yalbac
Belizean archaeology. *See* History of Maya archaeology in Belize
Belize Estate and Produce Company, 7, 190, 199
Belize Estates Archaeological Survey Team (BEAST), 168
Belize River, 4f, 71, 85f, 148, 161, 190, 220, 238f, 258
Belize River Archaeological Settlement Survey (BRASS), 161, 165
Belize River East Archaeology project, 43
Belize Valley, xviii, 11–12, 147–48, 167. *See also* El Pilar; Xunantunich
Belize Valley Archaeological Project (BVAP), 71, 74
Belize Valley Preclassic site case studies, 70–76
Belmopan, 148
Benches, 31, 37, 40, 41f, 93, 115, 124, 131, 177, 198
Benque Viejo. *See* Xunantunich
Berlin, Heinrich, 24
Bifaces, 79, 209
Bird-Jaguar, 178
Bital, 143*t*
Black, Stephen, 7
Blackman Eddy, 2, 4f, 46t, 54, 70–71, 74–76, 85f
Blue Creek (river). *See* Río Azul
Blue Creek (site), 10, 168, 169f, 170, 236t, 273
Bolon Tzuk Witz, 188
Bonampak, xviii, 59, 279

328   Index

Bones, 60, 91, 127, 139, 178, 216, 226
Booth's River, 169f, 170f, 180, 273
Booth's River Escarpment, 170f, 180, 200, 201
Booth's River Upland, 180
Boulder fill, 28–29, 89, 109, 125, 216, 278
Bowls, 116, 127, 184, 185, 196, 198f, 282
BRASS (Belize River Archaeological Settlement Survey), 161, 165
Braswell, Geoffrey, 244; Lubaantun, 104, 109, 110–11, 268–69; Nim Li Punit, 114, 116, 117, 268–69; Pusilhá, 86, 87, 90, 92, 94, 236t, 268, 273; Uxbenka, 100
Bravo Hills, 148, 170, 201
Bridges, 88f, 89, 95
British Honduras. *See* Belize
British Museum expeditions, 7, 86–87, 89, 120, 159
Brown, Mary Kathryn, 75, 184
Bryan & Murphy Causeway, 163f, 164–65, 249, 281
Buenavista del Cayo, 85f, 123, 147, 236t, 237f
Building platforms, 30f
"Build what you know" concept, 275–77, 283–84
Built environment, studying, 13–15
Bullard, William, 8
"Bulldozed Mound," 92, 112
Burials, 92, 133, 138, 145, 180, 198, 203, 207, 216, 228; female, 78, 130, 139; mass graves, 59, 78, 82; in ritual practices, 127; royal, 55, 93, 114, 196, 197f, 199, 207, 208, 209, 228–29
BV. *See* Belize Valley
BVAP (Belize Valley Archaeological Project), 71, 74

Caana, 129, 130f, 131f, 132f, 135f, 139–40, 144, 252, 254, 258; Caana plaza, 241t, 242
Cahal Pech, 2, 4f, 46t, 29f, 32f, 46t, 70–74, 75–76, 85f, 123
Cahal Pichik, 138
Calakmul, xviii, 5, 22, 38, 57, 58, 94, 179, 243, 275, 276, 277; Chiik Nahb murals, 34; Classic period political history, 57, 62–65, 142t, 143, 144, 146; "overkingship," 25–27, 64
Caledonia, 120
Calendar cycles, 61
Calendar Round cycles, 61
Calendrical systems, 61–62
Camp 6, 120

Canals, 80, 81f
CAP (Caracol Archaeological Project), 10, 42, 129, 131, 136, 138, 139
Capstones, 30f
Caracol, xviii, 4f, 46t, 94, 145–46; Caracol identity, 140, 145; chronology and political history, 138–44; comparisons, 233, 236t, 237f, 238f, 240t, 240–42, 243–44, 247–48, 262, 263, 271t; coordination, 251t, 252, 253t, 254; site description, 128–38, 144–45; standardization, 255, 256–57t, 258, 260, 261f; ties to other cities, 64, 93, 126–27, 140, 141, 142–43t, 143–44, 146
Caracol, the, 66
Caracol Archaeological Project (CAP), 10, 42, 129, 131, 136, 138, 139
Caribbean Sea, xviii, 1, 4f
Carnegie Institution expeditions, 6–7
Castillo, the, 31f, 66, 148, 149, 150f, 151f, 155f, 156, 157, 159, 160, 280; friezes, 151, 152f, 282; as "World Tree," 268
Catchment basins. *See* Water management features
Catherwood, Frederick, 6
Causeways (*sacbeob*), 18, 35; Altun Ha, 223f, 227, 230, 249; Caracol, 35, 136–38, 140, 145, 194–95, 247, 254, 275, 277, 282; Chan Chich (35, 192f, 193, 194, 200; comparisons, 236t, 248, 249, 254, 259, 274, 275, 277, 280, 282); Dos Hombres, 183f, 249, 274, 281; El Mirador, 14, 54; El Pilar (162f, 163f, 164–65, 166, 194; comparisons, 248, 249, 259, 275, 277, 281, 283); Kaxil Uinic, 195f; Labná, 275; La Milpa, 171–72, 173f, 249, 274, 280; Minanha, 122f, 123, 249; Nakbe, 14, 53; Nohmul, 204f, 249; Pusilhá, 88f, 90, 249; Tikal, 35, 248, 277; Xunantunich (150f, 153–54, 156, 160, 194; comparisons, 249, 254, 259, 268, 275, 280, 282, 283)
—comparisons, 236t, 240t–41t; coordination, 252, 253t, 256t; Petén template, 266, 268, 270, 271t, 275, 277
—as dams, 39, 40, 154, 165, 249
—intersite, 35, 123, 127, 129, 137f, 138, 247–48
—intrasite, 35, 129, 137f, 138, 156, 166, 172, 236t, 247–48
—sunken, 194, 248, 249, 250, 256t, 259, 274, 275, 277
—as urban features, 247–49

Cayes, 49, 67
CCAP (Chan Chich Archaeological Project), 190
Cenotes, 49, 66, 119
Center walls. *See* Spinewalls
Central Foothills, 119, 148
Ceramic cord holders, 41f
Ceramic lids, 18, 176, 185, 186f, 187f, 278
Cerros, xviii, 2, 4f, 9, 10, 46t, 54, 56, 169f, 201, 202; Corozal Project, 9, 69–70, 76, 112, 203, 207
Cerros Cooperative Archaeological Development Project, 76
Chaaca Patio, 150f, 154
Chak Tok Ich'aak I (Jaguar Paw), 62, 63, 101, 102
Chalcedonies, 202
Chan Chich, xviii, 4f, 35, 46t, 55, 85f, 169f, 200, 208; ball courts, 108, 155, 192f, 193, 194–95, 197, 198, 200, 247; chronology and political history, 196–99; comparisons, 236t, 237f, 238f, 239, 240t, 240–42, 244–45, 246, 248, 249, 250, 262, 263; coordination, 252, 253t, 254–55; meaning, 271t, 272, 274, 275, 277, 280, 282, 283; SfM mapping, 42–43f; site description, 189–96, 199–200; standardization, 256t–57t, 259, 260, 261f; ties to other cities, 199, 274, 283; ties to Petén political sphere, 199
Chan Chich Archaeological Project (CCAP), 190
Chan Chich Creek, 189–90, 192f
Chase, Arlen, 10, 53, 129, 136, 140, 205, 236t, 247, 248, 254
Chase, Diane, 10, 53, 129, 136, 140, 203, 205, 236t, 247, 248, 254
Chawak But'o'ob, 189. *See* Dos Hombres: ball courts
Chert, 50, 154, 202, 220; bifaces, 209; debitage, 78, 176, 229; drills, 153; eccentrics, 209, 227, 229, 282; tools, 76, 228
Chetumal Bay, 80, 201, 202, 209
Chetumal province, 67
Chiapas, 32, 47
Chichén Itzá, xviii, 1, 6, 65–66, 209
Chiik Nahb, 34
Ch'orti', 21
Chronicle of Maya Kings and Queens (Martin and Grube), 51

Chultuns, 27, 192f
City comparisons. *See* Comparisons and urban planning
City-state cultures, 26
City-state models of geopolitical organization, 25–26
Cival, 54, 70
Classic Ch'olti'an, 22
Classic Maya collapse. *See* Maya collapse
Classic period, 46t, 51, 56–57; cultural history, 57–60; political history, 60–65
"Classic period overburden," 70, 79
Cobble fill, 28–29, 278
Cobweb Swamp, 76
Cocos Bank, 148
Codex-style vessels, 59, 279
Codex Vienna, 264
Codices, 61
Colha, xviii, 2, 4f, 9–10, 46t, 50, 69–70, 169f, 201, 228; Colha Project, 76, 78–79, 82
Collapse, process of (buildings), 40–42
Collapses. *See* Abandonment of Maya centers; Maya collapse
Colonization of Maya area, 52
Comparisons and urban planning, 232, 236t, 237f, 238f, 240t–41t, 249–50, 262–64; coordination, 15, 250–55; rank ordering, 25, 232–37, 253t, 256t; standardization, 15, 250, 255–61; urban features (238; ball courts, 246–47; carved monuments, 242–46; causeways, 247–49; emblem glyphs, 239; plazas, 239–42)
Compound glyphs. *See* Emblem glyphs
Construction: materials, 27, 40, 86; scheduling, 22, 33; techniques, 28–33
Construction pens, 29
Contour lines, 42, 43f
Contour maps, 44f
Coordinated arrangement of buildings and spaces, 250–52
Coordination, 15, 250–55
Copán, xviii, 94, 110, 116, 117, 230; dynasty foundation, 63, 93, 141, 178
Corbeled vaults, 30f–31, 33
Core-outlier intrasite causeways, 35. *See also* Intersite causeways
Coronation scenes, 55, 199
Corozal Bay, 2, 76, 80, 81f
Corozal Project, 9, 69–70, 76, 112, 203, 207

Correlating Long Count dates, 62
Cosmograms as interpretive tools, 16–17, 160, 265, 266–69; critiques of, 269–70
Courtyard counting systems, 25, 233–34. *See also* Rank ordering
Courtyards, 28, 34, 37, 38; Altun Ha, 223f, 227, 228; Cahal Pech, 71, 72f; Caracol, 130f, 131f, 133, 135f, 136, 139, 145; Cerros, 81f; Chan Chich, 192f, 195; Colha, 80, 78; Dos Hombres, 181, 183f, 184, 185; El Pilar, 162f, 163f, 164; Lamanai, 212f, 215; La Milpa, 41f, 44f, 172, 173f, 174, 176, 177, 178; Lubaantun, 105f, 106; Minanha, 121, 122f, 123, 124, 125, 127; Nim Li Punit, 113f; Nohmul, 204f, 215–16; Pusilhá, 88f; Tikal, 145; Uxbenka, 96f, 97f, 98; Xunantunich, 150f, 154, 157
—Plaza Plan 2, 124
—royal, 123, 125, 127, 236t
—U-shaped, 122f, 123–24, 154
Craft specialization, evidence for, 2, 46t, 82–83
Creation mythology, depictions of, 269
Creeks. *See* Rivers
Cremations, 139, 141, 142t, 145
Crystal skull, alleged discovery of, 6, 103
Cuello, 2, 4f, 9, 46t, 59, 69–70, 76–78, 82, 169f, 201; Cuello Project, 77
Cultural history of Maya, 46t, 51–52, 68; Classic period (46t, 51, 56–60; political history, 60–65); Postclassic period, 46t, 51, 65, 66–67; Preclassic period, 51, 52–56
Cunil ceramics, 52, 71, 155, 156

Dams, 39–40, 154, 165, 174, 227, 249
Danta pyramid, 54, 56
de Fuensalida, Bartolomé, 210
del Rio, Antonio, 6
Demarest, Arthur, 60
Density of stelae, 240t–41t, 243–45
de Orbita, Juan, 210
Depopulation. *See* Maya collapse
Deterioration of Maya buildings, 40–42
Digital elevation models, 43
Directionality, 16–17, 266–69. *See also* Orientations
Divine kingship, evidence of, 46t, 54, 55, 56
Doorway jambs, 41f
Dos Arroyos Orange Polychrome vessel, 187f
Dos Hombres, 4f, 145, 169f, 179; chronology and political history, 184–88; comparisons, 236t, 237f, 238f, 240t, 241, 242, 244, 246, 247, 249, 262, 263; coordination, 252, 253t, 254; meaning, 271t, 272, 274, 275–76, 280, 281, 283; site description, 180–84, 188–89; standardization, 256t–57t, 258, 259, 260, 261f; ties to other cities, 188–89, 275
Dots and bars, 61
Double-emblem glyphs, 178, 179
Double-headed serpent bars, 100, 218
Drainage, 135, 164, 174, 227, 249, 278
Drains, 174, 278
Drones, 43
Droughts, 59–60
Dry-laid fill, 28, 216
Dunham, Peter, 104
Dunning, Nicholas, 50, 169, 190
Durst, Jeffrey, 184
"Dynastic axis." *See* North–south orientations
Dzuluinicob, 219

Earliest Maya in eastern lowlands, 70–76
Early Classic period, 46t, cultural history, 57–58; political history, 62–64
Early Postclassic period, 66–67
Early Preclassic period, 46t, 52
Ear spools, 184, 213
Eastern lowlands, xviii, 4f
Eastern structures, 53, 73, 126, 127, 136f, 193
East–west orientations, 56, 92, 96, 150, 172, 247, 259, 260, 266
Eccentrics, 79, 126, 282; with burials, 209, 229; caching of, 126, 227, 229; production of, 176
E-Groups and possible E-Groups, 53, 256t, 257–58; Blackman Eddy, 74; Cahal Pech, 71; Caracol, 134, 136f, 138, 144, 146, 262; Chan Chich, 191; El Pilar, 163f, 164, 166; La Milpa, 191; Minanha, 121–22, 123, 127, 281; Uaxactun, 54; Xunantunich, 152, 163, 164, 166
18 Jog (Waxaklajuun Ubaah K'awiil), 159, 188
El Cayo. *See* Cahal Pech
Elite culture, Maya cities as part of, 20, 26
El Mirador, xviii, 14, 54, 56, 57, 70, 79, 83, 266
El Perú/Waka', xviii, 62
El Pilar, xviii, 4f, 161–66; chronology and political history, 165–66; comparisons, 236t, 237f, 38f, 239, 240t–41t, 244, 249, 250, 262, 271t; coordination, 252, 253t, 254; site description, 161–65, 166; standardization, 256t–57t, 259, 261f

Index 331

El Pozito, 209, 231, 273
El Salvador, 1, 47
El Tigre, 54, 56
Emblem glyphs, 24–25, 117, 159, 199, 239, 240t, 243; Altun Ha (at Lamanai), 229; Caracol, 233; Lamanai, 219; La Milpa, 178, 179; Lubaantun, 110–11, 117, 247; Naranjo (at Xunantunich), 158, 159, 276; Nim Li Punit, 115, 116; Pusilhá, 233; Uxbenka, 101
Engineering concerns, 39–40
Entrada, the, 62–63, 101

False arches. *See* Corbeled vaults
Faults, 48–49
Fedick, Scott, 50, 171
Female human remains, 78, 130, 139
Female rulers, 218; Ix Ich'ak . . . K'inich (Ruler F), 93t; Lady Six Sky, 158, 159
Fiberglass replicas, 151, 152f, 213f
Field Museum Expeditions, 7
Fine Orange ceramics, 110
Fishing, evidence of, 77, 207
Foias, Antonia, 26
Ford, Anabel, 161, 164, 165, 166, 171, 236t
Formality and monumentality, 250, 251t, 252–54
Formative period. *See* Preclassic period
Freidel, David, 9, 76, 79, 80, 199
Freiwald, Carolyn, 158
Frequency of stelae, 240t–41t, 245–46
Freshwater Creek, 202
Friezes, 123, 149, 151, 157, 160, 216, 268, 281, 282; fiberglass replicas, 151, 152f; reconstruction drawing, 174f
Functional definitions of urbanism, 19–20
Funerary monuments, temples as, 14, 36, 55, 57, 89, 228

Gallon Jug Ranch, 168, 190
Gann, Thomas E. F., 6, 103–4, 120, 149, 159, 203, 210
Garber, James, 71, 74, 75, 147
Gardens. See *Chultuns*
Garrison, Thomas, 26, 27, 190, 194, 233, 234, 248, 258
Gateway boulders at Pusilhá, 89
Gateway Hill Acropolis, 87–89, 92, 93, 94
Geographic information system (GIS), 251, 254
Geographic setting of Maya area, 47–51

Geometric order, 250, 251t
Geopolitical organization, models of, 24–27
Gill, Richardson, 60
GIS (geographic information system), 251, 254
Global positioning systems, 42
Glyph blocks, 101, 110, 116, 134, 229
Glyphs. *See* Hieroglyphs
GMT correlation, 62
Golden Stream, 85f, 86
Goodman-Martinez-Thompson (GMT) correlation, 62
Graham, Elizabeth, 211, 218
Gran Cacao, 169, 170, 182, 236t, 237f, 273
Granite, 47, 48, 86
Grave goods, 180, 188, 196, 197f, 198f, 216, 226–27
Grube, Nikolai, 24, 25, 27, 51, 64–65, 141, 178
Guatemala. *See* Cival; El Mirador; Holmul; Kaminaljuyu; Kinal; La Honradez; Nakbe; Naranjo; Piedras Negras; Pilar Poniente; Quiriguá; Río Azul; San Bartolo; Tikal; Uaxactun; Xultun
Guderjan, Thomas, 171, 176, 181, 191, 196, 197, 234, 236t
Gulf of Mexico, xviii, 47, 49

Haab, 61
Hageman, Jon, 181, 185–86
Hammond, Norman, 6, 9, 16, 231, 273; Corozal Project, 69–70, 76; La Milpa, 171, 174, 176, 236t; Lubaantun, 87, 103, 104, 106, 109, 110, 236t, 244; Nim Li Punit, 112, 114; Nohmul, 203, 205, 206, 208, 209, 236t, 258
Harbor hypothesis, (Lamanai), 211, 212f, 220
Harrison-Buck, Eleanor, 209
Hartnett, Kristen, 198
Hats' Chaak ceramic phase, 156, 157, 160, 246
Hatzcap Keel, 7
Healy, Paul, 129, 136t
Hematite, 75, 184, 226
Hendon, Julia, 17
Hero Twins, 16, 267
Herrera, Peter, 181
Hester, Thomas, 9
Hieroglyphic stairs, 90, 92, 93t, 94
Hieroglyphic texts, languages of, 21–22
Hieroglyphs, 4–5, 38, 54–55, 56, 60–61, 84, 90, 92, 100, 115–16. *See also* Emblem glyphs
Highlands, xviii, 47–48

332   Index

High-level meaning, 17–18, 265–65, 278
High Temple, 54, 214f, 217, 241t, 252, 258
Historical overviews. *See* Cultural history of Maya; History of Maya archaeology in Belize
History of Maya archaeology in Belize, 5–10; Altun Ha, 221–22; Caracol, 128–29; Chan Chich, 190; Dos Hombres, 181–82; El Pilar, 161; Lamanai, 210–11; La Milpa, 171; Lubaantun, 103–4; Minanha, 120–21; Nim Li Punit, 112; Nohmul, 203; Pusilhá, 86–87; Uxbenka, 95; Xunantunich, 149
Holmul, xviii, 54, 70, 85f
Holmul 1 burials, 208
Holuitz, 199
Honduras. *See* Copán
Horticulture, evidence of, 52
Houk, Brett A., 14, 174, 188, 194, 236t, 241, 272–73, 275, 276, 278
Houston, Stephen, 21–22, 24
Human remains, 77, 92, 127, 138, 157, 158, 201; cremations, 139, 141, 142t, 145; female, 78, 130, 139; mass graves, 59, 78, 82; as offerings, 178; royal, 55, 93, 114, 196, 197f, 199, 209, 228–29
Human sacrifice, 2, 78, 82, 279; royalty, 59, 64

Iannone, Gyles, 161; Minanha, 120–21, 123, 124, 126, 127, 128, 144, 236t, 268, 275
Incensarios, 178, 185, 198
"Indian Church." *See* Lamanai
In-line triadic shrines, 53, 54, 71, 95, 152, 154, 160
Inner ring termini, 137f, 138
Inomata, Takeshi, 23, 34, 248, 279
Intersite causeways. *See under* Causeways
Intrasite causeways. *See under* Causeways
Ix Chel, 120
Ix Ich'ak . . . K'inich (Ruler F), 93t

Jackson, Sarah, 21
Jade, 47, 77, 215; anklets, 226; beads, 139, 185, 197f, 209, 227, 282; carved pendants, 197f, 221; carved plaques, 229; chips, 138; diadems, 114; ear ornaments, 197f, 209, 229; head of K'inich Ahau, 201, 225, 226; helmet-bib head pendants, 199, 208; jewels, 5560; masks, 138
Jade head at Altun Ha, 201, 225, 226

Jaguar bowl, 185
Jaguar masks, 216
Jaguar Paw. *See* Chak Tok Ich'aak I
Jasaw Chan K'awiil, 64
Jasaw Chan K'awiil II, 64
Jones, Grant, 109
Jones, Richard C., 233, 234
Joyce, Rosemary, 17
Joyce, Thomas A., 103–4, 120

K'uhul ajaw, centrality of, 21
K'ahk' Tiliw Chan Chaak, 158
K'ahk' Ujol K'inich I (Ruler I), 142t
K'ahk' Ujol K'inich II (Ruler VI), 142t, 144
K'ak' U Ti' Chan (Ruler B), 93t
Ka'Kabish, 236t, 237f
Kaminaljuyu, xviii, 6, 48
Kan dynasty, 57
Kan I, 142t
Kan II (Ruler V), 142t
K'an I (Ruler II), 142t
K'an II, 143–44
K'an III (Ruler XII), 143t
Karst depressions. *See Bajos*
Karstic landscape, xviii, 47–48, 119–20, 169–70
K'atuns, 61, 62, 240t–41t
Kawam, 116
K'awiil scepter, 116, 159
K'awil Chan K'inich (Ruler A), 93t
Kaxil Uinic, 7, 190, 194, 195f, 196, 198, 199, 200, 249
Keller, Angela, 150, 154, 160, 194, 268, 280, 282
Kennett, Douglas, 60
Kidder, A. V., 7
Kinal, 169f, 258
Kingdoms as territories, 26–27
Kings. *See* Rulers
K'inich Ahau, jade head of, 201, 225, 226
K'inich Joy K'awiil (Ruler IX), 143t, 144
K'inich Toobil Yopaat (Ruler X), 143t
K'inich Yax K'uk' Mo', 141
Kins, 61, 62
Knot Ajaw (Ruler IV), 135, 142t
K'uk'ulkan, 66

Labná, 275
Lady Penis-head of Xultun, 142t
Lady Six Sky, 158, 159

Lagoons, 49, 67, 76, 202; New River Lagoon, 169f, 201, 202, 210, 211, 212f
Laguna Bacalar, 48, 49
Laguna de On, 67
Laguna Seca, 168
La Honradez, 155, 160, 166, 169f, 193, 194, 199, 200, 248, 274, 275, 277
Lajun Ka'an, 116
Lake Petén Itzá, 49, 210
La Lucha Escarpment, 170f, 190
La Lucha uplands, 171
Lama'an/ayin. *See* Lamanai
Lamanai, xviii, 4f, 46t, 169f, 219–20; chronology and political history, 216–19; comparisons, 236t, 237f, 238f, 240t–41t, 244, 262, 271t; coordination, 252, 253t; site description, 210–16; standardization, 256t–57t, 258, 261f; ties to other cities, 218–19
Lamanai Archaeological Project (LAP), 211
Lamanai Building Type, 214, 215, 216, 217, 220, 225f, 226
LaMAP (La Milpa Archaeological Project), 171, 174, 175, 176, 177
Lamayna. *See* Lamanai
La Milpa, xviii, 4f, 44f, 46t, 169f; chronology and political history, 175–79; comparisons, 236t, 237f, 238f, 239, 240t, 241, 242, 243–44, 247, 248, 249, 262, 271t; coordination, 253t; site description, 171–75, 180; standardization, 256t–57t, 259, 260, 261f; ties to other cities, 178–79, 188–89, 275; ties to Petén political sphere, 179
La Milpa Archaeological Project (LaMAP), 171, 174, 175, 176, 177
La Milpa Centre, 171, 267. *See* La Milpa
La Milpa Core Project (LMCP), 171, 173f, 175, 177
La Milpa's minor centers: La Milpa East, 174, 177, 179, 180, 267; La Milpa North, 174, 177, 179, 180, 267; La Milpa South, 174, 177, 180, 267; La Milpa West, 174, 177, 179, 267
Languages as markers of social distinction, 21–22
LAP (Lamanai Archaeological Project), 211
Las Cuevas, 120
Las Pinturas, 55
Las Ruinas de Arenal, 123
Late Classic period, 46t; cultural history, 58–59; political history, 64–65

Late Postclassic period, 67
Late Preceramic period. *See* Archaic period
Late Preclassic period, 46t, 53–56
La Union, 170
Leventhal, Richard, 84, 90, 94, 149, 236t, 237; Southern Belize Archaeological Project, 87, 95, 96, 104, 112, 114, 115
LiDAR (light detection and ranging), 42, 43, 161, 168
Lids, 18, 116, 176, 185, 186f, 187f, 215, 278
Light detection and ranging (LiDAR), 42, 43, 161, 168
Limestone, 27, 32, 38, 50, 86, 103, 111
Limestone hills, 48, 49, 84, 95, 103, 119, 161, 180
Lintels, 27, 31, 40, 60, 128, 222, 243
Lithic debitage deposits, 9, 78–79, 154
Little Chan Chich Creek, 189–90
LMCP (La Milpa Core Project), 171, 173f, 175, 177
Local intrasite causeways, 35, 172. *See also* Intrasite causeways
Logographs, 60. *See also* Hieroglyphs
Lohse, Jon, 52, 70, 181, 188, 236t, 246, 247
Long Count system, 61–62
Looters, evidence of, 38, 242; Caracol, 129; Chan Chich, 190, 191, 196, 197; Dos Hombres, 182; El Pilar, 164, 165, 166; La Milpa, 175, 176; Pusilhá, 90; Uxbenka, 98
Lord Chaak, 65
Lords of the Underworld, 16
Lower-level meanings, 17–18
Lowlands, xviii, 48
Lowry's Bight, 202. *See also* Cerros
Lubaantun, xviii, 4f, 6, 7, 87, 94, 95, 117, 118; chronology and political history, 109–11; comparisons, 236t, 237f, 238f, 239, 240t–41t, 244, 246, 247; coordination, 252, 253t, 254; meaning, 268–69, 271t, 273, 274; site description, 102–9, 111; standardization, 256t–57t, 261f; ties to other cities, 110
Lubaantun (Hammond), 104
Lucero, Lisa, 23, 236t
Lundell, Cyrus, 51

Maax Na, 236t, 237f
Macal River, 71, 85f, 119, 120, 124, 128, 148
"Macaw Jaguar God of the Underworld," 116
Machaca River. *See* Pusilhá River

Mai, Rosa, 128
Maize God, 55
Maler, Teobert, 44
Malerization, 43–45
Mangrove swamps, 49, 51, 220
Mapping methods, 42–45
Marcus, Joyce, 24, 67
Markers. *See* Ball court markers
Markets, evidence of, 34, 154, 191
Martin, Simon, 27, 51, 64–65, 141
Martinez, 124
MASDP (Maya Archaeological Sites Development Programme), 104, 112, 114
Masks, jadeite, 138; jaguar, 216; stucco, 9, 36, 54, 55, 57, 75, 80, 213f, 214, 226
Mask Temple, 213f, 214, 217, 218
Masonry altars, 226, 230. *See also* Altars
Masonry benches, 31, 40, 41f
Masonry buildings, 29–33, 36, 37, 53, 80, 151
Mass graves, 59, 78, 82
Mat designs, 18, 116, 278
Materials, perishable, 27–28, 40, 86
Mathematical systems, 61
Mathews, Peter, 24, 25, 229
Maya Archaeological Sites Development Programme (MASDP), 104, 112, 114
Maya archaeology in Belize, history of, 5–10
Maya area, xviii, 47–51; eastern lowlands, 4f; northern Belize, 169f; southern and central Belize, 85f
Maya chronologies, 46t
Maya cities, understandings of, 19–20
Maya collapse, 8, 46t, 59–60, 64–65, 219. *See also* Abandonment of Maya centers
Maya Mountains, xviii, 4f, 48, 84–86, 95, 102–3, 111–12, 119–20, 238f
Mayapan, xviii, 7, 66–67, 219
Maya pyramids. *See* Temple-pyramids
McKillop, Heather, 6, 8, 51
Meadows, Richard, 198
Meanings in built environments, 15, 17–19, 277–78
Mercury, 215
Merwin, R. E., 103
Mesoamerican cosmology. *See* Cosmograms as interpretive tools
Metrology. *See* Orientation
Mexican contact. *See* Teotihuacan interaction, evidence of

Mexico. *See* Bonampak; Calakmul; Chichén Itzá; Labná; Mayapan; Palenque; Quintana Roo; Sayil; Tulum; Uxmal
Microwatersheds, 56, 174
Middle-level meanings, 17–18, 277–78
Middle Preclassic period, 46t, 52–53; Cahal Pech, 72–73
Midwinters Lagoon, 220
Militaristic imagery, 157, 159–60
Minanha, xviii, 120–28, 145–46; chronology and political history, 124–27; comparisons, 240t–41t, 256t–57t, 271t; coordination, 253t; site description, 120–24, 127–28; standardization, 256t–57t, 258, 261f; ties to other cities, 126-27, 275
Mirador Basin, 49, 56, 57
Mitchell-Hedges, Frederick, 6, 103, 106–7
Mixtec codices, 264
Moho Plaza, 90, 91f, 92, 94, 240, 241t, 247, 272
Moho River, 85f, 86
Monkey River, 85f, 86
Monument gardens, cities as, 100, 111, 244
Mopan River, 71, 85f, 119, 147–48
Mopan Valley, 154
Mopan Valley Preclassic Project (MVPP), 149, 156
Morley, Sylvanus, 87, 110
Morris, John, 161, 165
Motagua River, xviii, 47
Mountain Cow, 7, 120
Mudstone, 86
Mul tepal, 67. *See also* Shared rule
Murals: Bonampak, 59, 279; Chiik Nahb, 34; San Bartolo, 55, 70, 77, 199, 248, 258, 274, 279
Muyal Nah K'uhul [unreadable] K'ak'U (Ruler C), 93t
MVPP (Mopan Valley Preclassic Project), 149, 156
Mythological scenes, 54, 55

Naj Tunich cave, 110
Nakbe, 14, 53–54, 56, 70, 266
Naranjo, xviii, 85f; Caracol rivalry, 64, 120, 126, 127, 140, 142t, 144; emblem glyph, 158, 159, 276; intersite causeways, 138, 247; polychrome vessels, 158, 188; Xunantunich ties, 158–60, 275, 276
National Science Foundation (NSF), 8

Index   335

NB. *See* Northern Belize
NBCBZ (Northern Belize Chert Bearing Zone), 78, 169f, 220
Necropoli. *See* Royal tombs
Net sinkers, 207
New Archaeology, rise of, 8, 69
New River, 169f, 202, 210
New River Lagoon, 169f, 201, 202, 210, 215, 219, 231, 252, 261, 262
Nim Li Punit, xviii, 4f, 94, 95, 110, 230; chronology and political history, 115–17; comparisons, 236t, 237f, 238f, 240t–41t, 244, 245, 263, 268, 271t, 273; coordination, 252, 253t, 254; site description, 111–15, 117; standardization, 256t–57t, 259, 261f; ties to other cities, 116–17
Noblewomen, 63, 116. *See also* Female rulers
Nohmul, xviii, 4f, 9, 46t, 69, 169f, 231; chronology and political history, 207–9; comparisons, 236t, 237f, 238f, 239, 240t–41t, 244, 249, 271t; coordination, 252, 253t; interaction with northern lowlands, 209; site description, 202–7, 209; standardization, 256t–57t, 258, 260, 261f; ties to other cities, 208
Nohol Pilar, 161, 163f, 166
Non-elites, role of, 23
Norman's Temple group, 192f, 195, 196, 198, 255, 256
Normark, Johan, 164
Northeast Walkway, 150f, 154
Northern Belize, xviii, 11–12, 169f, 201–2, 231. *See also* Altun Ha; Lamanai; Nohmul
Northern Belize Chert Bearing Zone (NBCBZ), 78, 169f, 202, 220
Northern lowlands, xviii, 48
Northern River, 202
North-south orientations, 16, 38, 56, 74, 251, 253t, 256, 257t, 259–60, 266; Altun Ha, 222, 227, 272; Blackman Eddy, 74; Caracol, 130, 132, 272; Cerros, 82; Chan Chich, 195, 200, 260, 272; Dos Hombres, 182, 189, 200, 260, 272, 274, 275; El Pilar, 161, 166, 272; La Milpa, 171, 172, 189, 200, 260, 272, 274, 275; Lubaantun, 104, 106, 111, 268; Minanha, 121, 127, 268, 272; Nim Li Punit, 112, 268; Pusilhá, 260, 268, 272; Uxbenka, 95–96, 260, 272; Xunantunich, 150, 160, 260, 268, 272

North Stair, 150f, 154
Northwestern Belize, xviii, 11–12, 168–70, 200. *See also* Chich; Dos Hombres; La Milpa
NSF (National Science Foundation), 8
NWB. *See* Northwestern Belize

Observatories, 53, 66, 191
Obsidian, 47, 77, 126, 139, 154, 184, 208, 209, 282; gray obsidian, 139; green obsidian, 58, 139, 229
Ocellated turkey bowls, 185
Ochk'in K'aloomte', 93
Offerings, Postclassic, 157, 176, 178, 185, 198, 228
Orange Walk, 76, 201, 202, 203, 210
Organization models, geopolitical, 24–27
Orientations, 253t, 255t, 259–60, 261t; Altun Ha, 222, 227, 272; Blackman Eddy, 74; Caracol, 130, 132, 272; Cerros, 82; Chan Chich, 195, 200, 260, 272; Dos Hombres, 182, 189, 200, 260, 272, 274, 275; El Pilar, 161, 166, 272; La Milpa, 171, 172, 189, 200, 260, 272, 274, 275; Lubaantun, 104, 106, 111, 268; Minanha, 121, 127, 268, 272; Nim Li Punit, 112, 268; Pusilhá, 260, 268, 272; Uxbenka, 95–96, 260, 272; Xunantunich, 150, 160, 260, 268, 272
Orientations, east–west, 56, 92, 96, 150, 172, 247, 259, 260, 266
Orientations, north–south, 16, 38, 56, 74, 251, 253t, 256, 257t, 259–60, 266
Orientations, primary axis, 259–61
Orthogonal layouts, 250, 251t
Ottawa Group, 212f, 215–16
Outer ring termini, 137f, 138
"Overkingships," 25–27, 64

Pacbitun, 42, 85f, 236t, 237f
Pace and compass mapping, 42
Palaces, 36–37, 57, 257t; Barrio palace compound, 130f, 131f, 133–34, 140; Caana, 129, 130f, 131f, 132f, 135f, 139–40, 144, 252, 254, 258; Northeast Acropolis, 131f, 133, 140; Xunantunich Plaza A-III, 150f, 152, 154, 156, 158, 160
Palacio, Joseph O., 112
Palenque, xviii, 1, 5, 6, 58, 64, 242
Paleoindian period, 52
Pan-Mesoamerican cosmological concepts, 16

336   Index

Paradero Fluted Teotihuacan-style tripod cylinders, 176
Paradigm shifts in archaeology, 8
Parapets, 35, 137, 153, 154, 160, 164–65, 166, 194, 236t, 283
Pendants, 77, 197f, 221; shell
Pendergast, David, 6, 30, 33; Altun Ha, 220–21, 222, 225, 228, 229, 230, 236t; Lamanai, 210–11, 214, 215, 216, 236t
Perishable buildings, 27–28, 40–42; Chan Chich Structure A-5, 191, 192, 193f
Petén Karst Plateau, 169
Petén region, xviii, 1, 48–49
Petén template, 16–17, 265–679, 270–76, 283, 284
PFB (Programme for Belize), 10, 168, 171, 181
PfBAP (Programme for Belize Archaeological Project), 10, 168
Piedras Negras, xviii, 62
Pilar Poniente, 162f, 164, 165, 166
Pilgrim offerings, Postclassic, 141, 157, 176, 178, 185, 198, 228
Place names, 24
Plan maps, 73f, 206f
Plaster coating, 28, 29f, 30, 33
Plate, polychrome, 188
Platforms, construction of, 28, 29f, 30f, 33, 40, 108f, 125
Playing alleys. See Ball courts
Plaza Axcanan, 162, 163f, 165
Plaza Copal, 162, 163f, 165, 241t, 281
Plaza Duende, 162, 163f, 164, 281
Plaza Escoba, 164
Plaza Faisan, 163f, 164
Plaza of the Royal Tombs, 114
Plaza Plan 2 layouts, 124, 145, 162, 166
Plazas, 16, 28, 29, 34, 36, 38, 53, 55, 127, 231; Altun Ha, 222–25, 225f, 227–28, 264; Blackman Eddy, 74; Cahal Pech, 71, 72f–73f; Caracol (130f, 131f, 134, 135f, 137, 138, 139, 140, 144; comparisons, 242, 248, 262, 272); Cerros, 80, 81f; Chan Chich (43f, 190, 191–95, 196–98, 199–200; comparisons, 241, 256, 259, 260, 272, 274, 279, 283); Colha, 78; Dos Hombres (181, 182, 183f, 184, 185, 189; comparisons, 242, 252, 254, 247, 249, 272, 274, 275–76, 281); El Pilar, 161–65, 166, 241, 259, 272, 275, 281; Kaxil Uinic, 195f, 196; Lamanai, 211, 212f, 215, 216; La Milpa, 18–19, 171, 172, 173f, 174, 175–76, 177–80; comparisons, 239, 240–41, 242, 247, 249, 272, 274, 275–76, 278, 280; Lubaantun, 105f, 106–8, 109; Minanha, 121, 122f, 123, 127, 242, 268, 272, 281; Nim Li Punit, 112–14, 115; Nohmul, 204f, 205–7, 208, 241, 249, 260, 273; Pusilhá, 87–92, 94, 114, 240, 247, 260; Tikal, 58, 248; Uxbenka, 95–96f, 97f–98, 99, 100, 111, 240, 260; Xunantunich (150f, 151, 152–55, 156–57, 158, 159–60; comparisons, 254, 259, 260, 268, 280)
—comparisons, 233–35, 239–42, 279, 280, 281, 282, 283; coordination, 252–53; standardization, 255, 256t, 257, 258–61, 284; Petén template, 270–72, 273, 274; planning, 262, 263, 264
—special-function plazas, 138, 140, 248, 254, 258
—stela plazas. See Stelae and stela plazas
—as urban features, 239–42
Plazuela organization, 145, 205
Poité River, 86, 87
Political emulation, 17, 158, 160, 199, 200, 266, 274–75. See also "Build what you know" concept
Political history of Classic period, 62–65
Polychrome bench, 177
Polychrome vessels, 21, 59, 158, 185, 186f, 187f, 188, 196, 276
Ponds. See Aguadas
Positional notation, 61
Postclassic period, 46t, 51; cultural history, 65, 66–67
Pottery Cave, 87, 91–92
Power, structures as statements about, 14
Powis, Terry, 42, 72, 75, 211, 236t
Preclassic period, 51, 52–56
Predecessors of Maya, 52
Prestige languages, 21–22
Primary axis orientations, 259–61
Primary site axis, 256t–57t
Principal Bird Deity, 55
Pring, Duncan, 207
Prismatic maps, 44–45
Processual archaeology. See New Archaeology, rise of
Programme for Belize (PFB), 10, 168, 171, 181
Programme for Belize Archaeological Project (PfBAP), 10, 168

Progresso Lagoon, 67
Proskouriakoff, Tatiana, 62
Prufer, Keith, 95, 98, 100, 110, 114, 116, 117, 236t, 244, 273
Pulltrouser Swamp, 9, 202
Punta de Cacao, 169, 236t, 237f, 273
Punta Gorda, 103
Pusilhá, xviii, 4f, 7, 102, 104, 111, 112, 114, 230; chronology and political history, 91–94; comparisons, 233, 236t, 237f, 238f, 240t–41t, 242, 244, 247, 249, 262, 271t; coordination, 252, 253t, 254; site description, 86–91, 94–95; standardization, 256t–57t, 259, 261f; ties to other cities, 92t–93, 228
Pusilhá Archaeological Project, 87, 93. *See also* TRIP
Pusilhá River, 85f, 86, 87, 88f, 89, 92
Puuc cities, 49, 65, 66
Puuc Hills, xviii, 49
Puuc kingdoms' architectural style, 65
Pyburn, Anne, 203, 208
Pyramids. *See* Temple-pyramids

Quadrangle groups, 65, 130, 152, 182, 200, 276. *See also* Courtyards
Quarries, 39, 220, 230
Quarrying, modern, 203, 207, 221
Queens. *See* Female rulers
Quetzalcoatl, 66
Quintana Roo, 49, 79, 170, 199
Quiriguá, xviii, 94, 110, 116, 117, 242

Radial causeways, 194, 259, 274
Rainfall, 50, 59–60; effects on Maya structures, 31–32, 38, 39
Range buildings, 36–37; Caracol, 132, 134, 135f, 136, 248; Chan Chich, 191, 195, 198, 200, 280; Dos Hombres, 182; El Pilar, 164; Lamanai, 211; La Milpa, 172, 180, 278, 282; Minanha, 121; Nim Li Punit, 114; Nohmul, 205; Pusilhá, 90, 97f
Rank ordering, 25, 232–37, 253t, 256t
Rapoport, Amos, 17, 18, 265
RB-1, 181, 183. *See also* Dos Hombres
Rectified maps, 44–45
Red decoration, 72, 75, 80, 123, 177; ceramic vessels, 127
Reese-Taylor, Kathryn, 208

Regal-ritual centers, Maya cities as, 20–23, 26, 118
Regional-state models of geopolitical organization, 25–26
Relief maps, shaded, 43f
Replicas, fiberglass, 151, 152f, 213f
Research in Belize. *See* History of Maya archaeology in Belize
Reservoirs, 39, 131f, 135f, 173f
Richmond-Brown, Lady "Sammy," 6, 103
Ricketson, Oliver, 7
Río Azul (river), 169f, 170f, 180, 190
Río Azul (site), xviii, 63, 169f, 178, 179
Río Bravo Archaeological Project, 190
Río Bravo Conservation and Management Area, 168
Río Bravo Escarpment, 170f, 180, 181, 189, 190
Río Bravo sites. *See* Dos Hombres
Río Bravo Terrace Lowland, 189–90
Río Chiquibul, 85f, 128, 147–48
Río Columbia, 103
Río Grande, 85f, 86, 103
Río Grande Ruins, 103
Río Hondo, xviii, 4f, 76, 169f, 170, 190, 202, 209, 238f, 273
Río Machaquilá, 120
Ritual engineering, 18, 174
Rivers: Belize River, 4f, 71, 85f, 148, 161, 190, 220, 238f, 258; Booth's River, 169f, 170f, 180, 273; Chan Chich Creek, 189–90, 192f; Freshwater Creek, 202; Golden Stream, 85f, 86; Little Chan Chich Creek, 189–90; Macal River, 71, 85f, 119, 120, 124, 128, 148; Moho River, 85f, 86; Monkey River, 85f, 86; Mopan River, 71, 85f, 119, 147–48; Motagua River, xviii, 47; New River, 169f, 202, 210; Northern River, 202; Poité River, 86, 87; Pusilhá River, 85f, 86, 87, 88f, 89, 92; Río Azul, 169f, 170f; Río Chiquibul, 85f, 128, 147–48; Río Columbia, 103; Río Grande, 85f, 86, 103; Río Machaquilá, 120; Sarstoon River, 86
Road systems. *See* Causeways (*sacbeob*)
Robichaux, Hubert, 175, 178, 179, 181, 188, 276
Rockstone Pond. *See* Altun Ha
ROM (Royal Ontario Museum), 8, 210, 221–22, 226
Roof combs, 31, 36, 151

Royal courts, 20, 21–22, 57, 118, 125, 126–27, 152, 177, 246
Royal households, Maya cities as, 20
Royal Ontario Museum (ROM), 8, 210, 221–22, 226
"Royal precinct planning," 15
Royal tombs, 55, 57; Altun Ha, 228–29; Caracol, 134; Chan Chich, 196, 197f, 199, 208; Lamanai, 218, 225, 226–27; La Milpa, 176, 179, 199, 208, 227–28, 229; Nim Li Punit, 112, 114; Pusilhá, 94
Roys, Ralph, 67
Rubble fill, 28, 45, 185, 197
Rulers:
—Altun Ha: "Akbal Lord," 229; foreign lords, 228–30
—Bolon Tzuk Witz: Ah Muwaan, 188
—Calakmul: Sky Witness, 64, 143; Yuknoom Chan, 142t; Yuknoom the Great, 64; Yuknoom Yich'aak, 26, 64
—Caracol: K'ahk' Ujol K'inich I, 142t; K'ahk' Ujol K'inich II, 142t, 144; Kan I, 142t; Kan II, 142t; K'an I, 142t; K'an II, 143–44; K'an III, 143t; K'inich Joy K'awiil, 143t, 144; K'inich Toobil Yopaat, 143t; Knot Ajaw, 135, 142t; Te' K'ab Chaak, 141, 142t; Tum Yohl K'inich, 143t; Yajaw Te' K'inich I, 142t, 142t; Yajaw Te' K'inich II, 143
—Copán: K'ak' U Ti' Chan, 93t; K'inich Yax K'uk'Mo', 141
—female, 218; Ix Ich'ak . . . K'inich (Ruler F), 93t; Lady Six Sky, 158, 159
—La Milpa: Ukay ("18-?"), 178, 179, 188
—Naranjo: Lady Six Sky, 158, 159; K'ahk' Tiliw Chan Chaak, 158; Waxaklajuun Ubaah K'awiil (18 Jog), 159, 188
—Nim Li Punit: B'ahlam Te', 230; Lajun Ka'an, 116; "Macaw Jaguar God of the Underworld," 116
—Pusilhá: Ix Ich'ak . . . K'inich, 93t; K'awil Chan K'inich, 93t; Muyal Nah K'uhul [unreadable] K'ak'U, 93t; Ruler G, 93t, 94
—Teotihuacan: Spearthrower Owl, 63
—Tikal: Chak Tok Ich'aak I (Jaguar Paw), 62, 63, 101, 102; Jasaw Chan K'awiil, 64; Jasaw Chan K'awiil II, 64; Sihyaj Chan K'awiil II, 63; Wak Chan K'awiil, 64, 142t, 143; Yax Ehb' Xook, 55, 62; Yax Nuun Ahiin I, 63, 101

—Uxmal: Lord Chaak, 65
—Xultun: Lady Penis-head, 142t
—Yaxchilan: Bird-Jaguar, 178

Sabloff, Jeremy, 16–17, 160, 258, 259, 260, 265, 275
Sacbeob. *See* Causeways (*sacbeob*)
Sacralized warfare, 2
Sacrifice, human, 2, 78, 82, 279; of royalty, 59, 64
Sacrifice, mass, 59, 78, 82
Sagebiel, Kerry, 176, 178–79, 184
Sajalob, 21
Saktunja, 67
San Bartolo, xviii, 55, 70, 77, 169f, 194, 199, 248, 258, 274, 277, 279
Sand, calcareous. *See Sascab*
Sanders, William, 20
Sandstone, 27, 38, 86, 95, 103, 111
San Estevan, 8
San Ignacio, 71, 148
San José, 7, 85f, 169f, 199, 210, 236t, 237f
San Pablo Ridge, 201, 202. *See also* Booth's River Escarpment
Santa Rita Corozal, xviii, 67, 203
SARP (Social Archaeology Research Program), 121, 124, 128
Sarstoon River, 86
Sascab, 35, 50
Satterthwaite, Linton, 8, 128–29, 149
Saturday Creek, 43, 85f, 148, 155, 193, 275, 283
Saturno, William, 199
Sayil, xviii, 65, 275
Say Ka, 174, 177, 179
SB. *See* Southern Belize
Scarborough, Vernon, 22, 38, 39, 56, 171, 174, 218, 227
Scattering rituals, 116
Schele, Linda, 80, 199
Schwake, Sonja, 121, 136t
Secondary growth at Altun Ha, Pendergast on, 220–21
Seibert, Jeffrey, 123
Sequential construction phases, evidence of, 71–74, 74–75, 77–78
Serpent bars, double-headed, 100, 218
7 Ajaw glyph, 116

SfM (Structure from Motion) technology, 42–43
Shafer, Harry, 9
Shared rule, 65, 66, 67
Sharer, Robert, 28, 51, 54, 57
Shell, bowl resembling, 185
Shell artifacts, 77, 138, 139, 184, 185, 198, 215, 216
Sherds, 87, 124, 196, 207, 282
Short Count dating, 116–17
Short Count monument (Stela 3), 116–17, 245
Shrines, 34, 53, 55, 194, 249, 280. *See also* In-line triadic shrines
Sierra Red bowl, 184
Sierrita de Ticul. *See* Puuc Hills
Sihyaj Chan K'awiil II, 63
Sihyaj K'ahk' (Fire Is Born), 63, 101
Siltstone, 95, 103
Simmons, Scott, 211
Simplified plan maps, 73f
Simplified site maps, 261f
Sinkholes. See *Cenotes*
Site core areas, 236t, 237f, 238f
Site maps, simplified, 261f
Site-planning analysis, 13, 15–19
Sky Witness, 64, 143
Smith, Michael E.: ancient urban planning analysis, 10, 15, 19, 45, 232, 250, 251t, 262, 283, 284; coordination, 250, 251t; cosmograms, 17, 269; spatial patterns, 258; orientation, 259
"Smoking Shell," 218–19
Snake Kingdom. *See* Calakmul
Social Archaeology Research Program (SARP), 121, 124, 128
Social complexity, rise of, 2, 14, 46t, 52–53, 70
Soils, 47, 49–51, 76, 120
"Solar axis." *See* East-west orientations
Southern Belize, xviii, 11–12, 84–86, 117–18. *See also* Nim Li Punit; Lubaantun; Pusilhá; Uxbenka
Southern Belize Archaeological Project. *See* Leventhal, Richard
Southern lowlands, xviii, 48–49
Spatial patterns, 255t, 258–59
Spearthrower Owl, 63
Special Function Groups, 90–91, 95
Special-function plazas, 138, 140, 248, 258
Spinewalls, 30–31f

Spondylus shells, 77, 138, 184
Stairs, 29, 36, 54; Altun Ha, 222, 225–26; Blackman Eddy, 75; Cahal Pech, 74, 75; Caracol, 131, 132; Cerros, 80; Chan Chich, 191, 193f, 198, 280; El Pilar, 162, 163–64; Lamanai, 213f, 214, 215, 216, 220; La Milpa, 177, 178, 281; Lubaantun, 106, 107; Nim Li Punit, 114; Nohmul, 205; Pusilhá, 87, 89, 90, 93t, 94; Uxbenka, 97, 98; Xunantunich, 150f, 154
Standardization, 15, 250, 255–61
Stelae and stela plazas, 20, 38, 60, 62, 86, 118, 166, 178, 230; Altun Ha, 244; Blackman Eddy, 74; Cahal Pech, 71, 72f; Calakmul, 64, 65; Caracol, 129, 132, 134, 140, 142–43, 144, 243–44, 255; Chan Chich, 191, 196, 199, 244–45, 246; Cobá, 65; Copán, 63, 141, 144; Dos Hombres, 182, 185, 189, 244–45; El Pilar, 147, 166, 167, 244; El Mirador, 54; Kaxil Uinic, 195f, 198, 199, 200; Lamanai, 215, 218–19, 220, 244; La Milpa, 172, 176, 177, 178, 179, 180, 188, 189, 240, 243–44, 245, 246; Lubaantun, 104, 110, 111, 118, 244; Minanha, 121, 122, 123, 126, 127, 245–46; Nakbe, 53; Nim Li Punit, 112, 113f, 114, 115–17, 230 244, 255; Nohmul, 244; Pusilhá, 7, 87, 88f, 89–90, 91, 92, 93t, 94, 230, 244, 245; Río Azul, 179; Tikal, 63, 64, 243; Uxbenka, 96, 97f, 100–101, 102, 111, 240, 244, 255; Uxmal, 65; Xunantunich, 147, 153, 157, 159–60, 245–46, 276
—comparisons, 234, 235, 239, 240t–41t, 242–46, 259, 274, 276; processional architecture, 281; densities, 240t–41t, 243–45; frequencies, 240t–41t, 245–46; standardization, 256t, 259
—depictions of kings, 34, 57, 279; Caracol, 141, 142t–43t; Lamanai, 218–19; La Milpa, 178, 188; Nim Li Punit, 112, 115–16, 230; Pusilhá, 93t; Tikal, 63; Uxbenke, 100–101; Xunantunich, 159
—stela plazas, 241t, 242, 256t, 274; Nim Li Punit, 112–14, 240, 244; Pusilhá, 87, 88f, 89–90, 92, 114, 259, 240, 244, 259; Uxbenka, 96, 97f, 100, 114, 240, 244, 259
—wooden stelae, 243
Stephens, John Lloyd, 6
"Stone-binding" event, 159
Stone monuments, 38, 242–46. *See also* Altars; Ball court markers; Stelae and stela plazas

Stone tools, production of, 9, 78–79, 82, 154
Structure from Motion (SfM) technology, 42–43
Stuart, David, 24, 141
Stucco masks, 9, 36, 54, 55, 57, 75, 80, 213f, 214, 226
Summit temples, 131
Sunken causeways, 194, 248, 256t, 259, 274, 275, 277
Superimposed structures, maps of, 73f
Supernatural imagery. *See* Mythological scenes
Surveying, 42
Symbolic communication in built environments, 18–19, 174. *See also* Cosmograms as interpretive tools
Symbolic egalitarianism, 140, 141

Talud-tablero architectural style, 58, 63
Tandem range buildings, 36; Altun Ha, 222; Caracol, 131, 133; Chan Chich, 193f, 222; Dos Hombres, 182; El Pilar, 162f, 164; Minanha, 121; Xunantunich, 151
Tape and compass mapping, 42
Tate, Carolyn, 264
TDP (Tourism Development Project), 129, 149, 222
Te' K'ab Chaak, 141, 142t
Temple of the Warriors, 66
Temple-pyramids, 18, 36–37, 55, 57, 276; Altun Ha, 222–24, 224f, 227, 228, 229, 230; Blackman Eddy, 74–75; Cahal Pech, 71, 72f, 74; Caracol, 130f, 131f, 132f, 133f, 134, 135f, 258, 262; Cerros, 80, 81f, 82; Chan Chich (191, 192f; Norman's Temple group, 195, 196, 198, 255, 256); Cuello, 77; Dos Hombres, 182, 183f; El Mirador, 54, 56; El Pilar, 162f, 163f–64, 165, 281; Lamanai (211, 212f, 213, 219, 220; High Temple, 54, 214f, 217, 241t, 252, 258; Mask Temple, 213f, 214, 217; Temple of the Jaguar, 216); La Milpa, 172, 173f, 178, 280; Lubaantun, 105f, 106f, 108, 109, 110; Minanha, 121, 122f, 281; Nakbe, 53; Nim Li Punit, 113f, 114; Nohmul, 204f, 205, 206–7, 208; Pusilhá, 88f, 89, 94; Tikal, 66, 248; Uaxactun, 69; Uxbenka, 96f, 97f, 98, 99f; Xunantunich (150f, 152, 154, 155f, 156; the Castillo, 66, 150f, 151f)

—adornment of, 36, 54, 55, 57, 66, 75, 151, 213f, 214, 216
—as funerary monuments, 14, 36, 55, 57, 89, 228
—in-line triadic shrines, 53, 54, 71, 95, 152, 154, 160
—summit temples, 131
—triadic pyramids/temples, 53, 54, 56, 82, 130, 209, 212, 214, 217; comparisons, 256, 257t, 258, 262
—tripartite temples, 124
Temples, 36, 66, 80, 227
Teotihuacan interaction, evidence of, 58, 63, 65, 66, 229; Teotihuacan-style ceramics, 59, 139, 176, 179, 185, 188, 218, 229; Teotihuacan-style cremation, 141, 142t, 145
Teotihuacan-style ceramics, 59, 139, 176, 179, 185, 188, 218, 229
Tepeu 2 and Tepeu 3 ceramics, 109
Terminal Classic period, 46t, cultural history, 59–60; political history, 65–66
Terminal Preclassic period, 46t, 55–56
Termini, 129, 137f, 138, 145, 280; special-function termini, 138, 140, 248, 254, 262
Terminus shrines, 123, 194, 249
Territories, kingdoms as, 26–27
Textbooks on Maya cultural history, 51
Thompson, J. Eric S., 7, 19, 71, 95, 104, 138; Kaxil Uinic, 7, 190; Lamanai, 210; La Milpa, 171, 174; San José, 7, 236t; Xunantunich, 149
Three-dimensional mapping, 42
"Three-Hills-Water," 141. *See also* Caracol
Three Rivers region, 169f, 170f
Throne rooms, 123, 125, 179
Thrones, 38, 60, 177, 236t; polychrome, 177; wooden, 279. *See also* Altars
Tikal, xviii, 4, 66, 79, 94, 243, 276, 277; Calakmul rivalry, 38, 142t, 143, 179; Caracol ties, 141, 142t, 143, 247; causeways, 35, 248, 277; Classic period political history, 56, 57, 58, 62–64, 146; Dos Hombres ties, 188; Lamanai ties, 218; La Milpa ties, 178–79; "overkingship," 25–27; *plazuela* organization, 145; royal tombs, 55; Naranjo rivalry, 127; Nohmul ties, 208; Tikal Project, 7–8; Uxbenka ties, 100–102; water management, 22–23, 39, 40
Tikal Project, 7–9
Time keeping, 61–62

Tipan Chen Uitz, 236t, 237f
Tipu, 219
Toledo District, 87, 104. *See also* TRIP
Toledo Foothills, 84, 86, 103, 119
Toledo Regional Interaction Project (TRIP), 87, 104, 112, 114, 115, 116, 117
Toledo sandstone, 111
Toledo series, 95, 103, 111, 119
Tombs, 84; Barba Group, 185, 188; Caracol, 129, 130, 133, 136, 140, 184–85, 190; Chan Chich, 190; Dos Hombres, 184; Uxbenka, 96–97f, 98
Tonina, 62
Topographic maps, 42–43, 235
Total data stations, 42
Tourism Development Project (TDP), 129, 149, 222
Tourtellot, Gair, 44, 171, 176, 236t, 267
Tranchet bit tools, 79
Traxler, Loa, 51, 54, 57
Trees in Maya ruins, 40, 41f, 175f
Trent University's Social Archaeology Research Program (SARP), 121, 124, 128
Triadic pyramids/temples, 53, 54, 56, 82, 130, 209, 212, 214, 217; comparisons, 256, 257t, 258, 262
Trigger, Bruce, 14, 19
TRIP (Toledo Regional Interaction Project), 87, 104, 112, 114, 115, 116, 117
Tripartite stairs, 214
Tripartite temples, 124
Tripod cylinders, 176, 185
Tripod plates, 127
Tulum, xviii, 219
Tumble. *See* Collapse debris
Tum Yohl K'inich (Ruler VIII), 143t
Tuns, 61, 62
Turkey bowls, 185
Tzimin Kax, 7
Tzolk'in cycles, 61
"Tzul Causeway," 236t

Uaxactun, xviii, 6–7, 53, 54, 63, 69, 188, 199
Ucanal, 143t, 159
Uinals, 61, 62
Ukay ("18-?"), 178, 179, 188
Unfinished projects as subcategory of built environment, 14–15

University Museum of the University of Pennsylvania's Tikal Project, 7–9
UN World Heritage Sites, 7
Urban features, ball courts, 246–47; carved monuments, 242–46; causeways, 247–49; emblem glyphs, 239; plazas, 239–42
U-shaped courtyards, 122f, 123–24, 154
Uxbenka, xviii, 95–102; chronology and political history, 100–102; comparisons, 236t, 237f, 238f, 240t–41t, 271t; coordination, 253t; site description, 95–99, 102; standardization, 256t–57t; ties to other cities, 100–101
Uxbenka Archaeological Project, 95
Uxmal, xviii, 65
Uxwitza', 141. *See also* Caracol

Vaca Plateau, 4f, 119–20, 124, 125, 128, 148, 236t, 238f, 253t, 256t, 271t
Vaca Plateau and Maya Mountains, xviii, 4f, 11–12, 85f, 119–20, 145–46. *See also* Caracol; Minanha
Valdez, Fred, 10, 184
Vaulted structures, 30f–31, 33, 123, 131, 133
Vault stones, 30f, 198
Vegetation patterns, 50–51, 220–21
Vias, 129, 138
Vigesimal mathematical systems, 61
Villages: earliest, 2, 46t, 52–53; transition from, 72–73, 78, 80–82, 196, 217, 227–28; transition to, 52–53, 69, 70
Visibility. *See* Access and visibility
Volcanic resources, 47 (volcanic highlands, 1, 47–48)
VP. *See* Vaca Plateau and Maya Mountains

Wak Chan K'awiil, 64, 142t, 143
Walker, Chet, 42–43
Walker, Debra, 208
Wall cores, 30f
Wall facing stones, 30f
Walling, Stan, 181, 189
Wanyerka, Phillip, 84, 92, 93, 101, 116, 117, 229–30
Warfare, 2, 5, 25, 26, 59, 64, 126, 140
Water and Ritual (Lucero), 23
Water-lily jaguar, 116
Water lily symbols, 22

Water management features, 22–23, 39–40, 56, 249, 264. See also *Aguadas*; *Bajos*; *Cenotes*; Dams; Microwatersheds; Reservoirs
Water rituals, 23
Wattle and daub structures, 28, 72, 75, 77, 216
Waxaklajuun Ubaah K'awiil (18 Jog), 159, 188
Waybil, 120, 124
Webster, David, 20, 21, 22, 33, 58
Western Plaza, 192f, 195, 196, 198, 256
Western structures, 127, 172, 193
Wet-laid fill, 28
Wild Cane Caye, xviii, 67
Willey, Gordon, 8, 147
Willis, Mark, 42–43
Witz' monster pedestals, 116
Women in burials, 78, 130, 139
Women rulers, 218; Ix Ich'ak . . . K'inich (Ruler F), 93t; Lady Six Sky, 158, 159
Workshops, lithic, 9, 76, 78–79, 191, 198
World Heritage Sites, 7
"World Tree," Castillo as, 268
Worldview maps. *See* Microcosms
Writing, spread of, 46t, 54–55

Xaman Pilar, 161, 162f, 163f, 164, 166
XAP (Xunantunich Archaeological Project), 149, 151
Xnaheb, 104, 116
Xultun, 85f, 169, 171, 233, 258

Xunantunich, xviii, 4f, 7, 31f, 46t, 147, 160, 167; chronology and political history, 155–60; comparisons, 236t, 237f, 238f, 240t–41t, 245–46, 247, 249, 263, 280, 282, 283; coordination, 253t, 254; meaning, 267, 268, 270, 271t, 272, 274, 275, 276, 277; site description, 148–55, 160; standardization, 256t–57t, 259, 260, 261f; ties to other cities, 158–59, 160, 275–76, 283
Xunantunich Archaeological Project (XAP), 149, 151

Yaeger, Jason, 149, 152, 157–58, 236t, 268
Yajaw Te' K'inich I, 142t, 142t
Yajaw Te' K'inich II (Ruler III), 143
Yajaw, 188
Yalbac, 85f, 155, 193, 236t, 237f, 275, 283
Yalbac Hills, 167, 190
Yaloche Cream Polychrome lid, 186f
Yaxchilan, xviii, 178
Yax Ehb' Xook, 55, 62
Yax Nuun Ahiin I, 63, 101
Yaxuna, 65
Yucatán Peninsula, xviii, 1, 47–50, 52, 65, 66, 67, 103, 208, 209
Yuknoom Chan, 142t
Yuknoom the Great, 64
Yuknoom Yich'aak K'ahk', 26, 64

Zaro, Gregory, 14, 174, 278

BRETT A. HOUK is associate professor of archaeology at Texas Tech University. His first archaeological field school took place in Belize after his freshman year of college at Trinity University. He earned MA and PhD degrees in anthropology from The University of Texas at Austin, and, after a decade-long detour in cultural resource management, began teaching at Texas Tech University in 2006. As a student he worked on archaeological projects in Guatemala and Belize, and as a professor he continues to study the ancient Maya as the director of the Chan Chich Archaeological Project and the Belize Estates Archaeological Survey Team, which has the coolest project acronym ever—BEAST. He was born in New Orleans, grew up in Houston, was educated in San Antonio and Austin, and currently resides in Lubbock.

THE UNIVERSITY PRESS OF FLORIDA is the scholarly publishing agency for the State University System of Florida, comprising Florida A&M University, Florida Atlantic University, Florida Gulf Coast University, Florida International University, Florida State University, New College of Florida, University of Central Florida, University of Florida, University of North Florida, University of South Florida, and University of West Florida.

Ancient Cities of the New World

Edited by Michael E. Smith, Arizona State University; Marilyn A. Masson, University at Albany, SUNY; John W. Janusek, Vanderbilt University

Ancient Cities of the New World is devoted to the study of the ancient urban sites of Mesoamerica and South America. This series is designed to present theories, models, and approaches that shed light on the region's diverse, ancient urban patterns and polity organization. Major, overarching topics to be explored in the series are urban form (size, architecture, and layout) and urban lifestyles (ethnicity, gender, households, neighborhoods, and craft activities). Books include important works focused on a single key ancient city or analyzing a collection of cities and towns within their regional contexts. The series features cross-disciplinary works in archaeology, art history, and ethnohistory written for a broad scholarly audience.

Aztec City-State Capitals, by Michael E. Smith (2008)
Tenochtitlan: Capital of the Aztec Empire, by José Luis de Rojas (2012; first paperback edition, 2014)
Cusco: Urbanism and Archaeology in the Inka World, by Ian Farrington (2013; first paperback edition, 2014)
Ancient Maya Cities of the Eastern Lowlands, by Brett A. Houk (2015; first paperback edition, 2016)
The Ancient Urban Maya: Neighborhoods, Inequality, and Built Form, by Scott R. Hutson (2016)
The Casma City of El Purgatorio: Ancient Urbanism in the Andes, by Melissa A. Vogel (2016)

www.ingramcontent.com/pod-product-compliance
Lightning Source LLC
Chambersburg PA
CBHW020340240426
43662CB00048B/380